Ancient Philosophy

This is the remarkable story of the birth of philosophy, its flourishing in the ancient Mediterranean world, and the development of ideas which have shaped the course of Western thought and society.

Sir Anthony Kenny's stimulating account begins with Pythagoras and Thales, and ends with St Augustine, who handed on the torch of philosophy to the Christian age. At the centre of the narrative are the two great figures of Plato and Aristotle, who between them set the agenda for philosophy for the next two millenia, and whose influence is as profound today as ever.

The fruit of a lifetime's scholarship and insight, *Ancient Philosophy* sets the philosophers and their ideas in historical context, and explains the significance and impact of each wave of new ideas. It is the first volume in a magisterial new series, which brings the history of philosophy alive to anyone who wants to understand the roots of Western civilization.

Sir Anthony Kenny has been President of the British Academy, and Pro-Vice-Chancellor of the University of Oxford. He has written many acclaimed books on the philosophy of mind, the philosophy of religion, and the history of philosophy, including both scholarly and popular works on Aristotle, Aquinas, Descartes, and Wittgenstein.

A New History of Western Philosophy

Anthony Kenny

Volume 1: Ancient Philosophy

Volume 2: Medieval Philosophy

Volume 3: The Rise of Modern Philosophy

Volume 4: Philosophy in the Modern World

A NEW HISTORY OF WESTERN PHILOSOPHY

VOLUME I

Ancient Philosophy

ANTHONY
KENNY

CLARENDON PRESS · OXFORD

OXFORD
UNIVERSITY PRESS

Great Clarendon Street, Oxford OX2 6DP

Oxford University Press is a department of the University of Oxford.
It furthers the University's objective of excellence in research, scholarship,
and education by publishing worldwide in

Oxford New York

Auckland Cape Town Dar es Salaam Hong Kong Karachi
Kuala Lumpur Madrid Melbourne Mexico City Nairobi
New Delhi Shanghai Taipei Toronto

With offices in

Argentina Austria Brazil Chile Czech Republic France Greece
Guatemala Hungary Italy Japan Poland Portugal Singapore
South Korea Switzerland Thailand Turkey Ukraine Vietnam

Oxford is a registered trade mark of Oxford University Press
in the UK and in certain other countries

Published in the United States
by Oxford University Press Inc., New York

British Library Cataloguing in Publication Data
Data available

Library of Congress Cataloging in Publication Data
Data available

Typeset by SPI Publisher Services, Pondicherry, India

ISBN 0–19–875273–3   978–0–19–875273–8
ISBN 0–19–875272–5 (Pbk.)   978–0–19–875272–1 (Pbk.)

SUMMARY OF CONTENTS

List of Contents   vii

Map   x

Introduction   xi

1. Beginnings: From Pythagoras to Plato   *1*

2. Schools of Thought: From Aristotle to Augustine   *65*

3. How to Argue: Logic   *116*

4. Knowledge and its Limits: Epistemology   *145*

5. How Things Happen: Physics   *178*

6. What There Is: Metaphysics   *199*

7. Soul and Mind   *229*

8. How to Live: Ethics   *257*

9. God   *289*

Chronology   *317*

List of Abbreviations and Conventions   *319*

Bibliography   *323*

List of Illustrations   *331*

Index   *335*

CONTENTS

Map x

Introduction xi

1. **Beginnings: From Pythagoras to Plato** *1*

   The Four Causes *1*
   The Milesians *4*
   The Pythagoreans *9*
   Xenophanes *11*
   Heraclitus *12*
   Parmenides and the Eleatics *17*
   Empedocles *20*
   Anaxagoras *24*
   The Atomists *26*
   The Sophists *28*
   Socrates *32*
   The Socrates of Xenophon *35*
   The Socrates of Plato *37*
   Socrates' Own Philosophy *41*
   From Socrates to Plato *45*
   The Theory of Ideas *49*
   Plato's *Republic* *56*
   The *Laws* and the *Timaeus* *60*

2. **Schools of Thought: From Aristotle to Augustine** *65*

   Aristotle in the Academy *65*
   Aristotle the Biologist *69*
   The Lyceum and its Curriculum *73*
   Aristotle on Rhetoric and Poetry *75*
   Aristotle's Ethical Treatises *79*
   Aristotle's Political Theory *82*
   Aristotle's Cosmology *87*
   The Legacy of Aristotle and Plato *89*
   Aristotle's School *91*
   Epicurus *94*

CONTENTS

Stoicism   *96*

Scepticism in the Academy   *100*

Lucretius   *101*

Cicero   *103*

Judaism and Christianity   *104*

The Imperial Stoa   *106*

Early Christian Philosophy   *109*

The Revival of Platonism and Aristotelianism   *111*

Plotinus and Augustine   *112*

3. **How to Argue: Logic**   *116*

Aristotle's Syllogistic   *117*

The *de Interpretatione* and the *Categories*   *123*

Aristotle on Time and Modality   *129*

Stoic Logic   *136*

4. **Knowledge and its Limits: Epistemology**   *145*

Presocratic Epistemology   *145*

Socrates, Knowledge, and Ignorance   *148*

Knowledge in the *Theaetetus*   *152*

Knowledge and Ideas   *156*

Aristotle on Science and Illusion   *161*

Epicurean Epistemology   *166*

Stoic Epistemology   *169*

Academic Scepticism   *173*

Pyrrhonian Scepticism   *175*

5. **How Things Happen: Physics**   *178*

The Continuum   *178*

Aristotle on Place   *182*

Aristotle on Motion   *184*

Aristotle on Time   *186*

Aristotle on Causation and Change   *189*

The Stoics on Causality   *192*

Causation and Determinism   *194*

Determinism and Freedom   *196*

6. **What There Is: Metaphysics**   *199*

Parmenides' Ontology   *200*

CONTENTS

Plato's Ideas and their Troubles   *205*
Aristotelian Forms   *216*
Essence and Quiddity   *218*
Being and Existence   *223*

7. **Soul and Mind**   *229*

Pythagoras' Metempsychosis   *229*
Perception and Thought   *232*
Immortality in Plato's *Phaedo*   *234*
The Anatomy of the Soul   *237*
Plato on Sense-Perception   *240*
Aristotle's Philosophical Psychology   *241*
Hellenistic Philosophy of Mind   *248*
Will, Mind, and Soul in Late Antiquity   *251*

8. **How to Live: Ethics**   *257*

Democritus the Moralist   *257*
Socrates on Virtue   *260*
Plato on Justice and Pleasure   *264*
Aristotle on *Eudaimonia*   *266*
Aristotle on Moral and Intellectual Virtue   *269*
Pleasure and Happiness   *274*
The Hedonism of Epicurus   *277*
Stoic Ethics   *280*

9. **God**   *289*

Xenophanes' Natural Theology   *289*
Socrates and Plato on Piety   *290*
Plato's Evolving Theology   *293*
Aristotle's Unmoved Movers   *296*
The Gods of Epicurus and the Stoics   *302*
On Divination and Astrology   *308*
The Trinity of Plotinus   *311*

Chronology   *317*
List of Abbreviations and Conventions   *319*
Bibliography   *323*
List of Illustrations   *331*
Index   *335*

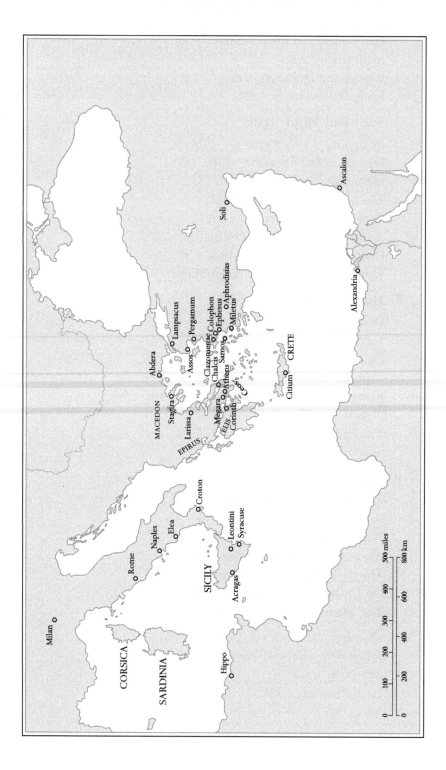

INTRODUCTION

Why should one study the history of philosophy? There are many reasons, but they fall into two groups: philosophical and historical. We may study the great dead philosophers in order to seek illumination upon themes of present-day philosophical inquiry. Or we may wish to understand the people and societies of the past, and read their philosophy to grasp the conceptual climate in which they thought and acted. We may read the philosophers of other ages to help to resolve philosophical problems of abiding concern, or to enter more fully into the intellectual world of a bygone era.

In this history of philosophy, from the beginnings to the present day, I hope to further both purposes, but in different ways in different parts of the work, as I shall try to make clear in this Introduction. But before outlining a strategy for writing the history of philosophy, one must pause to reflect on the nature of philosophy itself. The word 'philosophy' means different things in different mouths, and correspondingly 'the history of philosophy' can be interpreted in many ways. What it signifies depends on what the particular historian regards as being essential to philosophy.

This was true of Aristotle, who was philosophy's first historian, and of Hegel, who hoped he would be its last, since he was bringing philosophy to perfection. The two of them had very different views of the nature of philosophy. Nonetheless, they had in common a view of philosophical progress: philosophical problems in the course of history became ever more clearly defined, and they could be answered with ever greater accuracy. Aristotle in the first book of his *Metaphysics* and Hegel in his *Lectures on the History of Philosophy* saw the teachings of the earlier philosophers they recorded as halting steps in the direction of a vision they were themselves to expound.

Only someone with supreme self-confidence as a philosopher could write its history in such a way. The temptation for most philosopher historians is to see philosophy not as culminating in their own work, but rather as a gradual progress to whatever philosophical system is currently in fashion. But this temptation should be resisted. There is no force that guarantees philosophical progress in any particular direction.

Indeed, it can be called into question whether philosophy makes any progress at all. The major philosophical problems, some say, are all still being debated after centuries of discussion, and are no nearer to any definitive resolution. In the twentieth century the philosopher Ludwig Wittgenstein wrote:

> You always hear people say that philosophy makes no progress and that the same philosophical problems which were already preoccupying the Greeks are still troubling us today. But people who say that do not understand the reason why it has to be so. The reason is that our language has remained the same and always introduces us to the same questions. . . . I read 'philosophers are no nearer to the meaning of "reality" than Plato got'. What an extraordinary thing! How remarkable that Plato could get so far! Or that we have not been able to get any further! Was it because Plato was *so* clever? (MS 213/424)

The difference between what we might call the Aristotelian and the Wittgensteinian attitude to progress in philosophy is linked with two different views of philosophy itself. Philosophy may be viewed as a science, on the one hand, or as an art, on the other. Philosophy is, indeed, uniquely difficult to classify, and resembles both the arts and the sciences.

On the one hand, philosophy seems to be like a science in that the philosopher is in pursuit of truth. Discoveries, it seems, are made in philosophy, and so the philosopher, like the scientist, has the excitement of belonging to an ongoing, cooperative, cumulative intellectual venture. If so, the philosopher must be familiar with current writing, and keep abreast of the state of the art. On this view, we twenty-first-century philosophers have an advantage over earlier practitioners of the discipline. We stand, no doubt, on the shoulders of other and greater philosophers, but we do stand above them. We have superannuated Plato and Kant.

On the other hand, in the arts, classic works do not date. If we want to learn physics or chemistry, as opposed to their history, we don't nowadays read Newton or Faraday. But we read the literature of Homer and Shakespeare not merely to learn about the quaint things that passed through people's minds in far-off days of long ago. Surely, it may well be argued, the same is true of philosophy. It is not merely in a spirit of antiquarian curiosity that we read Aristotle today. Philosophy is essentially the work of individual genius, and Kant does not supersede Plato any more than Shakespeare supersedes Homer.

There is truth in each of these accounts, but neither is wholly true and neither contains the whole truth. Philosophy is not a science, and there is no state of the art in philosophy. Philosophy is not a matter of expanding knowledge, of acquiring new truths about the world; the philosopher is not in possession of information that is denied to others. Philosophy is not a matter of knowledge, it is a matter of understanding, that is to say, of organizing what is known. But because philosophy is all-embracing, is so universal in its field, the organization of knowledge it demands is something so difficult that only genius can do it. For all of us who are not geniuses, the only way in which we can hope to come to grips with philosophy is by reaching up to the mind of some great philosopher of the past.

Though philosophy is not a science, throughout its history it has had an intimate relation to the sciences. Many disciplines that in antiquity and in the Middle Ages were part of philosophy have long since become independent sciences. A discipline remains philosophical as long as its concepts are unclarified and its methods are controversial. Perhaps no scientific concepts are ever fully clarified, and no scientific methods are ever totally uncontroversial; if so, there is always a philosophical element left in every science. But once problems can be unproblematically stated, when concepts are uncontroversially standardized, and where a consensus emerges for the methodology of solution, then we have a science setting up home independently, rather than a branch of philosophy.

Philosophy, once called the queen of the sciences, and once called their handmaid, is perhaps better thought of as the womb, or the midwife, of the sciences. But in fact sciences emerge from philosophy not so much by parturition as by fission. Two examples, out of many, may serve to illustrate this.

In the seventeenth century philosophers were much exercised by the problem which of our ideas are innate and which are acquired. This problem split into two problems, one psychological ('What do we owe to heredity and what do we owe to environment?') and one belonging to the theory of knowledge ('How much of our knowledge depends on experience and how much is independent of it?'). The first question was handed over to scientific psychology, the second question remained philosophical.

But the second question itself split into a number of questions, one of which was 'Is mathematics merely an extension of logic, or is it an independent body of truth?' The question whether mathematics could be derived from pure logic was given a precise answer by the work of logicians and mathematicians in the twentieth century. The answer was not philosophical, but mathematical. So here we had an initial, confused, philosophical question which ramified in two directions—towards psychology and towards mathematics. There remains in the middle a philosophical residue to be churned over, concerning the nature of mathematical propositions.

An earlier example is more complicated. A branch of philosophy given an honoured place by Aristotle is 'theology'. When today we read what he says, the discipline appears a mixture of astronomy and philosophy of religion. Christian and Muslim Aristotelians added to it elements drawn from the teaching of their sacred books. It was when St Thomas Aquinas, in the thirteenth century, drew a sharp distinction between natural and revealed theology that the first important fission took place, removing from the philosophical agenda the appeals to revelation. It took rather longer for the astronomy and the natural theology to separate out from each other. This example shows that what may be sloughed off by philosophy need not be a science but may be a humanistic discipline such as biblical studies. It also shows that the history of philosophy contains examples of fusion as well as of fission.

Philosophy resembles the arts in having a significant relation to a canon. A philosopher situates the problems to be addressed by reference to a series of classical texts. Because it has no specific subject matter, but only characteristic methods, philosophy is defined as a discipline by the activities of its great practitioners. The earliest people whom we recognize as philosophers, the Presocratics, were also scientists, and several of them were also religious leaders. They did not yet think of themselves as belonging to a common profession, the one with which we twenty-first-century philosophers claim continuity. It was Plato who in his writings first used the word 'philosophy' in some approximation to our modern sense. Those of us who call ourselves philosophers today can genuinely lay claim to be the heirs of Plato and Aristotle. But we are only a small subset of their heirs. What distinguishes us from the other heirs of the great Greeks, and what entitles us to inherit their name, is that unlike the physicists, the astronomers, the medics, the linguists, we philosophers pursue the goals of Plato and Aristotle only by the same methods as were already available to them.

If philosophy lies somewhere between the sciences and the arts, what is the answer to the question 'Is there progress in philosophy?'

There are those who think that the major task of philosophy is to cure us of intellectual confusion. On this, modest, view of the philosopher's role, the tasks to be addressed differ across history, since each period needs a different form of therapy. The knots into which the undisciplined mind ties itself differ from age to age, and different mental motions are necessary to untie the knots. A prevalent malady of our own age, for instance, is the temptation to think of the mind as a computer, whereas earlier ages were tempted to think of it as a telephone exchange, a pedal organ, a homunculus, or a spirit. Maladies of earlier ages may be dormant, such as belief that the stars are living beings; or they may return, such as the belief that the stars enable one to predict human behaviour.

The therapeutic view of philosophy, however, may seem to allow only for variation over time, not for genuine progress. But that is not necessarily true. A confusion of thought may be so satisfactorily cleared up by a philosopher that it no longer offers temptation to the unwary thinker. One such example will be considered at length in the first volume of this history. Parmenides, the founder of the discipline of ontology (the science of being), based much of his system on a systematic confusion between different senses of the verb 'to be'. Plato, in one of his dialogues, sorted out the issues so successfully that there has never again been an excuse for mixing them up: indeed, it now takes a great effort of philosophical imagination to work out exactly what led Parmenides into confusion in the first place.

Progress of this kind is often concealed by its very success: once a philosophical problem is resolved, no one regards it as any more a matter of philosophy. It is like treason in the epigram: 'Treason doth never prosper, what's the reason? | For if it prosper none dare call it treason.'

The most visible form of philosophical progress is progress in philosophical analysis. Philosophy does not progress by making regular additions to a quantum of information; as has been said, what philosophy offers is not information but understanding. Contemporary philosophers, of course, know some things that the greatest philosophers of the past did not know; but the things that they know are not philosophical matters but the truths that have been discovered by the sciences begotten of philosophy. But there are also some things that philosophers of the present day understand which even the greatest philosophers of earlier generations failed to understand. For instance, philosophers clarify language by distinguishing between different senses of words; and once a distinction has been made, future philosophers have to take account of it in their deliberations.

Take, as an example, the issue of free will. At a certain point in the history of philosophy a distinction was made between two kinds of human freedom: liberty of indifference (ability to do otherwise) and liberty of spontaneity (ability to do what you want). Once this distinction has been made the question 'Do human beings enjoy freedom of the will?' has to be answered in a way that takes account of the distinction. Even someone who believes that the two kinds of liberty coincide has to provide arguments to show this; he cannot simply ignore the distinction and hope to be taken seriously on the topic.

It is unsurprising, given the relationship of philosophy to a canon, that one notable form of philosophical progress consists in coming to terms with, and interpreting, the thoughts of the great philosophers of the past. The great works of the past do not lose their importance in philosophy— but their intellectual contributions are not static. Each age interprets and applies philosophical classics to its own problems and aspirations. This is, in recent years, most visible in the field of ethics. The ethical works of Plato and Aristotle are as influential in moral thinking today as the works of any twentieth-century moralists—this is easily verified by taking any citation index—but they are being interpreted and applied in ways quite different from the ways in which they were applied in the past. These new inter-pretations and applications do effect a genuine advance in our understand-ing of Plato and Aristotle; but of course it is understanding of quite a different kind from what is given by a new study of the chronology of Plato's dialogues or a stylometric comparison between Aristotle's various ethical works. The new light we receive resembles rather the enhanced appreciation of Shakespeare we may get by seeing·a new and intelligent production of *King Lear*.

The historian of philosophy, whether primarily interested in philosophy or primarily interested in history, cannot help being both a philosopher and a historian. A historian of painting does not have to be a painter; a historian of medicine does not, *qua* historian, practise medicine. But a historian of philosophy cannot help doing philosophy in the very writing of history. It is not just that someone who knows no philosophy will be a bad historian of philosophy; it is equally true that someone who has no idea of how to cook will be a bad historian of cookery. The link between philosophy and its history is a far closer one. The historical task itself forces historians of philosophy to paraphrase their subjects' opinions, to offer reasons why past thinkers held the opinions they did, to speculate on the premises left tacit in their arguments, and to evaluate the coherence and cogency of the inferences they drew. But the supplying of reasons for philosophical conclusions, the detection of hidden premises in philosophical arguments, and the logical evaluation of philosophical inferences are themselves full-blooded philosophical activities. Consequently, any serious history of philosophy must itself be an exercise in philosophy as well as in history.

On the other hand, the historian of philosophy must have a knowledge of the historical context in which past philosophers wrote their works. When we explain historical actions, we ask for the agent's reasons; if we find a good reason, we think we have understood his action. If we conclude he did not have good reason, even in his own terms, we have to find, different, more complicated explanations. What is true of action is true of taking a philosophical view. If the philosophical historian finds a good reason for a past philosopher's doctrine, then his task is done. But if he concludes that the past philosopher has no good reason, he has a further and much more difficult task, of explaining the doctrine in terms of the context in which it appeared—social, perhaps, as well as intellectual.[1]

History and philosophy are closely linked even in the first-hand quest for original philosophical enlightenment. In modern times this has been most brilliantly illustrated by the masterpiece of the great nineteenth-century German philosopher Gottlob Frege, *The Foundations of Arithmetic*. Almost half of Frege's book is devoted to discussing and refuting the view of other philosophers and mathematicians. While he is discussing the opinions of others, he ensures that some of his own insights are artfully insinuated, and this makes easier the eventual presentation of his own theory. But the main purpose of his lengthy polemic is to convince readers of the seriousness of the problems to which he will later offer solutions.

[1] The magnitude of this task is well brought out by Michael Frede in the introduction to his *Essays in Ancient Philosophy* (Oxford: Clarendon Press, 1987).

Without this preamble, he says, we would lack the first prerequisite for learning anything: knowledge of our own ignorance.

Most histories of philosophy, in this age of specialization, are the work of many hands, specialists in different fields and periods. In inviting me to write, single-handed, a history of philosophy from Thales to Derrida, Oxford University Press gave expression to the belief that there is something to be gained by presenting the development of philosophy from a single viewpoint, linking ancient, medieval, early modern, and contemporary philosophy into a single narrative concerned with connected themes. The work will appear in four volumes: the first will cover the centuries from the beginning of philosophy up to the conversion of St Augustine in AD 387. The second will take the story from Augustine up to the Lateran Council of 1512. The third will end with the death of Hegel in 1831. The fourth and final volume will bring the narrative up to the end of the second millennium.

Obviously, I cannot claim to be an expert on all the many philosophers whom I will discuss in the volumes of this work. However, I have published books on major figures within each of the periods of the four volumes: on Aristotle (*The Aristotelian Ethics* and *Aristotle on the Perfect Life*), on Aquinas (*Aquinas on Mind* and *Aquinas on Being*), on Descartes (*Descartes: A Study of his Philosophy* and *Descartes: Philosophical Letters*), and on Frege and Wittgenstein (*Frege* and *Wittgenstein* as Penguin introductions and *The Legacy of Wittgenstein*). I hope that the work that went into the writing of these books gave me an insight into the philosophical style of four different eras in the history of philosophy. It certainly gave me a sense of the perennial importance of certain philosophical problems and insights.

I hope to write my history in a manner that takes account of the points I have raised in this Introduction. I do not suffer from any Whiggish illusion that the current state of philosophy represents the highest point of philosophical endeavour yet reached. On the contrary, my primary purpose in writing the book is to show that in many respects the philosophy of the great dead philosophers has not dated, and that today one may gain philosophical illumination by a careful reading of the great works that we have been privileged to inherit.

The kernel of any kind of historiography of philosophy is exegesis: the close reading and interpretation of philosophical texts. Exegesis may be of two kinds, internal or external. In internal exegesis the interpreter tries to render the text coherent and consistent, making use of the principle of charity in interpretation. In external exegesis the interpreter seeks to bring out the significance of the text by comparing it and contrasting it with other texts.

Exegesis may form the basis of the two quite different historical endeavours that I described at the beginning of this Introduction. In one, which we may call historical philosophy, the aim is to reach philosophical truth, or philosophical understanding, about the matter or issue under discussion in the text. Typically, historical philosophy looks for the reasons behind, or the justification for, the statements made in the text under study. In the other endeavour, the history of ideas, the aim is not to reach the truth about the matter in hand, but to reach the understanding of a person or an age or a historical succession. Typically the historian of ideas looks not for the reasons so much as the sources, or causes, or motives, for saying what is said in the target text.

Both of these disciplines base themselves on exegesis, but of the two, the history of ideas is the one most closely bound up with the accuracy and sensitivity of the reading of the text. It is possible to be a good philosopher while being a poor exegete. At the beginning of his *Philosophical Investigations* Wittgenstein offers a discussion of St Augustine's theory of language. What he writes is very dubious exegesis; but this does not weaken the force of his philosophical criticism of the 'Augustinian' theory of language. But Wittgenstein did not really think of himself as engaged in historical philosophy, any more than he thought of himself as engaged in the historiography of ideas. The invocation of the great Augustine as the author of the mistaken theory is intended merely to indicate that the error is one that is worth attacking.

In different histories of philosophy the skills of the historian and those of the philosopher are exercised in different proportions. The due proportion varies in accordance with the purpose of the work and the field of philosophy in question. The pursuit of historical understanding and the pursuit of philosophical enlightenment are both legitimate approaches to the history of philosophy, but both have their dangers. Historians who study the history of thought without being themselves involved in the philosophical problems that exercised past philosophers are likely to sin by superficiality. Philosophers who read ancient, medieval, or early modern texts without a knowledge of the historical context in which they were written are likely to sin by anachronism. Rare is the historian of philosophy who can tread firmly without falling into either trap.

Each of these errors can nullify the purpose of the enterprise. The historian who is unconcerned by the philosophical problems that troubled past writers has not really understood how they themselves conducted their thinking. The philosopher who ignores the historical background of past classics will gain no fresh light on the issues that concern us today, but merely present contemporary prejudices in fancy dress.

The two dangers threaten in different proportions in different areas of the history of philosophy. In the area of metaphysics it is superficiality which is most to be guarded against: to someone without a personal interest in fundamental philosophical problems the systems of the great thinkers of the past will seem only quaint lunacy. In political philosophy the great danger is anachronism: when we read Plato's or Aristotle's criticisms of democracy, we shall not make head or tail of them unless we know something about the institutions of ancient Athens. In between metaphysics and political philosophy stand ethics and philosophy of mind: here both dangers threaten with roughly equal force.

I shall attempt in these volumes to be both a philosophical historian and a historical philosopher. Multi-authored histories are sometimes structured chronologically and sometimes structured thematically. I shall try to combine both approaches, offering in each volume first a chronological survey, and then a thematic treatment of particular philosophical topics of abiding importance. The reader whose primary interest is historical will focus on the chronological survey, referring where necessary to the thematic sections for amplification. The reader who is more concerned with the philosophical issues will concentrate rather on the thematic sections of the volumes, referring back to the chronological surveys to place particular issues in context.

Thus in this first volume I offer in the first part a conventional chronological tour from Pythagoras to Augustine, and in the second part a more detailed treatment of topics where I believe we have still much to learn from our predecessors in classical Greece and imperial Rome. The topics of these thematic sections have been chosen partly with an eye to the development of the same themes in the volumes that are yet to come.

The audience I have in mind is at the level of second- or third-year undergraduate study. I realize, however, that many of those interested in the history of philosophy may themselves be enrolled in courses that are not primarily philosophical. Accordingly, I shall do my best not to assume a familiarity with contemporary philosophical techniques or terminology. I aim also to write in a manner clear and light-hearted enough for the history to be enjoyed by those who read it not for curricular purposes but for their own enlightenment and entertainment.

1

Beginnings:
From Pythagoras to Plato

The history of philosophy does not begin with Aristotle, but the historiography of philosophy does. Aristotle was the first philosopher who systematically studied, recorded, and criticized the work of previous philosophers. In the first book of the *Metaphysics* he summarizes the teachings of his predecessors, from his distant intellectual ancestors Pythagoras and Thales up to Plato, his teacher for twenty years. To this day he is one of the most copious, and most reliable, sources of our information about philosophy in its infancy.

The Four Causes

Aristotle offers a classification of the earliest Greek philosophers in accordance with the structure of his system of the four causes. Scientific inquiry, he believed, was above all inquiry into the causes of things; and there were four different kinds of cause: the material cause, the efficient cause, the formal cause, and the final cause. To give a crude illustration of what he had in mind: when Alfredo cooks a risotto, the material causes of the risotto are the ingredients that go into it, the efficient cause is the chef himself, the recipe is the formal cause, and the satisfaction of the clients of his restaurant is the final cause. Aristotle believed that a scientific understanding of the universe demanded an inquiry into the operation in the world of causes of each of these kinds (*Metaph. A* 3. 983^{a}24–^{b}17).

Early philosophers on the Greek coast of Asia Minor concentrated on the material cause: they sought the basic ingredients of the world we live in. Thales and his successors posed the following question: At a fundamental level is the world made out of water, or air, or fire, or earth, or a combination of some or all of these? (*Metaph. A* 3. 983^{b}20–84^{a}16). Even if we have an answer to this question, Aristotle thought, that is clearly not enough to satisfy our scientific curiosity. The ingredients of a dish do not put themselves together: there needs to be an agent operating upon them, by cutting, mixing, stirring, heating, or the like. Some of these early philosophers, Aristotle tells us, were aware of this and offered conjectures about the agents of change and development in the world. Sometimes it would be one of the ingredients themselves—fire was perhaps the most promising suggestion, as being the least torpid of the elements. More often it would be some agent, or pair of agents, both more abstract and more picturesque, such as Love or Desire or Strife, or the Good and the Bad (*Metaph. A* 3–4. 984^{b}8–31).

Meanwhile in Italy—again according to Aristotle—there were, around Pythagoras, mathematically inclined philosophers whose inquiries took quite a different course. A recipe, besides naming ingredients, will contain a lot of numbers: so many grams of this, so many litres of that. The Pythagoreans were more interested in the numbers in the world's recipe than in the ingredients themselves. They supposed, Aristotle says, that the elements of numbers were the elements of all things, and the whole of the heavens was a musical scale. They were inspired in their quest by their discovery that the relationship between the notes of the scale played on a lyre corresponded to different numerical ratios between the lengths of the strings. They then generalized this idea that qualitative differences might be the upshot of numerical differences. Their inquiry, in Aristotle's terms, was an inquiry into the formal causes of the universe. (*Metaph. A* 5. 985^{b}23–986^{b}2)

Coming to his immediate predecessors, Aristotle says that Socrates preferred to concentrate on ethics rather than study the world of nature, while Plato in his philosophical theory combined the approaches of the schools of both Thales and Pythagoras. But Plato's Theory of Ideas, while being the most comprehensive scientific system yet devised, seemed to Aristotle—for reasons that he summarizes here and develops in a number of his treatises—to be unsatisfactory on several grounds. There were so many things to explain, and the Ideas just added new items calling for explanation: they did not provide a solution, they added to the problem (*Metaph. A* 5. 990^{b}1 ff.).

Most dissertations that begin with literature searches seek to show that all work hitherto has left a gap that will now be filled by the author's original research. Aristotle's *Metaphysics* is no exception. His not too hidden agenda is to show how previous philosophers neglected the remaining member of the quartet of causes: the final cause, which was to play a most significant role in his own philosophy of nature (*Metaph. A* 5. 988^{b}6–15). The earliest philosophy, he concluded, is, on all subjects, full of babble, since in its beginnings it is but an infant (*Metaph. A* 5. 993^{a}15–7.)

A philosopher of the present day, reading the surviving fragments of the earliest Greek thinkers, is impressed not so much by the questions they were asking, as by the methods they used to answer them. After all, the book of Genesis offers us answers to the four causal questions set by Aristotle. If we ask for the origin of the first human being, for instance, we are told that the efficient cause was God, that the material cause was the dust of the earth, that the formal cause was the image and likeness of God, and that the final cause was for man to have dominion over the fish of the sea, the fowl of the air, and every living thing on earth. Yet Genesis is not a work of philosophy.

On the other hand, Pythagoras is best known not for answering any of the Aristotelian questions, but for proving the theorem that the square on the hypotenuse of a right-angled triangle is equal in area to the sum of the squares on the other two sides. Thales, again, was believed by later Greeks to have been the first person to make an accurate prediction of an eclipse, in the year 585 BC. These are surely achievements in geometry and astronomy, not philosophy.

The fact is that the distinction between religion, science, and philosophy was not as clear as it became in later centuries. The works of Aristotle and his master Plato provide a paradigm of philosophy for every age, and to this day anyone using the title 'philosopher' is claiming to be one of their heirs. Writers in twenty-first-century philosophy journals can be seen to be using the same techniques of conceptual analysis, and often to be repeating or refuting the same theoretical arguments, as are to be found in the writings of Plato and Aristotle. But in those writings there is much else that would not nowadays be thought of as philosophical discussion. From the sixth century BC onwards elements of religion, science, and philosophy ferment together in a single cultural cauldron. From our distance in time philosophers, scientists, and theologians can all look back to these early thinkers as their intellectual forefathers.

The Milesians

Only two sayings are recorded of Thales of Miletus (*c*.625–545 BC), traditionally the founding father of Greek philosophy. They illustrate the mélange of science and religion, for one of them was 'All things are full of gods', and the other was 'Water is the first principle of everything'. Thales was a geometer, the first to discover the method of inscribing a right-angled triangle in a circle; he celebrated this discovery by sacrificing an ox to the gods (D.L. 1. 24–5). He measured the height of the pyramids by measuring their shadows at the time of day when his own shadow was as long as he was tall. He put his geometry to practical use: having proved that triangles with one equal side and two equal angles are congruent, he used this result to determine the distance of ships at sea.

Thales also had a reputation as an astronomer and a meteorologist. In addition to predicting the eclipse, he is said to have been the first to show that the year contained 365 days, and to determine the dates of the summer and winter solstices. He studied the constellations and made estimates of the sizes of the sun and moon. He turned his skill as a weather forecaster to good account: foreseeing an unusually good olive crop, he took a lease on all the oil mills and made a fortune through his monopoly. Thus, Aristotle said, he showed that philosophers could easily be rich if they wished (*Pol.* 1. 11. 1259^{a}6–18).

If half the stories current about Thales in antiquity are true, he was a man of many parts. But tradition's portrait of him is ambiguous. On the one hand, he figures as a philosophical entrepreneur, and a political and military pundit. On the other hand, he became a byword for unworldly absent-mindedness. Plato, among others, tells the following tale:

Thales was studying the stars and gazing into the sky, when he fell into a well, and a jolly and witty Thracian servant girl made fun of him, saying that he was crazy to know about what was up in the heavens while he could not see what was in front of him beneath his feet. (*Theaetetus* 174a)

An unlikely story went around that he had met his death by just such a fall while stargazing.

Thales was reckoned as one of the Seven Sages, or wise men, of Greece, on a par with Solon, the great legislator of Athens. He is credited with a number of aphorisms. He said that before a certain age it was too soon for a man to marry; and after that age it was too late. When asked why he had no children, he said 'Because I am fond of children.'

Thales' remarks heralded many centuries of philosophical disdain for marriage. Anyone who makes a list of a dozen really great philosophers is likely to discover that the list consists almost entirely of bachelors. One plausible list, for instance, would include Plato, Augustine, Aquinas, Scotus, Descartes, Locke, Spinoza, Hume, Kant, Hegel, and Wittgenstein, none of whom were married. Aristotle is the grand exception that disproves the rule that marriage is incompatible with philosophy.

Even in antiquity people found it hard to understand Thales' adoption of water as the ultimate principle of explanation. The earth, he said, rested on water like a log floating in a stream—but then, asked Aristotle, what does the water rest on? (*Cael.* 2. 13. 294ᵃ28–34). He went further and said that everything came from and was in some sense made out of water. Again, his reasons were obscure, and Aristotle could only conjecture that it was because all animals and plants need water to live, or because semen is moist (*Metaph. A* 3. 983ᵇ17–27).

It is easier to come to grips with the cosmology of Thales' junior compatriot Anaximander of Miletus (d. *c.*547 BC). We know rather more about his views, because he left behind a book entitled *On Nature*, written in prose, a medium just beginning to come into fashion. Like Thales he was credited with a number of original scientific achievements: the first map of the world, the first star chart, the first Greek sundial, and an indoor clock as well. He taught that the earth was cylindrical in shape, like a stumpy column no higher than a third of its diameter. Around the world were gigantic tyres full of fire; each tyre was punctured with a hole through which the fire could be seen from outside, and the holes were the sun and moon and stars. Blockages in the holes accounted for eclipses of the sun and phases of the moon. The celestial fire which is nowadays

Anaximander with his sundial, in a Roman mosaic

largely hidden was once a great ball of flame around the infant earth; when this ball exploded, the fragments grew tyres like bark around themselves.

Anaximander was much impressed by the way trees grow and shed their bark. He used the same analogy to explain the origin of human beings. Other animals, he observed, can look after themselves soon after birth, but humans need a long nursing. If humans had always been as they are now, the race would not have survived. In an earlier age, he conjectured, humans had spent their childhood encased in a prickly bark, so that they looked like fish and lived in water. At puberty they shed their bark, and stepped out onto dry land, into an environment in which they could take care of themselves. Because of this, Anaximander, though not otherwise a vegetarian, recommended that we abstain from eating fish, as the ancestors of the human race (KRS 133–7).

Anaximander's cosmology is more sophisticated than Thales' in several ways. First of all, he does not look for something to support the earth: it stays where it is because it is equidistant from everything else and there is no reason why it should move in any direction rather than any other (DK 12 A11; Aristotle, *Cael.* 2. 13. 295^{b}10).

Secondly, he thinks it is an error to identify the ultimate material of the universe with any of the elements we can see around us in the contemporary world, such as water or fire. The fundamental principle of things, he said, must be boundless or undefined (*apeiron*). Anaximander's Greek word is often rendered as 'the Infinite', but that makes it sound too grand. He may or may not have thought that his principle extended for ever in space; what we do know is that he thought it had no beginning and no end in time and that it did not belong to any particular kind or class of things. 'Everlasting stuff' is probably as close a paraphrase as we can get. Aristotle was later to refine the notion into his concept of prime matter.[1]

Thirdly, Anaximander offered an account of the origin of the present world, and explained what forces had acted to bring it into existence, inquiring, as Aristotle would say, into the efficient as well as the material cause. He saw the universe as a field of competing opposites: hot and cold, wet and dry. Sometimes one of a pair of opposites is dominant, sometimes the other: they encroach upon each other and then withdraw, and their interchange is governed by a principle of reciprocity. As Anaximander put it poetically in his one surviving fragment, 'they pay penalty and render reparation to each other for their injustice under the arbitration of time' (DK 12 B1). Thus, one surmises, in winter the hot and the dry make reparation to the cold and the wet for the aggression they committed in summer. Heat and cold were the first of the opposites to make their appearance, separating off from an original cosmic egg of the everlasting indeterminate stuff. From them developed the fire and earth which, we have seen, lay at the origin of our present cosmos.

---

[1] See Ch. 5 below.

Anaximenes (fl. 546–525 BC), a generation younger than Anaximander, was the last of the trio of Milesian cosmologists. In several ways he is closer to Thales than to Anaximander, but it would be wrong to think that with him science is going backwards rather than forwards. Like Thales, he thought that the earth must rest on something, but he proposed air, rather than water, for its cushion. The earth itself is flat, and so are the heavenly bodies. These, instead of rotating above and below us in the course of a day, circle horizontally around us like a bonnet rotating around a head (KRS 151–6). The rising and setting of the heavenly bodies is explained, apparently, by the tilting of the flat earth. As for the ultimate principle, Anaximenes found Anaximander's boundless matter too rarefied a concept, and opted, like Thales, for a single one of the existing elements as fundamental, though again he opted for air rather than water.

In its stable state air is invisible, but when it is moved and condensed it becomes first wind and then cloud and then water, and finally water condensed becomes mud and stone. Rarefied air became fire, thus completing the gamut of the elements. In this way rarefaction and condensation can conjure everything out of the underlying air (KRS 140–1). In support of this claim Anaximenes appealed to experience, and indeed to experiment—an experiment that the reader can easily carry out for herself. Blow on your hand, first with the lips pursed, and then from an open mouth: the first time the air will feel cold, and the second time hot. This, argued Anaximenes, shows the connection between density and temperature (KRS 143).

The use of experiment, and the insight that changes of quality are linked to changes of quantity, mark Anaximenes as a scientist in embryo. Only in embryo, however: he has no means of measuring the quantities he invokes, he devises no equations to link them, and his fundamental principle retains mythical and religious properties.[2] Air is divine, and generates deities out of itself (KRS 144–6); air is our soul, and holds our bodies together (KRS 160).

The Milesians, then, are not yet real physicists, but neither are they myth-makers. They have not yet left myth behind, but they are moving away from it. They are not true philosophers either, unless by 'philosophy'

---

[2] See J. Barnes, *The Presocratic Philosophers*, rev. edn. (London: Routledge, 1982), 46–8.

one simply means infant science. They make little use of conceptual analysis and the a priori argument that has been the stock-in-trade of philosophers from Plato to the present day. They are speculators, in whose speculations elements of philosophy, science, and religion mingle in a rich and heady brew.

The Pythagoreans

In antiquity Pythagoras shared with Thales the credit for introducing philosophy into the Greek world. He was born in Samos, an island off the coast of Asia Minor, about 570 BC. At the age of 40 he emigrated to Croton on the toe of Italy. There he took a leading part in the political affairs of the city, until he was banished in a violent revolution about 510 BC. He moved to nearby Metapontum, where he died at the turn of the century. During his time at Croton he founded a semi-religious community, which outlived him until it was scattered about 450 BC. He is credited with inventing the word 'philosopher': instead of claiming to be a sage or wise man (*sophos*) he modestly said that he was only a lover of wisdom (*philosophos*) (D.L. 8. 8). The details of his life are swamped in legend, but it is clear that he practised both mathematics and mysticism. In both fields his intellectual influence, acknowledged or implicit, was strong throughout antiquity, from Plato to Porphyry.

The Pythagoreans' discovery that there was a relationship between musical intervals and numerical ratios led to the belief that the study of mathematics was the key to the understanding of the structure and order of the universe. Astronomy and harmony, they said, were sister sciences, one for the eyes and one for the ears (Plato, *Rep.* 530d). However, it was not until two millennia later that Galileo and his successors showed the sense in which it is true that the book of the universe is written in numbers. In the ancient world arithmetic was too entwined with number mysticism to promote scientific progress, and the genuine scientific advances of the period (such as Aristotle's zoology or Galen's medicine) were achieved without benefit of mathematics.

Pythagoras' philosophical community at Croton was the prototype of many such institutions: it was followed by Plato's Academy, Aristotle's

Pythagoras commending vegetarianism, as imagined by Rubens

Lyceum, Epicurus' Garden, and many others. Some such communities were legal entities, and others less formal; some resembled a modern research institute, others were more like monasteries. Pythagoras' associates held their property in common and lived under a set of ascetic and ceremonial rules: observe silence, do not break bread, do not pick up crumbs, do not poke the fire with a sword, always put on the right shoe before the left, and so on. The Pythagoreans were not, to begin with, complete vegetarians, but they avoided certain kinds of meat, fish, and poultry. Most famously, they were forbidden to eat beans (KRS 271–2, 275–6).

The dietary rules were connected with Pythagoras' beliefs about the soul. It did not die with the body, he believed, but migrated elsewhere, perhaps into an animal body of a different kind.[3] Some Pythagoreans extended this into belief in a three-thousand-year cosmic cycle: a human soul after death would enter, one after the other, every kind of land, sea, or

---

[3] See Ch. 7 below.

10

air creature, and finally return into a human body for history to repeat itself (Herodotus 2. 123; KRS 285). Pythagoras himself, however, after his death was believed by his followers to have become a god. They wrote biographies of him full of wonders, crediting him with second sight and the gift of bilocation; he had a golden thigh, they said, and was the son of Apollo. More prosaically, the expression 'Ipse dixit' was coined in his honour.

Xenophanes

The death of Pythagoras, and the destruction of Miletus in 494, brought to an end the first era of Presocratic thought. In the next generation we encounter thinkers who are not only would-be scientists, but also philosophers in the modern sense of the word. Xenophanes of Colophon (a town near present-day Izmir, some hundred miles north of Miletus) straddles the two eras in his long life (c.570–c.470 BC). He is also, like Pythagoras, a link between the eastern and the western centres of Greek cultures. Expelled from Colophon in his twenties, he became a wandering minstrel, and by his own account travelled around Greece for sixty-seven years, giving recitals of his own and others' poems (D.L. 9. 18). He sang of wine and games and parties, but it is his philosophical verses that are most read today.

Like the Milesians, Xenophanes propounded a cosmology. The basic element, he maintained, was not water nor air, but earth, and the earth reaches down below us to infinity. 'All things are from earth and in earth all things end' (D.K. 21 B27) calls to mind Christian burial services and the Ash Wednesday exhortation 'remember, man, thou art but dust and unto dust thou shalt return'. But Xenophanes elsewhere links water with earth as the original source of things, and indeed he believed that our earth must at one time have been covered by the sea. This is connected with the most interesting of his contributions to science: the observation of the fossil record.

Seashells are found well inland, and on mountains too, and in the quarries in Syracuse impressions of fish and seaweed have been found. An impression of a bay leaf was found in Paros deep in a rock, and in Malta there are flat shapes of all kinds of sea creatures. These were produced when everything was covered with mud long ago, and the impressions dried in the mud. (KRS 184)

Xenophanes' speculations about the heavenly bodies are less impressive. Since he believed that the earth stretched beneath us to infinity, he could not accept that the sun went below the earth when it set. On the other hand, he found implausible Anaximenes' idea of a horizontal rotation around a tilting earth. He put forward a new and ingenious explanation: the sun, he maintained, was new every day. It came into existence each morning from a congregation of tiny sparks, and later vanished off into infinity. The appearance of circular movement is due simply to the great distance between the sun and ourselves. It follows from this theory that there are innumerable suns, just as there are innumerable days, because the world lasts for ever even though it passes through aqueous and terrestrial phases (KRS 175, 179).

Though Xenophanes' cosmology is ill-founded, it is notable for its naturalism: it is free from the animist and semi-religious elements to be found in other Presocratic philosophers. The rainbow, for instance, is not a divinity (like Iris in the Greek pantheon) nor a divine sign (like the one seen by Noah). It is simply a multicoloured cloud (KRS 178). This naturalism did not mean that Xenophanes was uninterested in religion: on the contrary, he was the most theological of all the Presocratics. But he despised popular superstition, and defended an austere and sophisticated monotheism.[4] He was not dogmatic, however, either in theology or in physics.

> God did not tell us mortals all when time began
> Only through long-time search does knowledge come to man.
>
> (KRS 188)

Heraclitus

Heraclitus was the last, and the most famous, of the early Ionian philosophers. He was perhaps thirty years younger than Xenophanes, since he is reported to have been middle-aged when the sixth century ended (D.L. 9. 1). He lived in the great metropolis of Ephesus, midway between Miletus and Colophon. We possess more substantial portions of his work than of any previous philosopher, but that does not mean we find him easier to

[4] See Ch. 9 below.

understand. His fragments take the form of pithy, crafted prose aphorisms, which are often obscure and sometimes deliberately ambiguous. Heraclitus did not argue, he pronounced. His delphic style may have been an imitation of the oracle of Apollo which, in his own words, 'neither speaks, nor conceals, but gestures' (KRS 244). The many philosophers in later centuries who have admired Heraclitus have been able to give their own colouring to his paradoxical, chameleon-like dicta.

Even in antiquity Heraclitus was found difficult. He was nicknamed 'the Enigmatic One' and 'Heraclitus the Obscure' (D.L. 9. 6). He wrote a three-book treatise on philosophy—now lost—and deposited it in the great temple of Artemis (St Paul's 'Diana of the Ephesians'). People could not make up their minds whether it was a text of physics or a political tract. 'What I understand of it is excellent,' Socrates is reported as saying. 'What I don't understand may well be excellent also; but only a deep sea diver could get to the bottom of it' (D.L. 2. 22). The nineteenth-century German idealist Hegel, who was a great admirer of Heraclitus, used the same marine metaphor to express an opposite judgement. When we reach Heraclitus after the fluctuating speculations of the earlier Presocratics, Hegel wrote, we come at last in sight of land. He went on to add, proudly, 'There is no proposition of Heraclitus which I have not adopted in my own Logic.'[5]

Heraclitus, like Descartes and Kant in later ages, saw himself as making a completely new start in philosophy. He thought the work of previous thinkers was worthless: Homer should have been eliminated at an early stage of any poetry competition, and Hesiod, Pythagoras, and Xenophanes were merely polymaths with no real sense (D.L. 9. 1). But, again like Descartes and Kant, Heraclitus was more influenced by his predecessors than he realized. Like Xenophanes, he was highly critical of popular religion: offering blood sacrifice to purge oneself of blood guilt was like trying to wash off mud with mud. Praying to statues was like whispering in an empty house, and phallic processions and Dionysiac rites were simply disgusting (KRS 241, 243).

Again like Xenophanes, Heraclitus believed that the sun was new every day (Aristotle, *Mete.* 2. 2355[b]13–14), and, like Anaximander, he thought the

---

[5] *Lectures on the History of Philosophy*, ed. and trans. E. S. Haldane and F. H. Simpson (London: Routledge, 1968), 279.

sun was constrained by a cosmic principle of reparation (KRS 226). The ephemeral theory of the sun is indeed in Heraclitus expanded into a doctrine of universal flux. Everything, he said, is in motion, and nothing stays still; the world is like a flowing stream. If we step into the same river twice, we cannot put our feet twice into the same water, since the water is not the same two moments together (KRS 214). That seems true enough, but on the face of it Heraclitus went too far when he said that we cannot even step twice into the same river (Plato, *Cra.* 402a). Taken literally, this seems false, unless we take the criterion of identity for a river to be the body of water it contains rather than the course it flows. Taken allegorically, it is presumably a claim that everything in the world is composed of constantly changing constituents: if this is what is meant, Aristotle said, the changes must be imperceptible ones (*Ph.* 8. 3. 253^{b}9 ff.). Perhaps this is what is hinted at in Heraclitus' aphorism that hidden harmony is better than manifest harmony—the harmony being the underlying rhythm of the universe in flux (KRS 207). Whatever Heraclitus meant by his dictum, it had a long history ahead of it in later Greek philosophy.

A raging fire, even more than a flowing stream, is a paradigm of constant change, ever consuming, ever refuelled. Heraclitus once said that the world was an ever-living fire: sea and earth are the ashes of this perpetual bonfire. Fire is like gold: you can exchange gold for all kinds of goods, and fire can turn into any of the elements (KRS 217–19). This fiery world is the only world there is, not made by gods or men, but governed throughout by Logos. It would be absurd, he argued, to think that this glorious cosmos is just a piled-up heap of rubbish (DK 22 B124). 'Logos' is the everyday Greek term for a written or spoken word, but from Heraclitus onwards almost every Greek philosopher gave it one or more of several grander meanings. It is often rendered by translators as 'Reason'—whether to refer to the reasoning powers of human individuals, or to some more exalted cosmic principle of order and beauty. The term found its way into Christian theology when the author of the fourth gospel proclaimed, 'In the beginning was the Logos, and the Logos was with God, and the Logos was God' (John 1: 1).

This universal Logos, Heraclitus says, is hard to grasp and most men never succeed in doing so. By comparison with someone who has woken up to the Logos, they are like sleepers curled up in their own dream-world instead of facing up to the single, universal truth (S.E., *M.* 7. 132). Humans fall into three classes, at various removes from the rational fire that governs the universe. A philosopher like Heraclitus is closest to the fiery Logos and receives most warmth from it; next, ordinary people when awake draw light from it when they use their own reasoning powers; finally, those who are asleep have the windows of their soul blocked up and keep contact with nature only through their breathing (S.E., *M.* 7. 129–30).[6] Is the Logos God? Heraclitus gave a typically quibbling answer. 'The one thing that alone is truly wise is both unwilling and willing to be called by the name of Zeus.' Presumably, he meant that the Logos was divine, but was not to be identified with any of the gods of Olympus.

The human soul is itself fire: Heraclitus sometimes lists soul, along with earth and water, as three elements. Since water quenches fire, the best soul is a dry soul, and must be kept from moisture. It is hard to know exactly what counts as moisture in this context, but alcohol certainly does: a drunk, Heraclitus says, is a man led by a boy (KRS 229–31). But Heraclitus' use of 'wet' also seems close to the modern slang sense: brave and tough men who die in battle, for instance, have dry souls that do not suffer the death of water but go to join the cosmic fire (KRS 237).[7]

What Hegel most admired in Heraclitus was his insistence on the coincidence of opposites, such as that the universe is both divisible and indivisible, generated and ungenerated, mortal and immortal. Sometimes these identifications of opposites are straightforward statements of the relativity of certain predicates. The most famous, 'The way up and the way down are one and the same', sounds very deep. However, it need mean no more than that when, skipping down a mountain, I meet you toiling upward, we are both on the same path. Different things are attractive at different times: food when you are hungry, bed when you are sleepy (KRS 201). Different things attract different species: sea-water is wholesome for fish, but poisonous for humans; donkeys prefer rubbish to gold (KRS 199).

Not all Heraclitus' pairs of coinciding opposites admit of easy resolution by relativity, and even the most harmless-looking ones may have a more profound significance. Thus Diogenes Laertius tells us that the sequence fire–air–water–earth is the road downward, and the sequence earth–water–air–fire is the road upward (D.L. 9. 9–11). These two roads can

---

[6] Readers of Plato are bound to be struck by the anticipation of the allegory of the Cave in the *Republic*.

[7] See the discussion in KRS 208.

only be regarded as the same if they are seen as two stages on a continuous, everlasting, cosmic progress. Heraclitus did indeed believe that the cosmic fire went through stages of kindling and quenching (KRS 217). It is presumably also in this sense that we are to understand that the universe is both generated and ungenerated, mortal and immortal (DK 22 B50). The underlying process has no beginning and no end, but each cycle of kindling and quenching is an individual world that comes into and goes out of existence.

Though several of the Presocratics are reported to have been politically active, Heraclitus has some claim, on the basis of the fragments, to be the first to produce a political philosophy. He was not indeed interested in practical politics: an aristocrat with a claim to be a ruler, he waived his claim and passed on his wealth to his brother. He is reported to have said that he preferred playing with children to conferring with politicians. But he was perhaps the first philosopher to speak of a divine law—not a physical law, but a prescriptive law, that trumped all human laws.

There is a famous passage in Robert Bolt's play about Thomas More, *A Man for All Seasons*. More is urged by his son-in-law Roper to arrest a spy, in contravention of the law. More refuses to do so: 'I know what's legal, not what's right; and I'll stick to what's legal.' More denies, in answer to Roper, that he is setting man's law above God's. 'I'm not God,' he says, 'but in the thickets of the law, there I am a forester.' Roper says that he would cut down every law in England to get at the Devil. More replies, 'And when the last law was down, and the Devil turned round on you—where would you hide, Roper, the laws all being flat?'[8]

It is difficult to find chapter and verse in More's own writings or recorded sayings for this exchange. But two fragments of Heraclitus express the sentiments of the participants. 'The people must fight on behalf of the law as they would for the city wall' (KRS 249). But though a city must rely on its law, it must place a much greater reliance on the universal law that is common to all. 'All the laws of humans are nourished by a single law, the divine law' (KRS 250).

What survives of Heraclitus amounts to no more than 15,000 words. The enormous influence he has exercised on philosophers ancient and modern is a matter for astonishment. There is something fitting about his position

---

[8] Robert Bolt, *A Man for All Seasons* (London: Heinemann, 1960), 39.

in Raphael's fresco in the Vatican stanze, *The School of Athens*. In this monumental scenario, which contains imaginary portraits of many Greek philosophers, Plato and Aristotle, as is right and just, occupy the centre stage. But the figure to which one's eye is immediately drawn on entering the room is a late addition to the fresco: the booted, brooding figure of Heraclitus, deep in meditation on the lowest step.[9]

Parmenides and the Eleatics

In Roman times Heraclitus was known as 'the weeping philosopher'. He was contrasted with the laughing philosopher, the atomist Democritus. A more appropriate contrast would be with Parmenides, the head of the Italian school of philosophy in the early fifth century. For classical Athens, Heraclitus was the proponent of the theory that everything was in motion, and Parmenides the proponent of the theory that nothing was in motion. Plato and Aristotle struggled, in different ways, to defend the audacious thesis that some things were in motion and some things were at rest.

Parmenides, according to Aristotle (*Metaph.* A 5. 986^{b}21–5), was a pupil of Xenophanes, but he was too young to have studied under him in Colophon. He spent most of his life in Elea, seventy miles or so south of Naples. There he may have encountered Xenophanes on his wanderings. Like Xenophanes, he was a poet: he wrote a philosophical poem in clumsy verse, of which we possess about 120 lines. He is the first philosopher whose writing has come down to us in continuous fragments that are at all substantial.

The poem consists of a prologue and two parts, one called the path of truth, the other the path of mortal opinion. The prologue shows us the poet riding in a chariot with the daughters of the Sun, leaving behind the halls of night and travelling towards the light. They reach the gates which lead to the paths of night and day; it is not clear whether these are the same as the paths of truth and opinion. At all events, the goddess who welcomes him on his quest tells him that he must learn both:

---

[9] The figure traditionally regarded as Heraclitus does not figure on cartoons for the fresco. Michelangelo is said to have been Raphael's model, though R. Jones and N. Penny, *Raphael*, (London: Yale University Press, 1983) 77, doubt both traditions.

> Besides trustworthy truth's unquaking heart
> Learn the false fictions of poor mortals' art.
>
> (KRS 288. 29–30)

There are only two possible routes of inquiry:

> Two ways there are of seeking how to see
> One that it is, and is not not to be—
> That is the path of Truth's companion Trust—
> The other it is not, and not to be it must.   (KRS 291. 2–5)

(I must ask the reader to believe that Parmenides' Greek is as clumsy and as baffling as this English text.) Parmenides' Way of Truth, thus riddlingly introduced, marks an epoch in philosophy. It is the founding charter of a new discipline: ontology or metaphysics, the science of Being.

Whatever there is, whatever can be thought of, is for Parmenides nothing other than Being. Being is one and indivisible: it has no beginning and no end, and it is not subject to temporal change. When a kettle of water boils away, this may be, in Heraclitus' words, the death of water and the birth of air; but for Parmenides it is not the death or birth of Being. Whatever changes may take place, they are not changes from being to non-being; they are all changes within Being. But for Parmenides there are not, in fact, any real changes at all. Being is everlastingly the same, and time is unreal because past, present, and future are all one.[10]

The everyday world of apparent change is described in the second part of Parmenides' poem, the Way of Seeming, which his goddess introduces thus:

> I bring to an end my trusty word and thought,
> The tale of Truth. The rest's another sort—
> A pack of lies expounding men's beliefs.   (KRS 300)

It is not clear why Parmenides feels obliged to reproduce the false notions that are entertained by deluded mortals. If we took the second part of his poem out of its context, we would see in it a cosmology very much in the tradition of the Ionian thinkers. To the normal pairs of opposites Parmenides adds light and darkness, and he is given credit by Aristotle for introducing Love as the efficient cause of everything (*Metaph. A* 3. 984[b]27). The Way of Seeming in fact includes two truths not hitherto

---

[10] A detailed examination of Parmenides' ontology will be found in Ch. 6 below.

generally known: first, that the earth is a sphere (D.L. 9. 21), and secondly, that the Morning Star is the same as the Evening Star. Parmenides' disowned discovery was to provide philosophers of a later generation with a paradigm for identity statements.[11]

Parmenides had a pupil, Melissus, who came from Pythagoras' island of Samos and who was said to have studied also with Heraclitus. He was active in politics, and rose to the rank of admiral of the Samos fleet. In 441 BC Samos was attacked by Athens, and though Athens was finally victorious in the war Melissus is recorded as having twice inflicted defeat on the fleet of Pericles (Plutarch, *Pericles* 166c–d; D.L. 9. 4).

Melissus expounded the philosophy of Parmenides' poem in plain prose, arguing that the universe was unlimited, unchangeable, immovable, indivisible, and homogeneous. He was remembered for drawing two consequences from this monistic view: (1) pain was unreal, because it implied (impossibly) a deficiency of being; (2) there was no such thing as a vacuum, since it would have to be a piece of Unbeing. Local motion was therefore impossible, for the bodies that occupy space have no room to move into (KRS 534).

Another pupil of Parmenides was Zeno of Elea. He produced a set of more famous arguments against the possibility of motion. The first went like this: 'There is no motion, for whatever moves must reach the middle of its course before it reaches the end.' To get to the far end of a stadium, you have to run to the half-way point, to get to the half-way point you must reach the point half-way to that, and so ad infinitum. Better known is the second argument, commonly known as Achilles and the tortoise. 'The slower', Zeno said, 'will never be overtaken by the swifter, for the pursuer must first reach the point from which the fugitive departed, so that the slower must necessarily remain ahead.' Let us suppose that Achilles runs four times as fast as the tortoise, and that the tortoise is given a forty-metre start when they run a hundred-metre race against each other. According to Zeno's argument, Achilles can never win. For by the time he reaches the forty-metre mark, the tortoise is ahead by ten metres. By the time Achilles has run those ten, the tortoise is still ahead by two and a half metres. Each time Achilles makes up a gap, the tortoise opens up a new, shorter, gap, so he can never overtake him (Aristotle, *Ph.* 5. 9. 239^{b}11–14).

---

[11] The 19th-century philosopher Gottlob Frege used the example to introduce his celebrated distinction between sense and reference.

These and other similar arguments of Zeno assume that distances and motions are infinitely divisible. His arguments have been dismissed by some philosophers as ingenious but sophistical paradoxes. Others have admired them greatly: Bertrand Russell, for instance, claimed that they provided the basis of the nineteenth-century mathematical renaissance of Weierstrass and Cantor.[12] Aristotle, who preserved Zeno's puzzles for us, claimed to disarm them, and to re-establish the possibility of motion, by distinguishing between two forms of infinity: actual infinity and potential infinity.[13] But it was not for many centuries that the issues raised by Zeno were given solutions that satisfied both philosophers and mathematicians.

Empedocles

The most flamboyant of the early philosophers of Greek Italy was Empedocles, who flourished in the middle of the fifth century. He was a native of Acragas, the town on the south coast of Sicily which is now Agrigento. The town's port today bears the name Porto Empedocle, but this testifies not to an enduring veneration of the philosopher, but to the Risorgimento's passion for renaming sites in honour of Italy's past glories.

Empedocles came of an aristocratic family which owned a stud of prizewinning horses. In politics, however, he is reputed to have been a democrat; he is said to have foiled a plot to turn the city into a dictatorship. The grateful citizens, the story goes on, offered to make him king, but he refused the office, preferring his frugal life as a physician and counsellor (D.L. 8. 63). If free of ambition, however, he was not devoid of vanity, and in one of his poems he boasts that wherever he goes men and women throng to him for advice and healing. He claimed to possess drugs to ward off old age, and to know spells to control the weather. In the same poem he frankly professed himself to have achieved divine status (D.L. 8. 66).

Different biographical traditions, not all chronologically possible, make Empedocles a pupil of Pythagoras, of Xenophanes, and of Parmenides. Certainly he imitated Parmenides by writing a hexameter poem *On Nature*; this poem, dedicated to his friend Pausanias, contained about 2,000 lines, of which we possess about a fifth. He also wrote a religious poem, *Purifications*,

---

[12] *The Principles of Mathematics* (London: Allen & Unwin, 1903), 347.   [13] See Ch. 5 below.

of which less has been preserved. Scholars do not agree to which poem should be attached the many disjointed citations that survive; some, indeed, think that the two poems belonged to a single work. Further pieces of the textual jigsaw were recovered when forty papyrus fragments were identified in the archives of the University of Strasbourg in 1994. As a poet, Empedocles was more fluent than Parmenides, and also more versatile. According to Aristotle, he wrote an epic on Xerxes' invasion of Greece, and according to other traditions he was the author of several tragedies (D.L. 8. 57).

Empedocles' philosophy of nature can be regarded, from one point of view, as a synthesis of the thought of the Ionian philosophers. As we have seen, each of them had singled out some one substance as the basic or dominant stuff of the universe: Thales had privileged water, Anaximenes air, Xenophanes earth, and Heraclitus fire. For Empedocles all four of these substances stood on equal terms as the fundamental ingredients, or 'roots' as he put it, of the universe. These roots had always existed, he maintained, but they mingle with each other in various proportions in such a way as to produce the familiar furniture of the world and also the denizens of the heavens.

> From these four sprang what was and is and ever shall:
> Trees, beasts, and human beings, males and females all,
> Birds of the air, and fishes bred by water bright;
> The age-old gods as well, long worshipped in the height.
> These four are all there is, each other interweaving
> And, intermixed, the world's variety achieving.   (KRS 355)

What Empedocles called 'roots' were called by Plato and later Greek thinkers *stoicheia*, a word earlier used to indicate the syllables of a word. The Latin translation *elementum*, from which our 'element' is derived, compares the roots not to syllables, but to letters of the alphabet: an *elementum* is an LMNtum. Empedocles' quartet of elements was assigned a fundamental role in physics and chemistry by philosophers and scientists until the time of Boyle in the seventeenth century. Indeed, it can be claimed that it is still with us, in altered form. Empedocles thought of his elements as four different kinds of matter; we think of solid, liquid, and gas as three states of matter. Ice, water, and steam would be, for Empedocles, specific instances of earth, water, and air; for us they are three different

21

states of the same substance, H_2O. It was not unreasonable to think of fire, and especially the fire of the sun, as a fourth element of equal importance. One might say that the twentieth-century emergence of the science of plasma physics, which studies the properties of matter at the sun's temperature, has restored Empedocles' fourth element to parity with the other three.

Aristotle praised Empedocles for having realized that a cosmological theory must not just identify the elements of the universe, but must assign causes for the development and intermingling of the elements to make the living and inanimate compounds of the actual world. Empedocles assigns this role to Love and Strife: Love combines the elements, and Strife forces them apart. At one time the roots grow to be one out of many, at another time they split to be many out of one. These things, he said, never cease their continual interchange, now through love coming together into one, now carried apart from each other by Strife's hatred (KRS 348).

Love and Strife are the picturesque ancestors of the forces of attraction and repulsion which have figured in physical theory throughout the ages. For Empedocles, history is a cycle in which sometimes Love is dominant, and sometimes Strife. Under the influence of Love the elements combine into a homogeneous, harmonious, and resplendent sphere, reminiscent of Parmenides' universe. Under the influence of Strife the elements separate out, but when Love begins to regain the ground it had lost, all the different species of living beings appear (KRS 360). All compound beings, such as animals and birds and fish, are temporary creatures that come and go; only the elements are everlasting, and only the cosmic cycle goes on for ever.

To explain the origin of living species, Empedocles put forward a remarkable theory of evolution by survival of the fittest. First flesh and bone emerged as chemical mixtures of the elements, flesh being constituted by fire, air, and water in equal parts, and bone being two parts water to two parts earth and four parts fire. From these constituents unattached limbs and organs were formed: unsocketed eyes, arms without shoulders, and faces without necks (KRS 375–6). These roamed around until they chanced to find partners; they formed unions, which were often, at this preliminary stage, quite unsuitable. Thus there arose various monstrosities: human-headed oxen, ox-headed humans, androgynous creatures with faces and breasts on front and back (KRS 379). Most of these fortuitous organisms were fragile or sterile; only the fittest structures survived to be the human and animal species we know. Their fitness to reproduce was a matter of chance, not design (Aristotle, *Ph.* 2. 8. 198^{b}29).

Aristotle paid tribute to Empedocles for being the first to grasp the important biological principle that different parts of dissimilar living organisms might have homologous functions: e.g. olives and eggs, leaves and feathers (Aristotle, *GA* 1. 23. 731^{a}4). But he was contemptuous of his attempt to reduce teleology to chance, and for many centuries biologists followed Aristotle rather than Empedocles. Empedocles had the last laugh when Darwin saluted him for 'shadowing forth the principle of natural selection'.[14]

Empedocles employed his quartet of elements in giving an account of sense-perception, based on the principle that like is known by like. In his poem *Purifications* he combined his physical theory with the Pythagorean doctrine of metempsychosis.[15] Sinners—divine or human—are punished when Strife casts their souls into different kinds of creatures on land and sea. A cycle of reincarnation held out a hope of eventual deification for privileged classes of men: seers, bards, doctors, and princes (KRS 409). Empedocles, of course, had a claim to identify himself with all these professions.

In his writing, Empedocles moves seamlessly between an austerely mechanistic mode and a mystically religious one. He sometimes uses divine names for his four elements (Zeus, Hera, Aidoneus, and Nestis) and identifies his Love with the goddess Aphrodite, whom he celebrates in terms anticipating Schiller's great 'Ode to Joy' (KRS 349). No doubt his own claim to divinity can be deflated in the same way as he demythologizes the Olympian gods. But it caught the attention of posterity, especially in the legend of his death.

A woman called Pantheia, the story goes, given up for dead by the physicians, was miraculously restored to life by Empedocles. To celebrate, he offered a sacrificial banquet to eighty guests in a rich man's house at the foot of Etna. When the other guests went to sleep, he heard his name called from heaven. He hastened to the summit of the volcano, and then, in Milton's words,

---

[14] Appendix to 6th edn. of *The Origin of Species*, quoted in A. Gottlieb, *The Dream of Reason: A History of Western Philosophy from the Greeks to the Renaissance* (London: Allen Lane, 2000), 80.

[15] See Ch. 7 below.

> to be deemed
> A god, leaped fondly into Aetna flames.

> (*Paradise Lost* III. 470)

Matthew Arnold dramatized this story in his *Empedocles on Etna*. He places these verses in the mouth of the philosopher at the crater's rim:

> This heart will glow no more; thou art
> A living man no more, Empedocles!
> Nothing but a devouring flame of thought—
> But a naked, eternally restless mind!
> To the elements it came from
> Everything will return
> Our bodies to earth,
> Our blood to water,
> Heat to fire,
> Breath to air.
> They were well born, they will be well entomb'd—
> But mind?

> (lines 326–38)

Arnold gives the philosopher, before his final leap, the hope that in reward for his love of truth his intellect will never wholly perish.

Anaxagoras

If Empedocles achieved a kind of immortality as a precursor of Darwin, his contemporary Anaxagoras is sometimes regarded as an intellectual ancestor of the currently popular cosmology of the big bang. Anaxagoras was born around 500 BC in Clazomenae, near Izmir, and was possibly a pupil of Anaximenes. After the end of the wars between Persia and Greece, he came to Athens and was a client of the statesman Pericles. He thus stands at the head of the distinguished series of philosophers whom Athens either bred or welcomed. When Pericles fell from favour, Anaxagoras too became a target of popular attack. He was prosecuted for treason and impiety, and fled to Lampsacus on the Hellespont, where he lived in honourable exile until his death in 428.

Here is his account of the beginning of the universe: 'All things were together, infinite in number and infinite in smallness; for the small too was infinite. While all things were together, nothing was recognizable because of its smallness. Everything lay under air and ether, both infinite' (KRS 467). This primeval pebble began to rotate, throwing off the surrounding ether and air and forming out of them the stars and the sun and the moon. The rotation caused the separation of dense from rare, of hot from cold, of dry from wet, and bright from dark. But the separation was never complete, and to this day there remains in every single thing a portion of everything else. There is a little whiteness in what is black, a little cold in what is hot, and so on: things are named after the item that is dominant in it (Aristotle, *Ph.* 1. 4. 187ª23). This is most obvious in the case of semen, which must contain hair and flesh, and much, much more; but it must also be true of the food we eat (KRS 483–4, 496). In this sense, as things were in the beginning, so now they are all together.

The expansion of the universe, Anaxagoras maintained, has continued in the present and will continue in the future (KRS 476). Perhaps it has already generated worlds other than our own. As a result of the presence of everything in everything, he says,

men have been formed and the other ensouled animals. And the men possess farms and inhabit cities just as we do, and they have a sun and a moon and the rest just like us. The earth produces things of every sort for them to be harvested and stored, as it does for us. I have said all this about the process of separating off, because it would have happened not only here with us, but elsewhere too. (KRS 498)

Anaxagoras thus has a claim to be the originator of the idea, later proposed by Giordano Bruno and popular again today in some quarters, that our cosmos is just one of many which may, like ours, be inhabited by intelligent creatures.

The motion that sets in train the development of the universe is, according to Anaxagoras, the work of Mind. 'All things were together: then Mind came and gave them order' (D.L. 2. 6). Mind is infinite and separate, and has no part in the general commingling of elements; if it did, it would get drawn into the evolutionary process and could not control it. This teaching, placing mind firmly in control of matter, so struck his contemporaries that they nicknamed Anaxagoras himself the

Mind. It is difficult, however, to assess exactly what his doctrine, though it greatly impressed both Plato and Aristotle, actually meant in practice.

In Plato's dialogue *Phaedo*, Socrates, in his last days in prison, is made to express his gradual disillusionment with the mechanistic explanations of natural science to be found in the early philosophers. He was pleased, he said, when he heard that Anaxagoras had explained everything by *nous*, or mind; but he was disappointed by the total absence of reference to value in his work. Anaxagoras was like someone who said that all Socrates' actions were performed with his intelligence, and then gave the reason why he was sitting here in prison by talking about the constitution of his body from bones and sinews, and the nature and properties of these parts, without mentioning that he judged it better to sit there in obedience to the Athenian court's sentence. Teleological explanation was more profound than mechanistic explanation. 'If anyone wants to find out the reason why each thing comes to be or perishes or exists, this is what he must find out about it: how is it best for that thing to exist, or to act or be acted upon in any way?' (*Phd.* 97d).

Anaxagoras speaks about his Mind in ways appropriate to divinity, and this could have made him vulnerable to a charge, in the Athenian courts, of introducing strange gods. But in fact the charge of impiety seems to have been based on his scientific conjectures. The sun, he said, was a fiery lump of metal, somewhat larger than the Peloponnesus. This was taken to be incompatible with the veneration appropriate to the sun as divine. In exile in Lampsacus, Anaxagoras made his final benefaction to humanity: the invention of the school holiday. Asked by the authorities of the city how they should honour him, he said that children should be let off school in the month of his death. He had already earned the gratitude of students of science by being the first writer to include diagrams in his text.

The Atomists

The final and most striking anticipation of modern science in the Presocratic era was made by Leucippus of Miletus and Democritus of Abdera. Though they are always named together, like Tweedledum and Tweedledee, and considered joint founders of atomism, nothing really is known about Leucippus except that he was the teacher of Democritus. It is on the

surviving writings of the latter that we principally depend for our knowledge of the theory. Democritus was a polymath and a prolific writer,
author of nearly eighty treatises on topics ranging from poetry and
harmony to military tactics and Babylonian theology. All these treatises
are lost, but we do possess a copious collection of fragments from Democritus, more than from any previous philosopher.

Democritus was born in Abdera, on the coast of Thrace, and was thus
the first significant philosopher to be born on the Greek mainland. The
date of his birth is uncertain, but it was probably between 470 and 460 BC.
He is reported to have been forty years younger than Anaxagoras, from
whom he took some of his ideas. He travelled widely and visited Egypt and
Persia, but was not over-impressed by the countries he visited. He once said
that he would prefer to discover a single scientific explanation than to
become king of Persia (D.L. 9. 41; DK 68 B118).

Democritus' fundamental thesis is that matter is not infinitely divisible.
We do not know his exact argument for this conclusion, but Aristotle
conjectured that it ran as follows. If we take a chunk of any kind of stuff
and divide it up as far as we can, we will have to come to a halt at tiny bodies
which are indivisible. We cannot allow matter to be divisible to infinity: for let
us suppose that the division has been carried out and then ask: what would
ensue if the division was carried out? If each of the infinite number of parts
has any magnitude, then it must be further divisible, which contradicts our
hypothesis. If, on the other hand, the surviving parts have no magnitude,
then they can never have amounted to any quantity: for zero multiplied by
infinity is still zero. So we have to conclude that divisibility comes to an end,
and the smallest possible fragments must be bodies with sizes and shapes.
These tiny, indivisible bodies were called by Democritus 'atoms' (which is
just the Greek word for 'indivisible') (Aristotle, *GC* 1. 2. 316ª13–ᵇ16).[16]

Atoms, Democritus believed, are too small to be detected by the senses;
they are infinite in number and come in infinitely many varieties, and they
have existed for ever. Against the Eleatics, he maintained that there was no
contradiction in admitting a vacuum: there was a void, and in this infinite
empty space atoms were constantly in motion, just like motes in a sunbeam.
They come in different forms: they may differ in shape (as the letter A differs
from the letter N), in order (as AN differs from NA), and in posture (as N

---

[16] For Aristotle's counter to this argument, see Ch. 5 below.

differs from Z). Some of them are concave and some convex, and some are like hooks and some are like eyes. In their ceaseless motion they bang into each other and join up with each other (KRS 583). The middle-sized objects of everyday life are complexes of atoms thus united by random collisions, differing in kind on the basis of the differences between their constituent atoms (Aristotle, *Metaph. A* 4. 985^{b}4–20; KRS 556).

Like Anaxagoras, Democritus believed in plural worlds.

There are innumerable worlds, differing in size. In some worlds there is no sun and moon; in others there is a larger sun and a larger moon; in others there is more than one of each. The distances between one world and the next are various. In some parts of space there are more worlds, in others fewer; some worlds are growing, others shrinking; some are rising and some falling. They get destroyed when they collide with one another. There are some words devoid of animals or plants or moisture. (KRS 565)

For Democritus, atoms and the void are the only two realities: what we see as water or fire or plants or humans are only conglomerations of atoms in the void. The sensory qualities we see are unreal: they are due to convention.

Democritus explained in detail how perceived qualities arose from different kinds and configurations of atoms. Sharp flavours, for instance, originated from atoms that were small, fine, angular, and jagged, while sweet tastes were produced by larger, rounder, smoother atoms. The knowledge given us by the senses is mere darkness compared with the illumination that is given by the atomic theory. To justify these claims, Democritus developed a systematic epistemology.[17]

Democritus wrote on ethics as well as physics. Many aphorisms have been preserved, a number of which are, or have become, commonplace. But it is a mistake to think of him as a sententious purveyor of conventional wisdom. On the contrary, as will be shown in Chapter 8, a careful study of his remarks shows him to have been one of the first thinkers to have developed a systematic morality.

The Sophists

In the lifetime of Democritus, a younger compatriot from Abdera, Protagoras, was the doyen of a new class of philosopher: the sophists. Sophists

---

[17] See Ch. 4 below.

were itinerant teachers who went from city to city offering expert instruction in various subjects. Since they charged fees for imparting their skills, they might be called the first professional philosophers if it were not for the fact that they offered instruction and services over a much wider area than philosophy even in the broadest sense. The most versatile, Hippias of Elis, claimed expertise in mathematics, astronomy, music, history, literature, and mythology, as well as practical skills as a tailor and shoemaker. Some other sophists were prepared to teach mathematics, history, and geography; and all sophists were skilled rhetoricians. They did brisk business in mid-fifth-century Athens, where young men who had to plead in law courts, or who wished to make their way in politics, were willing to pay substantial sums for their instruction and guidance.

The sophists made a systematic study of forensic debate and oratorical persuasion. In this pursuit they wrote on many topics. They started with basic grammar: Protagoras was the first to distinguish the genders of nouns and the tenses and moods of verbs (Aristotle, *Rh.* 3. 4. 1407^{b}6–8). They went on to list techniques of argument, and tricks of advocacy. As interpreters of ambiguous texts, and assessors of rival orations, they were among the earliest literary critics. They also gave public lectures and performances, and set up eristic moots, partly for instruction and partly for entertainment (D.L. 9. 53). Altogether, their roles encompassed those in modern society of tutors, consultants, barristers, public relations professionals, and media personalities.

Protagoras first visited Athens as an ambassador for Abdera. He was held in honour by the Athenians and invited back several times. He was asked by Pericles to draw up a constitution for the new pan-Hellenic colony at Thurii in southern Italy in 444 BC. He gave his first public performance in Athens in the house of the tragedian Euripides. He read aloud a tract entitled *On the Gods*, whose opening words were long remembered: 'About the gods, I cannot be sure whether they exist or not, or what they are like to see; for many things stand in the way of the knowledge of them, both the opacity of the subject and the shortness of human life' (D.L. 9. 51). His most famous saying, 'Man is the measure of all things', encapsulated a relativist epistemology which will be examined in detail later in this book.[18]

---

[18] See Ch. 4 below.

Protagoras seems to have been prepared to argue on either side of any question, and he boasted that he could always make the worse argument the better. This may simply have meant that he could coach a weak client into the best presentation of his case; but by critics as different as Aristophanes and Aristotle he was taken to mean that he could make wrong seem right (Aristophanes, *Clouds* 112 ff., 656–7; Aristotle, *Rh.* 2. 24. 1402^{a}25). Protagoras' enemies liked telling the story of the time when he sued his pupil Eualthus for non-payment of fees. Eualthus had refused to pay up, saying he had not yet won a single case. 'Well,' said Protagoras, 'if I win this case, you must pay up because the verdict was given for me; if you win it, you must still pay up, because then you will have won a case' (D.L. 9. 56).

Another sophist, Prodicus from the island of Ceos in the Aegean, came to Athens, like Protagoras, on official business of his home state. He was a linguist, but more interested in semantics than grammar: he can perhaps be regarded as the first lexicographer. Aristophanes and Plato teased him as a pedant, who made quibbling distinctions between words that were virtually synonymous. In fact, however, some of the distinctions credited to him (such as that between two Greek equivalents of 'want', *boulesthai* and *epithumein*; Plato, *Protagoras* 340b2) were later of serious philosophical importance.

Prodicus is credited with a romantic moral fable about the young Heracles choosing between two female impersonations of Virtue and Vice. He also had a theory of the origin of religion. 'The men of old regarded the sun and the moon, rivers and springs, and whatever else is helpful for life, as gods, because we are helped by them, just as the Egyptians worship the Nile' (DK 84 B5). Thus, the worship of Hephaestus is really the worship of fire, and the worship of Demeter is really the worship of bread.

Gorgias, from Leontini in Sicily, once a pupil of Empedocles, was another sophist who came to Athens on an embassy, to seek help in a war against Syracuse. He was not only a persuasive orator, but a technician of rhetoric who categorized different figures of speech, such as antithesis and rhetorical questions. His style was much admired in his own day, but was later regarded as excessively florid. Of his writings there have survived two short works of philosophical interest.

The first is a rhetorical exercise defending Helen of Troy against those who slander her, arguing that she deserves no blame for running off with

Paris and thus sparking off the Trojan war. 'She did what she did either because of the whims of fortune, the decisions of the gods and the decrees of necessity, or because she was abducted by force, or persuaded by speech, or overwhelmed by love' (DK 82 B11, 21–4). Gorgias goes through these alternatives in turn, arguing in each case that Helen should be held free from blame. No human can resist fate, and it is the abductor, not the abductee, who merits blame. Thus far, Gorgias has an easy task: but in order to show that Helen should not be blamed if she succumbed to persuasion, he has to engage in an unconvincing, though no doubt congenial, encomium on the powers of the spoken word: 'it is a mighty overlord, insubstantial and imperceptible, but it can achieve divine effects'. In this case, too, it is the persuader, not the persuadee, who should be blamed. Finally, if Helen fell in love, she is blameless: for love is either a god who cannot be resisted or a mental illness which should excite our pity. This brief and witty piece is the ancestor of many a philosophical discussion of freedom and determinism, *force majeure*, incitement, and irresistible impulse.

Gorgias' work entitled *On What is Not* contained arguments for three sceptical conclusions: first, that there is nothing; secondly, that if there is anything it cannot be known; thirdly, that if anything can be known it cannot be communicated by one person to another. This suite of arguments has been handed down in two forms, once in the pseudo-Aristotelian treatise *On Melissus*, and once by Sextus Empiricus.

The first argument trades on the polymorphous nature of the Greek verb 'to be'. I shall not spell out the argument here, but I shall endeavour in Chapter 6 to sort out the crucial ambiguities involved. The second argument goes like this. Things that have being can only be objects of thought if objects of thought are things that have being. But objects of thought are not things that have being; otherwise everything one thinks would be the case. But you can think of a man flying or of a chariot driven over the sea without there being any such things. Therefore, things that have being cannot be objects of thought. The third argument, the most plausible of the three, argues that each individual's sensations are private and that all we can pass on to our neighbours is words and not experiences.

The arguments of this famous sophist for these distressing conclusions are indeed sophisms, and were no doubt dismissed as such by those who first encountered them. But it is easier to dismiss a sophism than to diagnose its nature, and it is harder to still to find its cure. The first sophism was disarmed essentially by Plato in his dialogue appropriately named *The Sophist*.[19] The second sophism involves a fallacious form of argument that sometimes occurs in Plato himself. Aristotle's logic, however, made clear to subsequent thinkers that 'Not all As are B' does not entail 'No B is an A'. The third argument, from the privacy of experience, was not given its definitive quietus until the work of Wittgenstein in the twentieth century.

Beside Protagoras, Hippias, Prodicus, and Gorgias there were other sophists whose names and reputations have come down to us. There was Callicles, for instance, the champion of the doctrine that might is right; and Thrasymachus, the debunker of justice as the self-interest of those in power. There were Euthydemus and Dionysidorus, a pair of logic choppers who would offer to prove to you that your father was a dog. These men, however, and even the better-known sophists whom we have considered, are known to us primarily as characters in Plato's dialogues. Their philosophical contentions are best studied in the context of those dialogues. Searching for the historical truth about the sophists is no more rewarding than trying to discover what King Lear or Prince Hamlet were like before Shakespeare got hold of them.

We shall say goodbye, therefore, to these sophists and turn to consider Socrates, who, according to one view, was the greatest of the sophists, and according to another, was a paradigm of the true philosopher at the opposite pole from any kind of sophistry.

Socrates

In the history of philosophy Socrates has a place without parallel. On the one hand, he is revered as inaugurating the first great era of philosophy, and therefore, in a sense, philosophy itself. In textbooks all previous thinkers are lumped together in textbooks as 'Presocratics', as if philosophy prior to his age was somehow prehistoric. On the other hand, Socrates left behind no writing, and there is hardly a single sentence ascribed to him that we can be sure was his own utterance rather than a literary creation of one of his admirers. Our first-hand acquaintance with his philosophy is less

---

[19] see Ch. 6 below.

than with that of Xenophanes, Parmenides, Empedocles, or Democritus. Yet his influence on subsequent philosophy, down to our own day, has been incomparably greater than theirs.

In antiquity many schools of thought claimed Socrates as a founder and many individuals revered him as a paragon philosopher. In the Middle Ages his history was not much studied, but his name appears on the page whenever a logician or metaphysician wishes to give an example: 'Socrates' was to scholastic philosophers what 'John Doe' long was to legal writers. In modern times Socrates' life has been held up as a model by philosophers of many different kinds, especially by philosophers living under tyranny and risking persecution for refusal to conform to unreasoned ideology. Many thinkers have made their own the dictum that has as good a claim as any to be his own authentic utterance: 'the unexamined life is not worth living'.

The hard facts of Socrates' life do not take long to tell. He was born in Athens about 469 BC, ten years after the Persian invasions of Greece had been crushed at the battle of Plataea. He grew up during the years when Athens, a flourishing democracy under the statesman Pericles, exercised imperial hegemony over the Greek world. It was a golden age of art and literature, which saw the sculptures of Phidias and the building of the Parthenon, and in which Aeschylus, Sophocles, and Euripides produced their great tragedies. At the same time Herodotus, 'the father of history', wrote his accounts of the Persian Wars, and Anaxagoras introduced philosophy to Athens.

The second half of Socrates' life was overshadowed by the Peloponnesian War (431–4), in which Athens was eventually forced to cede the leadership of Greece to victorious Sparta. During the first years of the war he served in the heavy infantry, taking part in three major engagements. He acquired a reputation for conspicuous courage, shown particularly during the retreat after a disastrous defeat at Delium in 422. Back in Athens during the last years of the war, he held office in the city's Assembly in 406. A group of commanders was tried for abandoning the bodies of the dead after a sea victory at Arginusae. It was unconstitutional to try the commanders collectively rather than individually, but Socrates was alone in voting against the illegality, and the accused were executed.

In 404, after the war had ended, the Spartans replaced Athenian democracy with an oligarchy, 'the Thirty Tyrants', long remembered for a reign

33

of terror. Instructed to arrest an innocent man, Leon of Salamis, Socrates took no notice. He refused to accept illegal orders, but seems to have taken no part in the revolution that overthrew the oligarchy and restored democracy. His uprightness had by now given both democrats and aristocrats a grievance against him, and the restored democrats remembered also that some of his close associates, such as Critias and Charmides, had been among the Thirty.

An aspiring democrat politician, Anytus, with two associates, caused an indictment to be drawn up against Socrates in the following terms: 'Socrates has committed an offence by not recognizing the gods whom the state recognizes but introducing other new divinities. He has also committed the offence of corrupting the young. Penalty demanded: death' (D.L. 2. 40). We have no record of the trial, though two of Socrates' admirers have left us imaginative reconstructions of his speech for the defence. Whatever he actually said failed to move a sufficient number of the 500 citizen jurors. He was found guilty, albeit by a small majority, and condemned to death. After a delay in prison, due to a religious technicality, Socrates died in spring 399, accepting a poisonous cup of hemlock from the executioner.

The allegation of impiety in the indictment of Socrates was not something new. In 423 the dramatist Aristophanes had produced a comedy, *The Clouds*, in which he introduces a character called Socrates, who runs a college of chicanery which is also an institute of bogus research. Students at this establishment not only learn to make bad arguments trump good arguments, but also study astronomy in a spirit of irreverent scepticism about traditional religion. They invoke a new pantheon of elemental deities: air, ether, clouds, and chaos (260–6). The world, they are told, is governed not by Zeus, who does not exist, but by Dinos (literally 'Vortex'), the rotation of the heavenly bodies (380–1). Much of the play is burlesque that is obviously not meant to be taken seriously: Socrates measures how many flea-feet a flea can leap, and explores the clouds in a ramshackle flying machine. But the allegation that astronomy was incompatible with piety, if it was a joke, was a dangerous one. After all, it was only in the previous decade that Anaxagoras had been banished for asserting that the sun was a fiery lump. At the end of the play Socrates' house is burnt down by an angry crowd of people who wish to punish him for insulting the gods and violating the privacy of the moon. To those who recalled

Aristophanes' comedy, the events of 399 must have seemed a sorry case of life imitating art.

Some of Socrates' traits in *The Clouds* are attributed to him also by other, more friendly writers. There is general agreement that he was pot-bellied and snub-nosed, pop-eyed and shambling in gait. He is regularly described as being shabby, wearing threadbare clothes, and liking to go barefoot. Even Aristophanes represents him as capable of great feats of endurance, and indifferent to privation: 'never numb with cold, never hungry for break-fast, a spurner of wine and gluttony' (414–17). From other sources it appears that he was a spurner of wine not in the sense of being a teetotaller, but as having an unusual ability to hold his liquor (Plato, *Smp.* 214a). Socrates married Xanthippe, with whom he had a son, Lamprocles; a stubborn, but perhaps ill-founded, tradition represents her as a shrew (D.L. 2. 36–7). According to some ancient writers he had two other sons by an official concubine, Myrto (D.L. 2. 26). In antiquity, however, he was best known for his attachment to the flamboyant aristocrat Alcibiades, some twenty years his junior: an attachment which, though passionate, remained, in the terminology of a later age, platonic.

The Socrates of Xenophon

On more important issues, there is little that is certain about Socrates' life and thought. For further information we are dependent above all on the two disciples whose works have come down to us intact, the soldierly historian Xenophon, and the idealist philosopher Plato. Both Xenophon and Plato composed, after the event, speeches for the defence at Socrates' trial. Xenophon in addition wrote four books of memoirs of Socrates (*memorabilia Socratis*) and a Socratic dialogue, the *Symposium*. Plato, besides his *Apology*, wrote at least twenty-five dialogues, in all but one of which Socrates figures. Xenophon and Plato paint pictures of Socrates which differ from each other as much as the picture of Jesus given in the gospel of Mark differs from that in the gospel of John. While in Mark Jesus speaks in parables, brief aphorisms, and pointed responses to questions, the Jesus of the fourth gospel delivers extensive discourses that resonate at several levels. There is a similar contrast between Xenophon's Socrates, who questions, argues, and exhorts in a workmanlike manner, and the Socrates of Plato's *Republic*, who delivers profound metaphysical lectures in a style of layered literary artifice. Just as it was John's presentation of Jesus that had the greatest impact on later theological development, so it is the Socrates of Plato whose ideas proved fertile in the history of philosophy.

According to Xenophon, Socrates was a pious man, punctiliously observant of ritual and respectful of oracles. In his prayers he let the gods decide what was good for him, since the gods were omnipresent and omniscient, knowing everyone's words, actions, and unspoken intentions (*Mem.* 1. 2. 20; 3. 2). He taught that the poor man's mite was as pleasing to the gods as the grand sacrifices of the rich (*Mem.* 1. 3. 3). He was a decent, temperate person, devoid of avarice and ambition, moderate in his desires, and tolerant of hardship. He was not an educator, though he taught virtue by practice as well as exhortation, and he discouraged vice by teasing and fable as well as by reproof. He was not to be blamed if some of his pupils went to the bad in spite of his example. Though critical of some aspects of Athenian democracy, he was a friend of the people, and totally innocent of crime and treason (*Mem.* 1. 2).

Xenophon's major concern in his memoirs was to exonerate Socrates from the charges made against him at his trial, and to show that his life was such that conservative Athenians should have revered him rather than condemned him to death. Xenophon is also anxious to place a distance between Socrates and the other philosophers of the age: unlike Anaxagoras he had no futile interest in physics or astronomy (*Mem.* 1. 1. 16), and unlike the sophists he did not charge any fees or pretend to expertise that he lacked (*Mem.* 1. 6–7).

Xenophon's Socrates is an upright, rather wooden person, capable of giving shrewd, commonsensical advice in practical and ethical matters. In discussion he is quick to resolve ambiguities and to deflate cant, but he rarely ventures upon philosophical argument or speculation. In a rare case when he does so it is, significantly, in order to prove the existence and providence of God. If an object is useful, Socrates argues, it must be the product of design, not chance; but our sense-organs are eminently useful and delicately constructed. 'Because our sight is delicate, it has been shuttered with eyelids which open when we need to use it, and close in sleep; so that not even the wind will damage it, eyelashes have been planted as a screen; and our foreheads have been fringed with eyebrows to prevent harm from the head's own sweat' (*Mem.* 1. 4. 6). Such contrivances, and the

36

implantation of the instincts for procreation and self-preservation, look like the actions of a wise and benevolent craftsman (*demiourgos*). It is arrogant to think that we humans are the only location of Mind (*nous*) in the universe. It is true that we cannot see the cosmic intelligence that governs the infinite multitudinous universe, but we cannot see the souls that control our own bodies either. Moreover, it is absurd to think that the cosmic powers that be have no concern for humans: they have favoured humans above all other animals by endowing them with erect posture, multi-purpose hands, articulate language, and all-year-round sex (*Mem.* 1. 4. 11–12).

Despite this anticipation of the perennial Argument from Design, there is little in Xenophon's work that would entitle Socrates to a prominent position in the history of philosophy. Several of the Presocratics would be more than a match for Xenophon's Socrates in scope, insight, and originality. The Socrates who has captured the imagination of succeeding generations of philosophers is the Socrates of Plato, and it is he with whom we shall henceforth be concerned.

The Socrates of Plato

It is, however, an oversimplification to speak of a Platonic Socrates, because Plato's dialogues do not assign a consistent role or personality to the character called Socrates. In some dialogues he is predominantly a critical inquirer, challenging the pretensions of other characters by a characteristic technique of question and answer—*elenchus*—which reduces them to incoherence. In other dialogues Socrates is quite willing to harangue his audience, and to present an ethical and metaphysical system in dogmatic form. In yet other dialogues he plays only a minor part, leaving the philosophical initiative to a different protagonist. Before going further, therefore, we must digress to consider when and where the dialogues can be taken to be presenting Socrates' actual views, and when and where the character Socrates is acting as a mouthpiece for Plato's own philosophy.

In recent centuries scholars have sought to explain these differences in chronological terms: the different role assigned to Socrates in different dialogues represents the development of Plato's thought and his gradual

Socrates and Plato as portrayed by Matthew Paris in the thirteenth century. Who is teaching whom?

emancipation from the teaching of his master. The initial clue to a chronological ordering of the dialogues was given by Aristotle, who tells us that Plato's *Laws* was written later than the *Republic* (*Pol.* 2. 6. 1264^b24–7).

There is indeed a tradition that the *Laws* was unfinished at Plato's death (D.L. 3. 37). On this basis nineteenth-century scholars sought to establish a grouping of the dialogues, beginning from the final stage of Plato's life. They studied the frequency in different dialogues of different features of style, such as the use of technical terms, preferences between synonymous idioms, the avoidance of hiatus, and the adoption of particular speech rhythms.

On the basis of these stylometric studies, which by the end of the nineteenth century had covered some 500 different linguistic criteria, a consensus emerged that a group of dialogues stood out by its similarity to the *Laws*. All scholars agreed on including in the group the dialogues *Critias*, *Philebus*, *Sophist*, *Statesman*, and *Timaeus*, and all agreed that the group represented the latest stage of Plato's writing career. There was no similar consensus about ordering within the group: but it is notable that the group includes all the dialogues in which Socrates' role is at a minimum. Only in the *Philebus* is he a prominent character. In *Laws* he does not appear at all, and in the *Timaeus, Critias, Sophist*, and *Politicus* he has only a walk-on part while the lead role is given to another: in the first two to the protagonist named in the dialogue's title, and in the latter two to a stranger from Parmenides' town of Elea. It seemed reasonable, therefore, to regard the dialogues of this group as expressing the views of the mature Plato rather than those of his long-dead teacher.

In dividing the earlier dialogues into groups, scholars could once again follow a clue given by Aristotle. In *Metaph.* M 4. 1078^{b}27–32 he sets out the prehistory of Plato's Theory of Ideas, and assigns the following role to Socrates: 'Two things may fairly be attributed to Socrates: inductive arguments and general definitions; both are starting points of scientific knowledge. But he did not regard the universal or the definitions as separate entities, but [the Platonists] did, and called them Ideas of things.' Expositions of the Theory of Ideas are placed in the mouth of Socrates in several important dialogues, notably *Phaedo, Republic*, and *Symposium*. In these dialogues Socrates appears not as an inquiring questioner, but as a teacher in full possession of a system of philosophy. By stylometric criteria these dialogues are closer than other dialogues to the late group already described. It is reasonable, therefore, to treat them as a middle group in the corpus, and to regard them as representing Plato's own philosophy rather than Socrates'.

A third group of dialogues can be identified by a set of common features: (1) they are short; (2) Socrates appears as an inquirer, not an instructor; (3) the Theory of Ideas is not presented; and (4) stylometrically they are at the greatest remove from the late group first identified. This group includes *Crito, Charmides, Laches, Lysis, Ion, Euthydemus,* and *Hippias Minor.* These dialogues are commonly accepted as those most likely to be presentations of the philosophical views of the historical Socrates. Here too belongs the *Apology,* in which Socrates is the sole speaker, on trial for his life, and which in philosophical content and stylometric features resembles the other dialogues of the group. The first book of the *Republic,* too, in both content and style, resembles this group more than it resembles the remaining books of the dialogue: some scholars suppose, with good reason, that it first existed as a separate dialogue, perhaps under the title *Thrasymachus.* It is difficult to assign a chronology within this early group, though some authors place the *Lysis* first and assign it before 399, on the basis of an ancient anecdote that it was read to Socrates himself, who said, 'what a load of lies this young man tells about me' (D.L. 3. 35).

In my view there is good reason to accept the general consensus that thus divides the Platonic dialogues into three groups, early, middle, and late. The division results from the striking coincidence of three independent sets of criteria, dramatic, philosophical, and stylometric. Whether we focus on the dramatic role given to Socrates, or the philosophical content of the dialogues, or tell-tale details of style and idiom, we reach the same threefold grouping. Twentieth-century developments in stylometry, with much more refined statistical techniques, and with vast amounts of new data obtained from computerised texts, have essentially done little more than confirm the consensus achieved in the late nineteenth and early twentieth century.[20]

A number of dialogues, however, do not fall clearly into one of the three groups, because the three criteria do not so happily coincide: the most important such cases are *Cratylus, Euthyphro, Gorgias, Meno, Phaedrus, Parmenides, Protagoras, Theaetetus.* Here more recent stylometric studies have thrown new light on the problems.[21] There is no space here to enter into the detailed

---

[20] The consensus has been significantly questioned only in respect of the *Timaeus* and its appendix, the *Critias.* The debate here will be examined later when I discuss Plato's Theory of Ideas.

[21] See L. Brandwood, *The Chronology of Plato's Dialogues* (Cambridge: Cambridge University Press, 1990); G. Ledger, *Re-counting Plato: A Computer Analysis of Plato's Style* (Oxford: Clarendon Press, 1989);

arguments for assigning each of these dialogues to a particular period, so I will simply state the chronology that appears to me most probable after an examination of the three sets of criteria.

Gorgias, *Protagoras*, and *Meno* seem to belong between the first and second group. Though the Theory of Ideas is absent from the discussion, the role of Socrates is closer to the didactic philosopher of the middle dialogues than to the agnostic inquirer of the early dialogues. The order suggested by philosophical considerations is *Protagoras*, *Gorgias*, *Meno*; the order that emerges from stylometric studies is *Meno*, *Protagoras*, *Gorgias*. The *Cratylus* in style is close to these three, but is difficult to place precisely. The *Euthyphro* is generally considered an early dialogue, but it contains a hint of the Theory of Ideas, and stylistic indicators place it close to the *Gorgias*. Accordingly, I would place it in this intermediate group.

The *Phaedrus* was sometimes thought in antiquity to be the earliest of Plato's dialogues (D.L. 3. 38), but on both doctrinal and stylistic grounds the dialogue fits reasonably well into the middle group. The case is not the same with two other very important dialogues that in style are close to the *Phaedrus*, namely the *Parmenides* and *Theaetetus*. In content these works stand at some distance from the classical Theory of Ideas, which is ignored in the *Theaetetus* and subjected to severe criticism in the *Parmenides*. In structure the *Parmenides* differs from all other dialogues; the *Theaetetus* resembles the dialogues of the early group. Internal references in the *Theaetetus* look backwards to the *Parmenides* (183e) and forwards to the *Sophist* (210d). On balance it seems sensible to place these two dialogues between the middle and the later dialogues, but a discussion of the problems in giving a coherent statement of Plato's philosophical position at this period will have to wait until we have given an account of the Theory of Ideas.

Socrates' Own Philosophy

It was necessary to establish a plausible chronology for the Platonic texts in order to indicate to what extent it is safe to rely on Plato as a source of information about the historical Socrates. Having done this, we can give an

J. T. Temple, 'A Multivariate Synthesis of Published Platonic Stylometric Data', *Literary and Linguistic Computing*, 11/2 (1996), 67–75.

account of Socrates' own philosophy as it is presented in the early dialogues of his pupil. In the *Apology* Plato is anxious, like Xenophon, to defend Socrates from the charge of atheism. He points to the inconsistency between the two charges, that he is an atheist and that he introduces strange divinities. He also distances him from the secular physicism of Anaxagoras. The denial in the *Apology* that he had ever discussed physics (19d) does not ring altogether true, even though it is echoed later by Aristotle (*Metaph. A* 6. 987^{b}2). If Socrates had never shown any interest in issues of cosmology, Aristophanes' mockery would have been so wide of the mark that the jokes would have fallen very flat. Moreover, Plato himself in his *Phaedo* represents Socrates as confessing that he at one time shared Anaxagoras' curiosity about whether the earth was flat or round and whether it was in the middle of the universe, and what was the reason for the motion and speed of the sun and moon and other heavenly bodies (*Phd.* 97b–99a).

It may have been Socrates' disillusionment with Anaxagoras that made him give up scientific inquiry and concentrate on the issues which, according to the *Apology* and Aristotle, dominated the latter part of his life. According to both Plato and Xenophon, another factor that directed his interest was an oracle uttered in the name of Apollo by the entranced priestess in the shrine at Delphi. When asked if there was anyone in Athens wiser than Socrates, the priestess replied in the negative. Socrates professed to be puzzled by this response, and began to question different classes of people who claimed to possess wisdom of various kinds. It soon became clear that politicians and poets possessed no genuine expertise at all, and that craftsmen who were genuine experts in a particular area would pretend to a universal wisdom to which they had no claim. Socrates concluded that the oracle was correct in that he alone realized that his own wisdom was worthless (23b).

It was in matters of morality that it was most important to pursue genuine knowledge and to expose false pretensions. For according to Socrates virtue and moral knowledge were the same thing: no one who really knew what was the best thing to do could do otherwise, and all wrongdoing was the result of ignorance.[22] This makes it all the more absurd that he should be accused of corrupting the young. Anyone would obviously prefer to live among good men than among bad men, who might harm him. He cannot, therefore, have any motive for corrupting

---

[22] For a fuller discussion of this remarkable doctrine, 'the Socratic Paradox', see Ch. 8 below.

the young on purpose; and if he is doing so unwittingly he should be educated rather than prosecuted (26a).

Socrates, in the *Apology*, did not claim to possess himself the wisdom that is sufficient to keep a man from wrongdoing. Instead, he said that he relied on an inner divine voice, which would intervene if ever he was on the point of taking a wrong step (41d). So far from being an atheist, his whole life was dedicated to a divine mission, the campaign to expose false wisdom which was prompted by the Delphic oracle. What would really be a betrayal of God would be to desert his post through fear of death. If he were told that he could go free on condition that he abandon philosophical inquiry, he would reply, 'Men of Athens, I honour and love you; but I shall obey God rather than you, and while I have life and strength I shall never cease from the practice and teaching of philosophy' (29d).

The early dialogues of Plato portray Socrates carrying out his philosophical mission. Typically, the dialogue will be named after a personage who claims knowledge of a certain subject or who can be taken to represent a certain virtue: thus the *Ion*, on poetry, is named after a prizewinning rhapsode (a reciter of Homer), and the *Laches*, on courage, is named after a distinguished general. *Charmides* and *Lysis*, on passion, temperance, and friendship, are named after two bright young men who commanded a circle of aristocratic admirers. In each dialogue Socrates seeks a scientific account or definition of the topic under discussion, and by questioning reveals that the eponymous protagonist is unable to give one. The dialogues all end with the ostensible failure of the inquiry, confirming the conclusion in the *Apology* that those who might most be expected to possess wisdom on particular topics fail, under examination, to exhibit it.

The search for definitions serves different purposes in different dialogues: a definition of justice is sought in *Republic* 1 in order to determine whether justice benefits its possessor, and a definition of piety is sought in the *Euthyphro* in order to settle a particular difficult case of conscience. But Aristotle was right to pick out the search as a notable feature of Socratic method. The method has sometimes been criticized as involving the fallacious claim that we cannot ever know whether some particular action is or is not, say, just or pious unless we can give a watertight definition of justice and piety. Such a claim would be inconsistent with Socrates' regular practice in the course of his *elenchus* of seeking agreement whether particular actions (such as returning a borrowed knife to a madman, or carrying out a strategic retreat in battle) do or do not exhibit particular virtues such as justice and courage. Socrates' method involves only the weaker claim that unless we have a general definition of a virtue we will not (*a*) be able to say whether the virtue universally has a particular property, such as being teachable, or being beneficial, or (*b*) be able to decide difficult borderline cases, such as whether a son's prosecuting his father for the manslaughter of an accused murderer is or is not an act of piety.

The other feature of Socrates' method emphasized by Aristotle, namely the use of inductive arguments, does in fact presuppose that we can be sure of truths about individual cases while still lacking universal definitions. Plato's Socrates does not claim to have a watertight definition of *techne*, or craft; but over and over again he considers particular crafts in order to extract general truths about the nature of a craft. Thus, in *Republic* 1 he wishes to show that the test of a good craftsman is not whether he makes a lot of money, but whether he benefits the objects of his craft. To show this he runs through the products of different crafts: a good doctor produces healthy patients, a good captain delivers safe navigation, a good builder constructs a good house, and so on. How much money these people make is not relevant to their goodness at their craft; it tells us only how efficient they are at the quite different craft of moneymaking (*Rep.* 1. 346a–e).

The two procedures identified by Aristotle are, in Socrates' method, closely related to each other. The inductive argument from particular instances to general truths is a contribution to the universal definition, even though the contribution in these dialogues is forever incomplete, never leading to an exception-proof definition. In the absence of the universal definition of a virtue, the general truths are applied to help settle difficult borderline cases of practice, and to evaluate preliminary hypotheses about the virtue's properties. Thus, in the *Republic* case, the induction is used to show that a good ruler is one who benefits his subjects, and therefore justice is not (as one of the characters in the dialogue maintains) simply whatever is to the advantage of those in power.

In these early dialogues about the virtues, in spite of Socrates' profession of ignorance, a number of theses emerge both about knowledge and about virtue. These will be explored in greater detail in later chapters on epistemology and ethics. For the moment we may notice that the issues converge on the question: Can virtue be taught? For if virtue is knowledge, then surely it must be teachable; and yet it is difficult to point to any successful teachers of virtue.

In Athens, however, there was no lack of people claiming to have the relevant expertise, namely the sophists. At the end of the early period, and before the central period of Plato's writing career, we find a series of dialogues named after major sophists—Hippias, Gorgias, Protagoras—which address the question whether virtue can be taught and which deflate the pretensions of the sophists to possess the secret of its teachability. The *Hippias Minor* sets out a serious difficulty for the idea that virtue is a craft that can be learnt. A craftsman who makes a mistake unknowingly is inferior to a craftsman who makes a mistake deliberately; so if virtue is a craft, one who sins deliberately is more virtuous than one who sins in ignorance (376b). The *Gorgias* argues that rhetoric, the main arrow in the sophist's quiver, is incapable of producing genuine virtue. The *Protagoras* seems to suggest—whether seriously or ironically—that virtue is indeed teachable, because it is the art of calculating the proportion of pleasure and pain among the consequences of one's actions.[23]

From Socrates to Plato

Whether or not this is Socrates' last word on the teachability of virtue, a reader of the dialogues soon finds a quite different answer being given, in the *Meno* and the *Phaedo*. Virtue, and the knowledge of good and evil, which according to Socrates is identical with virtue, cannot be taught in the present life: it can only be recovered by recollection of another and better world. This is presented not as a particular thesis about virtue, but as a general thesis about knowledge. In the *Meno* it is claimed that a slave-boy who has never been taught geometry can be brought, by suitable questioning, to recall significant geometrical truths (82b–86a). In the *Phaedo* it is argued that though we often see things that are more or less equal in size, we never see a pair of things absolutely equal to each other. The idea of absolute equality cannot therefore be derived from experience, but must have been acquired in a previous life. The same

---

[23] See Ch. 8 below.

goes for similar ideas such as that of absolute goodness and absolute beauty (74b–75b).

The *Meno* and the *Phaedo* therefore introduce two doctrines—the Theory of Ideas, and the thesis of recollection—which by the common consent of scholars belong to Plato, and not to the historical Socrates. They effect the 'separation', of which Aristotle spoke, between the universal definitions sought by Socrates and the empirical entities of our everyday world.

The *Phaedo* also contains Plato's account of the last days of Socrates in prison. Socrates' friend Crito has (in the dialogue named after him) failed to gain acceptance of a plan for escape. Socrates has rejected the proposal, saying that he owes so much to the laws of Athens, under which he was born and bred and lived contentedly, that he cannot now turn his back on his covenant with them and run away (51d–54c). The arrival of a ship from the sacred isle of Delos marks the end of the religious stay of execution, and Socrates prepares for death by engaging his friends in a long discussion of the immortality of the soul.[24] The discussion ends with Socrates' narrating a series of myths about the journeys in the underworld of the soul after it survives death.

Crito asks whether Socrates has any instructions about his burial; he is told to remember that he will be burying only the body, and not the soul, which is to go to the joys of the blessed. After his last bath Socrates says farewell to his family, jokes with his gaoler, and accepts the cup of hemlock. He is represented (with a degree of medical improbability) as composing himself serenely as sensation gradually deserts his limbs. His last words, like so many in his life, are puzzling: 'Crito, I owe a cock to Aesculapius [the god of healing]. Please remember to pay the debt.' Once again we ask ourselves whether he means his words literally or is employing his unique form of irony.

It is perhaps no coincidence that it is in one and the same dialogue that Plato records the last hours of Socrates and introduces clearly for the first time his own characteristic Theory of Ideas. As well as the physical death of Socrates, we witness the demise of his personal philosophy, to be reincarnated henceforth in the more metaphysical and mythical form of Platonism.

When Socrates died, Plato was in his late twenties, having been his pupil for about eight years. A member of an aristocratic Athenian family, Plato

---

[24] The philosophical content of this discussion is analysed below in Ch. 7.

A herm of Socrates, bearing a quotation from Plato's *Crito*

would have been just old enough to have fought in the Peloponnesian War, as his brothers Glaucon and Adeimantus certainly did. His uncles Critias and Charmides were two of the Thirty Tyrants, but he himself took no part in Athenian political life. At the age of 40 he went to Sicily and became an associate of Dion, the brother-in-law of the reigning monarch, Dionysius I; during this visit he made the acquaintance of the Pythagorean philosopher Archytas. On his return to Athens he founded a philosophical community, the Academy, in a private grove beside his own house. Here a group of thinkers, under his direction, shared with each other their interests in mathematics, astronomy, metaphysics, ethics, and mysticism. When 60 years old he was invited back to Sicily by Dion's nephew, who had now succeeded to the throne as Dionysius II; but his visit was not a success because Dion and Dionysius quarrelled with each other. A third visit as a royal adviser was equally abortive, and Plato returned home disillusioned in 360. He died peacefully at a wedding feast in Athens, himself unmarried, in the year 347, being aged about 80.

Writers in antiquity wove many stories around Plato's life, few of which deserve credence. If we wish to put flesh around the bare bones of his biography, we do best to read the Letters that have traditionally been included in his works. Though some, if not all, are the composition of other authors, they contain information that is much more plausible than the anecdotes to be found in the Life of Plato by Diogenes Laertius. They profess to be from the last two decades of Plato's life and principally concern his involvement in the government of Syracuse and his attempt to convert a tyranny into a constitution embodying his own political ideals.

Plato's works as handed down to us amount to some half a million words. Though probably some of the works in the corpus are spurious, there are no written works attributed to Plato in antiquity that have not survived today. However, later writers in antiquity, in addition to making copious citations of his dialogues, from time to time attach importance to an oral tradition of his lectures in the Academy.

Because Plato chose to write in dialogue form, and never himself appears in them as a speaker, it is difficult to be sure which of the varied philosophical theses expounded by his characters were ones to which he was himself committed. We have seen this par excellence in the case of his Socrates, but similar caution must be exercised in attributing to him the doctrines of the other main interlocutors in the dialogues,

Timaeus, the Eleatic Stranger in the *Sophist* and *Statesman*, and the Athenian Stranger in the *Laws*. The dialogue form enabled Plato to suspend judgement about difficult philosophical issues, while presenting the strongest arguments he could think of on both sides of the question (cf. D.L. 3. 52).

The Theory of Ideas

The best known of the doctrines to be found in Plato's dialogues is the Theory of Ideas. In the central dialogues, from the *Euthyphro* onwards, the theory is more often alluded to, taken for granted, or argued from, than explicitly stated and formally established. The clearest short statement of the theory is found not in the dialogues but in the seventh of the Letters traditionally attributed to Plato, which is largely devoted to a defence of his activities in Sicily. The authenticity of this letter has often been rejected in modern times. There is, however, no better ground for rejecting Plato's Seventh Epistle to the Syracusans than there is for rejecting Paul's Second Epistle to the Corinthians (which it resembles in several ways). Certainly there is no good stylometric reason for calling it into question.[25] If it is not authentic, then it is one of the clearest and most authoritative statements of the theory to be found in all the secondary literature on Plato. Hence it provides a useful starting point for the exposition of the theory.

The letter states the following as a fundamental doctrine that Plato has often expounded:

For each thing that there is three things are necessary if we are to come by knowledge: first, the name, secondly, the definition, and thirdly, the image. Knowledge itself is a fourth thing, and there is a fifth thing that we have to postulate, which is that which is knowable and truly real. To understand this, consider the following example and regard it as typical of everything. There is something called a circle; it has a name, which we have just this minute used. Then there is its definition, a compound of nouns and verbs. We might give 'The figure whose limit is at every point equidistant from its centre' as the definition of whatever is round, circular, or a circle. Thirdly, there is what we draw, or rub out, or rotate, or cancel. The circle itself which all these symbolize

---

[25] Ledger, *Re-counting Plato*, 148–50, 224, regards the Seventh Letter as authentic, and close in time to the *Philebus*, the first dialogue of the final period.

does not undergo any such change and is a quite different thing. In the fourth place we have knowledge, understanding, and true opinion on these matters—these, collectively, are in our minds and not in sounds or bodily shapes, and thus are clearly distinct from the circle itself and from the three entities already mentioned. Of all these items, it is understanding that is closest to the fifth in kinship and likeness; the others are at a greater distance. What is true of round is also true of straight, of colour, of good and beautiful, and just; of natural and manufactured bodies; of fire, water, and the other elements; of all living beings and moral characters; of all that we do and undergo. In each case, anyone who totally fails to grasp the first four things will never fully possess knowledge of the fifth. (342a–d)

If I follow Plato, then, I will begin by distinguishing four things: the word 'circle', the definition of circle (a series of words), a diagram of a circle, and my concept of a circle. The importance of being clear about these four items is to distinguish them from, and contrast them with, a fifth thing, the most important of all, which he calls 'the circle itself'. It is this that is one of the Ideas of which Plato's celebrated theory treats. The theory is a wide-ranging one, as is clear from the sentence at the end of the paragraph that lists the fields in which the theory applies. In his other writings Plato uses many other expressions to refer to Ideas. 'Forms' (*eide*) is probably the most common, but the Idea or Form of X may be called 'the X itself', 'that very thing that is X', or 'Xness', or 'what X is'.

It is important to note what is absent from Plato's list in the Seventh Letter. He does not mention, even at the lowest level, actual material circular objects such as cartwheels and barrels. The reason for his omission is clear from other passages in his writings (e.g. *Phd.* 74a–c). The wheels and barrel we meet in experience are never perfectly circular: somewhere or other there will be a bend or bump which will interfere with the equi-distance from the centre of every point on the circumference. This is true too, for that matter, of any diagram we may draw on paper or in the sand. Plato does not stress this point here, but it is the reason why he says that the diagram is at a greater distance from the circle itself than my concept is. My subjective concept of the circle—my understanding of what 'circle' means—is not the same as the Idea of the circle, because the Idea is an objective reality that is not the property of any individual mind. But at least the concept in my mind is a concept *of a perfect circle*; it is not merely an imperfect approximation to a circle, as the ring on my finger is.

In the passage I have cited, Plato arrives at the Idea of circle after starting from a consideration of the word 'circle' as it occurs in the subject-place of a sentence such as

> A circle is a plane figure whose circumference is everywhere equidistant from its centre.

However, he sometimes introduces the Idea of X by reflection on sentences in which 'X' appears not in subject-place, but as a predicate.

Consider the following. Socrates, Simmias, and Cebes are all called 'men'; they have it in common that they are all men. Now when we say 'Simmias is a man' we may wonder whether the word 'man' names or stands for something in the way that the name 'Simmias' stands for the individual man Simmias? If so, what? Is it the same thing as the word 'man' stands for in 'Cebes is a man'? In order to deal with questions of this kind, Plato introduces the Idea of Man. It is that which makes Simmias, Cebes, and Socrates all men; it is the prime bearer of the name 'Man'.

In many cases where we would say that a common predicate was true of a number of individuals, Plato will say that they are all related to a certain Idea or Form: where A, B, C, are all F, they are related to a single Form of F. Sometimes he will describe this relation as one of imitation: A, B, C, all resemble F. Sometimes he will talk rather of participation: A, B, C all share in F, they have F in common between them. It is not clear how universally we are to apply the principle that behind common predication there lies a common Idea. Sometimes Plato states it universally, sometimes he hesitates about applying it to certain particular sorts of predicate. Certainly he lists Ideas of many different types, such as the Idea of Good, the Idea of Bed, the Idea of Circle, the Idea of Being. He is prepared to extend the theory beyond single-place predicates such as 'is round' to two-place predicates like 'is distinct from'. When we say that A is distinct from B and when we say that B is distinct from A, although we use the word 'distinct' twice, each time we are applying it to a single entity.

We may state a number of Platonic theses about Ideas and their relations to ordinary things in the world.

(1) *The Principle of Commonality.* Wherever several things are F, this is because they participate in or imitate a single Idea of F (*Phd.* 100c; *Men.* 72c, 75a; *Rep.* 5. 476a10, 597c).

(2) *The Principle of Separation.* The Idea of F is distinct from all the things that are F (*Phd.* 74c; *Smp.* 211b).

(3) *The Principle of Self-Predication.* The Idea of F is itself F (*Hp. Ma.* 292e; *Prt.* 230c–e; *Prm.* 132a–b).

(4) *The Principle of Purity.* The Idea of F is nothing but F (*Phd.* 74c; *Smp.* 211e).

(5) *The Principle of Uniqueness.* Nothing but the Idea of F is really, truly, altogether F (*Phd.* 74d, *Rep.* 5. 479a–d).

(6) *The Principle of Sublimity.* Ideas are everlasting, they have no parts and undergo no change, and they are not perceptible to the senses (*Phd.* 78d; *Smp.* 211b).

The Principle of Commonality is not, by itself, uniquely Platonic. Many people who are unhappy with talk of 'participation' are content to speak of attributes as being 'in common' among many things which have them. They may say, for instance, 'If A, B, and C are all red, then this is because they have the property of being red in common, and we learn the meaning of 'red' by seeing what is common among the red things.' What is peculiar to Plato is that he seriously follows up what is implied if one uses the metaphor of 'having in common'.[26] For instance, there must be only a single Idea of F, otherwise we could not explain why the F things have something in common (*Rep.* 597b–c).

The Principle of Separation is linked with the notion of a hierarchy between Ideas and the individuals that exemplify them. To participate and to be participated in are two quite different relationships, and the two terms of these relationships must be on a different level.

The Principle of Self-Predication is important for Plato, because without it he could not show how the Ideas explain the occurrence of properties in individuals. Only what is hot will make something hot; and it is no good drying yourself with a wet towel. So, in general, only what is itself F can explain how something else is F. So if the Idea of Cold is to explain why snow is cold, it must itself be cold (*Phd.* 103b–e).

The Idea of F is not only F, it is a perfect specimen of an F. It cannot be diluted or adulterated by any element other than Fness: hence the Principle of Purity. If it were to possess any property other than being F, it would have to do so by participating in some other Idea, which would

---

[26] I owe this point to G. E. M. Anscombe, *Three Philosophers* (Oxford: Blackwell, 1961), 28.

surely have to be superior to it in the way that the Idea of F is superior to all the non-ideal Fs. The notion of stratified relationships between Ideas opens up a Pandora's box which Plato, when presenting the classical Theory of Ideas in his central dialogues, preferred to keep closed.

The Principle of Uniqueness is sometimes stated in a misleading way by commentators. Plato frequently says that only Ideas really are, and that the non-ideal particulars we encounter in sense-experience are between being and not being. He is often taken to be saying that only Ideas really exist, and that tangible objects are unreal and illusory. In context, it is clear that when Plato says that only Ideas really are, he does not mean that only Ideas really exist, but that only the Idea of F is really F, whatever F may be in the particular case. Particulars are between being and not being in that they are between being F and not being F—i.e. they are sometimes F and sometimes not F.[27]

For instance, only the Idea of Beauty is really beautiful, because particular beautiful things are (*a*) beautiful in one respect but ugly in another (in figure, say, but not in complexion), or (*b*) beautiful at one time but not another (e.g. at age 20 but not at age 70), (*c*) beautiful by comparison with some things, but not with others (e.g. Helen may be beautiful by comparison with Medea, but not by comparison with Aphrodite), (*d*) beautiful in some surroundings but not in others (*Smp.* 211 a–e).

An important feature of the classical Theory of Ideas is the Principle of Sublimity. The particulars that participate belong to the inferior world of Becoming, the world of change and decay; the Ideas that are participated in belong to a superior world of Being, of eternal stability. The most sublime of all Ideas is the Idea of the Good, superior in rank and power to all else, from which everything that can be known derives its being (*Rep.* 509c).

The problem with the Theory of Ideas is that the principles that define it do not seem to be all consistent with each other. It is difficult to reconcile the Principle of Separation with the Principles of Commonality and of Self-Predication. The difficulty was first expounded by Plato himself in the *Parmenides*, where he gives an argument along the following lines. Let us suppose that we have a number of particulars, each of which is F. Then, by (1) there is an Idea of F. This, by (3), is itself F. But now the Idea of F and the original particular Fs make up a new collection of F things. By (1) again, this

---

[27] I first learnt this from Vlastos's article 'Degrees of Reality in Plato', in R. Bambrough (ed.), *New Essays on Plato and Aristotle* (London: Routledge & Kegan Paul, 1965).

must be because they participate in an Idea of F. But by (2) this cannot be the Idea first postulated. So there must be another Idea of F; but this in turn, by (3), will be F, and so on *ad infinitum*. If we are to avoid this regress, we must abandon one or other of the principles that generate it. To this day scholars are divided as to how seriously Plato took this difficulty, and which, if any, of his principles he modified in order to solve it. I shall return to the question when we engage in a fuller discussion of Plato's metaphysics.[28]

Plato applied his Theory of Ideas to many philosophical problems: he offered them as the basis of moral values, the bedrock of scientific knowledge, and the ultimate origin of all being. One problem to which Plato offered his theory as an answer is often called the problem of universals: the problem of the meaning of universal terms such as 'man', 'bed', 'virtue', 'good'. Because Plato's answer turned out to be unsatisfactory, the problem was to remain on the philosophical agenda. In succeeding chapters we shall see how Aristotle handled the issue. The problem had a continuing history through the Middle Ages and up to our own time. A number of notions that occur in modern discussions of the problem bear a resemblance to Plato's Ideas.

Predicates. In modern logic a sentence such as 'Socrates is wise' is considered as having a subject, 'Socrates', and a predicate, which consists of the remainder of the sentence, i.e. '...is wise'. Some philosophers of logic, following Gottlob Frege, have regarded predicates as having an extramental counterpart: an objective predicate (Frege called it a 'function') corresponding to '...is a man' in a way similar to that in which the man Socrates corresponds to the name 'Socrates'. Frege's functions, such as the function *x is a man*, are objective entities: they are more like the fifth items of the Seventh Letter than like the fourth items. They share some of the transcendental properties of Ideas: the function *x is a man* does not grow or die as human beings do, and nowhere in the world can one view or handle the function *x is divisible by 7*. But functions do not conform to the Principles of Self-Predication or Uniqueness. How could one ever imagine that the function *x is a man*, and only that function, was really and truly a human being?

Classes. Functions serve as principles according to which objects can be collected into classes: objects that satisfy the function *x is human*, for instance, can be grouped into the class of human beings. Ideas in some way resemble classes: participation in an Idea can be assimilated to membership of a class. The difficulty in identifying Ideas with classes arises again over the Principle of Self-Predication. The class of men is not a man and we cannot say in general that the class of Fs is F. However, it seems at first sight as if there are, indeed, some classes that are members of themselves, such as the class of classes. But just as Plato was to find that the Principle of Self-Predication led him into serious problems, so modern philosophers discovered that if one was allowed total freedom to form classes of classes one would be led into paradoxes. Most notorious is the paradox of the class of all classes that are not members of themselves. Bertrand Russell pointed out that if this class is a member of itself it is not a member of itself, and if it is not a member of itself then it is a member of itself. It is no accident that Russell's paradox bears a striking resemblance to Plato's self-criticism in the *Parmenides*.

Paradigms. It has more than once been suggested that Platonic Ideas might be looked on as paradigms or standards: the relation between individuals and Ideas might be thought to be similar to that between metre-long objects and the Standard Metre by which the metre length was formerly defined.[29] This notion fits well the way in which for Plato particulars imitate or resemble Ideas: to be a metre long was, precisely, to resemble the Standard Metre, and if two things were each a metre long it was in virtue of their common resemblance to the paradigm. However, such paradigms fail the Principle of Sublimity: the Standard Metre was not in heaven but in Paris.

Concrete universals. Philosophers have sometimes toyed with the notion that in a sentence such as 'Water is fluid' the word 'water' is to be treated as the name of a single scattered object, the aqueous portion of the world, made up of puddles, rivers, lakes, and so on. This would give a clear sense to Plato's principle that particulars participate in Ideas: this particular bottle of water is quite literally a part of all-the-water-in-the-world. Moreover, water is undoubtedly water, and nothing that is not water is really and truly water. This notion also suits Plato's preference (not often shared by his commentators) for referring to Ideas by a concrete mode of speech (e.g.

---

[29] The idea originated with Wittgenstein. See P. T. Geach, 'The Third Man Again', in R. E. Allen (ed.), *Studies in Plato's Metaphysics* (London: Routledge & Kegan Paul, 1965).

'the beautiful') rather than an abstract one (e.g. 'beauty'). However, concrete universals fail the Principle of Sublimity and the Principle of Purity: the water in the universe can be located and can change in quantity and distribution, and it has many other properties besides that of being water.

None of these notions do full justice to the many facets of Plato's Ideas. If one wants to see how his six principles seemed plausible to Plato it is better to consider, not any modern logician's technical concept, but some more unreflective notion. Consider the points of the compass, north, south, west, and east. Take the notion, say, of the east as one might conceive it by naive reflection on the various idioms we in Britain use about the east. There are many places that are east of us, e.g. Belgrade and Hong Kong. Anything thus eastward is part of the east (participation) and is in the same direction as the east (imitation). That is what makes whatever is east of us east (1). The east, however, cannot be identified with any point in space, however eastward it may be (2). The east is of course east of us (3), and the east is nothing but east (4): if we say 'The east is red' we only mean that the eastern sky is red. Nothing but the east is unqualifiedly east: the sun is sometimes east and sometimes west, India is east of Iran but west of Vietnam, but in every time and place the east is east (5). The east has no history in time, and it cannot be seen, handled, or parcelled out (6).

I am not, of course, suggesting that points of the compass will supply an interpretation of Plato's principles that will make them all come out true: no interpretation could do that since the principles form an inconsistent set. I am merely saying that this interpretation will make the theses look prima facie plausible in a way that the interpretations previously considered will not. Functions, classes, paradigms, and concrete universals all raise problems of their own, as philosophers long after Plato discovered, and though we cannot go back to the classical Theory of Ideas, we have yet to give a fully satisfactory answer to the problems it was meant to address.

Plato's Republic

In Plato's most famous dialogue, the *Republic*, the Theory of Ideas is put to use not only for the logical and semantical purposes that we have just been considering, but also to address problems in epistemology, metaphysics, and ethics. These ramifications of the theory will be considered in later chapters. But the *Republic* is best known to the world at large not for its manifold exploitation of the theory, but for the political arrangements that are described in its central books.

The official topic of the dialogue is the nature and value of justice. After several candidate definitions for justice have been examined and found wanting in the first book (which probably originally existed as a separate dialogue), the main part of the work begins with a challenge to Socrates to prove that justice is something worthwhile for its own sake. Plato's brothers Glaucon and Adeimantus, who are characters in the dialogue, argue that justice is chosen as a way of avoiding evil. To avoid being oppressed by others, Glaucon says, weak human beings make compacts with each other neither to suffer nor to commit injustice. People would much prefer to act unjustly if they could do so with impunity—the kind of impunity a man would have, for instance, if he could make himself invisible so that his misdeeds passed undetected. Adeimantus supports his brother, saying that among humans the rewards of justice are the rewards of seeming to be just rather than the rewards of actually being just, and with regard to the gods the penalties of injustice can be bought off by prayer and sacrifice (2. 358a–367e).

We shall see in Chapter 8 how Socrates responds, through the remaining books of the dialogue, to this initial challenge. Now, in the interests of setting out Plato's political philosophy, we should concentrate on his immediate response. To answer the brothers he shifts from the consideration of justice, or righteousness, in the individual person to the larger issue of justice in the city-state. There, he says, the nature of justice will be written in bigger letters and therefore easier to read. The purpose of living in cities is to enable people with different skills to supply each other's needs by an appropriate division of labour. Ideally, if people were content as they once were with the satisfaction of their basic needs, a very simple community would suffice. But in the modern luxurious age citizens demand more than mere subsistence, and this necessitates more complicated political arrangements, including a well-trained professional army (2. 369b–374d).

Socrates now presents a blueprint for a city with three classes. Those among the soldiers best fitted to rule are selected by competition to form the upper class, called guardians; the remaining soldiers are described as auxiliaries, and the rest of the citizens belong to the class of farmers and artisans (2. 374d–376e). How are the working classes to be brought to accept the authority of the ruling classes? A myth must be propagated, a 'noble falsehood', to the effect that members of the three classes have different metals in their soul: gold, silver, and bronze respectively. Citizens in general are to remain in the class in which they were born, but Socrates allows a limited amount of social mobility (3. 414c–415c).

The rulers and auxiliaries are to receive an elaborate education in literature (based on a bowdlerized Homer), music (provided it is martial and edifying), and gymnastics (undertaken by both sexes in common) (2. 376e–3. 403b). Women as well as men are to be guardians and auxiliaries, but this involves severe restraints no less than privileges. Members of the upper classes are not allowed to marry; women are to be held in common and all sexual intercourse is to be public. Procreation is to be strictly regulated on eugenic grounds. Children are not to be allowed contact with their parents, but will be brought up in public creches. Guardians and auxiliaries may not own property or touch money; they will be given, free of charge, adequate but modest provisions, and they will live in common like soldiers in a camp (5. 451d–471c).

The state that Socrates imagines in books 3 to 5 of the *Republic* has been both denounced as a piece of ruthless totalitarianism and admired as an early exercise in feminism. If it was ever seriously meant as a blueprint for a real-life polity, then it must be admitted that it is in many respects in conflict with the most basic human rights, devoid of privacy and full of deceit. Considered as a constitutional proposal, it deserves all the obloquy that has been heaped on it by conservatives and liberals alike. But it must be remembered that the explicit purpose of this constitution-mongering was to cast light on the nature of justice in the soul, as Socrates goes on to do.[30] Plato, we know from other dialogues, delighted in teasing his readers; he extended the irony he had learnt from Socrates into a major principle of philosophical illumination.

However, having woven the analogy with his classbound state into his moral psychology, Plato in later books of the *Republic* returns to political theory. His ideal state, he tells us, incorporates all the cardinal virtues: the virtue of wisdom resides in the guardians, fortitude in the auxiliaries, temperance in the working classes, and justice is rooted in the principle of the division of labour from which the city-state took its origin. In a just

---

[30] See Ch. 7 below.

Despite Plato's proposals, it was rare for a woman to be admitted to a philosophical school as Hipparchia is here shown, in a fourth-century-BC fresco, joining her husband, Crates, founder of the Cynics

state every citizen and every class does that for which they are most suited, and there is harmony between the classes (4. 427d–434c).

In less ideal states there is a gradual falling away from this ideal. There are five possible types of political constitution (8. 544e). The first and best constitution is called monarchy or aristocracy: if wisdom rules it does not matter whether it is incarnate in one or many rulers. There are four other inferior types of constitution: timocracy, oligarchy, democracy, and despotism (8. 543c). Each of these constitutions declines into the next because of the downgrading of one of the virtues of the ideal state. If the rulers cease to be persons of wisdom, aristocracy gives place to timocracy, which is essentially rule by a military junta (8. 547c). Oligarchy differs from timocracy because oligarchic rulers lack fortitude and military virtues (8. 556d). Oligarchs do possess, in a rather miserly form, the virtue of temperance; when this is

59

abandoned oligarchy gives way to democracy (8. 555b). For Plato, any step from the aristocracy of the ideal republic is a step away from justice; but it is the step from democracy to despotism that marks the enthronement of injustice incarnate (8. 576a). So the aristocratic state is marked by the presence of all the virtues, the timocratic state by the absence of wisdom, the oligarchic state by the decay of fortitude, the democratic state by contempt for temperance, and the despotic state by the overturning of justice.

Plato recognizes that in the real world we are much more likely to encounter the various forms of inferior state than the ideal constitution described in the *Republic*. Nonetheless, he insists that there will be no happiness, public or private, except in such a city, and such a city will never be brought about unless philosophers become kings or kings become philosophers (5. 473c–d). Becoming a philosopher, of course, involves working through Plato's educational system in order to reach acquaintance with the Ideas.

The Laws *and the* Timaeus

Later in his life Plato abandoned the idea of the philosopher king and ceased to treat the Theory of Ideas as having political significance. He came to believe that the character of the ruler was less important to the welfare of a city than the nature of the laws under which it was governed. In his late and longest work, the *Laws*, he portrays an Athenian visitor discussing with a Cretan and a Spartan the constitution of a colony, Magnesia, to be founded in the south of Crete. It is to be predominantly agricultural, with the free population consisting mainly of citizen farmers. Manual work is done largely by slaves, and craft and commerce are the province of resident aliens. Full citizenship is restricted to 5,040 adult males, divided into twelve tribes. The blueprint for government that is presented as a result of the advice of the Athenian visitor stands somewhere between the actual constitutional arrangements of Athens and the imaginary structures of Plato's ideal republic.

Like Athens, Magnesia is to have an assembly of adult male citizens, a Council, and a set of elected officials, to be called the Guardians of the Laws. Ordinary citizens will take part in the administration of the laws by sitting on enormous juries. Various appointments are made by lot, so as to ensure wide political participation. Private property is allowed, subject to a highly progressive wealth tax (5. 744b). Marriage, far from being abolished, is imposed by law, and bachelors over 35 have to pay severe annual fines (6. 774b). Finally, legislators must realize that even the best laws are constantly in need of reform (6. 769d).

On the other hand, Magnesia has several features reminiscent of the *Republic*. Supreme power in the state rests with a Nocturnal Council, which includes the wisest and most highly qualified officials, specially trained in mathematics, astronomy, theology, and law (though not, like the guardians of the Republic, metaphysics). Private citizens are not allowed to possess gold or silver coins, and the sale of houses is strictly forbidden (5. 740c, 742a). Severe censorship is imposed on both texts and music, and poets must be licensed (7. 801d–2a). Female sex police, with right of entry to households, oversee procreation and enforce eugenic standards (6. 784a–b). In divorce courts there must be as many women judges as men (9. 930a). Women are to join men at the communal meals, and they are to receive military training, and provide a home defence force (7. 814a). Education is of great importance for all classes, and is to be supervised by a powerful Minister of Education reporting direct to the Nocturnal Council (6. 765d).

Substantive legislation is set out in the middle books of the dialogue. Each law must have a preamble setting out its purpose, so that citizens may conform to it with understanding. For instance, a law compelling marriage between the age of 30 and 35 should have a preamble explaining that procreation is the method by which human beings achieve immortality (4. 721b). The duties of the many administrative officials are set out in book 6, and the educational curriculum is detailed, from playschool upward, in book 7; the *Laws* itself is to be a set school text. Book 9 deals with forms of assault and homicide and sets out the procedure relating to capital offences such as temple robbery. Elaborate provision is made to ensure that the accused gets a fair trial. In civil matters the law goes into fine detail, laying down, for instance, the damages to be paid by a defendant who is shown to have enticed away bees from the plaintiff's hive (9. 843e). Hunting is to be very severely restricted: the only form allowed is the hunting of four-legged animals, on horseback, with dogs (7. 824a).

From time to time in the *Laws* Plato engages in theoretical discussion of sexual morality, though actual sexual legislation is restricted to a form of excommunication for adultery (7. 785d–e). In a way that has been very common during the Christian era, but was rare in pagan antiquity, he bases his sexual ethics on the notion that procreation is the natural purpose of sex. The Athenian says at one point that he would like to put into effect 'A law to permit sexual intercourse only for its natural purpose, procreation, and to prohibit homosexual relations; to forbid the deliberate killing of a human offspring and the casting of seed on rocks and stone where it will never take root and fructify' (8. 838e). He realizes, however, that it will be very difficult to ensure compliance with such a law, and instead he proposes other measures to stamp out sodomy and discourage all forms of non-procreative intercourse (8. 836e, 841d). We have reached a point in Plato's thinking far distant from the arch homosexual banter which is such a predominant feature of the Socratic dialogues.

One of the most interesting sections of the *Laws* is the tenth book, which deals with the worship of the gods and the elimination of heresy. Impiety arises, the Athenian says, when people do not believe that the gods exist, or believe that they exist but do not care for the human race. As a preamble to laws against impiety, therefore, the lawgiver must establish the existence of the divine. The elaborate argument he presents will be considered in a later chapter on philosophy of religion.

In the *Timaeus*, a dialogue whose composition probably overlapped with that of the *Laws*, Plato sets out the relationship between God and the world we live in. He returns to the traditional philosophical topic of cosmology, taking it up at the point where Anaxagoras had, in his view, left off unsatisfactorily. The world of the *Timaeus* is not a field of mechanistic causes: it is fashioned by a divinity, variously called its father, its maker, or its craftsman (*demiourgos*) (28c).

Timaeus, the eponymous hero of the dialogue, is an astronomer. He offers to narrate to Socrates the history of the universe, from the origin of the cosmos to the appearance of mankind. People ask, he says, whether the world has always existed or whether it had a beginning. The answer must be that it had a beginning, because it is visible, tangible, and corporeal, and nothing that is perceptible by the senses is eternal and changeless in the way that the objects of thought are (27d–28c). The divinity who fashioned it had his eye on an eternal archetype, 'for the cosmos is the most beautiful of the things that have come to be, and he is the best of all causes' (29a). Why did he bring it into existence? Because he was good, and what is good is utterly free from envy or selfishness (29d).

Like the Lord God in Genesis, the maker of the world looked at what he had made and found that it was good; and in his delight he adorned it with many beautiful things. But the Demiurge differs from the creator of Judaeo-Christian tradition in several ways. First of all, he does not create the world from nothing: rather, he brings it into existence from a primordial chaos, and his creative freedom is limited by the necessary properties of the initial matter (48a). 'God, wishing all things to be good and nothing, if he could help it, paltry, and finding the visible universe in a state not of peace but of inharmonious and disorderly motion, brought it from disorder into an order that he judged to be altogether better' (30a). Secondly, while the Mosaic creator infuses life into an inert world at a certain stage of its creation, in Plato both the ordered universe and the archetype on which it was patterned are themselves living beings. What is this living archetype? He does not tell us, but perhaps it is the world of Ideas which, he concluded belatedly in the *Sophist*, must contain life. God created the soul of the world before he formed the world itself: this world-soul is poised between the world of being and the world of becoming (35a). He then fastened the world on to it.

The soul was woven all through from the centre to the outermost heaven, which it wrapped itself around. By its own revolution upon itself it provided a divine principle of unending and rational life for all time. The body of the heaven was made visible, but the soul is invisible and endowed with reason and harmony. It is the best creation of the best of intelligible and eternal realities. (36e–37a)

In contrast to those earlier philosophers who spoke of multiple worlds, Plato is very firm that our universe is the only one (31b). He follows Empedocles in regarding the world as made up of the four elements, earth, air, fire, and water, and he follows Democritus in believing that the different qualities of the elements are due to the different shapes of the atoms that constitute them. Earth atoms are cubes, air atoms are octahedrons, fire atoms are pyramids, and water atoms are icosahedrons. Pre-existent space was the receptacle into which the maker placed the world, and in a mysterious way it underlies the transmutation of the four elements, rather as a lump of gold underlies the different shapes that a jeweller may give to it (50a). In this Plato seems to anticipate the prime matter of Aristotelian hylomorphism.[31]

[31] See Ch. 5 below.

Timaeus explains that there are four kinds of living creatures in the universe: gods, birds, animals, and fish. Among gods Plato distinguishes between the fixed stars, which he regards as everlasting living beings, and the gods of Homeric tradition, whom he mentions in a rather embarrassed aside. He describes the infusion of souls into the stars and into human beings, and he develops a tripartite division of the human soul that he had introduced earlier in the *Republic*. He gives a detailed account of the mechanisms of perception and of the construction of the human body.[32] This construction, he tells us, was delegated by God to the lesser divinities that he had himself made personally (69c). A full description is given of all our bodily organs and their function, and there is a listing of diseases of body and mind.

The *Timaeus* was for centuries the most influential of Plato's dialogues. While the other dialogues went into oblivion between the end of antiquity and the beginning of the Renaissance, much of the *Timaeus* survived in Latin translations by Cicero and a fourth-century Christian called Chalcidius. Plato's teleological account of the forming of the world by a divinity was not too difficult for medieval thinkers to assimilate to the creation story of Genesis. The dialogue was a set text in the early days of the University of Paris, and 300 years later Raphael in his *School of Athens* gave Plato in the centre of the fresco only the *Timaeus* to hold.

---

[32] See Ch. 7 below.

2

Schools of Thought:
From Aristotle to Augustine

The fourth century saw a shift in political power from the city-states of classical Greece to the kingdom of Macedonia to the north. In the same way, after the Athenians Socrates and Plato, the next great philosopher was a Macedonian. Aristotle was born, fifteen years after Socrates' death, in the small colony of Stagira, on the peninsula of Chalcidice. He was the son of Nicomachus, court physician to King Amyntas, the grandfather of Alexander the Great. After the death of his father he migrated to Athens in 367, being then 17, and joined Plato's Academy. He remained for twenty years as Plato's pupil and colleague, and it can safely be said that on no other occasion in history was such intellectual power concentrated in a single institution.

Aristotle in the Academy

Many of Plato's later dialogues date from these decades, and some of the arguments they contain may reflect Aristotle's contributions to debate. By a flattering anachronism, Plato introduces a character called Aristotle into the *Parmenides*, the dialogue that contains the most acute criticisms of the Theory of Ideas. Some of Aristotle's own writings also belong to this period, though many of these early works survive only in fragments quoted by later writers. Like his master, he wrote initially in dialogue form, and in content his dialogues show a strong Platonic influence.

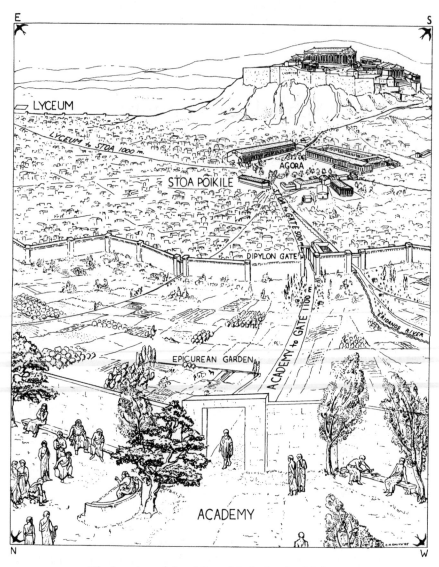

The location of the philosophical schools of Athens

In his lost dialogue *Eudemus*, for instance, Aristotle expounded a conception of the soul close to that of Plato's *Phaedo*. He argued vigorously against the thesis that the soul is an attunement of the body, claiming that it is imprisoned in a carcass and capable of a happier life when disembodied. The dead are more blessed and happier than the living, and have become greater and better. 'It is best, for all men and women, not to be born; and next after that—the best option for humans—is, once born, to die as quickly as possible' (fr. 44). To die is to return to one's real home.

Another Platonic work of Aristotle's youth is his *Protrepticus*, or exhortation to philosophy. This too is lost, but it was so extensively quoted in later antiquity that some scholars believe they can reconstruct it almost in its entirety. Everyone has to do philosophy, Aristotle says, for arguing against the practice of philosophy is itself a form of philosophizing. But the best form of philosophy is the contemplation of the universe of nature. Anaxagoras is praised for saying that the one thing that makes life worth living is to observe the sun and the moon and the stars and the heavens. It is for this reason that God made us, and gave us a godlike intellect. All else—strength, beauty, power, and honour—is worthless (Barnes, 2416).

The *Protrepticus* contains a vivid expression of the Platonic view that the soul's union with the body is in some way a punishment for evil done in an earlier life. 'As the Etruscans are said often to torture captives by chaining corpses to their bodies face to face, and limb to limb, so the soul seems to be spread out and nailed to all the organs of the body' (ibid.). All this is very different from Aristotle's eventual mature thought.

It is probable that some of Aristotle's surviving works on logic and disputation, the *Topics* and *Sophistical Refutations*, belong to this period. These are works of comparatively informal logic, the one expounding how to construct arguments for a position one has decided to adopt, the other showing how to detect weaknesses in the arguments of others. Though the *Topics* contains the germ of conceptions, such as the categories, that were to be important in Aristotle's later philosophy, neither work adds up to a systematic treatise on formal logic such as we are to be given in the *Prior Analytics*. Even so, Aristotle can say at the end of the *Sophistical Refutations* that he has invented the discipline of logic from scratch: nothing at all existed when he started. There are many treatises on rhetoric, he says, but

on the subject of deduction we had nothing of an earlier date to cite, but needed to spend a long time on original research. If, then, it seems to you on inspection that from such an unpromising start we have brought our investigation to a satisfactory condition comparable to that of traditional disciplines, it falls to you my students to grant me your pardon for the shortcomings of the inquiry, and for its discoveries your warm thanks. (*SE* 34. 184^{a}9–^{b}8)

It is indeed one of Aristotle's many claims on posterity that he was logic's founder. His most important works on the subject are the *Categories*, the *de Interpretatione*, and the *Prior Analytics*. These set out his teaching on simple terms, on propositions, and on syllogisms. They were grouped together, along with the two works already mentioned, and a treatise on scientific method, the *Posterior Analytics*, into a collection known as the *Organon*, or 'tool' of thought. Most of Aristotle's followers thought of logic not as itself a scientific discipline, but as a propaedeutic art which could be used in any discipline; hence the title. The *Organon*, though shown already in antiquity to be incomplete as a system of logic, was regarded for two millennia as providing the core of the subject.[1]

While Aristotle was at the Academy, King Philip II of Macedon, who succeeded his father in 359, adopted an expansionist policy and waged war on a number of Greek city-states, including Athens. Despite the martial eloquence of Aristotle's contemporary Demosthenes, who denounced the Macedonian king in his 'Philippics', the Athenians defended their interests only half-heartedly. After a series of humiliating concessions they allowed Philip to become, by 338, master of the Greek world. It cannot have been an easy time to be a Macedonian resident in Athens.

Within the Academy, however, relations seem to have remained cordial. Later generations liked to portray Plato and Aristotle embattled against each other, and some in antiquity likened Aristotle to an ungrateful colt who had kicked his mother (D.L. 5. 1). But Aristotle always acknowledged a great debt to Plato, whom on his death he described as the best and happiest of mortals 'whom it is not right for evil men even to praise'. He took a large part of his philosophical agenda from Plato, and his teaching is more often a modification than a repudiation of Plato's doctrines. The philosophical ideas that are common to the two philosophers are more important than the issues that divide them—just as, in the seventeenth and eighteenth centuries, the opposing schools of rationalists and empiricists had much more in common with each other than with the philosophers who preceded and followed them.

Already, however, during his period at the Academy, Aristotle began to distance himself from Plato's Theory of Ideas. In his pamphlet *On Ideas* he maintained that the arguments of Plato's central dialogues establish only

---

[1] Aristotle's logic is considered in detail in Ch. 3.

that there are, in addition to particulars, certain common objects of the sciences; but these need not be Ideas. He employs against Ideas a version of an argument that we have already encountered in Plato's own dialogues—he calls it the 'Third Man argument' (Barnes, 2435). In his surviving works Aristotle often take issue with the theory. Sometimes he does so politely, as where, in the *Nicomachean Ethics*, he introduces a series of arguments against the Idea of the Good with the remarks that he has an uphill task because the Forms were introduced by his good friends. However, his duty as a philosopher is to honour truth above friendship. In the *Posterior Analytics*, however, he dismisses Ideas contemptuously as 'tarradiddle' (1. 22. 83^{a}33).

More seriously, in his *Metaphysics* he argues that the theory fails to solve the problems it was meant to address. It does not confer intelligibility on particulars, because immutable and everlasting forms cannot explain how particulars come into existence and undergo change. Moreover, they do not contribute anything either to the knowledge or to the being of other things (*A* 9. 991^{a}8 ff.). All the theory does is to bring in new entities equal in number to the entities to be explained: as if one could solve a problem by doubling it (*A* 9. 990^{b}3).

Aristotle the Biologist

When Plato died in 347, his nephew Speusippus became head of the Academy, and Aristotle left Athens. He migrated to Assos on the north-western coast of what is now Turkey. The city was under the rule of Hermias, a graduate of the Academy, who had already invited a number of Academicians to form a new philosophical institute there. Aristotle became a friend of Hermias, and married a close relation of his, Pythias, with whom he had two children. In 343 Hermias met a tragic end: having negotiated, with Aristotle's help, an alliance with Macedon, he was treacherously arrested and eventually crucified by the Great King of Persia. Aristotle saluted his memory in an 'Ode to Virtue', his only surviving poem.

During his period in Assos, and during the next few years, when he lived at Mytilene on the island of Lesbos, Aristotle carried out extensive scientific research, particularly in zoology and marine biology. These researches were written up in a book later known, misleadingly, as the *History of Animals*, to which he added two shorter treatises, *On the Parts of Animals* and

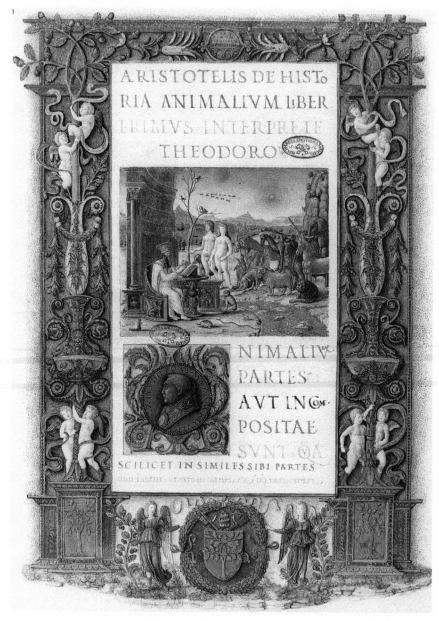

The frontispiece of a fifteenth-century manuscript translation of Aristotle's *History of Animals*

On the Generation of Animals. Aristotle does not claim to have founded the science of zoology, and his books contain copious citations of earlier writers, accompanied by a judicious degree of scepticism about some of their wilder reports. However, his detailed observations of organisms of very various kinds were quite without precedent, and in many cases they were not superseded until the seventeenth century.

Though he does not claim to be the first zoologist, Aristotle clearly saw himself as a pioneer, and indeed felt some need to justify his interest in the subject. Previous philosophers had given a privileged place to the observation of the heavens, and here was he prodding sponges and watching the hatching of grubs. In his defence he says that while the heavenly bodies are marvellous and glorious, they are hard to study because they are so distant and different from ourselves. Animals, however, are near at hand, and akin to our own nature, so that we can investigate them with much greater precision. It is childish to be squeamish about the observation of the humbler animals. 'We should approach the investigation of every kind of animal without being ashamed, for each of them will exhibit to us something natural and something beautiful' (*PA* 1. 5. 645^{a}20–5).

The scope of Aristotle's researches is astonishing. Much of his work is taken up with classification into genus (e.g. *Testacea*) and species (e.g. sea-urchin). More than 500 species figure in his treatises, and many of them are described in detail. It is clear that Aristotle was not content with the observation of a naturalist: he also practised dissection like an anatomist. He acknowledges that he found dissection distasteful, particularly in the case of human beings: but it was essential to examine the parts of any organism in order to understand the structure of the whole (*PA* 1. 5. 644^{b}22–645^{a}36).

Aristotle illustrated his treatises with diagrams, now sadly lost. We can conjecture the kind of illustrations he provided when we read passages such as the following, where he is explaining the relationship between the testicles and the penis.

In the accompanying diagram the letter A marks the starting point of ducts leading down from the aorta; the letters *KK* mark the heads of the testicles and the ducts that descend to them; the ducts leading from them through the testicles are marked *ΩΩ*, and the reverse ducts containing white fluid and leading to the testicles are marked *BB*; the penis *Δ*, the bladder *E*, and the testicles *ΨΨ*. (*HA* 3. 1. 510^{a}30–4)

Only a biologist could check the accuracy of the myriad items of information that Aristotle offers us about the anatomy, diet, habitat, modes of copulation, and reproductive systems of mammals, birds, reptiles, fish, and insects. The twentieth-century biologist Sir D'Arcy Thompson, who made the canonical translation of the *History of Animals* into English, constantly draws attention to the minuteness of his detailed investigations, coupled with vestiges of superstition. There are some spectacular cases where Aristotle's unlikely stories about rare species of fish were proved accurate many centuries later.[2] In other places Aristotle states clearly and fairly biological problems that were not solved until millennia had passed. One such case was the question whether an embryo contained all the parts of an animal in miniature form from the beginning, or whether wholly new structures were formed as the embryo develops (*GA* 2. 1. 734[a]1–735[a]4).

The modern layman can only guess which parts of passages like the following are accurate, and which are fantasy.

All animals that are quadrupedal, blooded, and viviparous are furnished with teeth; but, to begin with, some have teeth in both jaws, and some do not. For instance, horned quadrupeds do not; for they have not got the front teeth in the upper jaw; and some hornless animals, also, do not have teeth in both jaws, as the camel. Some animals have tusks, like the boar; and some have not. Further, some animals are saw-toothed, such as the lion, the leopard, and the dog; and some have teeth that do not interlock, as the horse and the ox; and by 'saw-toothed' we mean such animals as interlock the sharp-pointed teeth. (*HA* 2. 1. 501[a]8 ff.)

With such fish as pair, eggs are the result of copulation, but such fish have them also without copulation; and this is shown in the case of some river-fish, for the minnow has eggs when quite small—almost, one might say, as soon as it is born. These fishes shed their eggs, and, as is stated, the males swallow the greater part of them, and some portion of them goes to waste in the water; but such of the eggs as the female deposits in suitable places are saved. If all the eggs were preserved, each species would be vast in number. The greater number of these eggs are not productive, but only those over which the male sheds the milt; for when the female has laid her eggs, the male follows and sheds its milt over them, and from all the eggs so besprinkled young fishes proceed, while the rest are left to their fate. (*HA* 6. 3. 567[a]29–[b]6)

It is easier to form a quick judgement about Aristotle's attempts to link features of human anatomy to traits of character. He tells us, for instance,

[2] See G. E. R. Lloyd, *Aristotle: The Growth and Structure of his Thought* (Cambridge: Cambridge University Press, 1968), 74–81.

that those who have flat feet are likely to be rogues, and that those who have large and prominent ears have a tendency to irrelevant chatter (*HA* 1. 11. 492^{a}1).

Despite an admixture of old wives' tales, Aristotle's biological works must strike us as a stupendous achievement, when we remember the conditions under which he worked, unequipped with any of the aids to investigation that have been at the disposal of scientists since the early modern period. He, or one of his research assistants, must have been gifted with remarkably acute eyesight, since some of the features of insects that he accurately reports were not again observed until the invention of the microscope. His inquiries were conducted in a genuinely scientific spirit, and he is always ready to confess ignorance where evidence is insufficient. With regard to the reproductive mechanism in bees, for example, he has this to say:

The facts have not yet been sufficiently ascertained. If ever they are, then we must trust observation rather than theory, and trust theories only if their results conform with the observed phenomena. (*GA* 3. 10. 760^{b}28–31).

The Lyceum and its Curriculum

About eight years after the death of Hermias, Aristotle was summoned to the Macedonian capital by King Philip II as tutor to his 13-year-old son, the future Alexander the Great. We know little of the content of his instruction: the *Rhetoric for Alexander* that appears in the Aristotelian corpus is commonly regarded as a forgery. Ancient sources say that Aristotle did write essays on kingship and colonization for his pupil, and gave him his own edition of Homer. Alexander is said to have slept with this book under his pillow; and when he became king in 336 and started upon his spectacular military career, he arranged for biological specimens to be sent to his tutor from all parts of Greece and Asia Minor.

Within ten years Alexander had made himself master of an empire that stretched from the Danube to the Indus and included Libya and Egypt. While Alexander was conquering Asia, Aristotle was back in Athens, where he established his own school in the Lyceum, a gymnasium just outside the city boundary. Now aged 50, he built up a substantial library, and gathered around him a group of brilliant research students, called 'Peripatetics' from the name of the avenue (*peripatos*) in which they walked and held their discussions. The Lyceum was not a private club like the Academy; many of the lectures given there were open to the general public without fee.

Aristotle's anatomical and zoological studies had given a new and definitive turn to his philosophy. Though he retained a lifelong interest in metaphysics, his mature philosophy constantly interlocks with empirical science, and his thinking takes on a biological cast. Most of the works that have come down to us, with the exception of the zoological treatises, probably belong to this second Athenian sojourn. There is no certainty about their chronological order, and indeed it is probable that the main treatises—on physics, metaphysics, psychology, ethics, and politics—were constantly rewritten and updated. In the form in which they have survived it is possible to detect evidence of different layers of composition, though no consensus has been reached about the identification or dating of these strata.

In his major works Aristotle's style is very different from that of Plato or any of his other philosophical predecessors. In the period between Homer and Socrates most philosophers wrote in verse, and Plato, writing in the great age of Athenian tragedy and comedy, composed dramatic dialogue. Aristotle, an exact contemporary of the greatest Greek orator Demosthenes, preferred to write in prose monologue. The prose he wrote is commonly neither lucid nor polished, though he could compose passages of moving eloquence when he chose. It may be that the texts we have are the notes from which he lectured; perhaps even, in some cases, notes taken at lectures by students present. Everything Aristotle wrote is fertile of ideas and full of energy; every sentence packs a massive intellectual punch. But effort is needed to decode the message of his jagged clauses. What has been delivered to us from Aristotle across the centuries is a set of telegrams rather than epistles.

Aristotle's works are systematic in a way that Plato's never were. Even in the *Laws*, which is the closest to a textbook that Plato ever wrote, we flit from topic to topic, and indeed from discipline to discipline, in a disconcerting manner. None of the other major dialogues can be pigeon-holed as relating to a single area of philosophy. It is, of course, anachronistic to speak of 'disciplines' when discussing Plato: but the anachronism is not great because the notion of a discipline, in the modern academic sense, is made very explicit by Aristotle in his Lyceum period.

There are three kinds of sciences, Aristotle tells us in the *Metaphysics* (*E* 1. 1025ᵇ25): productive, practical, and theoretical sciences. Productive sciences are, naturally enough, sciences that have a product. They include engineering and architecture, with products like bridges and houses, but also disciplines such as strategy and rhetoric, where the product is something less concrete, such as victory on the battlefield or in the courts. Practical sciences are ones that guide behaviour, most notably ethics and politics. Theoretical sciences are those that have no product and no practical goal, but in which information and understanding is sought for its own sake.

There are three theoretical sciences: physics, mathematics, and theology (*Metaph. E* 1. 1026ᵃ19). In this trilogy only mathematics is what it seems to be. 'Physics' means natural philosophy or the study of nature (*physis*). It is a much broader study than physics as understood nowadays, including chemistry and meteorology and even biology and psychology. 'Theology' is, for Aristotle, the study of entities above and superior to human beings, that is to say, the heavenly bodies as well as whatever divinities may inhabit the starry skies. His writings on this topic resemble a textbook of astronomy more than they resemble any discourse on natural religion.

It may seem surprising that metaphysics, a discipline theoretical *par excellence*, does not figure in Aristotle's list of theoretical sciences, since so much of his writing is concerned with it, and since one of his longest treatises bears the title *Metaphysics*. The word, in fact, does not occur in Aristotle's own writings and first appears in the posthumous catalogue of his works. It simply means 'after physics' and refers to the works that were listed after his *Physics*. But he did in fact come to recognize the branch of philosophy we now call 'metaphysics': he called it 'First Philosophy' and he defined it as the discipline that studies Being as Being.³

Aristotle on Rhetoric and Poetry

In the realm of productive sciences Aristotle wrote two works, the *Rhetoric* and the *Poetics*, designed to assist barristers and playwrights in their respective tasks. Rhetoric, Aristotle says, is the discipline that indicates in any given case the possible means of persuasion: it is not restricted to a

---

³ See Ch. 5 below.

particular field, but is topic-neutral. There are three bases of persuasion by the spoken word: the character of the speaker, the mood of the audience, and the argument (sound or spurious) of the speech itself. So the student of rhetoric must be able to reason logically, to evaluate character, and to understand the emotions (1. 2. 1358^{a}1–1360^{b}3).

Aristotle wrote more instructively about logic and character in other treatises, but the second book of the *Rhetoric* contains his fullest account of human emotions. Emotions, he says, are feelings that alter people's judgements, and they are accompanied by pain and pleasure. He takes each major emotion in turn, offering a definition of the emotion and a list of its objects and causes. Anger, for instance, he defines as a desire, accompanied by pain, for what appears to be revenge for what appears to be an unmerited slight upon oneself or one's friends (2. 2. 1378^{a}32–4). He gives a long list of the kinds of people who make us angry: those who mock us, for instance, or those who stop us drinking when we are thirsty, or those who get in our way at work.

Also those who speak ill of us, and show contempt for us, in respect of the things we most care about. Thus those who seek a reputation as philosophers get angry with those who show disdain for their philosophy; those who pride themselves upon their appearance get angry with those who disparage it, and so on. We feel particularly angry if we believe that, either in fact or in popular belief, we are totally or largely lacking in the respective qualities. For when we are convinced that we excel in the qualities for which we are mocked, we can ignore the mockery. (2. 2. 1379^{a}32–^{b}1)

Aristotle takes us on a detailed tour of the emotions of anger, hatred, fear, shame, pity, indignation, envy, and jealousy. In each case his treatment is clear and systematic, and often shows—as in the above passage—acute psychological insight.

The *Poetics*, unlike the *Rhetoric*, has been very widely read throughout history. Only its first book survives, a treatment of epic and tragic poetry. The second book, on comedy, is lost. Umberto Eco, in *The Name of the Rose*, wove a dramatic fiction around its imagined survival and then destruction in a fourteenth-century abbey.

To understand Aristotle's message in the *Poetics* one must know something of Plato's attitude to poetry. In the second and third books of the *Republic* Homer is attacked for misrepresenting the gods and for encouraging debased emotions. The dramatic representations of the tragedians, too, are attacked as deceptive and debasing. In the tenth book the Theory of Ideas provides the basis for a further, and more fundamental, attack on the poets. Material objects are imperfect copies of the truly real Ideas; artistic representations of material objects are therefore at two removes from reality, being imitations of imitations (597e). Drama corrupts by appealing to the lower parts of our nature, encouraging us to indulge in weeping and laughter (605d–6c). Dramatic poets must be kept away from the ideal city: they should be anointed with myrrh, crowned with laurel, and sent on their way (398b).

One of Aristotle's aims was to resolve this quarrel between poetry and philosophy. Imitation, he says, so far from being the degrading activity that Plato describes, is something natural to humans from childhood. It is one of the features that makes men superior to animals, since it vastly increases their scope for learning. Secondly, representation brings a delight all of its own: we enjoy and admire paintings of objects which in themselves would annoy or disgust us (*Po.* 4. 1448^{b}5–24).

Aristotle offers a detailed analysis of the nature of tragic drama. He defines tragedy in the following terms.

A tragedy is a representation of a grand, complete, and significant action, in language embellished appropriately in the different parts of the work, in dramatic, not narrative form, with episodes arousing pity and fear so as to achieve purification (*katharsis*) of these emotions. (6. 1449^{b}24 ff.).

No one is quite sure what Aristotle meant by *katharsis*, or purification. Perhaps what he wanted to teach is that watching tragedy helps us to put our own sorrows and worries into perspective, as we observe the catastrophes that have overtaken people who were far superior to the likes of ourselves. Pity and fear, the emotions to be purified, are most easily aroused, he says, if the tragedy exhibits people as the victims of hatred and murder where they could most expect to be loved and cherished. That is why so many tragedies concern feuds within a single family (14. 1453^{b}1–21).

Six things, Aristotle says, are necessary for a tragedy: plot, character, diction, thought, spectacle, and melody (6. 1450^{a}11 ff.). It is the first two of these that chiefly interest him. Stage setting and musical accompaniment are dispensable accessories: what is great in a tragedy can be appreciated from a mere reading of the text. Thought and diction are more important:

it is the thoughts expressed by the characters that arouse emotion in the hearer, and if they are to do so successfully they must be presented convincingly by the actors. But it is character and plot that really bring out the genius of a tragic poet, and Aristotle devotes a long chapter to character, and no less than five chapters to plot.

The main character or tragic hero must be neither supremely good nor supremely bad: he should be a person of rank who is basically good, but comes to grief through some great error (*hamartia*). A woman may have the kind of goodness necessary to be a tragic heroine, and even a slave may be a tragic subject. Whatever kind of person is the protagonist, it is important that he or she should have the qualities appropriate to them, and should be consistent throughout the drama. (15. 1454^{a}15 ff.). Every one of the dramatis personae should possess some good features; what they do should be in character, and what happens to them should be a necessary or probable outcome of their behaviour.

The most important element of all is plot: the characters are created for the sake of the plot, and not the other way round. The plot must be a self-contained story with a clearly marked beginning, middle, and end; it must be sufficiently short and simple for the spectator to hold all its details in mind. Tragedy must have a unity. You do not make a tragedy by stringing together a set of episodes connected only by a common hero; rather, there must be a single significant action on which the whole plot turns (8. 1451^{a}21–9).

In a typical tragedy the story gradually gets more complicated until a turning point is reached, which Aristotle calls a 'reversal' (*peripeteia*). That is the moment at which the apparently fortunate hero falls to disaster, perhaps through a 'revelation' (*anagnorisis*), namely his discovery of some crucial but hitherto unknown piece of information (15. 1454^{b}19). After the reversal comes the denouement, in which the complications earlier introduced are gradually unravelled (18. 1455^{b}24 ff.).

These observations are illustrated by constant reference to actual Greek plays, in particular to Sophocles' tragedy *King Oedipus*. Oedipus, at the beginning of the play, enjoys prosperity and reputation. He is basically a good man, but has the fatal flaw of impetuosity. This vice makes him kill a stranger in a scuffle, and marry a bride without due diligence. The 'revelation' that the man he killed was his father and the woman he married was his mother leads to the 'reversal' of his fortune, as he is banished from his kingdom and blinds himself in shame and remorse.

Aristotle's theory of tragedy enables him to respond to Plato's complaint that playwrights, like other artists, were only imitators of everyday life, which was itself only an imitation of the real world of the Ideas. His answer is given when he compares drama with history.

From what has been said it is clear that the poet's job is to describe not something that has actually happened, but something that might well happen, that is to say something that is possible because it is necessary or likely. The difference between a historian and a poet is not a matter of prose v. verse—you might turn Herodotus into metre and it would still be history. It is rather in this matter of writing what happens rather than what might happen. For this reason poetry is more philosophical and more important than history; for poetry tells us of the universal, history tells us only of the particular. (9. 1451^{b}5–9)

What Aristotle says here of poetry and drama could of course be said of other kinds of creative writing. Much of what happens to people in everyday life is a matter of sheer accident; only in fiction can we see the working out of character and action into their natural consequences.

Aristotle's Ethical Treatises

If we turn from the productive sciences to the practical sciences, we find that Aristotle's contribution was made by his writings on moral philosophy and political theory. Three treatises of moral philosophy have been handed down in the corpus: the *Nicomachean Ethics* (*NE*) in ten books, the *Eudemian Ethics* (*EE*) in seven books, and the *Magna Moralia* in two books. These texts are highly interesting to anyone who is interested in the development of Aristotle's thought. Whereas in the physical and metaphysical treatises it is possible to detect traces of revision and rewriting, it is only in the case of ethics that we have Aristotle's doctrine on the same topics presented in three different and more or less complete courses. There is, however, no consensus on the explanation of this phenomenon.

In the early centuries after Aristotle's death no great use was made of his ethical treatises by later writers; but the *EE* is more often cited than the *NE*, and the *NE* does not appear as such in the earliest catalogues of his *Works*. Indeed there are traces of some doubt whether the *NE* is a genuine work of Aristotle or perhaps a production of his son Nicomachus. However, from the time of the commentator Aspasius in the second century AD it has been almost universally agreed that the *NE* is not only genuine but also the most important of the three works. Throughout the Middle Ages, and since the revival of classical scholarship, it has been treated as *the* Ethics of Aristotle, and indeed the most generally popular of all his surviving works.

Very different views have been taken of the other works. While the *NE* has long appealed to a wide readership, the *EE*, even among Aristotelian scholars, has never appealed to more than a handful of fanatics. In the nineteenth century it was treated as spurious, and republished under the name of Aristotle's pupil Eudemus of Rhodes. In the twentieth century scholars have commonly followed Werner Jaeger[4] in regarding it as a genuine but immature work, superseded by an *NE* written in the Lyceum period. As for the *Magna Moralia*, some scholars followed Jaeger in rejecting it as post-Aristotelian, whereas others have argued hotly that it is a genuine work, the earliest of all three treatises.

There is a further problem about the relationship between the *NE* and the *EE*. In the manuscript tradition three books make a double appearance: once as books 5, 6, and 7 of the *NE*, and once as books 4, 5, and 6 of the *EE*. It is a mistake to try to settle the relationship between the *NE* and the *EE* without first deciding which was the original home of the common books. It can be shown on both philosophical and stylometric grounds that these books are much closer to the *EE* than to the *NE*. Once they are restored to the *EE* the case for regarding the *EE* as an immature and inferior work collapses: nothing remains, for example, of Jaeger's argument that the *EE* is closer to Plato, and therefore earlier, than the *NE*. Moreover, internal historical allusions suggest that the disputed books, and therefore now the *EE*, belong to the Lyceum period.

There are problems concerning the coherence of the *NE* itself. At the beginning of the twentieth century the Aristotelian Thomas Case, in a celebrated article in the eleventh edition of the *Encyclopaedia Britannica*, suggested that 'the probability is that the *Nicomachean Ethics* is a collection of separate discourses worked up into a tolerably systematic treatise.' This remains highly probable. The differences between the *NE* and the *EE* do not admit of a simple chronological solution: it may be that some of the discourses worked up into the *NE* antedate, and others postdate, the *EE*,

---

[4] *Aristotle: Fundamentals of the History of his Development*, trans. R. Robinson (Oxford: Clarendon Press, 1948).

which is itself a more coherent whole. The stylistic differences that separate the *NE* not only from the *EE* but also from almost all Aristotle's other works may be explicable by the ancient tradition that the *NE* was edited by Nicomachus, while the *EE*, along with some of Aristotle's other works, was edited by Eudemus. As for the *Magna Moralia*, while it follows closely the line of thought of the *EE*, it contains a number of misunderstandings of its doctrine. This is easily explained if it consists of notes made by a student at the Lyceum during Aristotle's delivery of a course of lectures resembling the *EE*.[5]

The content of the three treatises is, in general, very similar. The *NE* covers much the same ground as Plato's *Republic*, and with some exaggeration one could say that Aristotle's moral philosophy is Plato's moral philosophy with the Theory of Ideas ripped out. The Idea of the Good, Aristotle says, cannot be the supreme good of which ethics treats, if only because ethics is a practical science, about what is within human power to achieve, whereas an everlasting and unchanging Idea of the Good could only be of theoretical interest.

In place of the Idea of the Good, Aristotle offers happiness (*eudaimonia*) as the supreme good with which ethics is concerned, for, like Plato, he sees an intimate connection between living virtuously and living happily. In all the ethical treatises a happy life is a life of virtuous activity, and each of them offers an analysis of the concept of virtue and a classification of virtues of different types. One class is that of the moral virtues, such as courage, temperance, and liberality, that constantly appeared in Plato's ethical discussions. The other class is that of intellectual virtues: here Aristotle makes a much sharper distinction than Plato ever did between the intellectual virtue of wisdom, which governs ethical behaviour, and the intellectual virtue of understanding, which is expressed in scientific endeavour and contemplation. The principal difference between the *NE* and the *EE* is that in the former Aristotle regards perfect happiness as constituted solely by the activity of philosophical contemplation, whereas in the latter it consists of the harmonious exercise of all the virtues, intellectual and moral.[6]

[5] The account here given of the relationship between the Aristotelian ethical treatises is controversial. I have expounded and defended it in *The Aristotelian Ethics* (Oxford: Clarendon Press, 1978) and, with corrections and modifications, in *Aristotle on the Perfect Life* (Oxford: Clarendon Press, 1992).

[6] Aristotle's ethical teaching is explained in detail in Ch. 8 below.

Aristotle's Political Theory

Even in the *EE* it is 'the service and contemplation of God' that sets the standard for the appropriate exercise of the moral virtues, and in the *NE* this contemplation is described as a superhuman activity of a divine part of ourselves. Aristotle's final word here is that in spite of being mortal we must make ourselves immortal as far as we can. When we turn from the *Ethics* to their sequel, the *Politics*, we come down to earth. 'Man is a political animal', we are told: humans are creatures of flesh and blood, rubbing shoulders with each other in cities and communities.

Like his work in zoology, Aristotle's political studies combine observation and theory. Diogenes Laertius tells us that he collected the constitutions of 158 states—no doubt aided by research assistants in the Lyceum. One of these, *The Constitution of Athens*, though not handed down as part of the Aristotelian corpus, was found on papyrus in 1891. In spite of some stylistic differences from other works, it is now generally regarded as authentic. In a codicil to the *NE* that reads like a preface to the *Politics*, Aristotle says that, having investigated previous writings on political theory, he will inquire, in the light of the constitutions collected, what makes good government and what makes bad government, what factors are favourable or unfavourable to the preservation of a constitution, and what constitution the best state should adopt (*NE* 10. 9. 1181^{b}12–23).

The *Politics* itself was probably not written at a single stretch, and here as elsewhere there is probably an overlap and interplay between the records of observation and the essays in theory. The structure of the book as we have it corresponds reasonably well to the *NE* programme: books 1–3 contain a general theory of the state, and a critique of earlier writers; books 4–6 contain an account of various forms of constitution, three tolerable (monarchy, aristocracy, polity) and three intolerable (tyranny, oligarchy, and democracy); books 7 and 8 are devoted to the ideal form of constitution. Once again, the order of the discourses in the corpus probably differs from the order of their composition, but scholars have not reached agreement on the original chronology.

Aristotle begins by saying that the state is the highest kind of community, aiming at the highest of goods. The most primitive communities are families of men and women, masters and slaves. He seems to regard the division between master and slave as no less natural than the division between men and women, though he complains that it is barbaric to treat women and slaves alike (1. 2. 1252^{a}25–^{b}6). Families combine to make a village, and several villages combine to make a state, which is the first self-sufficient community, and is just as natural as is the family (1. 2. 1253^{a}2). Indeed, though later than the family in time, the state is prior by nature, as an organic whole like the human body is prior to its organic parts like hands and feet. Without law and justice, man is the most savage of animals. Someone who cannot live in a state is a beast; someone who has no need of a state must be a god. The foundation of the state was the greatest of benefactions, because only within a state can human beings fulfil their potential (1. 2. 1253^{a}25–35).

Among the earlier writers whom Aristotle cites and criticizes Plato is naturally prominent. Much of the second book of the *Politics* is devoted to criticism of the *Republic* and the *Laws*. As in the *Ethics* there is no Idea of the Good, so in the *Politics* there are no philosopher kings. Aristotle thinks that Platonic communism will bring nothing but trouble: the use

Aristotle saw women as inferior to men. Legend took revenge, as in this illustration to a text of Petrarch, showing him ridden and beaten by his wife, Phyllis.

of property should be shared, but its ownership should be private. That way owners can take pride in their possessions and get pleasure out of sharing them with others or giving them away. Aristotle defends the traditional family against the proposal that women should be held in common, and he frowns even on the limited military and official role assigned to women in the *Laws*. Over and over again he describes Plato's proposals as impractical; the root of his error, he thinks, is that he tries to make the state too uniform. The diversity of different kinds of citizen is essential, and life in a city should not be like life in a barracks (2. 3. 1261^{a}10–31).

However, when Aristotle presents his own account of political constitutions he makes copious use of Platonic suggestions. There remains a constant difference between the two writers, namely that Aristotle makes frequent reference to concrete examples to illustrate his theoretical points. But the conceptual structure is often very similar. The following passage from book 3, for instance, echoes the later books of the *Republic*.

The government, that is to say the supreme authority in a state, must be in the hands of one, or of a few, or of the many. The rightful true forms of government, therefore, are ones where the one, or the few, or the many, govern with a view to the common interest; governments that rule with a view to the private interest, whether of the one, or the few, or the many, are perversions. Those who belong to a state, if they are truly to be called citizens, must share in its benefits. Government by a single person, if it aims at the common interest, we are accustomed to call 'monarchy'; similar government by a minority we call 'aristocracy', either because the rulers are the best men, or because it aims at the best interests of the state and the community. When it is the majority that governs in the common interest we call it a 'polity', using a word which is also a generic term for a constitution . . .
Of each of these forms of government there exists a perversion. The perversion of monarchy is tyranny; that of aristocracy is oligarchy; that of polity is democracy. For tyranny is a monarchy exercised solely for the benefit of the monarch, oligarchy has in view only the interests of the wealthy, and democracy the interests only of the poorer classes. None of these aims at the common good of all. (3. 6. 1279^{a}26–^{b}10)

Aristotle goes on to a detailed evaluation of constitutions of these various forms. He does so on the basis of his view of the essence of the state. A state, he tells us, is a society of humans sharing in a common perception of what is good and evil, just and unjust; its purpose is to provide a good and happy life for its citizens. If a community contains an individual or family of outstanding excellence, then monarchy is the best constitution. But such a case is very rare, and the risk of miscarriage is great: for monarchy corrupts into tyranny, which is the worst of all constitutions. Aristocracy, in theory, is the next best constitution after monarchy, but in practice Aristotle preferred a kind of constitutional democracy, for what he called 'polity' is a state in which rich and poor respect each others' rights, and in which the best-qualified citizens rule with the consent of all the citizens (4. 8. 1293^{b}30 ff.). The corruption of this is what Aristotle calls 'democracy', namely, anarchic mob rule. Bad as democracy is, it is in Aristotle's view the least bad of the perverse forms of government.

At the present time we are familiar with the division of government into three branches: the legislature, the executive, and the judiciary. The essentials of this system is spelt out by Aristotle, though he distributes the powers in a somewhat different way from, say, the US constitution. All constitutions, he tells us, have three elements: the deliberative, the official, and the judicial. The deliberative element has authority in matters of war and peace, in making and unmaking alliances; it passes laws, controls the carrying out of judicial sentences, and audits the accounts of officers. The official element deals with the appointment of ministers and civil servants, ranging from priests through ambassadors to the regulators of female affairs. The judicial element consists of the courts of civil and criminal law (4. 12. 1296^{b}13–1301^{a}12).

Two elements of Aristotle's political teaching affected political institutions for many centuries: his justification of slavery and his condemnation of usury. Some people, Aristotle tells us, think that the rule of masters over slaves is contrary to nature, and is therefore unjust. They are quite wrong: a slave is someone who is by nature not his own but another man's property. Slavery is one example of a general truth, that from their birth some people are marked out for rule and others to be ruled (1. 3. 1253^{b}20–3; 5. 1254^{b}22–4).

In practice much slavery is unjust, Aristotle agrees. There is a custom that the spoils of war belong to the victors, and this includes the right to make slaves of the vanquished. But many wars are unjust, and victories in such wars entail no right to enslave the defeated. Some people, however, are so inferior and brutish that it is better for them to be under the rule of a kindly master than to be left to their own devices. Slaves, for Aristotle, are living tools—and on this basis he is willing to grant that if non-living tools could achieve the same purpose there would be no need for slavery. 'If every instrument could achieve its own work, obeying or anticipating the will of others, like the statues of Daedalus . . . if the shuttle could weave and the plectrum pluck the lyre in a similar manner, overseers would not need servants, nor masters slaves' (1. 4. 1253^{b}35–54^{a}1). So perhaps, in an age of automation, Aristotle would no longer defend slavery.

Though not himself an aristocrat, Aristotle had an aristocratic disdain for commerce. Our possessions, he says, have two uses, proper and improper. The proper use of a shoe, for instance, is to wear it: to exchange it for other goods or for money is an improper use (1. 9. 1257^{a}9–10). There is nothing wrong with basic barter for necessities, but there is nothing natural about trade in luxuries, as there is in farming. In the operation of retail trade money plays an important part, and money too has a proper and an improper use.

The most hated sort of wealth-getting is usury, which makes a profit out of money itself, rather than from its natural purpose, for money was intended to be used for exchange, not to increase at interest. It got the name 'interest' (*tokos*), which means the birth of money from money, because an offspring resembles its parent. For this reason, of all the modes of getting wealth this is the most unnatural. (1. 10. 1258^{b}5–7)

Aristotle's hierarchical preference places farmers at the top, bankers at the bottom, with merchants in between. His attitude to usury was one source of the prohibition, throughout medieval Christendom, of the charging of interest even at a modest rate. 'When did friendship', Antonio asks Shylock in *The Merchant of Venice*, 'take a breed for barren metal of his friend?'

One of the most striking features of Aristotle's *Politics* is the almost total absence of any mention of Alexander or Macedon. Like a modern member of Amnesty International, Aristotle comments on the rights and wrongs of every country but his own. His own ideal state is described as having no more than a hundred thousand citizens, small enough for them all to know one another and to take their share in judicial and political office. It is very different from Alexander's empire. When Aristotle says that monarchy is the best constitution if a community contains a person or family of outstanding excellence, there is a pointed absence of reference to the royal family of Macedon.

Indeed, during the years of the Lyceum, relations between the world-conqueror and his former tutor seem to have cooled. Alexander became more and more megalomaniac and finally proclaimed himself divine. Aristotle's nephew Callisthenes led the opposition to the king's demand, in 327, that Greeks should prostrate themselves before him in adoration. He was falsely implicated in a plot, and executed. The magnanimous and magnificent man who is the hero of the earlier books of the *NE* has some of the grandiose traits of Alexander. In the *EE*, however, the alleged virtues of magnanimity and magnificence are downgraded, and gentleness and dignity take centre stage.[7]

Aristotle's Cosmology

The greater part of Aristotle's surviving works deal not with productive or practical sciences, but with the theoretical sciences. We have already considered his biological works: it is time to give some account of his physics and chemistry. His contributions to these disciplines were much less impressive than his researches in the life sciences. While his zoological writings were still found impressive by Darwin, his physics was superannuated by the sixth century AD.

In works such as *On Generation and Corruption* and *On the Heavens* Aristotle bequeathed to his successors a world-picture that included many features inherited from the Presocratics. He took over the four elements of Empedocles, earth, water, air, and fire, each characterized by the possession of a unique pair of the properties heat, cold, wetness, and dryness: earth being cold and dry, air being hot and wet, and so forth. Each element had its natural place in an ordered cosmos, and each element had an innate tendency to move towards this natural place. Thus, earthy solids naturally fell, while fire, unless prevented, rose ever higher. Each such motion was natural to its element; other motions were possible, but were 'violent'. (We preserve a relic of Aristotle's distinction when we contrast natural with violent death.)

In his physical treatises Aristotle offers explanations of an enormous number of natural phenomena in terms of the elements, their basic properties, and their natural motion. The philosophical concepts which he employs in constructing these explanations include an array of different notions of causation (material, formal, efficient, and final), and an analysis

[7] See my *The Aristotelian Ethics*, 233.

of change as the passage from potentiality to actuality, whether (as in substantial change) from matter to form or (as in accidental change) from one to another quality of a substance. These technical notions, which he employed in such an astonishing variety of contexts, will be examined in detail in later chapters.

Aristotle's vision of the cosmos owes much to his Presocratic precursors and to Plato's *Timaeus*. The earth was in the centre of the universe: around it a succession of concentric crystalline spheres carried the moon, the sun, and the planets in their journeys around the visible sky. The heavenly bodies were not compounds of the four terrestrial elements, but were made of a superior fifth element or quintessence. They had souls as well as bodies: living supernatural intellects, guiding their travels through the cosmos. These intellects were movers which were themselves in motion, and behind them, Aristotle argued, there must be a source of movement not itself in motion. The only way in which an unchanging, eternal mover could cause motion in other beings was by attracting them as an object of love, an attraction which they express by their perfect circular motion. It is thus that Dante, in the final lines of his *Paradiso*, finds his own will, like a smoothly rotating wheel, caught up in the love that moves the sun and all the other stars.

Even the best of Aristotle's scientific work has now only a historical interest. The abiding value of treatises such as his *Physics* is in the philosophical analyses of some of the basic concepts that pervade the physics of different eras, such as space, time, causation, and determinism. These are examined in detail in Chapter 5. For Aristotle biology and psychology were parts of natural philosophy no less than physics and chemistry, since they too studied different forms of *physis*, or nature. The biological works we have already looked at; the psychological works will be examined more closely in Chapter 7.

The Aristotelian corpus, in addition to the systematic scientific treatises, contains a massive collection of occasional jottings on scientific topics, the *Problems*. From its structure this appears to be a commonplace book in which Aristotle wrote down provisional answers to questions that were put to him by his students or correspondents. Because the questions are grouped rather haphazardly, and often appear several times—and are sometimes given different answers—it seems unlikely that they were generated by Aristotle himself, whether as a single series or over a lifetime.

But the collection contains many fascinating details that throw insight into the workings of his omnivorous intellect.

Some of the questions are the kind of thing a patient might bring to a doctor. Ought drugs to be used, rather than surgery, for sores in the armpits and groin? (1. 34. 863ª21). Is it true that purslane mixed with salt stops inflammation of the gums? (1. 38. 863ᵇ12). Does cabbage really cure a hangover? (3. 17. 873ᵇ1). Why is it difficult to have sex under water? (4. 14. 878ª35). Other questions and answers make us see Aristotle more in the role of agony aunt. How should one cope with the after-effects of eating garlic? (13. 2. 907ᵇ28–908ª10). How does one prevent biscuit from becoming hard? (21. 12. 928ª12). Why do drunken men kiss old women they would never kiss when sober? (30. 15. 953ᵇ15). Is it right to punish more seriously thefts from a public place than thefts from a private house? (29. 14. 952ª16). More seriously, why is it more terrible to kill a woman than a man, although the male is naturally superior to the female? (29. 11. 951ª12).

A whole book of the *Problems* (26) is devoted essentially to weather forecasting. Other books contain questions that simply reflect general curiosity. Why does the noise of a saw being sharpened set our teeth on edge? (7. 5. 886ᵇ10). Why do humans not have manes? (10. 25. 893ᵇ17). Why do non-human animals not sneeze or squint? (Don't they?) (10. 50. 896ᵇ5; 54. 897ª1). Why do barbarians and Greeks alike count up to ten? (15. 3. 910ᵇ23). Why is a flute better than a lyre as an accompaniment to a solo voice? (19. 43. 922ª1). Very often, the *Problems* ask 'Why is such and such the case?' when a more appropriate question would have been '*Is* such and such the case?' For instance, Why do fishermen have red hair? (37. 2. 966ᵇ25). Why does a large choir keep time better than a small one? (19. 22. 919ª36).

The *Problems* let us see Aristotle with his hair down, rather like the table talk of later writers. One of his questions is particularly endearing to those who may have found it hard to read their way through his more difficult works: Why is it that some people, if they begin to read a serious book, are overcome by sleep even against their will? (18. 1. 916ᵇ1).

The Legacy of Aristotle and Plato

When Alexander the Great died in 323, democratic Athens became uncomfortable even for an anti-imperialist Macedonian. Saying that he did not wish the city that had executed Socrates 'to sin twice against philosophy', Aristotle escaped to Chalcis, where he died in the following year. His will, which survives, makes thoughtful provision for a large number of friends and dependants. His library was left to Theophrastus, his successor as head of the Lyceum. His own papers were vast in size and scope—those that survive today total around a million words, and it is said that we possess only one-fifth of his output. As we have seen, in addition to philosophical treatises on logic, metaphysics, ethics, aesthetics, and politics, they included historical works on constitutions, theatre and sport, and scientific works on botany, zoology, biology, psychology, chemistry, meteorology, astronomy, and cosmology.

Since the Renaissance it has been traditional to regard the Academy and the Lyceum as two opposite poles of philosophy. Plato, according to this tradition, was idealistic, utopian, other-worldly; Aristotle was realistic, utilitarian, commonsensical. Thus, in Raphael's *School of Athens* Plato, wearing the colours of the volatile elements air and fire, points heavenwards; Aristotle, clothed in watery blue and earthy green, has his feet firmly on the ground. 'Every man is born an Aristotelian or a Platonist,' wrote S. T. Coleridge. 'They are the two classes of men, besides which it is next to impossible to conceive a third.' The philosopher Gilbert Ryle in the twentieth century improved on Coleridge. Men could be divided into two classes on the basis of four dichotomies: green versus blue, sweet versus savoury, cats versus dogs, Plato versus Aristotle. 'Tell me your preference on one of these pairs', Ryle used to say, 'and I will tell you your preference on the other three.'[8]

In fact, as we have already seen and will see in greater detail later, the doctrines that Plato and Aristotle share are more important than those that divide them. Many post-Renaissance historians of ideas have been less perceptive than the many commentators in late antiquity who saw it as their duty to construct a harmonious concord between the two greatest philosophers of the ancient world.

It is sometimes said that a philosopher should be judged by the importance of the questions he raises, not the correctness of the answers he gives. If that is so, then Plato has an uncontestable claim to pre-eminence as a philosopher. He was the first to pose questions of great profundity, many of

[8] Preference for an item on the left of a pair was supposed to go with preference for the other leftward items, and similarly for rightward preferences.

which remain open questions in philosophy today. But Aristotle too can claim a significant contribution to the intellectual patrimony of the world. For it was he who invented the concept of Science as we understand it today and as it has been understood since the Renaissance.

First, he is the first person whose surviving works show detailed observations of natural phenomena. Secondly, he was the first philosopher to have a sound grasp of the relationship between observation and theory in scientific method. Thirdly, he identified and classified different scientific disciplines and explored their relationships to each other: the very concept of a distinct discipline is due to him. Fourthly, he is the first professor to have organized his lectures into courses, and to have taken trouble over their appropriate place in a syllabus (cf. *Pol.* 1. 10. 1258ᵃ20). Fifthly, his Lyceum was the first research institute of which we have any detailed knowledge in which a number of scholars and investigators joined in collaborative inquiry and documentation. Sixthly, and not least important, he was the first person in history to build up a research library—not simply a handful of books for his own bookshelf, but a systematic collection to be used by his colleagues and to be handed on to posterity.[9] For all these reasons, every academic scientist in the world today is in Aristotle's debt. He well deserved the title he was given by Dante: 'the master of those who know'.

Aristotle's School

Theophrastus (372–287), Aristotle's ingenious successor as head of the Lyceum, continued his master's researches in several ways. He wrote extensively on botany, a discipline that Aristotle had touched only lightly. He improved on Aristotle's modal logic, and anticipated some later Stoic innovations. He disagreed with some fundamental principles of Aristotle's cosmology, such as the nature of place and the need for a motionless mover. Like his master, he wrote copiously, and the mere list of the titles of his works takes up sixteen pages in the Loeb edition of his life by Diogenes Laertius. They include essays on vertigo, on honey, on hair, on jokes, and on the eruption of Etna. The best known of his surviving works is a book

---

[9] See L. Casson, *Libraries in the Ancient World* (New Haven: Yale University Press, 2001), 28–9.

A Venetian representation of King Ptolemy and his library at Alexandria

entitled *Characters*, modelled on Aristotle's delineation in his *Ethics* of individual virtues and vices, but sketching them with greater refinement and with a livelier wit. He was a diligent historian of philosophy, and the part of his doxography that survives, *On the Senses*, is one of our main sources for Presocratic theories of sensation.

One of Theophrastus' pupils, Demetrius of Phaleron, was an adviser to one of Alexander's generals, Ptolemy, who made himself king of Egypt in 305. It is possible that it was he who suggested the creation in the new city of Alexandria of a library modelled on that of Aristotle, a project that was carried out by Ptolemy's son Ptolemy II Philadelphus. The history of Aristotle's own library is obscure. On Theophrastus' death it seems to have been inherited not by the next head of the Lyceum, the physicist Strato, but by Theophrastus' nephew Neleus of Skepsis, one of the last surviving pupils of Aristotle himself. Neleus' heirs are said to have hidden the books in a cave in order to prevent them from being confiscated by agents of King Eumenes, who was building up a library at Pergamon to rival that of Alexandria. Rescued by a bibliophile and taken to Athens, the story goes, the books were confiscated by the Roman general Sulla when he captured the city in 86 BC, and shipped to Rome, where they were finally edited and published by Andronicus of Rhodes around the middle of the first century BC (Strabo 609–9; Plutarch, *Sulla* 26).[10]

Every detail of this story has been called in question by one or another scholar,[11] but if true it would account for the oblivion that overtook Aristotle's writings between the time of Theophrastus and that of Cicero. It has been well said that 'If Aristotle could have returned to Athens in 272 BC, on the fiftieth anniversary of his death, he would hardly have recognized it as the intellectual milieu in which he had taught and researched for much of his life.'[12]

It was not that philosophy at that date was dormant in Athens: far from it. Though the Lyceum under Strato was a shadow of itself, and the

---

[10] Puzzlingly, our best ancient catalogue of the Andronican edition appears to have been made by a librarian at Alexandria. Is it possible that Mark Antony acquired the corpus from an heir of the proscribed Sulla and shipped them off to Cleopatra to fill the gaps in her recently destroyed library, just as her earlier lover Julius Caesar had pillaged the Pergamum library for her benefit?

[11] See J. Barnes, in J. Barnes and M. Griffin, *Philosophia Togata*, vol. ii (Oxford: Clarendon Press, 1997), 1–23.

[12] Introd. to LS, 1.

Platonic Academy under its new head Arcesilaus had given up metaphysics in favour of a narrow scepticism, there were two flourishing new schools of philosophy in the city. The best-known philosophers in Athens were members neither of the Academy nor of the Lyceum, but were the founders of these new schools: Epicurus, who established a school known as The Garden, and Zeno of Citium, whose followers were called Stoics because he taught in the Stoa, or painted portico.

Epicurus

Epicurus was born into a family of Athenian expatriates in Samos, and paid a brief visit to Athens in the last year of Aristotle's life. During early travels he studied under a follower of Democritus, and established more than one school in the Greek islands. In 306 he set up house in Athens and lived there until his death in 271. His followers in the Garden included women and slaves; they lived in seclusion and ate simple fare. He wrote 300 books, we are told, but all that survive intact are three letters and two groups of maxims. His philosophy of nature is set out in a letter to Herodotus and a letter to Pythocles; in the third letter, to Menoecus, he summarizes his moral teaching. The first set of maxims, forty in number, has been preserved, like the three letters, in the life of Epicurus by Diogenes Laertius: it is called *Kyriai Doxai*, or major doctrines. Eighty-one similar aphorisms were discovered in a Vatican manuscript in 1888. Fragments from Epicurus' lost treatise *On Nature* were buried in volcanic ash at Herculaneum when Vesuvius erupted in AD 79. Painstaking efforts to unroll and decipher them, begun in 1800, continue to the present day. But for most of our knowledge of his teachings, however, we depend on the surviving writings of his followers, especially a much later writer, the Latin poet Lucretius.

The aim of Epicurus' philosophy is to make happiness possible by removing the fear of death, which is the greatest obstacle to tranquillity. Men struggle for wealth and power so as to postpone death; they throw themselves into frenzied activity so that they can forget its inevitability. It is religion that causes us to fear death, by holding out the prospect of suffering after death. But this is an illusion. The terrors held out by religion are fairy tales, which we must give up in favour of a scientific account of the world.

This scientific account is taken mainly from Democritus' atomism. Nothing comes into being from nothing: the basic units of the world are everlasting, unchanging, indivisible units or atoms. These, infinite in number, move about in the void, which is empty and infinite space: if there were no void, movement would be impossible. This motion had no beginning, and initially all atoms move downwards at constant and equal speed. From time to time, however, they swerve and collide, and it is from the collision of atoms that everything in heaven and earth has come into being. The swerve of the atoms allows scope for human freedom, even though their motions are blind and purposeless. Atoms have no properties other than shape, weight, and size. The properties of perceptible bodies are not illusions, but they are supervenient on the basic properties of atoms. There is an infinite number of worlds, some like and some unlike our own (Letter to Herodotus, D.L. 10. 38–45).

Like everything else, the soul consists of atoms, differing from other atoms only in being smaller and subtler; these are dispersed at death and the soul ceases to perceive (Letter to Herodotus, D.L. 10. 63–7). The gods too are built out of atoms, but they live in a less turbulent region, immune to dissolution. They live happy lives, untroubled by concern for human beings. For that reason belief in providence is superstition, and religious rituals a waste of time (Letter to Menoecus, D.L. 10. 123–5). Since we are free agents, thanks to the atomic swerve, we are masters of our own fate: the gods neither impose necessity nor interfere with our choices.

Epicurus believed that the senses were reliable sources of information, which operate by transmitting images from external bodies into the atoms of our soul. Sense-impressions are never, in themselves, false, though we may make false judgements on the basis of genuine appearances. If appearances conflict (if, for instance, something looks smooth but feels rough) then the mind must give judgement between these competing witnesses.

Pleasure, for Epicurus, is the beginning and end of the happy life. This does not mean, however, that Epicurus was an epicure. His life and that of his followers was far from luxurious: a good piece of cheese, he said, was as good as a feast. Though a theoretical hedonist, in practice he attached importance to a distinction he made between different types of pleasure. There is one kind of pleasure that is given by the satisfaction of our desires for food, drink, and sex, but it is an inferior kind of pleasure, because it is bound up with pain. The desire these pleasures satisfy is itself painful, and its satisfaction leads to a renewal of desire. The pleasures to be aimed at are quiet pleasures such as those of private friendship (Letter to Menoecus, D.L. 10. 27–32).

To his last, Epicurus insisted that for a philosopher pleasure, in any circumstances, could outweigh pain. On his deathbed he wrote the following letter to his friend Idomeneus: 'I write this to you on the blissful day that is the last of my life. Strangury and dysentery have set in, with the greatest possible intensity of pain. I counterbalance them by the joy I have in the memory of our past conversations' (D.L. 10. 22). He lived up to his conviction that death, though inescapable, is, if we take a truly philosophical view of it, not an evil.

Stoicism

Stoics, like Epicureans, sought tranquillity, but by a different route. The founder of Stoicism was Zeno of Citium (334–262 BC). Zeno was born in Cyprus, but migrated to Athens in 313. He read Xenophon's memoir of Socrates, which gave him a passion for philosophy. He was told that the nearest contemporary equivalent of Socrates was Crates the Cynic. Cynicism was not a set of philosophical doctrines, but a way of life expressing contempt for wealth and disdain for conventional propriety. Its founder was Diogenes of Sinope, who lived like a dog ('cynic' means 'dog-like') in a tub for a kennel, wearing coarse clothes and subsisting on alms. A contemporary of Plato, for whom he had no great respect, Diogenes was famous for his snub to Alexander the Great. When the great man visited him and asked, 'What can I do for you', Diogenes replied, 'You can move out of my light' (D.L. 6. 38). Crates, impressed by Diogenes, gave his wealth to the poor and imitated his bohemian lifestyle; but he was less misanthropic, and had a keen sense of humour that he expressed in poetic satire.

Zeno was Crates' pupil for a time, but he did not become a cynic and drop out of society, though he avoided formal dinners and was fond of basking in the sun. After some years as a student of the Academy, he set up his own school in the Stoa Poikile. He instituted a systematic curriculum of philosophy, dividing it into three main disciplines, logic, ethics, and physics. Logic, said his followers, is the bones of philosophy, ethics the flesh, and physics the soul (D.L. 7. 37). Zeno studied under the great Megarian

Alexander standing in Diogenes' light (Rome, Villa Albani)

logician Diodorus Cronos, and was a fellow pupil of Philo, who laid the
ground for a development of logic which marked, in some areas, an
improvement on Aristotle.[13] He himself, however, was more interested in
ethics.

It may seem surprising that a moralist like Zeno should give physics the
highest place in the curriculum. But for Zeno, and later Stoics, physics is
the study of nature and nature is identified with God. Diogenes Laertius
tells us, 'Zeno says that the whole world and heaven are the substance of

---

[13] On Diodorus and Philo, see Ch. 3 below.

God' (7. 148). God is an active principle, matter is an active principle; both of them are corporeal, and together they constitute an all-pervasive cosmic fire (LS 45G).

Zeno's writings do not survive: the most famous of them in antiquity was his *Republic*. This combined Platonic utopianism with some cynic elements. Zeno rejected the conventional educational system, and thought it a waste of effort to build gymnasia, law courts, and temples. He recommended community of wives, and thought that men and women should wear the same, revealing, clothing. Money should be abolished and there should be a single legal system for all mankind, who should be like a herd grazing together nurtured by a common law (LS 67A).

In spite of these communistic proposals, which many of his own later disciples found shocking, Zeno in his lifetime was held in honour by the Athenians, who gave him the freedom of the city. King Antigonus of Macedon invited him to become his personal philosopher, but Zeno pleaded old age and sent to court instead two of his brightest pupils.

After Zeno's death his place as head of the Stoa was taken by Cleanthes (331–232), a converted boxer of a religious bent. Cleanthes wrote a hymn to Zeus, later quoted by St Paul in a sermon in Athens, which exalted the Stoic active principle in terms that were appropriate enough for Judaeo-Christian monotheism. The underlying Stoic conception of God is very different, however, from that of the biblical religions. God is not separate from the universe but is a material constituent of the cosmos. In his prose writings Cleanthes expounded in detail the way in which the divine fiery element provided the vital power for all the living beings in the world (Cicero, *ND* 2. 23–5).[14]

Cleanthes was succeeded as head of the school by Chrysippus of Soli, who governed it from 232 to 206. Chrysippus had been Cleanthes' pupil, but he seems to have had no great respect for his teacher. 'You tell me your theorems', he is said to have told him, 'and I'll supply them with proofs.' He spent some time as a student at the Academy, inoculating himself against scepticism. He was the most intelligent and the most industrious of the Hellenistic Stoics. His literary output was prodigious: his housekeeper reported that he wrote at a rate of 500 lines a day, and he left 705 books

---

[14] On Cleanthes' theology, see Ch. 9 below.

behind. Nothing but fragments survive. But it is clear that it was he who rounded Stoicism into a system; it used to be said, 'If there had been no Chrysippus, there had been no Stoa' (D.L., 6. 183).

It is difficult to separate out precisely the contributions of the three early Stoics, since their works have all been lost. However, there is little doubt that Chrysippus deserves the main share of the credit for the significant advances in logic that will be examined in detail in the next chapter. In physics he substituted breath (*pneuma*) for Cleanthes' fire as the vital principle of animals and plants. He accepted the Aristotelian distinction between matter and form, but as a good materialist he insisted that form too was bodily, namely *pneuma*. The human soul and mind are made out of this *pneuma*; so too is God, who is the soul of the cosmos, which, in its entirety, constitutes a rational animal. If God and the soul were not themselves bodily, Stoics argued, they would not be able to act on the material world.

The fully developed Stoic physical system can be summarized as follows. Once upon a time, there was nothing but fire; gradually there emerged the other elements and the familiar furniture of the universe. Later, the world will return to fire in a universal conflagration, and then the whole cycle of its history will be repeated over and over again. All this happens in accordance with a system of laws which may be called 'fate' (because the laws admit of no exception), or 'providence' (because the laws were laid down by God for beneficent purposes). The divinely designed system is called Nature, and our aim in life should be to live in accord with Nature.

Chrysippus was also the principal author of the Stoic ethical system, which is based on the principle of submission to Nature. Nothing can escape Nature's laws, but despite the determinism of fate human beings are free and responsible. If the will obeys reason it will live in accordance with Nature. It is this voluntary acceptance of Nature's laws that constitutes virtue, and virtue is both necessary and sufficient for happiness.[15]

The Stoics all agreed that because society is natural to human beings, a good man, in his aim to be in harmony with Nature, will play some part in society and cultivate social virtues. But Chrysippus had a number of ethical and political views that marked him out from other Stoics. Like Zeno, he

---

[15] The Stoic ethical system is considered in greater detail in Ch. 8 below.

wrote a *Republic*, in which he is alleged to have defended incest and cannibalism (LS 67F). Chrysippus differed from some of his fellows in insisting that a philosopher need not devote himself to scholarship: for a Stoic it was acceptable, indeed praiseworthy, to take part in public life (LS 67w).

Scepticism in the Academy

During the latter part of the third century Stoic doctrine came under attack from the Academy. The academic heirs of Plato began to take their inspiration from Plato's questioning master, Socrates, and turned to a form of scepticism. The leader of the Academy from 273 to 242 was Arcesilaus, a pupil of Pyrrho of Elis, a man often regarded as the founder of philosophical scepticism. Pyrrho, an older contemporary of Epicurus, who had served as a soldier in Alexander's army, taught that nothing could be known and, accordingly, wrote no books. It was Arcesilaus and another of Pyrrho's pupils, Timon, who brought scepticism to Athens in the early years of the third century. Timon denied the possibility of finding any self-evident principles to serve as the foundation of sciences. In the absence of such axioms, all lines of reasoning must be circular or endless.

The scepticism of Timon and Arcesilaus came to fruition, in a modified and more sophisticated form, with the work of Carneades, who headed the Academy from 155 to 137. Like Pyrrho, Carneades left no writings, but his arguments were recorded by a pupil who attended his highly popular lectures. They have come down to us principally through the good offices of Cicero, who was once taught by Carneades' pupil Philo. In 155 Carneades was sent by Athens, along with a Stoic and a Peripatetic philosopher, on an embassy to Rome. During this embassy he displayed his rhetorical skill by arguing on successive days for and against justice. Cato the Roman Censor, who heard his performance, sent him packing as a subversive influence (LS 68M).

Arcesilaus criticized the Stoics because they had claimed to found their search for truth upon mental impressions incapable of falsehood: there were, he argued, no such impressions. Carneades too attacked Stoic epistemology, and taught that probability, not unattainable truth, should be the guide to life. Though not himself an atheist, he ridiculed mercilessly both the traditional pantheon and Stoic pantheism. His arguments against the Stoic theory of divination were adopted and skilfully developed by Cicero.[16]

Lucretius

No philosopher of the second century was as intelligent or persuasive as Carneades, and in the first century primacy in philosophy passed from Greek to Latin authors. Latin philosophy, like Greek philosophy, began in verse and only later turned to prose. The first complete Latin philosophical work that has reached us is a long and magnificent poem in hexameter verse, *On the Nature of Things*, by Lucretius.

Almost nothing is known of Lucretius' life: we can conjecture the rough dating of his poem by noting that it was read by Cicero in 54, and was dedicated to one C. Memmius, who stood for the consulship in 53. Lucretius was an adoring admirer of Epicurus, and the six books of the poem set out the Epicurean system in verse which, as Cicero observed, always displays great artistry and sometimes shows flashes of genius. Lucretius himself described his poetic skill as honey to disguise the worm-wood of philosophy (1. 947). Parts of the poem were translated into English by John Dryden. Had he completed the task, his version would have been a worthy rival of Pope's *Essay on Man*.

Lucretius begins his poem by praising the bravery of Epicurus in throwing off the fear of religion. People cannot stand up to the tyranny of priests, because they fear eternal punishment; but that is only because they don't understand the nature of the soul. In his first book Lucretius sets out Epicurean atomism: nature consists of simple bodies and empty void, bodies perceived by sense, and void established by reason. Bodies are made out of atoms as words are made out of letters: the words 'ignis' and 'lignum' are made up of almost the same letters, just as the things they signify, namely fire and wood, are made up of almost the same atoms (1. 911–14).

In a famous passage early in the second book Lucretius describes the philosopher looking down, from the heights of virtue, on the petty struggles of mankind. He extols the Epicurean pursuit of simple pleasures and avoidance of unnecessary desires.

---

[16] The debate between Stoics and Sceptics is considered in detail in Ch. 4 below.

> O wretched man! in what a mist of life
> Enclosed with dangers and with noisy strife
> He spends his little span; and overfeeds
> His crammed desires, with more than nature needs!
> For nature wisely stints our appetite
> And craves no more than undisturbed delight;
> Which minds unmixed with cares and fears obtain;
> A soul serene, a body void of pain.
> So little this corporeal frame requires,
> So bounded are our natural desires,
> That wanting all, and setting pain aside,
> With bare privation sense is satisfied.   (2. 16–28)

The third book sets out the Epicurean theory of the soul and the mechanisms of sensation. Once we understand the material nature of the soul, we realize that fears of death are childish. A dead body cannot feel, and death leaves no self behind to suffer. It is those who survive who have the right to grieve. Give up fear of death, Lucretius tells his patron,

> For thou shalt sleep, and never wake again,
> And, quitting life, shalt quit thy living pain.
> But we, thy friends, shall all those sorrows find
> Which in forgetful death thou leav'st behind;
> No time shall dry our tears, nor drive thee from our mind.
> The worst that can befall thee, measured right,
> Is a sound slumber, and a long goodnight.   (3. 90–6)

Even Epicurus had to die, though his genius shone so brightly in comparison with other thinkers that he reduced them to nothing just as the rising sun puts out the stars (3. 1042–4).

Lucretius' fourth book, on the nature of love, is full of lively description of sexual activity, as well as atomistic explanations of the underlying physiology. No doubt it was the content of this book that gave rise to the legend, reported by St Jerome and dramatized by Tennyson, that Lucretius wrote the poem in the lucid intervals of a madness brought on by over-indulgence in an aphrodisiac.

St Jerome also preserves a tradition that the poem was left unfinished and edited, after the poet's death, by Cicero. This seems unlikely, for Cicero, having expressed his admiration on first reading of the poem, never mentions it in his own philosophical writing, even though he devotes considerable attention to the Epicurean system.

Cicero

Cicero himself was eclectic in his philosophy, which is a boon to the historian, since his writings provide information about a variety of philosophical tendencies. He made his first acquaintance with the different philosophical schools when he studied in Athens in his late twenties. Later he studied at Rhodes under the Stoic Posidonius. He was greatly influenced by Philo of Larissa, the last head of the Academy, who came to Rome from Athens in 88 BC. He kept in his house, as personal guru, the Stoic Diodotus until his death in 60.

For a long time Cicero's busy life in politics and in the courts did not leave him much leisure for any philosophy except political philosophy. In the late 50s he imitated Plato by writing a *Republic* and a *Laws*, which have survived only in part. He withdrew from public life, however, when Julius Caesar came to supreme power after a civil war in which he himself had taken the opposite side. Cicero spent much of Caesar's dictatorship in literary activity, and after the death of his only daughter, Tullia, in February 45 he wrote ever more frantically so as to forget his grief. Most of his philosophical works were written in the years 45 and 44.

The two first in the series are now lost, a *Consolatio* on the death of Tullia, and the *Hortensius*, an exhortation to the study of philosophy that was to play a dramatic part in the life of St Augustine. Ten other works, however, survive, impressive in their range and eloquence.

Cicero set himself the task of creating a Latin philosophical vocabulary, so that Romans could study philosophy in their own language. Many, indeed, of the philosophical terms of modern languages derive from his Latin coinages. In his own opinions, he took elements from different philosophical tendencies. In epistemology he favoured the moderate sceptical opinion that he had learnt from Philo: he presents the academic system and its variants in his *Academica*, which appeared in two different versions. In ethics he favoured the Stoic rather than the Epicurean tradition. He looked to moral philosophy for consolation and reassurance. In his *de Finibus* and *Tusculan Disputations* he writes, often with great passion and beauty, on the relation between emotion, virtue, and happiness. His works *On the Nature of the Gods* and *On Fate* contain interesting discussions of philosophical theology and the issue of determinism, and his *On*

Divination puts to good use arguments he had learnt, at a remove, from Carneades.[17]

Cicero wrote philosophy without profundity, but his arguments are often acute, his style is always elegant, and he is capable of great warmth. His essays on friendship and old age have been popular throughout the ages. His final work on moral philosophy, *On Duties (de Officiis)*, was addressed to his son shortly after the assassination of Julius Caesar in March 44. It was, during various periods of history, regarded as an essential item in the education of a gentleman.

After Caesar's death Cicero returned to politics with a series of bitter attacks on the Caesarian consul Mark Antony. After Antony went into partnership with Caesar's adopted son Octavian, Cicero was executed in the putsch that they jointly organized. He did not live to see the quarrel between the two that led to Antony's defeat at Actium in 31. He was dead before Octavian became the first Roman emperor, changing his name to Augustus.

Judaism and Christianity

For the long-term development of philosophy the most important event in the first century of the Roman Empire was the career of Jesus of Nazareth. The impact of his teaching on philosophy was, of course, delayed and indirect, and his own moral doctrine was not without precedent. He taught that we should not render evil for evil; but so had Plato's Socrates. He urged his hearers to love their neighbours as themselves; but he was quoting the ancient Hebrew book of Leviticus. He told us that we must refrain not just from wrong deeds, but from wrong thoughts and desires; Aristotle too had said that the really virtuous person is one who never even wants to do wrong. Jesus taught his disciples to despise the pleasures and honours of the world; but so, in their different ways, did the Epicureans and the Stoics. Considered as a moral philosopher, Jesus was not a great innovator: but that, of course, was not at all how he and his disciples saw his role.

The framework of Jesus' teaching was the world-view of the Hebrew Bible, according to which the Lord God Yahweh had created, by mere fiat,

---

[17] See Ch. 9 below.

heaven and earth and all in them. The Jews were God's chosen people, uniquely privileged by their possession of the divine law revealed to Moses. Like Heraclitus and other Greek and Jewish thinkers, Jesus predicted that there would be a divine judgement on the world, amid cosmic catastrophe. Unlike the Stoics, who placed the cosmic denouement in the indefinite and distant future, Jesus saw it as an imminent event, in which he would himself play a crucial role as the Messiah.

Around the time of Jesus' crucifixion (c. AD 30) Jewish ideas were gaining a hearing in Rome. Since the Hebrew Scriptures had been translated into Greek in Alexandria in the time of the first Ptolemys, there had been a substantial Greek-speaking Jewish diaspora. In the first century AD the outstanding representative of Hellenistic Jewish culture was Philo, who led a delegation to the emperor Caligula in 40 to protest against the persecution of the Jews in Alexandria and the imposition of emperor-worship. He wrote a life of Moses and a series of commentaries on the Pentateuch designed to make the Hebrew Scriptures intelligible and palatable to those educated in Greek culture.

In its early days Christianity spread through the empire via the Greek-speaking diaspora, but it soon came into contact with Gentile philosophy. St Paul, preaching the gospel in Athens, held a debate with Epicurean and Stoic philosophers, and the sermon against idolatry placed in his mouth in the Acts of the Apostles is skilfully crafted, and shows an awareness of matters at issue between the philosophical sects. Taking his cue from the altar of the unknown God, Paul undertook to show the philosophers the god whom they worshipped in ignorance.

[God] is not far from every one of us. For in him we live, and move, and have our being; as certain also of your own poets have said, for we are also his offspring. Forasmuch then as we are the offspring of God we ought not to think that the Godhead is like unto gold or silver or stone, graven by art and man's device. (Acts 17: 27–9)

The 'poet' Paul quoted was Cleanthes, the second head of the Stoa. Later legend imagined Paul in philosophical discourse with the Stoic philosopher Seneca. The story was no doubt untrue, but it was not wholly fanciful. Paul once appeared in court before Seneca's brother Gallio, and he had friends in the palace of Seneca's master Nero.

The Imperial Stoa

Seneca was the most significant philosopher of the first century. Born in Spain, at Cordoba, at the beginning of the Christian era, he was in 49 made tutor to the 12-year-old Nero. When Nero came to the throne in 54 he became a senior adviser, and guided the emperor through a period of comparatively good government, which came to an end in the year 59 when Nero murdered his own mother. Seneca lost all influence on Nero after 62 and gradually withdrew from public life. In 65 he was forced to slit his veins for alleged participation in a plot against the tyrant, and died a Socratic death.

Seneca wrote a number of tragedies, and left a scrapbook of questions on physical phenomena, but his reputation as a philosopher rests on his ten ethical dialogues, and his 124 moral epistles, mostly written during the period of his retirement. Seneca's style is more exhortatory than argumentative; he prefers preaching to debate. He was not interested in logic, and he had a philistine attitude to the liberal arts: he compared a person over-learned in literature to a man with an over-furnished house (Ep. 88. 36). He had a certain interest in the physical sciences, and wrote a treatise *On Natural Questions*, but he likes to draw a moral from natural phenomena, and of the three branches of Stoic philosophy it is ethics that is his main concern.

He urges us to strive towards liberation from the passions. In the longest and best known of his dialogues, *On Anger*, he insists on the crucial difference between bodily turmoil on the one hand, and the false judgements which were the essential element from which we need purification. On this issue, earlier Stoics had not spoken with a single voice. 'None of those things that strike the mind fortuitously should be called passions: they are not things the mind causes but things that happen to it. It is not passion to be affected by the appearances of things that present themselves; passion consists in surrendering oneself to them and following up this fortuitous impact' (2. 3. 1). Weeping, turning pale, sudden intakes of breath, and sexual arousal are not passions, but mere bodily phenomena: it is what happens in the mind that matters. Seneca is able to conduct the Stoic crusade against the passions with greater clarity and energy once this distinction has been made.

Seneca was a materialist, accepting the Stoic doctrine that the human mind was a material part of a material divine world-soul (Ep. 66. 12). But he often writes about the relation between soul and body in a manner that is distinctly other-worldly. 'The human heart is never more divine than when it meditates on its own mortality, and realises that a human being is born in order to give up life, and that this body is not a home but a short-term hostelry which one must leave as soon as one sees one is becoming a burden on one's host' (120. 14). Seneca recognizes the difficulty of the Stoic path to virtue. He distinguishes between three stages in moral progress. There are those who have given up some vices but not all—they are without avarice, but not without anger; without lust but not without ambition; and so on. Then there are those who have given up all passions but are not yet safe from relapse. The third class, the closest approximation to wisdom, consists of those who are beyond relapsing, but have not yet acquired secure self-confidence in their virtue (Ep. 75. 8–14).

Seneca also made popular the distinction in Stoicism between doctrines and precepts. The doctrines provided the general philosophical framework; the precepts enabled the true concept of the highest good to find expression in specific prescriptions to individuals (Ep. 94. 2). This distinction enabled Stoics to counter the allegation that their system was too elevated to be of any practical use, and justified the philosopher in giving the kind of pastoral advice of which Seneca's own letters are full.

Many, in both ancient and modern times, have regarded Seneca as a hypocrite: a man who praised mercy but was implicated in a tyrant's crimes; a man who preached the worthlessness of earthly goods but piled up a gigantic fortune. In his defence it can be said that he acted as a restraining influence on Nero, and that in his last years he sought genuine detachment from the world. He was under no illusion that he lived up to Stoic standards. 'I am a long way, not only from perfection, but from being a halfway decent person,' he wrote (Ep. 57. 3).

Seneca was the founding father of the Imperial Stoa. Two other prominent members of the school show how wide was the appeal of Stoicism under the empire: the slave Epictetus and the emperor Marcus Aurelius. The Stoics of the imperial period were far less interested in logic and physics than their predecessors in Hellenistic times, and like Seneca both Epictetus and Marcus are remembered principally for their moral philosophy.[18]

[18] J. Barnes, *Logic and the Imperial Stoa* (Leiden: Brill, 1997) has made a gallant case for the logical competence of Epictetus.

Epictetus' dates are uncertain, but we know that he was banished from Rome, along with other philosophers, by the emperor Domitian in AD 89. Freed from slavery, though permanently lamed, he set up a school in Epirus; his admirer Arrian published four books of his discourses and a handbook of his main teachings (*enchiridion*). Epictetus is one of the most readable of the Stoics, and has a rugged and jocular style, making constant use of cross-talk with imaginary interlocutors. Because of this, many people beside philosophers have found him attractive. Matthew Arnold lists him, along with Homer and Sophocles, as one of three men who have most enlightened him:

> He, whose friendship I not long since won,
> That halting slave, who in Nicopolis
> Taught Arrian, when Vespasian's brutal son
> Cleared Rome of what most shamed him.

Typical of Epictetus' style is the following passage on suicide, where he imagines people suffering from tyranny and injustice addressing him thus:

Epictetus, we can no longer endure imprisonment in this bodikin, feeding it and watering it and resting it and washing it, and being brought by it into contact with so-and-so and such-and-such. Aren't these things indifferent, indeed a very nothing, to us? Death isn't an evil, is it? Aren't we God's kin, and don't we come from him? Do let us go back where we came. (1. 9. 12)

He responds as follows:

Men, wait for God. When he gives the signal and releases you from this service, then you may go to him. For the time being, though, stay at the post where he has stationed you.

Rather than seek refuge in suicide, we should realize that none of the world's evils can really harm us. To show this, Epictetus identifies the self with the moral will (*prohairesis*).

When the tyrant threatens and summons me, I answer, 'Who is it that you are threatening?' If he says, 'I will put you in chains,' I respond, 'It is my hands and my feet he is threatening.' If he says, 'I will behead you,' I respond, 'It is my neck he is threatening.' . . . So doesn't he threaten *you* at all? No, not so long as I regard all this as nothing to me. But if I let myself fear any of these threats, then yes, he does threaten me. Who then is left for me to fear? A man who can master the things in my own power?—There is no such man. A man who can master the things that are not in my power?—Why should I trouble myself about him? (Disc. 1. 29)

In many periods Epictetus' writings have been found comforting by those who have had to live under the rule of tyrants. But in his own time the person who was most impressed by them was himself the ruler of the Roman world. Marcus Aurelius Antoninus became emperor in 161 and spent much of his life defending the frontiers of the Roman Empire, now at its furthest extent. Though himself a Stoic, he founded chairs of philosophy at Athens for all of the major schools, Platonic, Peripatetic, and Epicurean. During his military campaigns he found time to make entries into a philosophical notebook, which has been known in modern times as the *Meditations*. It is a collection of aphorisms and discourses on themes such as the brevity of life, the need to work for the common good, the unity of mankind, and the corrupting nature of power. He sought to combine patriotism with a universalist viewpoint. 'My city and country,' he says, 'so far as I am Antoninus, is Rome; but so far as I am a man, it is the world.' He hails the universe as 'Dear City of Zeus'.

One of Marcus Aurelius' friends was the medical doctor Galen, who came to Rome after being physician to the gladiators of Pergamum. His voluminous writings belong rather to the history of medicine than to that of philosophy, though he was a serious logician and once wrote a treatise with the title *That a Good Doctor Must Be a Philosopher*. He corrected Aristotle's physiology on an important point which was crucial for a true appreciation of the mind–body relationship. Aristotle had believed that the heart was the seat of the soul, regarding the brain as a mere radiator to cool the blood. Galen discovered that nerves arising from the brain and spinal cord are necessary for the initiation of muscle contraction, and hence he regarded the brain, and not the heart, as the primary seat of the soul.

Early Christian Philosophy

With Marcus Aurelius, Stoicism took its last bow, and Epicureanism was already in retirement. Among the schools of philosophy to whom the emperor assigned chairs in Athens, one was conspicuous by its absence: Christianity. Indeed, Marcus instituted a cruel persecution of Christians, and dismissed their martyrdoms as histrionic. One of those who was executed in his reign was Justin, the first Christian philosopher, who had dedicated to him an *Apologia* for Christianity.

The campaigns of Marcus Aurelius, depicted on his column in Rome

It was at the end of the second century that Christians first made substantial attempts to harmonize the religion of Jesus and Paul with the philosophy of Plato and Aristotle. Clement of Alexandria published a set of Miscellanies (*Stromateis*), written in the style of table talk, in which he argued that the study of philosophy was not only permissible, but necessary, for the educated Christian. The Greek thinkers were pedagogues for the world's adolescence, divinely appointed to bring it to Christ in its maturity. Clement enrolled Plato as an ally against dualist Christian heretics, he experimented with Aristotelian logic, and he praised the Stoic ideal of freedom from passion. In the manner of Philo, he explained away as allegorical aspects of the Bible, and especially the Old Testament, which repelled educated Greeks. In this he founded a tradition that was to have a long history in Alexandria.

Clement was an anthologist and a popularizer; his younger Alexandrian contemporary Origen (185–254) was an original thinker. Though he thought of himself primarily as a student of the Bible, Origen had sat at the feet of the Alexandrian Platonist Ammonius Saccas, and he incorporated into his system many philosophical ideas which mainstream Christians regarded as heretical. He believed, with Plato, that human souls existed before birth or conception. Formerly free spirits, human souls in their embodied state could use their free will to ascend, aided by the grace of Christ, to a heavenly destiny. In the end, he believed, all rational beings, sinners as well as saints, and devils as well as angels, would be saved and find blessedness. There would be a resurrection of the body which (according to some of our sources) he believed would take spherical form, since Plato had decreed that the sphere was the most perfect of all shapes.

Origen's eccentric teaching brought him into conflict with the local bishops, and his loyalty to Christianity laid him under the ban of the empire. He was exiled to Palestine, where, against his pagan fellow Platonist Celsus, he used philosophical arguments to defend Christian belief in God, freedom, and immortality. He died in 254 after repeated torture in the persecution of the emperor Decius.

The Revival of Platonism and Aristotelianism

While Christian philosophy was in its infancy, and while Stoicism and Epicureanism were in decline, there had been a fertile revival of the philosophy of Plato and Aristotle. Plutarch (c.46–c.120) was born in Boeotia and spent most of his life there, but he had studied at Athens and at least once gave lectures in Rome. He is best known as a historian for his parallel lives of twenty-three famous Greeks paired with twenty-three famous Romans, which in an Elizabethan translation by Sir Thomas North provided the plot and much of the inspiration for Shakespeare's Roman plays. But he also wrote some sixty short treatises on popular philosophical topics, which were collected under the title *Moralia*. He was a Platonist and commented on the *Timaeus*. He wrote a number of polemical treatises against the Stoics and Epicureans which contributed to the decline of those systems: they bear parallel titles such as *On the Contradictions of the Epicureans* and *On the Contradictions of the Stoics* or *On Free Will in Reply to Epicurus* and *On Free Will in Reply to the Stoics*. One of the longest of his surviving essays bears the title *That Epicurus Actually Makes a Pleasant Life Impossible*, and another is an attack on an otherwise unknown work by Colotes, one of Epicurus' earliest disciples. Though his works are not often read by philosophers for their own sake, they have long been quarried by historians for the information they provide about their targets of attack.

More important, initially, than the incipient revival of Platonism was the beginning of a tradition of scholarly commentary on the Aristotelian corpus. The oldest surviving commentary on a text is the second-century work of Aspasius on the *Ethics*, which inaugurates the custom of treating the *Nicomachean Ethics* as canonical. At the end of the century Alexander of Aphrodisias was appointed to the Peripatetic chair in Athens, and he produced extensive commentaries on the *Metaphysics*, the *de Sensu*, and some of the logical works. In pamphlets on the soul, and on fate, he presented his own developments of Aristotelian ideas. Aristotle had spoken, obscurely, of an active intellect that was responsible for concept formation in human beings. Alexander identified this active intellect with God, an interpretation that was to have a great influence on Aristotle's later Arab followers, while being rejected by Christians, who regarded the active intellect as a faculty of each individual human being.

Plotinus and Augustine

It was Plato, however, not Aristotle, who was to be the dominant philosophical influence during the twilight of classical antiquity. Contemporary with the Christian Origen, and a fellow pupil of Ammonius Saccas, was the last great pagan philosopher, Plotinus (205–70). After a brief military career Plotinus settled in Rome and won favour at the imperial court. He toyed with the idea of founding a Platonic republic in Campania. His works were edited after his death in six groups of nine treatises (Enneads) by his disciple and biographer Porphyry. Written in a taut and difficult style, they cover a variety of philosophical topics: ethics and aesthetics, physics and cosmology, psychology, metaphysics, logic, and epistemology.

The dominant place in Plotinus' system is occupied by 'the One': the notion is derived, through Plato, from Parmenides, where Oneness is a key property of Being. The One is, in a mysterious way, identical with the Platonic Idea of the Good: it is the basis of all being and the standard of all value, but it is itself beyond being and beyond goodness. Below this supreme and ineffable summit, the next places are occupied by Mind (the locus of Ideas) and Soul, which is the creator of time and space. Soul looks upward to Mind, but downward to Nature, which in turn creates the physical world. At the lowest level of all is bare matter, the outermost limit of reality.

These levels of reality are not independent of each other. Each level depends for its existence and activity on the level above it. Everything has its place in a single downward progress of successive emanations from the One. This impressive and startling metaphysical system is presented by Plotinus not as a mystical revelation but on the basis of philosophical principles derived from Plato and Aristotle. It will be examined in detail in Chapter 9 below.

Plotinus' school in Rome did not survive his death, but his pupils and their pupils carried his ideas elsewhere. A Neoplatonic tradition throve in Athens until the pagan schools were closed down by the Christian emperor Justinian in 529. But it was Christians, not pagans, who transmitted Plotinus' ideas to the post-classical world, and foremost among them was St Augustine of Hippo, who was to prove the most influential of all Christian philosophers.

Augustine was born in a small town in present-day Algeria in 354. The son of a Christian mother and a pagan father, he was not baptized as an infant, though he received a Christian education in Latin literature and rhetoric. Most of what we know of his early life comes from his own autobiography, the *Confessions*, a portrait, by a biographer nearly as gifted as Boswell, of a mind more capacious than Johnson's.

Having acquired a smattering of Greek, Augustine qualified in rhetoric and taught the subject at Carthage, a city which he described as 'a cauldron of unholy loves'. At the age of 18, reading Cicero's *Hortensius*, he was fired with a love of Plato. For about ten years he was a follower of Manichaeism, a syncretic religion which taught that there were two worlds, one of spiritual goodness and light created by God, and one of fleshly darkness created by the devil. The distaste for sex left a permanent mark on Augustine, though for several years in early manhood he lived with a mistress and had with her a son, Adeodatus.

In 383 he crossed the sea to Rome and quickly moved to Milan, then the capital of the western part of the now divided Roman Empire. There he became friends with Ambrose, the bishop of Milan, a great champion of the claims of religion and morality against the ruthless secular power of the emperor Theodosius. The influence of Ambrose, and of his mother, Monica, turned Augustine in the direction of Christianity. After a period of hesitation he was baptized in 387.

For some time after his baptism Augustine remained under the philosophical influence of Plotinus. A set of dialogues on God and the human soul articulated a Christian Neoplatonism. *Against the Academics* set out a detailed line of argument against Academic Scepticism. In *On Ideas* he presented his own version of Plato's Theory of Ideas: the Ideas have no extra-mental existence, but they exist, eternal and unchangeable, in the mind of God. He wrote *On Free Choice* on human freewill, choice, and the origin of evil, a text still used in a number of philosophy departments. He also wrote a donnish Platonic tract, the *83 Different Questions*. He also wrote six books on music, and an energetic work *On the Teacher*, reflecting imaginatively on the nature and power of words.

All these works were written before Augustine found his final vocation and was ordained as a priest in 391. He became after a short period bishop of Hippo in Algeria, where he resided until his death in 430. He had a prodigious writing career ahead of him, including his masterpiece *The City of God*, but the year 391 marks an epoch. Up to this point Augustine showed himself the last fine flower of classical philosophy. From then onwards he writes not as the pupil of the pagan Plotinus, but as the father of the Christian philosophy of the Middle Ages. We shall follow him into this creative phase in the next volume of this work.

Augustine did not see himself, in his maturity, as a philosophical innovator. He saw his task as the expounding of a divine message that had come to him from Plato and Paul, men much greater than himself, and from Jesus, who was more than man. But the way in which succeeding generations have conceived and understood the teaching of Augustine's masters has been in great part the fruit of Augustine's own work. Of all the philosophers in the ancient world, only Aristotle had a greater influence on human thought.

3

How to Argue:
Logic

Logic is the discipline that sorts out good arguments from bad arguments. Aristotle claimed to be its founder, and his claim is no idle boast. Of course, human beings had been arguing, and detecting fallacies in other people's arguments, since human society began; as John Locke said, 'God did not make men barely two legged and leave it to Aristotle to make them rational.' None the less, it is to Aristotle that we owe the first formal study of argumentative reasoning. But here as elsewhere, there is first of all a debt to Plato to be acknowledged. Following the lead of Protagoras, Plato made important distinctions between parts of speech, distinctions that form part of the basis on which logic is built. In the *Sophist* he introduces a distinction between nouns and verbs, verbs being signs of actions, and names being signs of the agents of those actions. A sentence, he insists, must consist of at least one noun and at least one verb: two nouns in succession, or two verbs in succession, will never make a sentence. 'Walks runs' is not a sentence, nor is 'Lion stag'. The simplest kind of sentence will be something like 'A man learns' or 'Theaetetus flies', and only something with this kind of structure can be true or false (*Sph.* 262a–263b). The splitting of sentences into smaller units—of which this is only one possible example—is an essential first step in the logical analysis of argument.

Aristotle left a number of logical treatises, which are traditionally placed at the beginning of the corpus of his works in the following order: *Categories, de Interpretatione, Prior Analytics, Posterior Analytics, Topics, Sophistical Refutations*. This order is neither the one in which the works were written nor the one in which it is most fruitful to read them. It is best to begin with the consideration of the *Prior Analytics*, the most substantial and the least controversial of his contributions to the discipline of logic which he founded.

Aristotle's Syllogistic

The *Prior Analytics* is devoted to the theory of the syllogism, a central method of inference that can be illustrated by familiar examples such as

> Every Greek is human.
> Every human is mortal.
> Therefore,   Every Greek is mortal.

Aristotle sets out to show how many forms syllogisms can take, and which of them provide reliable inferences.

For the purposes of this study, Aristotle introduced a technical vocabulary which, translated into many languages, has played an important part in logic throughout its history (1. 1. 24^{a}10–^{b}15). The word 'syllogism' itself is simply a transliteration into English of the Greek word 'syllogismos' which Aristotle uses for inferences of this pattern. It is defined at the beginning of the *Prior Analytics*: a syllogism is a discourse in which from certain things laid down something different follows of necessity (1. 1. 24^{b}18).

The example syllogism above contains three sentences in the indicative mood and each such sentence is called by Aristotle a *proposition* (*protasis*): a proposition is, roughly speaking, a sentence considered in respect of its logical features. The third of the propositions in the example—the one preceded by 'therefore'—is called by Aristotle the *conclusion* of the syllogism. The other two propositions we may call *premisses*, though Aristotle does not have a consistent technical term to differentiate them.

The propositions in the above example begin with the word 'every': such propositions are called by Aristotle *universal* propositions (*katholou*). They are not the only kind of universal propositions: equally universal is a proposition such as 'No Greeks are horses'; but whereas the first kind of proposition was a universal *affirmative* (*kataphatikos*), the second is a universal *negative* (*apophatikos*).

Contrasted with universal propositions there are *particular* propositions (*en merei*) such as 'Some Greeks are bearded' (a particular affirmative) or 'Some Greeks are not bearded' (a particular negative). In propositions of all these kinds, Aristotle says, something is *predicated* of something else: e.g. mortal is predicated of human in one case, and horse of Greek in another. The presence or absence of a negative sign determine whether these predications are affirmations or negations respectively (1. 1. 24^{b}17).

The items that enter into predications in propositions are called by Aristotle *terms* (*horoi*). It is a feature of terms, as conceived by Aristotle, that they can either figure as predicates themselves or have other terms predicated of them. Thus, in our first example, human is predicated of something in the first sentence and has something predicated of it in the second.

Aristotle assigns the terms occurring in a syllogism three distinct roles. The term that is the predicate of the conclusion is the *major* term; the term of which the major is predicated in the conclusion is the *minor* term; and the term that appears in each of the premisses is the *middle* term (1. 4. 26^{a}21–3).[1] Thus, in the example given 'mortal' is the major term, 'Greek' the minor term, and 'human' the middle term.

In addition to inventing these technical terms, Aristotle introduced the practice of using schematic letters to bring out patterns of argument: a device that is essential for the systematic study of inference and which is ubiquitous in modern mathematical logic. Thus, the pattern of argument we illustrated above is set out by Aristotle not by giving an example, but by the following schematic sentence:

> If A belongs to every B, and B belongs to every C, A belongs to every C.[2]

If Aristotle wishes to produce an actual example, he commonly does it not by spelling out a syllogistic argument, but by giving a schematic sentence and then listing possible substitutions for A, B, and C (e.g. 1. 5. 27^{b}30–2).

---

[1] Aristotle's use of these terms in the *Prior Analytics* is not consistent: the account given here, from which he departs in considering the second and third figures of syllogism, has been accepted as canonical since antiquity (see W. C. Kneale and M. Kneale, *The Development of Logic* (Oxford: Clarendon Press, 1962), 69–71).

[2] Note that beside being cast in schematic form, Aristotle's exposition of syllogisms follows the pattern 'If *p* and *q*, then necessarily *r*' rather than '*p*, *q* therefore *r*'.

All syllogisms will contain three terms and three propositions; but given that there are the four different kinds of proposition Aristotle has distinguished, and that there are different orders in which the terms can appear in the premisses, there will be many different syllogistic inference patterns. Unlike our initial example, which contained only affirmative universal propositions, there will be triads containing negative and particular propositions. Again, unlike our example in which the middle term appeared in the first premiss as a predicate and in the second as a subject, there will be cases where the middle is subject in each premiss and cases where it is predicate in each premiss. (By Aristotle's preferred definition, the conclusion will always have the minor term as its subject and the major as its predicate.)

Aristotle grouped the triads into three figures (*schemata*) on the basis of the position occupied in the premisses by the middle term. The first figure, illustrated by our initial example, has the middle once as predicate and once as subject (the order in which the premisses are stated is immaterial). In the second figure the middle term appears twice as subject, and in the third figure it appears twice as predicate. Thus, using S for the minor, M for the middle, and P for the major term, we have these figures:

	(1)	(2)	(3)
	S–M	M–S	S–M
	M–P	M–P	P–M
Therefore,	S–P	S–P	S–P

Aristotle was mainly interested in syllogisms of the first figure, which he regarded as alone being 'perfect', by which he probably meant that they had an intuitive validity that was lacking to syllogisms in other figures (1. 4. 25^{b}35).

Predication occurs in all propositions, but it comes in different forms in the four different kinds of proposition: universal affirmative, universal negative, particular affirmative, particular negative. Thus the predication S–P can be either 'All S is P', 'No S is P', 'Some S is P', or 'Some S is not P'. Within each figure, therefore, we have many possible patterns of inference. In the first figure, for instance, we have, among many possibilities, the two following.

Every Greek is human.	Some animals are dogs.
No human is immortal.	Some dogs are white.
No Greek is immortal.	Every animal is white.

Triads of these different kinds were, in later ages, called 'moods' of the syllogism. Both of the given triads exemplify the pattern of a syllogism of the first figure, but there is obviously a great difference between them: the first is a valid argument, the second is invalid, having true premisses and a false conclusion.[3]

Aristotle sets himself the task of determining which of the possible moods produces a valid inference. He addresses it by trying out the various possible pairs of premisses and asking whether any conclusion can be drawn from them. If no conclusion can be validly drawn from a pair of premisses, he says that there is no syllogism. For instance, he says that if B belongs to no C, and A belongs to some B, there cannot be a syllogism; and he gives the terms 'white', 'horse', 'swan' as the test instance (1. 3. 25ª38). What he is doing is inviting us to consider the pair of premisses 'No swan is a horse' and 'Some horses are white' and to observe that from these premisses no conclusion can be drawn about the whiteness or otherwise of swans.

His procedure appears, at first sight, to be both haphazard and intuitive; but in the course of his discussion he is able to produce a number of general rules which, between them, are adequate to determine which moods yield a conclusion and which do not. There are three rules which apply to syllogisms in all figures:

(1) At least one premiss must be universal.
(2) At least one premiss must be affirmative.
(3) If either premiss is negative, the conclusion must be negative.

These rules are of universal application, but they take more specific form in relation to particular figures. The rules peculiar to the first figure are

(4) The major premiss (the one containing the major term) must be universal.
(5) The minor premiss (the one containing the minor term) must be affirmative.

---

[3] No valid argument has true premisses and a false conclusion, but of course there can be valid arguments from false premisses to false conclusions, and invalid arguments for true conclusions.

If we apply these rules we find that there are four, and only four, valid moods of syllogism in the first figure.

Every S is M	Every S is M	Some S is M	Some S is M
Every M is P	No M is P	Every M is P	Every M is not P
Every S is P	No S is P	Some S is P	Some S is not P

Aristotle also offers rules to determine the validity of moods in the second and third figures, but we do not need to go into these since he is able to show that all second- and third-figure syllogisms are equivalent to first-figure syllogisms. In general, syllogisms in these figures can be transformed into first-figure syllogisms by a process he calls 'conversion' (*antistrophe*).

Conversion depends on a set of relations between propositions of different forms that Aristotle sets out early in the treatise. When we have particular affirmative and universal negative propositions, the order of the terms can be reversed without alteration of sense: Some S is P if and only if some P is S, and no S is P if and only if no P is S (1. 2. 25^{a}5–10). (By contrast, 'Every S is P' may be true without 'Every P is S' being true.)

Consider the following syllogism in the third figure: 'No Greek is a bird; but all ravens are birds; therefore no Greek is a raven'. If we convert the minor premiss into its equivalent 'No bird is a Greek' we have a first-figure syllogism in the second of the moods tabulated above. Aristotle shows in the course of his treatise that almost all second- and third-figure syllogisms can be reduced to first-figure ones by conversion in this manner. In the rare cases where this is not possible he transforms the second- and third-figure syllogisms by a process of *reductio ad absurdum*, showing that if one premiss of the syllogism is taken in conjunction with the negation of its conclusion as a second premiss, it will yield (by a deduction in the first figure) the negation of the original second premiss as a conclusion (1. 23. 41^{a}21 ff.).

Aristotle's syllogistic was a remarkable achievement: it is a systematic formulation of an important part of logic. Some of his followers in later times—though not in antiquity or the Middle Ages—thought that syllogistic was the whole of logic. Immanuel Kant, for instance, in the preface to the second edition of his *Critique of Pure Reason*, said that since Aristotle logic had neither advanced a single step nor been required to retrace a single step.

121

In fact, however, syllogistic is only a fragment of logic. It deals only with inferences that depend on words like 'all' or 'some', which classify the premisses and conclusions of syllogisms, not with inferences that depend on words like 'if' and 'then', which, instead of attaching to nouns, link whole sentences. As we shall see, inferences such as 'If it is not day, it is

A head of Aristotle attributed to Lysippus (fourth century BC)

night; but it is not day; therefore it is night' were formalized later in antiquity. Another gap in Aristotle's syllogistic took longer to fill. Though it was concerned above all with words like 'all', 'every', and 'some' (quantifiers, as they were later to be called), it could not cope with inferences in which such words occurred not in subject place but somewhere in the grammatical predicate. Aristotle's rules would not provide for assessing the validity of inferences containing premisses such as 'Every boy loves some girl' or 'Nobody can avoid every mistake.' It took more than twenty centuries before such inferences were satisfactorily formalized.

Aristotle may perhaps, for a moment, have thought that his syllogistic was sufficient to deal with every possible valid inference. But his own logical writings show that he realized that there was much more to logic than was dreamt of in his syllogistic.

The de Interpretatione *and the* Categories

The *de Interpretatione* is principally interested, like the *Prior Analytics*, in general propositions beginning with 'every', 'no', or 'some'. But its main concern is not to link them to each other in syllogisms, but to explore the relations of compatibility and incompatibility between them. 'Every man is white' and 'No man is white' can clearly not both be true together: Aristotle calls such propositions *contraries (enantiai)* (7. 17^b4–15). They can, however, both be false, if, as is the case, some men are white and some men are not. 'Every man is white' and 'Some man is not white', like the earlier pair, cannot be true together; but—on the assumption that there are such things as men—they cannot be false together. If one of them is true, the other is false; if one of them is false, the other is true. Aristotle calls such a pair *contradictory (antikeimenai)* (7. 17^b16–18).

Just as a universal affirmative is contradictory to the corresponding particular negative, so too a universal negative contradicts, and is contradicted by, a particular affirmative: thus 'No man is white' and 'Some man is white'. Two corresponding particular affirmatives are neither contrary nor contradictory to each other: 'Some man is white' and 'Some man is not white' can be, and in fact are, both true together. Given that there are men, the propositions cannot, however, both be false together. This relationship was not given a name: later followers called it the relationship of subcontrariety.

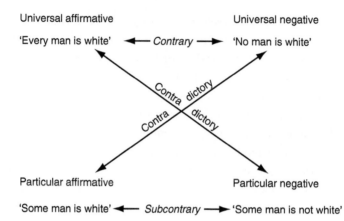

The relationships set out in the *de Interpretatione* can be set out, and have been set out for centuries by Aristotle's followers, in a diagram known as a square of opposition.

The propositions that enter into syllogisms and into the square of opposition are all general propositions, whether they are universal or particular. That is to say, none of them are propositions about individuals, containing proper names, such as 'Socrates is wise'. Of course, Aristotle was familiar with singular propositions, and one such, 'Pittacus is generous', turns up in an example in the final chapter of the *Prior Analytics* (2. 27. 70ª25). But its appearance is incongruous in a treatise whose standard assumption is that all premisses and conclusions are quantified general propositions. In the *de Interpretatione* singular propositions are mentioned from time to time, principally to point a contrast with general propositions. It is a simple matter, for instance, to form the contradictory of 'Socrates is white': it is 'Socrates is not white' (7. 17ᵇ30). But to find a systematic treatment of singular propositions we must turn to the *Categories*.

Whereas the *Analytics* operates with a distinction between propositions and terms, the *Categories* starts by dividing 'things that are said' into complex (*kata symploken*) and simple (*aneu symplokes*) (2. 1ª16). An example of a complex saying is 'A man is running'; simple sayings are the nouns and verbs that enter into such complexes: 'man', 'ox', 'run', 'win', and so on. Only complex sayings can be statements, true or false; simple sayings are neither true nor false. A similar distinction appears in the *de Interpretatione*, where we learn that a sentence (*logos*) has parts that signify on their own, while on the other hand there are signs that have no significant parts. These simple signs come in two different kinds, names (*Int.* 2. 16^{a}20–^{b}5) and verbs (*Int.* 3. 16^{b}6–25): the two are distinguished from each other, we learn, because a verb, unlike a noun, 'signifies time in addition', i.e. has a tense. But in the *Categories* there is a much richer classification of simple sayings. In the fourth chapter of the treatise Aristotle has this to say:

Each one signifies either substance (*ousia*), or how big, or what sort, or in relation to something, or where, or when, or posture, or wearing, or doing, or being acted on. To give a rough idea substance is e.g. human, horse; how big is e.g. four-feet, six-feet; what sort is e.g. white, literate; in relation to something is e.g. double, half, bigger than; where is e.g. in the Lyceum, in the forum; when is e.g. yesterday, tomorrow, last year; posture is e.g. is lying, is sitting; wearing is e.g. is shod, is armed; doing is e.g. cutting, burning; being acted on is e.g. being cut, being burnt. (4. 1^{b}25–2^{a}4)

This compressed and cryptic passage has received repeated commentary and has exercised enormous influence over the centuries. These ten things signified by simple sayings are the *categories* that give the treatise its name. Aristotle in this passage indicates the categories by a heterogeneous set of expressions: nouns (e.g. 'substance'), verbs (e.g. 'wearing'), and interrogatives (e.g. 'where?' or 'how big?'). It became customary to refer to every category by a more or less abstract noun: substance, quantity, quality, relation, place, time, posture, vesture, activity, passivity.

What are categories and what is Aristotle's purpose in listing them? One thing, at least, that he is doing is listing ten different kinds of expression that might appear in the predicate of a sentence about an individual subject. We might say of Socrates, for example, that he was a man, that he was five feet tall, that he was wise, that he was older than Plato, and that he lived in Athens in the fifth century BC. On a particular occasion his friends might have said of him that he was sitting, wearing a cloak, cutting a piece of cloth, and being warmed by the sun. Obviously, the teaching of the *Categories* makes room for a variety of statements much richer than the regimented propositions of the *Prior Analytics*.

The text makes clear, however, that Aristotle is not only classifying expressions, pieces of language. He saw himself as making a classification of extra-linguistic entities, things signified as opposed to the signs that signify them. In Chapter 6 we shall explore the metaphysical implications of the doctrine of the categories. But one question must be addressed immediately. If we follow Aristotle's lead, we shall easily be able to categorize the predicates in sentences such as 'Socrates was pot-bellied', 'Socrates was wiser than Meletus'. But what are we to say about the 'Socrates' in such sentences? Aristotle's list seems to be a list of predicates not of subjects.

The answer to this is given in the succeeding chapter of the *Categories*.

Substance—strictly so called, primarily and *par excellence*—is that which is neither said of a subject nor is in a subject, e.g. such-and-such a man, such-and-such a horse.

Second substances are the species and genera to which the primary substances belong. Thus, such-and-such a man belongs in the species human, and the genus of this species is animal; so both human and animal are called second substances. (5. 2ª11–19)

When Aristotle speaks of a subject in this passage, it is clear that he is talking not about a linguistic expression, but about what the expression stands for. It is the man Socrates, not the word 'Socrates', that is the first substance. The substance that appeared first in the list of categories, it now emerges, was second substance: so the sentence 'Socrates was human' predicated a second substance (a species) of a first substance (an individual). When Aristotle in this passage contrasts a first substance with things that are *in a subject*, what he has in mind as being in a subject are the items signified by predicates in the other categories. Thus, if 'Socrates is wise' is true, then Socrates' wisdom is one of the things that are in Socrates (cf. 2. 1ª25).

Aristotle goes through the categories, discussing them in turn. Some, such as substance, quantity, and quality, are treated at length; others, such as activity and passivity, are briefly touched on; yet others, such as posture and vesture, pass into oblivion. Detailed logical points are made in order to mark the distinctions between different categories. For example, qualities often admit of degrees, while particular quantities do not: one thing can be darker than another, but cannot be more four-foot-long than another (7. 6ª19; 8. 10ᵇ26). Within individual categories, further subclasses are identified. There are, for instance, two types of quantity (discrete and continuous) and four types of quality, which Aristotle illustrates with the following examples: virtue, healthiness, darkness, shape. The criteria by which he distinguishes these types are not altogether clear, and the reader is left in doubt whether a particular item can occur in more than one of these classes, or indeed in more than one category. Aristotle's commentators through the ages have laboured to fill his gaps and reconcile his inconsistencies.

The *Categories* contains more than the theory of categories: it deals also with a mixed bag of other logical topics. It is clear that the treatise we have was not written as a single whole by Aristotle, though there is no need to question, as some scholars have done, that it is his authentic work.[4]

One cluster of topics discussed is that of homonymy and synonymy. These words are transliterations of the Greek words Aristotle uses; but whereas the English words signify properties of bits of language, the Greek words as he uses them signify properties of things in the world. Aristotle's account can be paraphrased thus: if A and B are called by the same name with the same meaning, then A is synonymous with B; if A and B are called by the same name with a different meaning, then A is homonymous with B. Because of peculiarities of Greek idiom, we have to tweak Aristotle's examples in English, but it is clear enough what he has in mind. A Persian and a tabby are synonymous with each other because they are both called cats; but they are only homonymous with the nine-tailed whip that is also called a cat. The difference between homonymous and synonymous things, Aristotle says, is that homonymous things have only the name in common, whereas synonymous things have both the name and its definition in common.

Aristotle's distinction between homonymous and synonymous things is an important one which is easily adapted—and was indeed later adapted by himself—into a distinction between homonymous and synonymous bits of language, that is to say between expressions that have only the symbol in common and those that have also the meaning in common.

The study of homonymy was important for the treatment of fallacies in arguments due to the ambiguity of terms used. It is undertaken for these purposes in the *Topics*, and Aristotle gives rules for detecting it. 'Sharp', for instance, has one meaning as applied to knives, and another as applied to musical notes: the homonymy is made obvious because in the case of knives the opposite of 'sharp' is 'blunt', whereas in the case of notes the opposite is 'flat' (*Top.* 1. 15. 106ª13–14). In the course of his studies Aristotle came to draw a distinction between mere chance homonymy (as in the English word 'bank', which is used both for the side of a river and for a

---

[4] With the exception of 8. 11ª10–18, an editorial insertion to link together two of the disparate elements and to explain gaps in the treatment of the later categories.

moneylending institution) and homonymy of a more interesting kind, which his followers called 'analogy' (*NE* 1. 6. 1096ª27 ff.). His standard example of an analogical expression is 'medical': a medical man, a medical problem, and a medical instrument are not all medical in the same way. However, the use of the words in these different contexts is not a mere pun: medicine, the discipline that is practised by the medical man, provides a primary meaning from which the others are derived (*EE* 7. 2. 1236ª15–22). Aristotle made use of this doctrine of analogy in a variety of ethical and metaphysical contexts, as we shall see.

In Aristotle's logical writings we find two different conceptions of the structure of a proposition and the nature of its parts. One conception can trace its ancestry to Plato's distinction between nouns and verbs in the *Sophist*. Any sentence, Plato there insisted, must consist of at least one verb and one noun (262a–263b). It is this conception of a sentence as constructed from two quite heterogeneous elements that is to the fore in Aristotle's *Categories* and *de Interpretatione*. This conception of propositional structure has also been paramount in modern logic since the time of Gottlob Frege, who made a sharp distinction between words that name objects, and predicates that are true or false of objects.

In the syllogistic of the *Prior Analytics* the proposition is conceived in quite a different way. The basic elements out of which it is constructed are *terms*: elements that are not heterogeneous like nouns and verbs, but that can occur indifferently, without change of meaning, either as subjects or as predicates.[5] To be sure, two terms in succession (like 'man animal') do not compose a sentence: other elements, a quantifier and a copula, such as 'is', must enter in if we are to have a proposition capable of occurring in a syllogism, such as 'Every man is an animal'. Aristotle shows little interest in the copula, and his attention now focuses on the quantifiers and their relations to each other. The features that differentiate subjects from predicates drop out of consideration.[6]

One of the dysfunctional features of the doctrine of terms is that it fosters confusion between signs and what they signify. When Plato talks

[5] Cf. 43ª25–31. Instead of a distinction between noun and verb we here have a distinction between proper names (which are not predicates but of which things are predicated) and terms (which are both predicates and predicated of).

[6] Modern admirers of Frege naturally regard the theory of terms as a disaster for the development of logic. Peter Geach has written, 'Aristotle was logic's Adam; and the doctrine of terms was Adam's fall' (*Logic Matters* (Oxford: Blackwell, 1972), 290).

about nouns and verbs, he makes quite clear that he is talking about signs. He clearly distinguishes between the name 'Theaetetus' and the person Theaetetus whose name it is; and he is at pains to point out that the sentence 'Theaetetus flies' can occur even though what it tells us, namely the flying of Theaetetus, is not among the things there are in the world. It takes him some trouble to bring out the distinction between signs and signified, because of the lack of inverted commas in ancient Greek. This valuable device of modern languages makes it easy for us to distinguish the normal case where we are using a word to talk about what it signifies, and the special case in which we are mentioning a word to talk about the word itself, as in ' "Theaetetus" is a name'. The doctrine of terms, on the other hand, makes it all too easy to confuse use with mention.

Take a syllogism whose premisses are 'Every human is mortal', 'Every Greek is human'. Shall we say, as Aristotle's language sometimes suggests, (e.g. *APr.* 1. 4. 25^{b}37–9) that here mortal is predicated of human, and human is predicated of Greek? This does not seem quite right: what occurs as a predicate is surely a piece of language, and so perhaps we should say instead: 'mortal' is predicated of human and 'human' is predicated of Greek. But then we seem to have four terms, not three, in our syllogism, since ' "human" ' is not the same as 'human'. We cannot remedy this by rephrasing the first proposition thus: 'mortal' is predicated of 'human'. It is human beings themselves, not the words they use to refer to themselves, that are mortal. There is no doubt that Aristotle sometimes fell into confusion between use and mention; the wonder is that, given the quicksand provided by the doctrine of terms, he did not do so more often.

Aristotle on Time and Modality

A feature of propositions as discussed in the *Categories* and the *de Interpretatione* is that they can change their truth-values. At *Cat.* 1. 5. 4^{a}24, when discussing whether it is peculiar to substances to be able to take on contrary properties, he says 'The same statement seems to be both true and false. If, for example, the statement that somebody is sitting is true, after he has stood up that same statement will be false.' According to a common modern conception of the nature of the proposition, no proposition can be at one time true and at another false. A sentence such as 'Theaetetus is sitting', which is true when Theaetetus is sitting, and false at another time, would on this view be said to express a different proposition at different times, so that at one time it expresses a true proposition, and at another time a false one. And a sentence asserting that 'Theaetetus is sitting' *was true* at time *t* is commonly treated as asserting that the proposition that ascribes *sitting at time t* to Theaetetus is true timelessly. On this account, no proposition is significantly tensed, but any proposition expressed by a tensed sentence contains an implicit reference to time and is itself timelessly true or false.

Aristotle nowhere puts forward such a theory according to which tensed sentences are incompletely explicit expressions of timeless propositions. For him uttered sentences do indeed express something other than themselves, namely thoughts in the mind; but thoughts change their truth-values just as sentences do (*Cat.* 1. 5. 4^{a}26–8).[7] For Aristotle, a sentence or proposition such as 'Theaetetus is sitting' is significantly tensed, and is at some times true and at others false. It becomes true whenever Theaetetus sits down, and becomes false whenever Theaetetus ceases to sit.

There is, for Aristotle, nothing in the nature of the proposition as such that prevents it from changing its truth-value: but there may be something about the content of a particular proposition that entails that its truth-value must remain fixed.

Logicians in later ages regularly distinguished between propositions that can, and propositions that cannot, change their truth-value, calling the former *contingent* and the latter *necessary* propositions. The roots of this distinction are to be found in Aristotle, but he speaks by preference of predicates, or properties, necessarily or contingently belonging to their subjects. In both the *de Interpretatione* and the *Categories* he discusses propositions such as 'A must be B' and 'A can be not B': propositions later called by logicians 'modal propositions'.

In the *de Interpretatione* he introduces the topic of modal propositions by saying that whereas 'A is not B' is the negation of 'A is B', 'A can be not B' is not the negation of 'A can be B'. A piece of cloth, for instance, has the possibility of being cut, but it also has the possibility of being uncut. However, contradictories cannot be true together. Hence the negation of 'A can be B' is not 'A can be not B' but rather 'A cannot be B'. In the

---

[7] The truth-value of a proposition is its truth or its falsity, as the case may be.

straightforward categorical statement, whether we take the 'not' as going with the 'is' or the 'B' makes no practical difference. In the modal statement, whether we take the 'not' as going with the 'can' or the 'B' makes a great difference. Aristotle likes to bring out this difference by rewriting 'A can be B' as 'It is possible for A to be B', rewriting 'A can be not B' as 'It is possible for A to be not B', and rewriting 'A cannot be B' as 'It is not possible for A to be B' (*Int.* 12. 21ª37–ᵇ24). This rewriting allows the negation sign to be unambiguously placed, and brings out the relationship between a modal proposition and its negation.

Modal expressions other than 'possible', such as 'impossible' and 'necessary', are to be treated similarly. The negation of 'It is impossible for A to be B' is not 'It is impossible for A not to be B' but 'It is not impossible for A to be B'; the negation of 'It is necessary for A to be B' is not 'It is necessary for A to be not B' but 'It is not necessary for A to be B' (*Int.* 13. 22ª2–10).

These modal notions are interrelated. 'Impossible' is obviously enough the negation of 'possible', but more interestingly 'necessary' and 'possible' are interdefinable. What is necessary is what is not possible not to be, and what is possible is what is not necessary not to be. If it is necessary for A to be B, then it is not possible for A not to be B, and vice versa. Moreover, if something is necessary, then a fortiori it is possible, and if it is not possible, then a fortiori it is not necessary. Aristotle arranges the different cases in a square of opposition similar to that I exhibited above for categorical propositions.

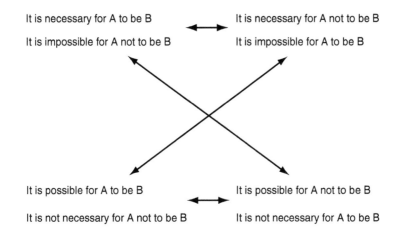

In each corner of this diagram the pairs of propositions are equivalent to each other: this brings out the interdefinability of the modal terms. The operators 'necessary', 'possible', and 'impossible' in this square of opposition are related to each other in a way parallel to the quantifiers 'all', 'some', and 'no' in the categorical square of opposition. As in the categorical case, the propositions in the upper corners are contraries: they cannot both be true together, but they can both be false together. Propositions in one corner are the contradictories of propositions in the diagonally opposite corner. The pair of propositions in the upper corners entail the pair of propositions immediately below them, but not conversely. Propositions in the lower corners are compatible with each other: they can both be true together, but they cannot both be false together (*Int*. 13. 22^{a}14–35).

In this scheme all necessary propositions are also possible, though the converse is not true. There is, however, as Aristotle remarks, another use of 'possible' in which it is contrasted with 'necessary' and inconsistent with it. In this other use, 'It is possible that A is not B' is not just consistent with 'It is possible that A is B' but actually follows from it (*Int*. 12. 21^{b}35). In this use 'possible' would be equivalent to 'neither necessary nor impossible'. There is another word, 'contingent' (*endechomenon*), which is available to replace 'possible' in this second use, and Aristotle often uses it for that purpose (e.g. *Apr*. 1. 13. 32^{a}18–21; 15. 34^{b}25). Thus propositions can be divided into three classes: the necessary, the impossible, and between the two, the contingent (i.e. those that are neither necessary nor impossible).

One of the most interesting passages in Aristotle's *Organon* is the ninth chapter of the *de Interpretatione*, in which he discusses the relation between tense and modality in propositions. He begins by saying that for what is and what has been, it is necessary that the affirmation or the negation should be true or false (18^{a}27–8). It transpires that he is not saying simply that if '*p*' is a present- or past-tense proposition, then 'Either *p* or not *p*' is necessarily true: that is something that holds of all propositions, no matter what their tense (19^{a}30). Nor is he saying just that if '*p*' is a present- or past-tense proposition, it is either true or false: it turns out later that he thinks this is true also of future-tense propositions. What he is saying is that if '*p*' is a present- or past-tense proposition, then '*p*' is a necessary proposition. The necessity in question is clearly not logical necessity: it is not a matter of logic that Queen Anne is dead. The necessity is the kind of necessity that is expressed in the proverbs that what's done cannot be undone, and that it is no use crying over spilt milk (cf. *NE* 6. 2. 1139^b7–11).

The central part of *de Interpretatione* 9 is an inquiry into whether this kind of necessity that applies to present and past propositions applies also to all future propositions. There are, no doubt, universally necessary truths that apply to the future as well as to the present and to the past: but Aristotle's attention focuses on singular propositions such as 'This coat will be cut up before it wears out', 'There will be a sea-battle tomorrow'. The truth or falsity of such propositions is not, on the face of it, entailed by any universal generalization.

However, it is possible to construct a powerful argument to the effect that such a proposition about the future, if it is true, is necessarily true. If A says that there will be a sea-battle tomorrow, and B says that there will not be, then one or other will be speaking the truth. Now there are relations between propositions in different tenses: for instance, if 'Socrates will be white' is now true, then 'Socrates will be white' has been true in the past, and indeed was always true in the past. So—the argument goes—

> If it was always true to say it is or will be, then it is impossible for that not to be or to be going to be. But if it is impossible for something not to come about, then it cannot not come about. But if it cannot not come about, then it is necessary for it to come about. Therefore everything that is going to come about is, of necessity, to come about. (9. 18^b11–25)

The argument that Aristotle is considering began by supposing that someone says, for example, 'There will be a sea-battle tomorrow' and someone else 'There will not be a sea-battle tomorrow' and pointing out that one or the other is speaking truly. But, he goes on, a similar prediction might have been made long ago, 'There will be a sea-battle ten thousand years hence', and this too, or its contradictory, will be true. Indeed, it makes no difference whether any prediction has ever been made. If in the whole of time either the proposition or its contradictory has been the truth, it was necessary for the thing to come about. Since of whatever happens 'It will happen' was always previously true, everything must happen of necessity (9. 18^b26–19^a5).

It will follow, Aristotle says, that nothing is a matter of chance or happenstance. Worse, there will be no point in deliberating and choosing between alternatives. But in fact, he says, there are many obvious examples of things turning out one way when they could have turned out another, like a cloak that could have been cut up but wore out first. 'So it is clear that not everything is or happens of necessity, but some things are a matter of happenstance, and the affirmation is not true rather than the negation; and with other things one is true rather and for the most part, but still it is open for either to happen and the other not' (9. 19ª18–22).

How then are we to deal with the argument to the effect that everything happens of necessity? Because Aristotle says that in some cases 'the affirmation is not true rather than the negation', some have thought that his solution was that future contingent propositions lack a truth-value: not only are they not necessarily true or false, they are not true or false at all. However, this can hardly be what he means; for at 18ᵇ17 he says that it is not open to us to say that neither 'It will be the case that p' nor 'It will not be the case that p' is true. One reason he gives for this is that it is obviously impossible that they should both be false; but that does not rule out their both having some third value. His argument to rule this out is not altogether clear, but it appears to be something like this: if neither 'There will be a sea-battle tomorrow' nor 'There will not be a sea-battle tomorrow' is true today, then neither 'There is a sea-battle today' nor 'There is not a sea-battle today' will be true tomorrow.

At the end of the discussion it seems clear that Aristotle accepts that future contingent propositions can be true, but that they are not necessary in the way that present and past propositions are. Everything is necessary-when-it-is, but that does not mean it is necessary, period. It is necessary that there should or should not be a sea-battle tomorrow, but it is not necessary that there should be a sea-battle and it is not necessary that there should not be a sea-battle (9. 19ª30–2).

What is less clear is how Aristotle disarms the powerful argument he built up in favour of universal necessity. The distinction just enunciated is not sufficient by itself to do so, for it does not take account of the appeal to the past truth of future contingents that was part of the argument. Since on his own admission the past is necessary, past truths about future events must be necessary, and therefore the future events themselves must be necessary. The solution must come through an analysis of the notion of past truths: we must distinguish between truths that are stated in the past tense, and truths that are made true by events in the past. 'It was true ten thousand years ago that there was going to be a sea-battle tomorrow', for all its past tense, is not really a proposition about the past. But this solution is nowhere clearly enunciated by Aristotle, and the problem he set out recurred in many different forms in later antiquity and in the Middle Ages.[8]

In the *Prior Analytics* Aristotle explores the possibility of constructing syllogisms out of modal propositions. His attempt to construct a modal syllogistic is nowadays universally regarded as a gallant failure; and even in antiquity its faults were realized. His successor Theophrastus worked on it and improved it, but even so it must be regarded as unsatisfactory. The reason for the lack of success has been well explained by Martha Kneale: it is Aristotle's indecision about the best way to analyse modal propositions.

If modal words modify predicates, there is no need for a special theory of *modal* syllogisms. For these are only ordinary assertoric syllogisms of which the premises have peculiar predicates. On the other hand, if modal words modify the whole statements to which they are attached, there is no need for a special modal *syllogistic*, since the rules determining the logical relations between modal statements are independent of the character of the propositions governed by the modal words.[9]

The necessary basis for a modal logic, she concludes, is a logic of unanalysed propositions such as was developed by the Stoics. This statement needs qualification. It is true that the flowering of modal logic in the twentieth century depended on just such a propositional calculus. But there were also significant developments in modal logic in the Middle Ages within an Aristotelian context, when Aristotle's own modal syllogistic was superseded by much more sophisticated systems. Again, not all propositions in which words such as 'can' and 'must' occur within the predicate can be replaced by propositions in which the modal operator attaches to an entire nested proposition. 'I can speak French', for instance, does not have the same meaning as 'It is possible that I am speaking French'. Aristotle makes a distinction between two-way possibilities (such as a man's ability to walk, or not to walk, as he chooses) and one-way possibilities (fire can burn

---

[8] This passage of the *de Interpretatione* has also been the subject of voluminous discussion in modern times. My interpretation owes a lot to that of G. E. M. Anscombe, whose 'Aristotle and the Sea-Battle' of 1956 (*From Parmenides to Wittgenstein* (Oxford: Blackwell, 1981)) is still, nearly fifty years on, one of the best commentaries on the passage. For a carefully argued alternative account, see S. Waterlow, *Passage and Possibility: A Study of Aristotle's Modal Concepts* (Oxford: Clarendon Press, 1982), 78–109.
[9] Kneale and Kneale, *The Development of Logic*, 91.

wood, and if it has wood placed on it, it *will* burn it, and there are no two ways about it) (*Int.* 22ᵇ36–23ᵃ11). The logic of the two-way abilities exercised in human choice has not, to this day, been adequately formalized.

Stoic Logic

In the generation after Aristotle modal logic was developed in an interesting way in the school of Megara. For Diodorus Cronos a proposition is possible iff it either is or will be true, is impossible iff it is false and will never be true, and is necessary iff it is true and will never be false.[10] Diodorus, like Aristotle, accepted that propositions were fundamentally tensed and could change their truth-values; but unlike Aristotle he does not need to make a sharp distinction between actuality and potentiality, since potentialities are defined in terms of actualities. Propositions, on Diodorus' definitions, change not only their truth-values but also their modalities. 'The Persian Empire has been destroyed' was untrue but possible when Socrates was alive; after Alexander's victories it was true and necessary (LS 38ᴇ). For Diodorus, as for Aristotle, a special necessity applies to the past.

It is a feature of Diodorus' definition of possibility that there are no possibilities that are forever unrealized: whatever is possible is or will be one day true. This appears to involve a form of fatalism: no one can ever do anything other than what they in fact do. Diodorus seems to have supported this by a line of reasoning that became known (we know not why) as the Master Argument. Starting from the premiss (1) that past truths are necessary, Diodorus offered a proof that nothing is possible that neither is nor will be true. Let us suppose (taking an example used in ancient discussions of the argument) that there is a shell in shallow water, let us call it Nautilus, which will never in fact be seen. We can construct an argument from this premiss to show that it is impossible for it to be seen.

(2) Nautilus will not ever be seen.
(3) It has always been the case that
    Nautilus will not ever be seen.   (a plausible consequence of (2))

---

[10] 'Iff' is a logician's abbreviation for 'if and only if'.

Chrysippus, greatest of Stoic logicians, in a statue in the Louvre (third century AD)

(4) It is necessary that Nautilus will
     not ever be seen.   (from (4) and (1))
(5) It is impossible that Nautilus
     will ever be seen.   (necessarily not =
                                          impossible that)

Though we do not know the precise form of Diodorus' proof, it is easy enough to generalize this line of argument to show that only what will happen, can happen.

The argument is obviously akin to one that we met in discussing Aristotle's treatment of future contingents. Diodorus' argument appears to be flawed by an ambiguity in the premiss that past truths are necessary. What is a past truth? If it means a true proposition in the past tense, then there is no guarantee that it is necessary. To see this, we have only to think of a negative proposition in the past tense, such as 'The Persian Empire has not been destroyed.' This proposition was true in the time of Socrates, but it was not necessary: it was about to change its truth-value from true to false. On the other hand, if a past truth is a proposition that is made true by an event in the past, then past truths are indeed necessary; but a proposition such as (4) is not a past truth and hence does not entail (5).[11]

Diodorus' pupil Philo abandoned his master's modal definitions, and explained possibility in terms of the internal properties of a proposition rather than in terms of its truth-values over time. We do not know how his explanation went, but we know that on his account a piece of wood would be capable of being burnt even if it was never burnt and even if it spent its whole existence on the bed of the ocean (LS 38B).

Philo's major contribution to logic was his definition of the conditional. 'If p, then q', he said, was false in the case in which p was true and q false, and true in the three other possible cases. The truth of a conditional proposition, on this view, does not depend at all on the content of the antecedent or the consequent, but only on their truth-values. Thus, 'If it is night, it is day' will be true whenever it is daytime, and on the assumption that the atomic theory is true, 'If there are no atoms, there are atoms' is true. In treating the conditional in this way Philo anticipated the truth-functional definition of material implication used in modern propositional logic.

---

[11] See A. N. Prior, *Time and Modality* (Oxford: Clarendon Press, 1957), 86–7; Jonathan Barnes in *CHHP* 89–92.

However, the truth-values that determine the truth or falsity of his conditionals are changeable truth-values. This has disadvantages for the formulation of logic, since 'If p, then p' is no longer a logical law: 'If I am sitting, I am sitting' comes out false, as a Philonian conditional, if I rise to my feet between the antecedent and the consequent.

Nonetheless, Philo's definition seems to have been adopted by the Stoic logicians who were the first to offer a formalization of propositional logic. Where Aristotle used letters as variables in his logical texts, the Stoics used numbers; this is a trivial difference, but more importantly, where Aristotle's variables stood in for terms, Stoic variables stood in for whole sentences, or rather for elements that are capable of being whole sentences. In 'If the stars are shining, it is night' neither the antecedent, 'the stars are shining', nor the consequent, 'it is night', are complete sentences, but each set of words is capable of standing on its own as a complete sentence.

Stoic propositional logic was embedded in an elaborate theory of language and signification. The Stoics made a distinction between sound (*phone*), speech (*lexis*), and saying (*logos*). The roar of a beast or of the sea is a sound, but only articulate sound counts as speech. Not all speech, however, is meaningful: humans can utter nonsense words like 'hey nonny no'. Only meaningful speech counts as saying anything (D.L. 7. 57). The sounds and speech of a Greek can be taken in by a non-Greek-speaking barbarian, but the meaning is understood only by someone who knows the language (S.E., *M* 8. 11–12).

The word 'logos', which I have translated 'saying', is a Greek word of very wide meaning: in different contexts it can mean 'word', 'sentence', 'language', 'reason'. It is a noun connected with the common verb 'legein', meaning 'to say'. The Stoics coined a new word from this verbal root, 'lekton'. This means literally 'thing said', but I will leave the word as an untranslated technicality, since there is no exact English equivalent.

The *lekton* plays an important part in the Stoic treatment of the distinction between signs and what they signify. Consider a sentence such as 'Dion is walking', a proposition which may be true or false. Sextus Empiricus, discussing some such sentence, tells us this:

The Stoics said that three items are linked together, the signification, the signifier, and the topic (*tunchanon*). The signifier is a sound, such as 'Dion', the signification is the matter that is portrayed (*deloumenon*) by it. . . . and the topic is the external object such as Dion himself. Of these three items two, the sound and the topic, are material, but one is intangible, the matter signified, i.e. the *lekton*, which is what is true or false. (S.E., *M* 8. 11–12)

The *lekton* is what is said by the sentence, namely *that Dion is walking*. This, as Sextus says, is not a tangible entity like Dion himself, or the name 'Dion', or the whole sentence 'Dion is walking'. Dion, the man, is the topic of the sentence, that is to say, what the sentence is *about*. Whether the sentence is true or false depends on whether the *matter* it portrays[12] obtains or not, i.e. on whether Dion is or is not walking. On the basis of passages such as this, then, we can say that a *lekton* is the content of a sentence in the indicative (cf. Seneca, Ep. 117. 13).

Two qualifications need to be made, however, to this definition of *lekton*.

First, Diogenes Laertius tells us that the Stoics distinguished between self-standing and defective *lekta*. He offers 'active and passive predicates' as a gloss on 'incomplete *lekton*', and explains that a defective *lekton* is one that has a linguistic expression that is incomplete, such as 'is writing', which evokes the question 'Who?' A defective *lekton*, therefore, would be what is said by a predicate, e.g. we may say of someone *that he is writing*. Such a *lekton* remains defective until we make clear who we are talking about, thus specifying a topic, e.g. Socrates (D.L. 7. 63).

Secondly, indicative sentences are not the only ones whose contents provide examples of *lekta*. There are also interrogative sentences, which come in two kinds: the questions that can be answered by 'yes' or 'no', such as 'Is it day?', and the questions that need more complicated answers such as 'Where do you live?' Again, there are commands, like 'Take a bath' and exclamations like 'Isn't the Parthenon beautiful!' (D.L. 7. 66–7).

In fact, the definition I offered of *lekton* as the content of a sentence in the indicative really fits only one particular, though most important, kind of *lekton*. This is what the Stoics called an *axioma*. Several definitions of *axioma* are offered. 'An *axioma* is what is true or false, a complete matter capable of assertion in and by itself.' 'An *axioma* is something which can be asserted or denied in and by itself, such as "it is day" or "Dion is walking" ' (D.L. 7. 65). While an *axioma* is capable of being a self-standing assertion, it need not be

---

[12] The customary translation of *deloumenon* as 'revealed' is unsatisfactory since you can only reveal what is in fact the case. If the sentence is false, there is no matter to be revealed.

asserted. Neither of the two quoted *axiomata* are asserted in 'If Dion is walking, then it is day'. Hence some authors translate the word as 'assertable'.[13] The translation is accurate, but cumbrous, and instead I shall use 'proposition' to render *axioma*, since the meaning of the Greek word, as explained, is close to one of the standard meanings of the English word. It is important to remember, however, that a Stoic proposition is unlike an Aristotelian proposition in that it is not a sentence itself, but something abstract that is said by a sentence; and that it is unlike a proposition as discussed by modern logicians since it is something that can change its truth-value over time.

The Stoics distinguished between simple and non-simple propositions. Simple propositions are constantly illustrated by 'It is day' and 'It is night'; but they include three kinds of subject–predicate propositions, which differ depending on whether their subject is a demonstrative, a proper name, or a pronoun functioning as a quantifier. 'That one is walking' they called a definite proposition, 'Someone is walking' an indefinite proposition, and 'Socrates is walking' an intermediate proposition. Non-simple propositions are those that are compounded out of different propositions by means of one or more connectives (*sundesmoi*). Examples are 'If it is day, it is light', 'Since it is day, it is light', 'Either it is day or it is night' (D.L. 7. 71).

It is in their treatment of non-simple propositions that the Stoics approached most nearly to the modern propositional calculus based on truth-functional operators.[14] A number of differences, however, need to be marked.

In the modern calculus the negation sign is treated as a truth-functional operator, on a par with binary connectives such as 'and', 'or', and 'if'. The Stoics, by contrast, classified negative propositions as simple propositions. They did, however, recognize the possibility of negating a proposition by attaching a negative sign to the entire proposition and not just to the predicate, the procedure that is essential to the operation of the propositional calculus. Thus, they preferred 'Not: it is day' to 'It is not day'. They recognized further that negation could be applied to complex as well as simple propositions; and they realized that in such a case care needed to be

---

[13] e.g. Suzanne Bobzien in *CHHP* 93 ff.

[14] A logical operator (i.e. a symbol that forms a new proposition out of one or more other propositions) is truth-functional iff the truth-value of the new proposition depends only on the truth-value of the original propositions, and not on their content.

exercised in order to sort out genuine from spurious contradictories. 'It is day and it is light' was not the contradictory of 'It is day and it is not light'. The contradictory must be formed by attaching the negation sign at the beginning so that it governs the entire proposition. Thus the notion of *scope* enters into the history of logic, (S.E., *M*. 8. 88–90).

Another difference between Stoic logic and modern propositional logic comes out in the treatment of individual connectives. 'Or' in modern propositional logic is treated by convention as an inclusive connective: this is to say, '*p* or *q*' comes out true if *p* and *q* are both true and not just when only one of them is true. The Stoics seem to have been undecided between this view and the exclusive interpretation according to which '*p* or *q*' is true if and only if one and only one of the constituent propositions is true. Moreover, the Stoics allowed among the connectives that form complex propositions some that are not truth-functional. Whether a proposition of the form 'Since *p* then *q*' is true is determined not simply by the truth-values of the constituent propositions.

With regard to the conditional connective 'if', there is some uncertainty how far the Stoics accepted Philo's truth-functional interpretation of it, according to which 'If *p* then *q*' is true in every case except when '*p*' is true and '*q*' is false. Sextus Empiricus roundly attributes this view to them in the following passage:

A sound conditional is one that does not have a true antecedent and a false consequent. A conditional may have a true antecedent and a true consequent, e.g. 'If it is day it is light'. It may have a false antecedent and a false consequent, e.g. 'If the earth flies, the earth has wings'. It may have a true antecedent and a false consequent, e.g. 'If the earth exists, the earth flies'. Or it may have a false antecedent and a true consequent, e.g. 'If the earth flies, the earth exists'. Of these they say that only the one with the true antecedent and the false consequent is unsound, all the others are sound. (S.E., *P*. 2. 104–6)

The examples given here support Sextus' assertion that the Stoics interpreted the conditional truth-functionally. It is characteristic of such an interpretation that the truth of a conditional does not demand any link between the content of the antecedent and the content of the consequent. While 'If the earth flies, the earth has wings' may be linked by the thought that whatever flies has wings, no such link connects 'the earth exists' with 'the earth flies'. Of course, the conditionals in which the Stoics were most interested were ones in which such a link did exist; as in an example given by Sextus shortly afterwards: 'If she has milk, she has conceived'. But the same would be true of most of the examples in a modern textbook even though the logic it expounds is firmly based on a truth-functional interpretation of the basic form of conditional.

On the other hand, there are passages suggesting that at least some Stoics took a different view of the truth-conditions of conditional propositions. Chrysippus is reported as saying that in 'If *p* then *q*' the connective declared that *q followed from p*. This was glossed, by himself or by another Stoic, in the following way:

A conditional is true when the contradictory of its consequent conflicts with its antecedent. For instance, 'If it is day, it is light' is true because 'It is not light', the contradictory of the consequent, conflicts with 'It is day'. A conditional is false when the contradictory of its consequent does not conflict with the antecedent, such as 'If it is day, Dion is walking' because 'Not: Dion is walking' does not conflict with 'It is day'. (D.L. 7. 73)

Here it seems clear that 'conflict' must refer to some kind of incompatibility of content between antecedent and consequent, and not just a difference of truth-value. But the exact nature of the incompatibility (is it logical? is it discovered empirically?) remains unclear.

It is, fortunately, not necessary to resolve these uncertainties in order to present and evaluate the Stoic theory of inference. Whereas Aristotle had indicated each of his syllogisms by listing the conditional necessary truths corresponding to them, the Stoics present their arguments in the form of inference schemata, sometimes using numbers as variables and sometimes using standard examples, and sometimes a mixture of the two as in 'If Plato is alive, Plato is breathing. But the first, therefore the second.' An inference, most Stoics said, must consist of a first premiss (*lemma*), a second premiss (*proslepsis*), and a conclusion (*epiphora*). It was a minority view that an inference might sometimes have only a single premiss (D.L. 7. 76).

The criterion for the invalidity of an inference was analogous to the one Chrysippus offered for the truth-value of a conditional. An inference was valid (*perantikos*) if the contradictory of the conclusion conflicted with the conjunction of the premisses; if it did not conflict, then the inference was invalid. A typical invalid inference was 'If it is day, it is light. But it is day. Therefore Dion is walking' (D.L. 7. 77). Nowadays we are accustomed to distinguish between valid inferences and sound inferences. An inference may be valid but unsound if one or more of its premisses is untrue. The Stoics made a similar distinction, but used the Greek word for 'true', *alethes*, to correspond to 'sound' and 'false' to correspond to 'unsound'. An inference was unsound, they said, if either it was invalid or it contained some falsity in its premisses (D.L. 7. 79).

Inferences came in various forms, called 'moods'. Chrysippus listed five basic forms of valid inference, or 'indemonstrable moods' (D.L. 7. 79). They may be set out as follows, using cardinal numbers rather than ordinals.

(A) If 1 then 2; but 1; therefore 2.
(B) If 1 then 2; but not 2; therefore not 1.
(C) Not both 1 and 2; but 1; therefore not 2.
(D) Either 1 or 2; but 1; therefore not 2.
(E) Either 1 or 2; but not 2; therefore 1.

All valid inferences, Chrysippus believed, could be reduced to these primitive forms, and in his many lost works he seems to have proved many theorems which reduced more complex and derivative moods to these simple patterns. Thus, if we take

(F) If 1, then if 1 then 2; but 1; therefore 2,

we can show this is a valid inference schema by deriving from the two premisses in accordance with (A) 'If 1 then 2', and then using (A) once more to derive, from this conclusion and the second premiss '2' (S.E., *M* 8. 234–6).

On the face of it, Chrysippus' five primitive schemata form neither a complete nor an irreducible basis for deductions within the propositional calculus. There is no primitive proposition to justify the inference of 'p' from 'both p and q'; this, no doubt, is because of the reluctance to consider inferences with only a single premiss. The fourth primitive schema is valid only if 'or' is given its exclusive interpretation; but if it is, then it is not needed, since any inference that it validates will already have been validated by (C).

In late antiquity Aristotelian logic and Stoic logic were regarded as rivals, and while the Stoics' own writings have not survived, we have much evidence of polemics between supporters of the two systems. With the hindsight of millennia we can see that the systems were not in general incompatible with each other, but were formulations of different areas of logic, each of them precursors of different, but complementary, modern developments, in the propositional and predicate calculus.

4

Knowledge and its Limits: Epistemology

There is a branch of philosophy nowadays called epistemology: the inquiry into what can be known, and how we can know it. We all have many beliefs on many topics; which, if any of them, can count as real knowledge? What is the mark of genuine knowledge and how does it differ from mere belief? Is there a reliable way to acquire knowledge of the truth to eliminate false beliefs that are mere seemings? These questions occupied the attention of Greek thinkers from an early stage.

Presocratic Epistemology

Parmenides might well claim to be the founder of epistemology: at least he is the first philosopher to make a systematic distinction between knowledge and belief. At the beginning of his great poem a goddess promises that he will learn all things, both reliable truth and the untrustworthy opinions of mortals. The poem is in two parts: the way of truth and the way of seeming. The way of truth sets out Parmenides' theory of Being, which we will consider in Chapter 6 on metaphysics. The way of seeming deals with the world of the senses, the world of change and colour, the world of empty names. Mortals who do not accept the way of truth, sunk in metaphysical error, know nothing at all. Deaf, dazed, and blind, they can be called 'two-headed' because of the internal inconsistencies of their beliefs (KRS 293).

A sharp contrast between reality and appearance also appears in the writing of a very different philosopher, Democritus. For him, atoms and the void are the only two realities and the qualities perceived by the senses are mere appearances. To show that sense-appearances cannot be the truth about things, he argues that they conflict with each other. The sick and the healthy do not agree about the taste of things, men disagree with other animals, and sensory properties appear different even to the same individual at different times (Aristotle, *Metaph Γ* 5. 1009^{b}7). Sense-appearances lead only to belief, not to truth. 'By convention sweet,' he is quoted as saying, 'by convention bitter; by convention hot, by convention cold; by convention colour, but in reality atoms and void' (KRS 549). To say that a proposition such as 'The wind is cold' enunciates a false belief seems not quite the same as saying that it enunciates something that is true only by convention; but whatever exactly Democritus meant, it is clear that he maintained that the senses did not deliver truths about an independent reality.

If I stand in the same wind as you and pronounce it hot, while you pronounce it cold, Democritus would say that neither of us is speaking the truth. The sophist Protagoras took up a quite opposite position: he claimed that each of us is speaking the truth. (Plato, *Tht.* 151e). 'Man is the measure of all things,' he famously said; 'both of things that are that they are, and of things that are not that they are not' (KRS 551). Whatever appears true to a particular person *is* true for that person. All beliefs, therefore, are true: but they have only a relative truth. There is no such thing as the independent, objective truth that Democritus sought, and failed to find, in sense-appearance. Democritus objected that Protagoras' doctrine was self-refuting. If all beliefs are true, then among true beliefs is the belief that not every belief is true (DK 68 A114).

Protagoras might have tried to counter this objection by restricting his claim to the case of sense-perception. The expression 'It appears to me that . . .', and its equivalent in Greek, can cover either sense-impressions or opinions, and this fact is exploited by Democritus in his refutation. Historically, however, Protagoras did not take this route of escape: his interests extended far wider than the realm of sense-perception. Diogenes Laertius tells us that he said that there were two opposed accounts of every matter, and Seneca that he claimed that on every issue one could argue equally well on either side.[1] If A offers arguments for *p*, and B offers arguments for

[1] D. L. 9. 51; DK 80 A20. See J. Barnes, *The Presocratic Philosophers*, rev. edn. (London: Routledge, 1982), ii. 243.

not-*p*, and both sets of arguments are equally good, how should I decide between them? Protagoras appears to suggest that I should not decide, but accept both. But does not this involve accepting both sides of a contradiction? On the contrary, Protagoras denied that contradiction was possible (D.L. 9. 53). What is really accepted is not '*p*' and 'not-*p*' but ' "*p*" is true for A' and ' "not-*p*" is true for B'.

For Protagoras, all truth is relative, and not just truth about obviously subjective matters such as the feel of the wind. For this thesis, so far as we know, he did not offer any argument, merely the analogy between sense-appearances and beliefs, and a personal claim to be able to match any argument pro with an argument contra. But the thesis does give him an escape from Democritus' trap. He can accept 'Some beliefs are false' as true—but true *for Democritus*. He can continue to believe that 'No beliefs are false' is true—true, of course, for himself, for Protagoras. There has to be some other way of sorting out the issue between the two of them—a way which Plato, as we shall see, attempted to provide.

Protagoras is sometimes described as a sceptic. In one way this is an odd description. A sceptic is someone who thinks the discovery of truth is difficult, perhaps impossible. For Protagoras it is all too easy: you only have to frame a belief and, hey presto, it is true. But from the point of view of someone like Democritus, the replacement of a universal, objective concept of truth with a relative one is itself a very deep form of scepticism. The only kind of truth really worth seeking is, for a relativist, impossible to discover because it does not exist.

Democritus himself, however, was in no strong position to reject scepticism. He claimed that there were two kinds of knowledge, one through the senses and one through the intellect. Only intellectual knowledge is legitimate knowledge; the five senses deliver only a bastard version (S.E., *M*. 7. 130–9). There is, however, a problem: the intellectual knowledge expressed in the atomic theory is based in part on empirical evidence: and this comes from the cheating senses. Galen, quoting the dictum about the conventionality of sense-properties, says, 'Having slandered appearances, [Democritus] makes the senses address the intellect thus: "Mind, you wretch! You take your evidence from us and then you throw us over! Our overthrow is your downfall too" ' (KRS 552).

Logically, then, perhaps Democritus should have ended up not as an atomist but as a sceptic. One of his pupils, Metrodorus of Chios, is known to have made an extreme statement of scepticism: 'None of us knows anything, not even whether we know or do not know, nor even what knowing and not knowing are' (DK 70 B1). But this was at the beginning of a book of atomistic physics, so it is hard to know how seriously to take this manifesto. The sophist Gorgias, on the other hand, offered an argument to show that knowledge of reality was impossible. It went like this. If objects of thought (*ta phronoumena*) are not real (*onta*), then what is real is not an object of thought. But objects of thought are not real; for if any of them are, all of them are, just as they are thought. But just because someone thinks of a man flying or chariots running on the sea, that does not mean that there is a flying man or chariots running on the sea. Hence it is not the case that what is thought of is real; and therefore what is real is not an object of thought (DK 82 B3).

We do not know whether Gorgias meant this argument seriously or not. We need not question that if no object of thought is a reality, then no reality is an object of thought. The weak point in the argument seems to be the claim that if some object of thought is real, then all objects of thought are real. The very choice of examples suggests that we can distinguish between those cases where an object of thought is not real and those cases where it is real (i.e. when the thought has a reality corresponding to it).

Socrates, Knowledge, and Ignorance

Protagoras and Gorgias were sophists, and it was a regular complaint against the sophists that they were purveyors of scepticism. Some thought that Socrates was tarred with the same brush. Socrates certainly went round puncturing other people's claims to knowledge, and prided himself on his awareness of his own ignorance. But he never challenged claims to knowledge when made by craftsmen and experts in their own particular fields. Indeed, over and over again, in Plato's Socratic dialogues, we are given a run through half a dozen arts and crafts—shoemaking, shipbuilding, navigation, cookery, medicine—to provide a paradigm of knowledge against which to test and find wanting the pretensions of those who claim moral and political knowledge. If Socrates was a sceptic, his scepticism was of a limited and contingent kind. It was only of certain important things that knowledge was unavailable; and it was not necessarily

Socrates seen through Roman eyes in a wall-painting from Ephesus

unavailable to human beings, it was just not to be found in the Athens of the day.

But in order to evaluate Socrates' epistemology, and still more in order to understand the epistemological theses that Plato in his dialogues puts in Socrates' mouth, it is necessary to discuss the different Greek words that correspond more or less to the English word 'knowledge'. The word 'epistemology' itself is derived from the Greek word 'episteme' a word that is often used to indicate knowledge of a rather grand kind, so that one of its English equivalents is 'science'. Besides the verb 'epistamai' which goes with this noun, there are humbler words for more everyday knowledge and acquaintance. Hence, someone who denies the possibility of *episteme* in a particular area is not necessarily a sceptic ruling out the possibility of all knowledge.

The Delphic oracle pronounced that no one was wiser than Socrates. After interrogating those who had a reputation for wisdom (*sophia*), Socrates came to the conclusion that he was wiser than them in that he did not falsely believe he knew matters that he did not know. Questioning the politicians and the poets, he concluded that they did not have any real knowledge of the areas in which they had made their reputation. When he went to the craftsmen, however, he did find that they had knowledge (*episteme*) of many things where he was ignorant, and to that extent they were wiser than he was. The problem was that on the basis of their particular expertise, they foolishly thought themselves wise on totally different, and more important, topics. Socrates decided that he was better off than they, lacking both their wisdom and their ignorance (*Apol.* 22d–e).

In Plato's Socratic dialogues there is always someone who claims knowledge in a particular area; typically, a character will claim to know the nature of a particular virtue or craft. Thus, Euthyphro claims to have knowledge of piety and impiety (*Euthphr.* 4e–5a), Meno is happy to accept that he knows what virtue is (*Men.* 71d–e), and even the modest Charmides thinks he knows what modesty is. Socrates then questions such a character in order to get the knowledge expressed in a definition. As each definition is produced, he declares it deficient, either producing counter-examples or revealing ambiguities in its terms. Counter-examples can take two forms: they can show either that the definition covers more than it should, or that it covers less than it should. Thus, when Cephalus in *Republic* 1 says that justice is telling the truth and returning what is borrowed, Socrates complains that returning a borrowed weapon to a mad friend is not just (*Rep.* 331c–d). On the other hand, when Laches, in the dialogue called after him, says that courage is standing at one's post without running away, Socrates points out that tactical retreat can be an expression of courage (191c). Sooner or later, the alleged expert has to admit that his definition breaks down; and the failure to be able to produce a satisfactory definition is taken to show that the claim to knowledge was unjustified.

The questioning Socrates, in Plato's dialogues, is never satisfied with being offered a list of items falling under a certain concept such as *virtue* or *knowledge*. Meno tells him that there are many different kinds of virtue: one for males, one for females, one for children; one for slaves and one for freemen; one for the young and one for the old. Socrates says that this is no use: it is like telling someone who wants to know what a bee is that there are many different kinds of bee. Bees of different kinds, Socrates says, do not differ from one another in so far as they are bees; and what we want to find out is that very thing in which they are all the same and do not differ from one another (*Men.* 72c). So too with virtue. Socrates, we might say, is looking for the *essence* of virtue.

Knowledge of the essence of something is clearly a very special kind of knowledge: and ever since Plato's Socrates it has been for many philosophers a paradigm of knowledge. Other philosophers, in recent times, have criticized Socratic insistence on knowledge of essences. Wittgenstein pointed out that among the items that most interest philosophers some may not have such an essence at all. He denied, for instance, that everything we call language possesses one feature in common which makes us use the same word for all. Rather, these phenomena are related to one another in many different ways, just as different members of the same family will resemble each other in different features such as build, gait, colour, temperament, and so on.[2] Even where X does have an essence, being able to define that essence or to articulate an exceptionless criterion for distinguishing Xs from not Xs is not a necessary condition for being genuinely able to tell an X when one sees one. Thus, I can know that a computer is not alive without being able to produce a watertight criterion to separate life from non-life.[3]

---

[2] L. Wittgenstein, *Philosophical Investigations* (Oxford: Blackwell, 1958), 1. 66–7.
[3] The denial of this is called by Peter Geach 'the Socratic Fallacy' (*God and the Soul* (London: Routledge, 1969), 40).

We can agree that knowledge, in the everyday sense of the English word, can be present in the absence of the power to define and delimit. It might well be thought, however, to be the special task of the philosopher to seek for essences, or, as the case may be, to lay out the family resemblances between different applications of a concept. The goal of this special task is to reach a level of knowledge, or at least understanding, that is superior to that possessed by the ordinary informal employer of a concept. And it was for this level of insight that Plato, in his mature dialogues, came to reserve the Greek word 'episteme'.

Knowledge in the Theaetetus

One of the richest of Plato's dialogues, the Theaetetus, is devoted to the question: What is knowledge (episteme)? (145e). This dialogue, though not an early one, has the structure usual for a Socratic dialogue: the protagonist (in this case a brilliant young mathematician) offers a series of definitions, all in turn are rejected by Socrates, and the drama ends with a proclamation of ignorance. The young Theaetetus, at the beginning of the dialogue, is pregnant with a reply to the question, 'What is knowledge?' Socrates offers himself as midwife to bring it to birth (149a–151d); but the pregnancy turns out to be imaginary, with only a phantom offspring.

Theaetetus' first proposal is that knowledge consists of things like geometry and astronomy, on the one hand, and shoemaking and carpentry on the other (146d). This will not do: Socrates is never happy with a list, and he says that if we tried to define geometry and carpentry the word 'knowledge' itself would turn up in the definition. Theaetetus next suggests that knowledge is perception: to know something is to perceive it with the senses (151e). Socrates observes that since only what is true can be known, knowledge can be sense-perception only if such perception is always correct. But this can only be the case if we accept the thesis of Protagoras that whatever seems to a particular person is true for him.

With regard to momentary sensations, Protagoras' thesis may be given plausibility by the thesis of Heraclitus that the world is in constant flux. The colours we see are not stable objects: when my eye encounters a piece of marble, the whiteness of the marble and my vision of that whiteness are two momentary items, twins begotten together by the encounter of the parent eye and the parent marble (156c–d). If, then, on a particular occasion I say 'This is white', I cannot be wrong: no one else is in a position to contradict me. The same is true of other kinds of sense-perception (157a).

Let us suppose we concede to Protagoras that, in such a case, what the perceiver says goes. Still, Socrates insists, there are many other kinds of case where it would be absurd to make such a claim. We have dreams in which we think we are flying; a man may go mad and think he is a god. Surely these are cases where what seems to a person is not true? And even the ordinary cases, where the perception is not erroneous, cannot be cases of real knowledge. For how can we be sure that we are not dreaming? Half our life is spent abed, and it is a commonplace that it is impossible to prove that one is awake and not asleep (158c–e).

At this point Socrates offers Theaetetus (and Protagoras) a response—rather a feeble response, since it deals with the case not of dreamers or madmen, but of sick people whose senses are affected by their disease. Suppose Socrates falls ill, and sweet wine begins to taste sour to him. On the Heraclitean account, the taste of the wine is the offspring of the wine and the taster. Socrates sick is a different taster from Socrates healthy, and with a different parent naturally the offspring differs. It may not be true that the wine is sour, but it is, in his sickness, sour for Socrates. So we do not have here a case of erroneous perception, and the equivalence of knowledge and perception is not yet defeated.

Socrates in the dialogue moves on to different terrain. There are cases of perception without knowledge: we can hear a foreign language spoken, and yet not know the language (163b). There are cases of knowledge without perception: when we shut our eyes and recall something we have seen, we know what it looks like and yet are no longer seeing it (164a). But if knowing = perception, then both these must be cases of simultaneously knowing and not knowing, and surely that is an absurdity? But even now, Socrates is willing to allow Protagoras a way out. It is easy to have cases of simultaneous perception and non-perception: if you wear an eyepatch you see something with one eye but not with the other. So if perception = knowledge, it is no surprise that you can both know and not know at the same time (165c).

In discussing Theaetetus' identification of knowledge and perception, Plato's Socrates gives Protagoras a surprising amount of rope. But he is, in the end, confident that Protagoras hangs himself on Democritus' hook. It seems to all men that some men know better than others: if so, that must—according to Protagoras—be true for all men. It seems to most people that Protagoras' thesis is false; if so, his thesis must be, on his own account, more false than true, since the unbelievers outnumber the believers (170b–171d). But his thesis can be attacked more directly. However plausible it may be if applied to sense-perception, it cannot apply to medical diagnosis or political prediction. Even if each man is an authority on what he senses *now*, he is not the measure of what he *will* feel or perceive: a physician knows better than a patient whether the patient will later feel hot or cold, and a vintner will know better than a drinker whether a wine, come next year, will taste sweet or dry (178c).

The final argument by which Socrates leads Theaetetus to abandon the proposal that knowledge is perception is this. The objects of the senses are delivered to us through different channels: we see with our eyes and hear with our ears. Colours are not the same as sounds; we cannot hear colours and we cannot see sounds. But what of the judgement 'Colours are not the same as sounds'? Where does that piece of knowledge come from? It cannot come from the eyes, since they cannot see sounds; it cannot come from the ears, since they cannot hear colours. Moreover, there are no organs for detecting sameness, in the way that there are organs for seeing and hearing. The soul itself contemplates the common terms that apply to the deliverances of all of the senses (184b–185d).

Theaetetus, in response to this argument, moves to a second proposed definition of knowledge. Knowledge is not perception (*aesthesis*); it is thought (*doxa*), and thought is an activity of the soul by itself. When the mind is thinking, it is as if it were talking to itself, asking and answering questions, and silently forming opinions. Knowledge cannot be identified outright with thought, because there are false thoughts; but perhaps we can say that knowledge is true thought (187a5).

Socrates, after an interesting diversion in which he points out that the notion of 'false thought' is not without its problems, offers an objection to this definition. There are cases where people have true thoughts, and form true opinions, without having actual knowledge. If a jury is persuaded by a clever attorney to bring in a certain verdict, then if the verdict accords with the facts, the jurors will have formed a true opinion. But do their true thoughts amount to knowledge? Not really, says Socrates: only an eyewitness is in a position really to know what happened in a case of alleged assault or robbery. So knowledge cannot be defined as true thought.

Socrates showed earlier that knowledge is not perception by giving an example of a piece of knowledge for which perception was insufficient. He has now shown that knowledge is not true opinion by giving an example of a piece of knowledge for which perception was necessary. It might be expected that Theaetetus might have responded by offering an account of knowledge embracing both perception and thought in some relation to each other. Instead he offers an elaboration of his second definition. Knowledge, he now suggests, is true thought plus a *logos*; and he proposes three forms that the *logos* may take (206c).

'Logos', as has been remarked, is a difficult word to translate because it corresponds to many different English words: 'word' itself, 'sentence', 'discourse', 'reason'. In the present context it is clear that for Theaetetus a true thought with a *logos* is a thought that is somehow articulated in a way that a thought without a *logos* is not: but I shall leave the word untranslated while explaining the different kinds of articulation he has in mind.

One way in which one can give a *logos* of a thought is by expressing it in words. But being able to articulate a thought in this sense cannot be what makes the difference between true thought and knowledge, since anyone who is not dumb is capable of doing so (206d–e).

More plausibly, a *logos* may be a kind of analysis. To know what X is is to be able to analyse it into its elements. Thus one can exhibit knowledge of a word by spelling it out in letters. If that is what knowledge is, then knowledge of reality must be exhibited in analysing it into the ultimate elements of which it is composed. But the analogy with spelling places us in a difficulty. The word 'Socrates' can be analysed into its elements, such as the letter S. But the letter S cannot be further analysed; unlike the word 'Socrates', the letter S has no spelling. So if knowledge involves analysis, the ultimate, unanalysable elements of the universe cannot be known. And if the elements of a complex cannot be known, how can the complex itself be known? Moreover, a mere listing of the elements of a complex is insufficient for knowledge unless the elements are put together in the correct way (207b).

Theaetetus' final account of giving a *logos* of an object is giving a description that is uniquely true of it: thus one might give a *logos* of the sun by saying that it is the brightest of the heavenly bodies. But does this amount to real knowledge of the sun? Surely, being able to offer some definite description of X is a necessary condition of having any thought at all about X; it is not sufficient to turn a true thought about X into a piece of genuine knowledge.

At this point Theaetetus gives up. The thoughts he has delivered with the aid of Socrates' midwifery turn out to be mere wind-eggs. We are far from having reached a definition of knowledge; and hence all the use of words like 'know' and 'not know' throughout the dialogue turns out to have been illegitimate (196e).

Perhaps Theaetetus gave up too soon. If he had offered a fourth account of 'logos' as meaning something like 'justification', 'reason', or 'evidence', then his definition of knowledge as true belief plus *logos* would have been found satisfactory by many a philosopher during the subsequent millennia of philosophy. But Plato's Socrates was a hard man to satisfy, and Plato himself, in the sixth and seventh books of his *Republic*, has his Socrates present quite a different epistemology in quite a different style.

Knowledge and Ideas

The presentations in the two dialogues differ above all because the *Republic* appeals, as the *Theaetetus* does not, to Plato's Theory of Ideas. Common to both dialogues is the principle that what is known must be true; knowledge can only be of what *is*. The Ideas are relevant in the *Republic* because Plato is committed to the thesis that only the Ideas really *are*: that is to say, everything other than an Idea is what it is only in a qualified sense. Beautiful things other than the Idea of Beauty, for instance, are beautiful only at one time and not another, or beautiful only in one part and not in another. Nothing except the Idea of Beauty is just beautiful, period (*Smp.* 211a). The Ideas make their first appearance in the *Republic* in the fifth book, where Plato is describing the philosopher. He describes him as the lover of truth, and distinguishes him from the mere dilettante, the lover of sights and sounds.

The non-philosopher does not know the difference between beautiful objects and beauty itself: he is living in a dream, mistaking an image for reality (*Rep.* 476c–d). For the state of mind (*dianoia*) of such a person, Plato uses the word 'doxa', which in the *Theaetetus* was used for thought, or belief. He contrasts it with the knowledge that belongs to the philosopher—here called *gnome*. If knowledge must be knowledge of what *is*, and only an Idea utterly *is*, then knowledge must be knowledge of Ideas. If there is anything at the opposite pole from an Idea, something that utterly *is not*, that is totally unknowable. But most things that are F are partly F and partly not F, F in one respect and not in another. They are set in between what is utterly F and what is utterly not F. These are the objects of *doxa*.

At this point a fundamental difference emerges between the *Republic* and the *Theaetetus*. In the *Theaetetus* we sought to locate the essential characteristic of knowledge as a feature of the state of mind of the knower: is it a matter of sensation? must it include a *logos*? But in the *Republic* the difference between knowledge and belief is a difference between objects: between *what* is known and *what* is thought of. This point is made quite explicitly. Knowledge and thought, Plato says, are *powers* (*dynameis*), just as sight and hearing are powers. Powers do not have colours or shapes by which we can tell one from another. 'In the case of a power I look only at what it is concerned with and what it does to it, and by reference to that I call each the power it is' (477d). Sight is a power to discriminate colour, and hearing a power to discriminate sound: it is the difference between the objects, colour and sound, that distinguishes these two powers from each other. Similarly, Plato proposes, the difference between knowledge and belief is to be determined by noting the differences between the two kinds of object with which they deal (478b6 ff.).

In book 6 Plato takes this line of argument further, and subdivides *gnome* and *doxa*. *Doxa*, or thought, has the visible world as its realm, but it comes in two different forms that have different objects. One form is imagination (*eikasia*), whose objects are shadows and reflections; another form is belief (*pistis*), whose objects are the living creatures about us and the works of nature or of human hands. The realm of *gnosis*, of knowledge, is likewise divided into two. Knowledge *par excellence* is *noesis*, or understanding, whose object is the Ideas that are the province of the philosopher. But there is also another kind of knowledge, typical of the mathematician, to which Plato gives the name *dianoia* (509c5 ff.). The abstract objects of the mathematician share with the Ideas the characteristic of eternity and unchangeability: they

According to Plato, human knowledge is like that of prisoners chained in a cave who can see nothing except shadows cast on the inner wall by puppets on a screen at the entrance. Only the mathematician and the philosopher can escape from the cave into the real world of daylight. (Flemish school, sixteenth century)

belong to the world of being, not of becoming. But they also share a characteristic with ordinary terrestrial objects, namely they are multiple and not single. The geometer's circles, unlike the Ideal Circle, can intersect with each other; and the arithmetician's twos, unlike the one and only Idea of Two, can be added to each other to make four (cf. 525c–526a).

Plato distinguishes between the mathematician and the philosopher on the basis not only of the different objects of their disciplines, but also of the different methods of their investigation. Mathematicians, he complains, start from hypotheses which they treat as obvious and do not feel called upon to give an account of. The philosopher, however, though starting likewise from hypotheses, does not, like the mathematician, immediately move down from hypotheses to conclusions, but ascends first from hypotheses to an unhypothetical principle, and only then redescends from premiss to conclusion. Philosophical method is called by Plato 'dialectic'; and dialectic, he says, 'treats its assumptions, not as first principles, but literally as hypotheses, like stepping stones or starting points on a journey up to an unhypothetical first principle'. Having grasped this principle, dialectic 'goes into reverse, and, keeping hold of what follows from the principle, finally comes down to a conclusion' (511b). The upward path of dialectic is described again in book 7 as a course of 'taking up what has been laid down and travelling up to the first principle of all'. 'Taking up what has been laid down' is equivalent to unhypothesizing the hypotheses, which in a particular case may mean either abandoning a hypothesis, or placing it on an unhypothetical foundation (533c).

Scholars have not been able to reach agreement on the precise nature of dialectic, as envisaged by Plato, but in broad outline we can say that the dialectician operates as follows. He takes a hypothesis, a questionable assumption, and tries to show that it leads to a contradiction. When he reaches a contradiction, he abandons the hypothesis and goes on to test the other premisses used to derive the contradiction, and so on until he reaches a premiss that is unquestionable. The procedure can be illustrated in the *Republic* itself.

In book 1 three characters in the dialogue, Cephalus, Polemarchus, and Thrasymachus, each offer definitions of justice, which are shown by Socrates to be unsatisfactory. Cephalus' proposal that justice is telling the truth and returning what is borrowed is refuted because, Socrates claims, it is not just to return a weapon to a mad friend (331c). But this refutation depends on an implicit definition of justice as doing good to one's friends and harm to one's enemies. When this definition is made explicit by Polemarchus (332b ff.), it is refuted on the grounds that it is never just to harm any man at all. This refutation, in its turn, depends on the premiss that justice is human goodness: it is surely preposterous to think that a good man could exercise his goodness in making others less good. But Thrasymachus leaps in to challenge this premiss: justice is not goodness, but weakness and foolishness (338c). Eventually, Thrasymachus too is refuted, when he is forced to agree that the just man will have a better life than the unjust (354a). His surrender is exacted by a number of hypotheses that are themselves questionable and most of which are questioned elsewhere in the *Republic*.

For instance, one hypothesis assumed against Thrasymachus is that it is the soul's function to direct the person whose soul it is. This hypothesis is reviewed when, in book 4, Socrates divides the soul into three parts: this directing function belongs not to the whole soul but only to reason. In establishing the trichotomy Socrates appeals to the following principle: it is not the case 'that the same thing can ever act or be acted upon in two opposite ways, or be two opposite things, at the same time, in respect of the same part of itself, and in relation to the same object' (437a). This, which seems at first to be a harmless principle of non-contradiction, turns out to be, in Plato's eyes, a hypothesis that is not true of anything except the Ideas. So the dialectician on his upward path has to move into the realm of Ideas.

The path to a full understanding of the nature of justice would go through the different degrees of cognition identified by Plato on book 6. The first degree is what Plato calls imagination. Someone who reads the poets and watches dramatic spectacles (provided the texts are of an approved kind) will have seen justice triumphing on the stage and will have learnt that the gods are unchanging, good, and truthful (382c). From this he will proceed to true belief about justice: this will be equivalent to competence in the human justice that operates in the law courts. But to learn what ideal justice is, and to see how it takes its place in the system of Ideas which is presided over by the supreme Idea, the Idea of Good, will be the task of dialectic. Sadly, as he approaches the end of the upward path of dialectic, to learn from goodness itself the first principles of law and morality, the Socrates of the *Republic*, like Moses on Mount Sinai, disappears into a cloud. He can talk only in metaphor, and cannot give even a provisional account of goodness itself (506d).

The obscurity of the Theory of Ideas, and in particular of the Idea of the Good, means that there is a hole at the centre of the epistemology of the *Republic*. What it is to have knowledge of an Idea, and how such knowledge is acquired, is never there explained. Other dialogues—the *Phaedo*, the *Meno*—put forward a startling suggestion to fill this gap. Knowledge of Ideas is essentially recollection: recollection of acquaintance in an earlier, more spiritual life. This proposal, more metaphysical than epistemological, will be considered in a later chapter.

160

Aristotle on Science and Illusion

In epistemology, as in other matters, Aristotle's agenda was set by Plato. He accepted Plato's distinction between the senses and the intellect, and attached great importance to it, often attacking earlier thinkers, such as Empedocles and Democritus, for failing to appreciate the distinction between sensation and thought (e.g. *Metaph. Γ* 5.1009^{b}14 ff.). With the *Theaetetus* in mind, he addressed once again the Protagorean question of the reliability and fallibility of the senses. Finally, he took over and developed the Platonic catalogue of different intellectual states; and set out criteria for the attainment of the highest such state, namely scientific knowledge.

Plato frequently emphasized the unstable and confusing nature of sense-experience. For instance, in the tenth book of the *Republic* he wrote, 'Things look crooked when seen in water and straight when seen out of it; things can look both concave and convex because colours mislead the eye; and all kinds of similar confusion are manifest in our souls' (602c–d). He contrasted this with the constancy of the results of the calculations and measurements carried out by the reasoning part of the soul.

Aristotle considers the epistemic status of the senses in the course of defending the principle of contradiction against Protagorean arguments in *Metaphysics Γ* (5. 1009^{b}1 ff.). The problem arises from the occurrence of conflicting sense-impressions. We have these four propositions.

(1) Sense says that *p*.
(2) Sense says that not-*p*.
(3) What Sense says is true.
(4) Not both *p* and not-*p*.

This is an inconsistent quartet: any three of the propositions can be used to prove the falsity of the fourth. This possibility is used in different ways by different protagonists in to the debate that Aristotle is addressing. Democritus and Plato, followed by sceptics ancient and modern, accept (1), (2), and (4) as showing the falsity of (3). Aristotle's Protagoreans accept (1), (2), and (3) as showing the falsity of (4). In modern times some philosophers have sought to defend (3) and (4) by qualifying (1) and (2) and introducing the notion of sense-data. Sense, according to these philosophers, does not really say that the stick is straight and that the stick is not straight; it says that here and now there is a visual non-straight-looking sense-datum, and here and now there is a tactile straight-feeling sense-datum.

Aristotle, like the sense-datum theorists, deals with the inconsistent quartet by qualifying (1) and (2). But he does not do so by altering the content of *p*. The senses do tell us about external realities and not about an alleged purely mental entity such as a sense-datum. He solves his problems by focusing on Sense. Wherever we have an apparent case of Sense saying that *p*, and Sense saying that not-*p*, we really have a case of one sense S1 saying that *p*, and another sense S2 saying that not-*p*. Not all that the senses tell us is true, and if S1 and S2 tell us different stories we can give reasons for making a choice between them.

It is an essential part of the Protagorean contention that where two judgements of sense conflict, there should be no reason for preferring the one to the other in regard of truth. But someone might say that in the case of the conflict of tastes between healthy and sick, we are to prefer the report of the healthy, since this is the opinion of the majority. The reply to this that Aristotle offers Protagoras is that we cannot treat majority opinion as the criterion of truth. If a worldwide epidemic broke out, those now called healthy might be outnumbered, and there would no longer be reason to accept as true their opinion that honey is sweet (*Metaph.* Γ. 5. 1009^{a}1–5).

Aristotle can agree that the reason for preferring healthy perception to diseased perception must be something other than statistical. But he counters the Protagorean conclusion by saying that everyone does in fact grade appearances and no one treats them as all equally trustworthy. If you doze off in Libya and dream you are in Athens, you do not, on waking, set off for the Athens theatre (*Metaph.* Γ. 5. 1010^{b}11). Aristotle offers a number of criteria for ranking sense-appearances when it is necessary to choose between them, the most important of which is that a sense has priority when it is judging its proper object.

The proper object of each sense is defined in the *de Anima* (2. 6. 418^{a}12) as being that which cannot be perceived by another sense, and that about which it is impossible to be deceived: colour is the proper object of sight, sound of hearing, and flavour of taste. Aristotle's first point is clear enough: we cannot taste a colour, hear a flavour, or see a sound. But what is meant by saying that a sense cannot be deceived about its proper object? Aristotle is quick to explain that if I see something white, I can be mistaken about whether it is a man or something else, but not about whether it is white or not (3. 6. 430^{b}29). This makes it look as if he is saying simply that if when you use your eyes, and confine yourself to making statements about how things look to you here and now, then you cannot go wrong. But this cannot be what he means, for he clearly envisages there being genuine conflicts between two deliverances of a single sense, and he offers rules for sorting them out: in the case of sight, for instance, prefer a closer glimpse to a more distant one.

So the infallibility of the senses about their proper objects, for Aristotle, does not mean that whatever appears to a particular sense within its own competence is true. Not all statements made about colour on the basis of using our eyes are true: what appears to be red may not be red. Statements such as 'That is red' made on the basis of visual experience are not incorrigible. What is special about them is that they can be corrected only by a further use of the same sense. If we are not sure whether a thing really is the colour it looks from here to me now, we check by having a better look, by looking closer, by looking in a better light. Against the verdict of any particular look an appeal lies; but where what is in question is colour, the appeal can never go to a court higher than that of sight. With qualities proper to other senses, or senses perceptible by more than one sense (the 'common sensibles'), sight does not have the final verdict (*Metaph. Γ. 5.* 1010^{b}15–18). So, generalizing: each sense is the final judge in the case of its proper object, though it has to get into the right condition and position to judge. Where S1 and S2 tells us different things about sensory properties, S1 is to be preferred over S2 if S1 is the proper sense, and S2 is the alien sense, for the property in question. Between two verdicts of the proper sense, we are to choose the one delivered in optimum conditions: near, not far; healthy, not ill; awake not asleep; and so on.

It is thus that Aristotle seeks to avoid both Protagoras' phenomenalism and Plato's intellectualism. He insists that our knowledge depends on the senses both for the concepts we employ and for the unproved premises from which we start. We form concepts thus: first there is sensation and then there is memory; memories build up into experience and out of individual experience we form a universal concept, which is the basis of both practical skill (*techne*) and theoretical knowledge (*episteme*) (*APo.* 19. 100^{a}3). It is for experience, Aristotle says in the *Prior Analytics* (1. 30 46^{a}17–22), to provide the principles of any subject. Astronomers begin with their

163

experience of the heavens, and only after mastering astronomical phenomena do they go on to seek causes and offer proofs. A similar method should be adopted in the life sciences (*APr.* 1. 1. 639^{b}7–10, 640^{b}14–18).

Science begins, but does not end, with experience, and, like Plato, Aristotle has an elaborate classification of cognitive and intellectual states. Both philosophers regard moral virtue and intellectual excellence as two species of a particular genus; but whereas Plato (no doubt under the influence of Socrates) tended to treat virtue as if it was a special kind of science, Aristotle treats science as a special kind of virtue. The Aristotelian counterpart of Plato's anatomy of knowledge occurs in one of the common books of the *Ethics* (*NE* 6, *EE* 5) where he is dealing with intellectual virtues. The Greek word 'arete' corresponds to both 'virtue' and 'excellence'; so I shall leave it, in the present context, untranslated.

The nature of the *arete* of anything depends upon its *ergon*, that is to say its job or characteristic output. The *ergon* of the mind and all its faculties is the production of true and false judgements (*NE* 6. 2. 1139^{a}29). That, at least, is its *ergon* in the sense of its characteristic activity, its output whether it is working well or ill; its activity when it is working well and doing its job, and therefore its *ergon* in the strict sense, is truth alone (2. 1139^{b}12). The intellectual *aretai*, then, are excellences that make an intellectual part of the soul come out with truth. There are five states of mind that have this effect—*techne, episteme, phronesis, sophia, nous*—which we may translate as skill, science, wisdom, understanding, and insight (3. 1139^{b}16–17).

Skill and wisdom are both forms of practical knowledge: knowledge of what to do and how to bring things about. Skills, such as architecture or medicine, are exercised in the production (*poiesis*) of something other than their exercise, whether their output is concrete, like a house, or abstract, like health. Wisdom, on the other hand, is concerned with human activity (*praxis*) itself rather than with its output: it is defined as a ratiocinative excellence that ascertains the truth concerning what is good and bad for human beings (4. 1140^{b}5, ^{b}21).

It is characteristic of the wise man to deliberate well about goods attainable by action: he is not concerned with things that cannot be other than they are (7. 1141^{b}9–13). Thus wisdom differs from science and understanding, which are concerned with unchanging and eternal matters. The rational part of the soul is divided into two parts: the *logistikon* that deliberates and the *epistemonikon* that is concerned with the eternal truths. Each of these parts has its proper *arete*: wisdom for the former and understanding for the latter. Other intellectual virtues turn out to be parts of either *phronesis* or *sophia*: *sophia*, for instance, consists of *nous* plus *episteme* (7. 1141^{b}3–4).

Sophia, Aristotle tells us, has as its subject matter divine, honourable, and useless things: it is what was practised by famous philosophers such as Thales and Anaxagoras. What *nous* is, is not immediately clear: it is a word often used for the whole human intellectual apparatus, for the cognitive as opposed to the affective part of the mind (cf. 1. 1139^{a}17, 2. 1139^{b}5). Here, however, it appears to mean insight into the first principles of theoretical science: the understanding of unproven necessary truths which is the basis of *episteme* (6. 1140^{b}31–41^{a}9). It is this which, in conjunction with *episteme*, constitutes *sophia*, the highest human intellectual achievement.

The *Ethics* does not spell out what is involved in *episteme* or science. That is laid out, explicitly and at length, in the first six chapters of *Posterior Analytics* 1. Aristotle accepts that to know something is the case is to be genuinely acquainted with the explanation of its being the case and to be aware that it cannot be otherwise. If that is what knowledge is, Aristotle says, 'It is necessary for demonstrative knowledge to depend on things that are true and primitive and immediate and better known than the conclusion, to which they must also be prior and of which they must be explanatory' (*APo.* 1. 2. 70^{a}20–2). A body of scientific knowledge is built up out of demonstrations. A demonstration is a particular kind of syllogism: one whose premises can be traced back to principles that are true, necessary, universal, and immediately intuited. These first, self-evident principles are related to the conclusions of science as axioms to theorems.

There is an unsolved problem about the account of science in the *Posterior Analytics*: it bears no resemblance to the substantial corpus of Aristotle's own scientific works. Generations of scholars have tried in vain to find in his writings a single instance of a demonstrative syllogism. To be sure, the *Posterior Analytics* is not a treatise on scientific method, but a set of guidelines for scientific exposition.[4] But Aristotle's treatises are themselves expository, not methodological, and they do not even approximate to the pattern of the *Posterior Analytics*.

---

[4] See J. Barnes, 'Aristotle's Theory of Demonstration', in J. Barnes, M. Schofield, and R. Sorabji (eds.), *Articles on Aristotle*, i: *Science* (London: Duckworth, 1975).

It is not only the Aristotelian corpus that lacks an Aristotelian science: the whole history of scientific endeavour contains no perfect instance of any such science. Many of the examples given by Aristotle are drawn from arithmetic or geometry, and his thought was clearly influenced by the mathematicians of his time. When, after Aristotle's death, Euclid presented his axiomatized geometry, it looked as if the scientific ideal of the *Posterior Analytics* had been fulfilled: but after more than two millennia it was discovered that one of Euclid's axioms lacked the necessary self-evidence. A similar fate, in the twentieth century, overtook Gottlob Frege's project of axiomatizing logic and arithmetic. Spinoza's seventeenth-century attempt to axiomatize philosophy itself served only to show that the ideal held up in the *Posterior Analytics* was a will-o'-the-wisp.

Epicurean Epistemology

In the Hellenistic period epistemology came to occupy a more fundamental position in philosophy than it had done for either Plato or Aristotle. It was Epicurus who first gave it a name as a separate branch of philosophy. He called it 'canonic', from the Greek word 'kanon', meaning a rule or measuring rod. More often than 'canon' Epicurus and other Hellenistic philosophers made use of the word 'criterion'. According to Epicurus the three criteria of truth are sensations, concepts (*prolepseis*), and feelings.

Sensation is the foundation of knowledge for Epicurus, and he held a strong form of the thesis that the senses are infallible with regard to their proper objects. This is set forth elegantly by Lucretius:

> Truth's very notion from the senses came.
> What witness, then, to challenge them can claim?
> Against the senses' faith to win the day
> What greater truth can chase the false away?
> What right has reason sense to criticize
> When from false sense that reason took its rise?
> If what the senses tell us is not true
> Then reason's self is naught but falsehood too.
> Can ears deliver verdict on the eyes?
> Can touch convict the ears, or taste the touch, of lies?
>
> (4. 478–87)

The opening of a book of Lucretius' *De Rerum Natura* in an illuminated manuscript from the British Library

Lucretius, like Aristotle, points out that one sense cannot be corrected by another with regard to its proper object. But the Epicureans go further than Aristotle in claiming a sense cannot even correct its own impressions: each impression is of equal reliability and hence whatever appears to a sense at any time is true (Lucretius 4. 497–9; D.L. 10. 31).

By treating all appearances as on a par, instead of grading them in terms of reliability, Epicureans rule out Aristotle's method of dealing with conflicting impressions, such as that of a tower that looks round from a distance but square close up. Instead, they claim that in such a case we have two equally valid impressions, but impressions of different objects. Sextus Empiricus explains how Epicurus would deal with the problem, by invoking his atomistic explanation of sight as an encounter with a stream of images flowing from an object of vision.

I would not say that sight is deceived when from a great distance it sees a tower as small and round, and from nearby as large and square. Rather, it is quite correct. When what is perceived appears small and so-shaped, it really is small and shaped like that, because the edges of the images have been rubbed off as a result of their journey through the air. And when it appears big and of a different shape, once again it really is big and of that shape. But the two are not the same. (M. 7. 208)

Our common impression that these are two glimpses of the same thing, Epicurus says, is due not to perception but to 'distorted belief'. He deals in a similar way with other objections to the infallibility of sensation, such as dreams and delusions. When Orestes thought he saw the Furies, his sight was not deceived because there were genuine images present; it was his mind that erred in taking them as solid bodies (S.E., M. 8. 63). We must distinguish sharply between a sense-impression (*phantastike epibole*) and an accompanying, but distinct, belief (D.L. 10. 51).

Sensations, therefore, the first criteria of truth, in spite of their infallibility, provide only a rather slender base for the structure of our knowledge. We need to turn to the second set of criteria, namely concepts. Epicurus' word 'prolepsis' is often translated 'preconceptions', but that is misleading, partly because it suggests prejudice, partly because it suggests something that would be expressed by a whole proposition, while most of the examples we are given are expressed by single words, such as 'body', 'man', 'cow', 'red'. A concept is a general notion of what kind of thing is signified by such a word (which may, of course, be expressed in a sentence of paraphrase, such as 'A cow is an animal of such-and-such a kind'). The 'pro' in 'prolepsis' is meant to indicate that a concept of X is not a set of information about X derived from experience, but rather a template by which we recognize in advance whether an individual presented in experience is or is not an X. Concepts are not things that have to be proved: they are themselves employed in any proof (D.L. 10. 33, 38). It remains obscure, in both Epicurus and his followers, whence concepts originate. They cannot all be the result of experience, since they provide the means by which we sort sensations, which are the basis of experience. But some of them do seem to be the result of experience—perhaps misinterpreted experience, like the concept of God (Lucretius 5. 1169–71).

Sensations and concepts, for Epicurus, are both 'evident' (so too are feelings, but they will be considered in a different context). It is on these evident elements that we must base our beliefs in what is not evident. We start with the senses, he said, and then must infer the non-evident by reasoning from their testimony (D.L. 10. 39). Conjectures and theories are false if the senses bear witness against them (D.L. 10. 50–1). A conjecture is true if it is confirmed by the senses; a theory is true if it is not impugned by the senses (S.E., M. 213). The latter claim seems surprising: may not more than one incompatible theory be consistent with the evidence? The Epicureans accepted this possibility; thus Lucretius accepts that there may be different explanations of the movements of the stars, just as there may be different hypotheses about the cause of death of a corpse on a slab (6. 703–11). In such a case they should all be accepted: each of them is likely to be true in one or other of the many worlds in the universe, even if we do not know which is true in our world (5. 526–33).

Stoic Epistemology

The early Stoics shared with the Epicureans a number of assumptions about the nature of knowledge. Like them, they believed it must have a dual basis of infallible sense-impressions and primitive and acquired concepts. On the topic of concepts they are more informative than the Epicureans, and they give an account of their origin that closely resembles Aristotle's. When a man is born, his mind is like a blank sheet of paper, and as he develops towards the use of reason, concepts are written on the page. The earliest concepts come from the senses: individual experiences leave behind memory, and memory builds up experience. Some concepts are acquired from teaching or devised for a purpose; others arise naturally and spontaneously, and it is these that deserve the name 'prolepsis' (LS 39E). Concepts of this kind are common to all humans: disagreement arises only when they are applied to particular cases, as when the same action is described by one man as courageous and by another as lunatic (Epictetus 1. 22. 3).

The Stoics developed a more elaborate classification of mental states than ever the Epicureans did. They wanted to propound an epistemology that would withstand sceptical challenge. In addition to the two states of knowledge (*episteme*) and belief (*doxa*) that had been contrasted since Plato, they introduced a third state, cognition (*katalepsis*).[5] The Stoics, Sextus Empiricus tells us,

> say there are three things connected to each other, knowledge and belief and located between them cognition. Knowledge is cognition that is sound and firm and unchangeable by argument; belief is weak and false assent, and cognition is in between the two: it is assent to a cognitive appearance. (*M* 7. 150–1)

A new element is here added to the definition of knowledge: knowledge is unchangeable by argument. This seems a sound insight. If I claim to know that *p*, I am claiming, among other things, that no one is going to (rightly) argue me out of believing that *p*. This is unlike the case where I believe that *p* but am open to conviction that not-*p*. This latter is what is meant by saying that belief is weak assent. It is also (possibly) false: there is nothing absurd in saying 'X believes that *p*, but it is false that *p*' as there is in saying 'X knows that *p*, but it is false that *p*'. But the most interesting point in this passage is the definition of cognition in terms of cognitive appearance (*phantasia kataleptike*).

'Appearance' is a broad term, including not only what appears to the senses but candidates for belief of other kinds. Cognitions, likewise, may result from the senses or from reason (D.L. 7. 52). An appearance is not the

---

[5] This translation is now standard, being used by Long and Sedley (LS 254) and Frede (*CHHP* 296 ff.). I use it with reluctance, since the word 'cognition' is associated with much confusion in modern philosophy of mind.

same thing as a belief: belief involves an extra item, namely assent; assent, unlike appearance, is a voluntary matter. An appearance is cognitive if it is worthy of assent. Cognition is between knowledge and belief in that, unlike belief, it is never false, and unlike knowledge, it does not involve the resolution never to change one's mind.[6]

A cognitive appearance, we are told, is 'that which arises from what is and is stamped and impressed exactly in accordance with what is' (D.L. 7. 46; Cicero, *Acad.* 2. 77). Well and good: clearly such an impression (as we may call it) is worthy of assent. A wise man will have no mere beliefs, Zeno said (Cicero, *Acad.* 2. 77); and no doubt this can be achieved if the wise man assents only to cognitive appearances. But how do I know whether an appearance is cognitive or not? Is it a matter of an appearance being so clear and distinct that it actually forces my assent, so that I cannot help but believe? Or does it have certain features that I can use as a criterion by which I decide to confer an assent that I might have withheld? Our evidence is not totally clear, but we are given some indications by the examples that survive.

First, we are told that the impressions of the insane are not cognitive. (Sometimes, indeed, the Stoics denied that they were genuine impressions, calling them instead 'phantasms'; D.L. 7. 49.) They 'arise purely externally and fortuitously, so that they are often not positive about them and do not assent to them' (S.E., *M.* 7. 248). But suppose they do assent to them: clearly that does not make them cognitive, since they are not true and only a true appearance can be cognitive. But what epistemological rule have the insane violated? Well, perhaps they have not examined the degree of detail in their impression: for a second piece of information we are given is that a cognitive impression must be highly comprehensive, so that all the characteristics of its original are reproduced. 'Just as the seals on rings always stamp their features accurately on the wax, so those impressions that create cognition of objects should incorporate all their peculiarities' (S.E., *M.* 2. 750). However, if cognitive impressions are ones that are fully comprehensive in detail, they must be very few and far between.

Perhaps, we might conjecture, cognitive impressions have a specially persuasive quality that marks them out. The Stoics did indeed classify impressions in terms of their persuasiveness into four classes:

---

[6] So Frede, *CHHP* 296 ff.

(1) Persuasive; e.g. 'It is day', 'I am talking'.
(2) Unpersuasive; e.g. 'If it is dark, it is day'.
(3) Persuasive and unpersuasive; e.g. philosophical paradoxes.
(4) Neither persuasive nor unpersuasive; e.g. 'The number of all the stars is odd'.

However, persuasiveness is not a guarantee of truth: the bent appearance of an oar in water is persuasive enough, but is a false impression for all that. No doubt a man who is wise will resist the temptation to accept all persuasive appearances, and will restrict his assent to appearances that are not only persuasive but reasonable. Thus, Posidonius tells us, in addition to offering cognitive impressions as the criterion of truth, some older Stoics identified the criterion as being right reason (D.L. 7. 54).

However, the matter is further complicated. In addition to cognitive impressions there are reasonable impressions. A Stoic, trapped by King Ptolemy Philopator into taking wax pomegranates for the genuine article, replied that he had given his assent not to the proposition that they were pomegranates, but to the proposition that it was reasonable (*eulogon*) to believe that they were. A reasonable impression, he said, was compatible with falsehood (D.L. 7. 177) If so, it seems, the assessment of whether an appearance is or is not cognitive cannot be a matter of reason. The early Stoics give us no further assistance in determining the identifying feature of cognitive impressions.

The weakness of the Stoic position was exposed by Arcesilaus, the head of the New Academy during the latter part of the third century. He challenged the Stoic definition of a cognitive impression as 'something stamped and impressed from something that is, exactly as it is'. Could there not be, he asked, a false impression indiscernible from a true one? Zeno agreed that if an impression was such that there could be a false one exactly like it, then (even if true) it could not be a cognitive impression. Accordingly he modified the definition, adding 'and of such a kind that it could not arise from what is not' (Cicero, *Acad.* 2. 77; S.E., *M.* 7. 251). But it is not clear how the Stoics were to establish in which cases such unmistakable distinguishing marks were to be found, or respond to a sceptical claim that wherever there was a true appearance a false indiscernible replica could be imagined.

Academic Scepticism

It is not surprising that Stoic epistemology should be challenged from a sceptical angle. It was surprising, however, that the challenge should come from the Academy, from the heirs of Plato. Surely the Platonic corpus contains some of the most dogmatic philosophy ever to be devised. The leaders of the later Academy, however, Arcesilaus and his successor, Carneades, traced their ancestry further back. They appealed to Socrates, whose question and answer technique so famously punctured false claims to knowledge (Cicero, *Fin.* 2. 2). Socrates himself claimed no philosophical knowledge, and left no philosophical writings; and Arcesilaus and Carneades followed him in both respects. But they went further than Socrates in commending a much more radical scepticism: a suspension of belief not only on philosophical but also on the most everyday topics.

Though Arcesilaus and Carneades left no writings, we are reasonably well informed about their philosophical teachings because Cicero, who had been taught by Carneades' pupil Philo, was much attracted to Academic Scepticism, and left a lively account of the to and fro of sceptical debate in his *Academica*. From him and other sources we learn that the Academics presented a battery of arguments to show that there could be no infallible impressions.

There is no true impression arising from sensation that cannot be paired with another impression, indistinguishable from it, which is non-cognitive. But if two impressions are indistinguishable, it cannot be the case that one of them is cognitive and the other not. Therefore no impression, even if true, is cognitive. To illustrate this argument, consider the case of identical twins, Publius Geminus and Quintus Geminus. If someone looking at Publius thinks he is looking at Quintus, he has an impression that corresponds in every detail to the one he would have if he were in fact looking at Quintus. Hence, his impression is not a cognitive one: it does not answer to the final clause of Zeno's definition: 'of such a kind as could not arise from what is not' (Cicero, *Acad.* 2. 83–5).

In reply, the Stoics seem to have denied the possibility of any pair of objects resembling each other in every respect. They propounded the thesis later known as the identity of indiscernibles: no two grains of sand, no two wisps of hair, were totally alike. The Academics complained that the thesis was gratuitous; but it is surely no more gratuitous than their own claim that true impressions are *always* liable to be confused with false replicas.

In fact, the Stoic reply seems to be either unnecessary or insufficient, depending on how we interpret the sceptical challenge. If only a genuine possibility of a mistake prevents an impression from being cognitive, then in order to preserve cognitive impressions the Stoic need not claim that in all cases a true impression will be irreplaceable by a false one: he need only claim that there are some cases in which this is so. On the other hand, if the mere imaginability of a deceptive replica is sufficient to undermine the cognitivity of an impression, then the identity of indiscernibles will not restore it. I may be as certain as I am of anything that I am talking to you: but isn't it imaginable that you have an identical twin, quite unknown to me, and that it is he whom I am addressing?

There are various degrees of scepticism. A sceptic may simply be some-one who denies the possibility of genuine knowledge (in some, or all, areas of inquiry). Such a sceptic need have no objection to the holding of beliefs on various topics, provided that the person holding them does not claim that those beliefs have the status of knowledge. He may very well have a set of beliefs himself, including the belief that there is no such thing as knowledge. There is no inconsistency here, provided he does not claim to *know* that there is no knowledge. Arcesilaus went so far as to reprove Socrates for claiming to know that he knew nothing (Cicero, *Acad.* 1. 45).

A more radical sceptic, however, may question not only the possibility of knowledge but also the propriety of belief. He may recommend abstinence from not only the resolute assent characteristic of certainty, but also the tentative assent characteristic of opinion. Arcesilaus appears to have been a sceptic of this kind: he maintained, Cicero tells us (*Acad.* 1. 44; LS 68A), 'no one should assert or affirm anything or offer it assent; instead we should curb our rashness and hold it back from any slip. It would be rash indeed to approve something false or unknown, and nothing is more disgraceful than to allow assent and approval to outrun cognition.' Arcesilaus made a practice of offering arguments pro and con every thesis, so as to facilitate the suspension of assent that he recommended (*Fin.* 5. 10). Scholars are uncertain whether his arguments were all purely *ad hominem* or whether he did (inconsistently) assert as true his own sceptical philosophical position.[7]

---

[7] See Schofield, in *CHHP* 334.

According to some of our ancient sources, Carneades was a sceptic of the less radical kind who, while rejecting the possibility of knowledge, accepted that the wise man could legitimately hold mere belief. The two Academics focus their attack on Zeno at different points. Zeno held that no wise man would hold mere belief, but if he relied only on cognitive impressions his assents would all count as knowledge. Arcesilaus and Carneades agree with each other that there are no cognitive impressions and therefore no knowledge, but the former concludes that the wise man will give no assent, while the latter concludes that the wise man will hold mere belief (Cicero, *Acad.* 2. 148).

On another account, however, in evaluating Carneades' position we need to make a more subtle analysis of the mental phenomena studied by the epistemologist. Instead of simply distinguishing between an appearance and assent to the appearance, we have to introduce a new notion of impulse (*horme*). While assent is voluntary and can be withheld, appearance, we know, is outside our control. But appearance is inevitably followed by impulse, and it is possible to follow this without the mental assent in which truth is to be found and falsehood to be avoided (Plutarch, *adversus Coloten* 1122 LS 69A; Cicero, *Acad.* 2. 103–4 LS 69I).

This distinction appears to have been introduced in order to answer a common objection to radical scepticism: if the sceptic suspends judgement, how can he live a normal life. How can he get into a bath if, for all he knows, it is a chasm? The answer is that he does not judge, rashly, that it really is a bath; but he is swept along by his bath-entering impulse. In non-philosophical discussions a wise man may even follow his impulses so far as to give the answers 'yes' and 'no' to questions.

Pyrrhonian Scepticism

In the first century BC there grew up a new fundamentalist school of scepticism which regarded the Academics as having watered down scepticism in unacceptable ways. The founder of this school was Aenesidemus, but he and his followers described their version of scepticism as Pyrrhonism, after Pyrrho of Elis, a soldier in the army of Alexander the Great, whom they regarded as their founding father. Aenesidemus wrote a lost book of Pyrrhonian discourses that set out his differences with Academic

Scepticism. He collected together sceptical arguments of the kind that we have encountered in this chapter, and grouped them under ten headings, which achieved fame as the Ten Tropes of Aenesidemus. Our knowledge of them, as of much else in ancient scepticism, derives from the writings of Sextus Empiricus, a Pyrrhonian sceptic of the second century AD.

Sextus left three books of *Outlines of Pyrrhonism* and eleven books *Against the Professors*. In these books appear almost all the sceptical arguments from illusion that appeared in the later literature, and many that no one cared to use again. We find in him the yellow look of jaundice, the after-image on the book, vision distorted by pressure on the eyeball, concave and convex mirrors, wine which tastes sour after figs and sweet after nuts, ships apparently stationary on the horizon, oars bent in water, smells more pungent in the bathroom, the fleeting flashes of colour on the necks of pigeons, and, of course, our old friend the tower that looks round from afar and square close at hand.

Sextus' own version of scepticism turns out not to be as different from Academic Scepticism as he would have us believe. Sceptics, without giving assent to anything, still seem, for him, to be able to have views, not only about perceptual matters of everyday life, but even on philosophical issues. Sextus' works are of value to us, not because they give a new turn to the sceptical discussion, but because they are a treasury of information about the reasoning of earlier and more original sceptics. He brought to an end the sceptical tradition he chronicled.

The study of ancient epistemology can teach us much about the nature of knowledge and the limits of scepticism. Several insights became part of the patrimony of all future philosophy: knowledge can only be of what is true; knowledge is only knowledge if it can appeal implicitly or explicitly to some kind of support, whether from experience, reasoning, or some other source; and one who claims knowledge must be resolute, excluding the possibility of being rightly converted, at a later stage, to a different view.

However, ancient epistemology is bedevilled by two different but related fallacies. Both of them are generated by a misunderstanding of the truth that whatever is knowledge must be true. One of the fallacies haunts classical epistemology, up to the time of Aristotle; the other fallacy haunts Hellenistic and imperial epistemology.

The first fallacy is this. 'Whatever is knowledge must be true' may be interpreted in two ways.

(1) Necessarily, if p is known, p is true

or

(2) If p is known, p is necessarily true.

(1) is true but (2) is false. It is a necessary truth that if I know you are sitting down, then you are sitting down; but if I know you are sitting down it is not a necessary truth that you are sitting down; you may get up at any moment. Plato and Aristotle, over and over again, seem to regard (2) as indistinguishable from (1). Given the necessary connection between know-ledge and truth, they seem to think, only what is necessary can be known. From the acceptance of (2) there flows the construction of the theory of eternal and immutable Ideas, and there flows the impossible ideal of Aristotelian science.

If whatever is knowledge must be true, then it may seem that knowledge must be the exercise of a faculty that cannot err. This is the form that the fallacy takes in Hellenistic times. The Epicureans and Stoics, unlike Plato and Aristotle, are prepared to countenance knowledge not just of eternal truths, but of mundane contingencies such as that Dion is now walking. But this, they claim, is possible only if we have faculties—whether sense or reason—that are capable of infallible operation. This Hellenistic fallacy is just the mirror image of the classical fallacy. Let F stand for some faculty. Then it is true that

It is impossible, if F knows that p, that F has gone wrong.

But that is not the same as, nor is it true that,

If F knows that p, then it was impossible for F to go wrong.

The epistemological fallacy, both in its classical and in its Hellenistic form, would cast long shadows through philosophy's history.

5

How Things Happen:
Physics

In earlier chapters we saw how Greek thinkers, from Thales to Plato, developed an elaborate picture of the universe we live in. Though of great historic interest, their physical theories have been superseded by the progress of science, and can no longer offer us enlightenment about the world. The same is true of Aristotle's world-picture; but in addition to physical speculation, Aristotle offered, to a much greater extent than any of his predecessors, a philosophical examination of underlying concepts that are basic to physical explanation of many different kinds. His philosophy of physics, unlike his physical system itself, contains much that remains of abiding interest.

The second of Aristotle's categories is the category of quantity: this is the one that answers to the question 'how big?', and Aristotle has in mind answers such as 'four feet long', 'six feet high' (*Cat.* 4. 1^{b}28). There are two kinds of quantities, he tells us, discrete and continuous. A discrete quantity would be, for example, an army of a thousand men (cf. *Metaph. Δ* 13. 1020^{a}7); as examples of continuous quantities, we are given lines, surfaces, bodies, time, and place (*Cat.* 6. 4^{b}20 ff.). Aristotle's treatment of the continuum and of continuous quantities is fundamental to his philosophy of physics, and the first part of this chapter will be devoted to these topics.

The Continuum

At the beginning of book 6 of the *Physics* Aristotle introduces three terms to indicate different relationships between quantified items: they may be successive (*ephexes*), adjacent (*hama*), or continuous (*syneches*). Two items are successive if between them there is nothing of the same kind as themselves. Thus, two islands in an archipelago are successive if there is only sea between them; two days are successive if there is no day, but only night, between them. Two items are adjacent, Aristotle says, if they have two boundaries in contact with each other, and they are continuous if there is only a single common boundary between them (231ª18–25). He uses these definitions to base an argument that a continuum cannot be composed of indivisible atoms.

A line, for instance, cannot be composed of points that lack magnitude. Since a point has no parts, it cannot have a boundary distinct from itself: two points therefore cannot be either adjacent or continuous. If you say that the boundary of a point is identical with the point itself, then two points that were continuous would be one and the same point. Nor can points be successive to each other: between any two points on a continuous line we can always find other points on the same line (231ª29–ᵇ15).

Similar reasoning, Aristotle says, applies to spatial magnitude, to time, and to motion: all three are continua of the same kind. Time cannot be composed of indivisible moments, because between any two moments there is always a period of time; and an atom of motion would in fact have to be a moment of rest.

Divisibility, indeed, is a defining feature of quantity or magnitude, and is so used in Aristotle's lexicon of philosophical terms in *Metaphysics* Δ (1020ª7): 'We call a quantity whatever is divisible into two or more constituent parts of which each is of a kind to be a single individual entity.' We shall have to explore later what 'being of a kind to be an individual' amounts to.

Points or moments, therefore, which were indivisible would lack magnitude, and zero magnitude, however often repeated, could never add up to any magnitude. By another route, therefore, we reach the conclusion that a continuous quantity is not composed of indivisible items. If a magnitude can only be divided into other magnitudes, and every magnitude must be divisible, it follows that every magnitude is infinitely divisible.

Aristotle's notion of infinite divisibility is not easy to grasp, and he was fully aware of this. In *On Generation and Corruption* he spells out at length a line of objection to his thesis, and suggests that it was the line of argument that led Democritus to espouse atomism. The argument goes like this.

If matter is divisible to infinity, then let us suppose that this division has been carried out—for if matter is genuinely so divisible, there will be nothing incoherent in this supposition. How large are the fragments resulting from this division? If they have any magnitude at all, then, on the hypothesis of infinite divisibility, it would be possible to divide them further; so they must be fragments with no extension, like a geometrical point. But whatever can be divided can be put together again: if we saw a log into many pieces, even pieces as small as sawdust, we can put them together again into a log of the same size. But if our fragments have no magnitude, then how can they ever have added up to make the extended chunk of matter with which we began? Matter cannot consist of mere geometrical points, not even of an infinite number of them, so we have to conclude that divisibility comes to an end, and the smallest possible fragments must be bodies with sizes and shapes (1. 2. 316^{a}14–317^{a}3).

Aristotle in several places sets out to answer this difficulty (*Ph.* 3. 6. 206^{a}18–25; 7. 207^{b}14). 'Divisible to infinity', he insists, means 'unendingly divisible', not 'divisible into infinitely many parts'. However often a magnitude has been divided, it can always be divided further. It is infinitely divisible in the sense that there is no end to its divisibility. The continuum does not have an infinite number of parts; indeed Aristotle regarded the idea of an actually infinite number as incoherent. The infinite, he says, has only a potential existence (3. 6. 206^{a}18).

This is a sound answer to the Democritean argument: but Aristotle goes on to gild the lily. He offers a distinction between different kinds of potentiality. A block of marble has the potentiality to become a statue: when this is realized, the statue will be there, all of it at once. But the parts into which a temporal period or series can be divided have a different kind of potentiality. They cannot be all there at once: when I wake up, the day ahead contains both morning and afternoon, but they cannot both occur at once.

This seems an injudicious move, on several counts. First of all, Aristotle is defending a thesis about the continuum in general: it seems perverse to defend it by appealing to a property which may be peculiar to a particular form of continuum, namely time. Secondly, the argument for the infinite divisibility of the continuum is not concerned with the process of division. Democritus, in the argument Aristotle offers him, says that if something is infinitely divisible, it does not matter whether the division can be carried out simultaneously, the question is whether the result of the division is something coherently conceivable (*GC* 1. 2. 316ᵃ18). Thirdly, the contrast with the potentiality of producing a statue is a false trail.

In one of his sonnets Michelangelo gives a powerful evocation of the potentialities inherent in a block of marble.

> There's not a concept in an artist's mind,
> However great, but in a marble block
> It's hidden there for someone to unlock
> Whose intellect can teach his hand to find.[1]

The simultaneous actualization, from a single block of marble, of all the concepts of all the greatest artists would be just as impossible as the simultaneous actualization of all the parts of the continuum. In general, it is a fallacy to argue from

(1) It is both possible that *p* and possible that *q*

to

(2) It is possible that both *p* and *q*,

and to see this one has only to look at the case where '*q*' is 'not *p*'. Hence, in order to answer Democritus, Aristotle does not need to introduce his distinction between powers that are, and powers that are not, simultaneously actualizable. It is sufficient to point out (as he does; *GC* 1. 2. 317ᵃ8) that there is a difference between saying that whatever is continuous can be divided at *any* point and saying that whatever is continuous can be divided at *every* point.

But we should look more closely at the sonnet. While the hand and intellect of Michelangelo were unsurpassed at realizing the potentialities of marble, it may be questioned whether his poem shows an adequate philosophical grasp of the nature of potentiality. Clearly, he thinks of potential statues as shadowy realities, already present there in some mysterious way within the uncut marble. If one conceives of potentialities as shadow actualities, then it seems that one can count them and

---

[1] Non ha l'ottimo artista alcun concetto
Ch'un marmo solo in sè non circoscriva
Col suo soverchio, e solo a quello arriva
La man che ubbidisce all'intelletto.

quantify over them. Whatever is infinitely divisible, in that case, would have an infinite number of parts. But the temptation to think of potentialities in this way must be resisted, whether in Michelangelo or in Democritus.

Aristotle on Place

The fifth of Aristotle's categories is place, the answer to the question 'where?', of which a typical answer is 'in the Lyceum' (*Cat.* 4. 2^{a}1). We are not told anything further about this category in the *Categories*, but the fourth book of the *Physics* contains six chapters on place (a difficult topic, he tells us, on which he has found no help from his predecessors; 4. 1. 208^{a}32–3). Every body, prima facie at least, is in some place, and can move from place to place. The same place can be occupied at different times by different bodies, as a flask can contain first water and then air. So place cannot be identical with the body that occupies it (4. 1. 208^{b}29–209^{a}8). What, then, is it?

The answer that Aristotle eventually reaches is that the place of a thing is the first motionless boundary of whatever is containing it. Thus, the

Medieval imagination here shows Alexander the Great as Aristotle's research assistant exploring the sea-bed in a glass diving bell

place of a pint of wine is the inner surface of the flask containing it—provided the flask is stationary. But suppose the flask is in motion, on a punt perhaps floating down a river? Then the wine will be moving too, from place to place, and its place has to be given by specifying its position relative to the motionless river banks (4. 5. 212^{b}15). So too with a tree in a stream, surrounded by rushing water: its place is given by the unmoving bed in which it is rooted.[2]

As is clear from these examples, for Aristotle a thing is not only in the place defined by its immediate container, but also in whatever contains that container. Thus, just as a child may write out his address as 1 High Street, Oxford, England, Europe, The Earth, The Universe, so Aristotle says, 'You are now in the universe because you are in the atmosphere and the atmosphere is in the universe; and you are in the atmosphere because you are on the earth, and you are on the earth because you are in your own particular place.' The universe is the place that is common to everything.

If to be in place is to be within a container, it follows that the universe is not in place at all: and this is a conclusion that Aristotle himself draws. 'The universe is not anywhere; for whatever is somewhere must not only exist itself, but also have something alongside it in which it is and which contains it. But there is nothing outside the entire universe' (*Ph.* 4. 5. 212^{b}14–17). And if the universe is not in place, it cannot move from place to place.

It is clear that place as described by Aristotle is quite different from space as often conceived since Newton as an infinite extension or cosmic grid. Newtonian space would exist whether or not the material universe had been created. For Aristotle, if there were no bodies there would be no place; there can, however, be a vacuum, a place empty of bodies, but only if the place is bounded by actual bodies (4. 1. 208^{b}26). His concept of place, therefore, can avoid the difficulties that have led philosophers such as Kant to deny the reality of space. However, he adds to his basic concept a significant element that is irredeemably anachronistic: the notion of natural place.

In an ordered cosmos, Aristotle believed, each of the four elements, earth, air, fire, and water, had a natural place, which exercised a causal

[2] See W. D. Ross, *Aristotle*, 86; id., *Aristotle's Physics* (Oxford: Clarendon Press, 1936), 575.

influence: air and fire were by nature carried upward, water and earth were carried downward. Each such motion was natural to its element; other motions were possible, but were 'violent'. In the universe as we find it, these natural motions are hindered by various factors, so that few things are actually in their natural place; but the actual distribution of the elements is to be explained *inter alia* by their tendency to seek their natural place, the place where it is best for them to be (4. 1. 208^{b}9–22). We preserve a relic of Aristotle's distinction between natural and violent motions when we contrast natural with violent death. But none of Aristotle's modern admirers defends this rather class-bound vision of the universe, in which each element knows its place and is happiest to be in the station to which nature has assigned it.

Aristotle on Motion

Aristotle's fundamental account of motion, however, is not vitiated by the antiquated theory with which it was conjoined: indeed it was one of the most subtle components of his philosophy of physics. 'Motion' (*kinesis*) was for him a broad term, including changes in several different categories, such as growth in size or change in colour (*Ph.* 3. 1. 200^{b}32). Movement from place to place, however, local motion, provides a paradigm which can be used to expound his theory.

The definition of motion that Aristotle offers in the third book of the *Physics* is not, at first glance, very illuminating. 'Motion', he says, 'is the actuality of what is in potentiality, in so far as it is in potentiality.' Let us spell this out. If a body X is to move from point A to point B, it must be able to do so: when it is at A it is only potentially at B. When this potentiality has been realized, then X is at B. But it is then at rest, and not in motion. So motion from A to B is not simply the actualization of a potential at A for being at B. Shall we say that it is a partial actualization of that potentiality? That will not quite do, either, because a body stationary at the mid-point between A and B might be said to have partially actualized that potentiality. We have to say that it is an actualization of a potentiality that is still being actualized: and that is what Aristotle's definition amounts to. While at A, the body has in fact two different potentialities: a potentiality to be at B, and a potentiality to move to B. Aristotle illustrates the point with other examples of *kinesis*: the gradual heating of a body, the carving of a statue, the healing of a patient, the building of a house (3. 1. 201^{a}10–15).

Motion, he says, is a notion difficult to grasp, and this is because it is as it were halfway between straight potentiality and straight actuality. He sums up his account in a slogan, saying that motion is an incomplete or imperfect actuality of an imperfect potentiality (3. 2. 201^{b}31). Being at B would be the perfect actuality; moving to B is the imperfect actuality. The potentiality for being at B is the perfect potentiality; the potentiality for moving to B is the imperfect potentiality.

Motion is a continuum: a mere series of positions between A and B is not a motion from A to B. If X is to move from A to B, it has to pass through any intermediate point between A and B; but passing through a point is not the same as being located at that point. Aristotle argues that whatever is moving already has been moving. If X, travelling from A to B, passes through the mid-point K, it must already have passed through an earlier point J halfway between A and K. However short the distance between A and J, that too is divisible, and so on ad infinitum. At any point at which X is moving, there will be an earlier point at which it was already moving (cf. *Ph.* 6. 5. 236^{b}33–5). It follows that there is no such thing as a first instant of motion.

Aristotle's account of motion is embedded within a careful analysis of the semantic properties of Greek verbs. English, unlike Greek, has a special continuous form of each tense. The difference between 'He runs' and 'He is running' is clear enough in English. So too is the difference between 'Whatever moves has moved before' (which is doubtful) and 'Whatever is moving has been moving before' (which is true). In Greek Aristotle has to go to some pains to make clear that he is talking not about whatever moves, but whatever is moving. He does, however, maintain not just that whatever is moving has been moving before, but that whatever is moving *has moved* before (*Ph.* 5. 6. 237^{b}5).

For Aristotle, there are some verbs that signify *kineseis* (motions) and some that signify *energeiai* (actualities) (*Metaph.* θ 6. 1048^{b}18–36). *Kinesis*, as has been said, includes not only motion but many different kinds of change and production: Aristotle gives as examples learning something, building a particular house, walking to a particular place. As examples of *energeiai* he gives seeing, knowing, and being happy. He distinguishes between his two classes of verbs by means of subtle linguistic points.

Verbs of the first kind signify activities that are imperfect in the following sense: if I am φing, then I have not yet φd (if I am still building this house, I have not yet built it, and so on). The activities they signify are activities that take time (*NE* 10. 4. 1174^{b}8). Activities or achievements of the second kind, however, do not *take* time, but rather *last* or continue over time. A *kinesis* can be faster or slower, and can be completed or interrupted; not so an *energeia*. I may learn something quickly, but I cannot know it quickly; I may be interrupted while learning, but not while knowing (*NE* 10. 4. 1173^{a}33; *Metaph.* Θ 6. 1048^{b}19).

Energeiai such as knowing are states. Besides states such as knowledge, there are secondary *energeiai*, or actualities that are the exercise of such states. Thus, we have a triadic sequence: I learn Greek, I know Greek, I speak Greek. Secondary actualities have some of the features of motions and some of the features of activities: speaking Greek is not an imperfect process towards a terminus, in the way that learning Greek is; on the other hand it can be interrupted in a way that knowing Greek cannot.

Aristotle's classifications can be looked on as a study in what grammarians call the *aspect* of verbs, which, in Greek rather more than in English, often gets entangled with the *tense* of verbs. We still use Aristotle's terminology in distinguishing, for instance, between the imperfect tense (which tells was what *was happening*) and the perfect tense (which tells us what *has been done*). We have already encountered Aristotle's treatment of tense, when in Chapter 3 we studied his treatment of past- and future-tense propositions in the *de Interpretatione*. It is now appropriate to look at his formal treatment of the topic of time in the *Physics* (4. 10–14).

Aristotle on Time

For Aristotle extension, motion, and time are three fundamental continua, in an intimate and ordered relation to each other. His paradigm of change is local motion, motion over distance: motion acquires its continuity from the continuum of spatial extension. Time, in its turn, derives its continuity from the continuity of motion (*Ph.* 4. 11. 219^{a}10–14). Thus Aristotle's account of time is parasitic on his account of motion: his formal definition, indeed, is this: time is the number of motion in respect of before and after (4. 11. 219^{b}1).

Clearly motion and time are closely linked; but might not one question the priority that Aristotle thus gives to motion? Motions, and changes of any kind, are clearly impossible without time. If X is to move from A to B, it must *first* be at A and *then* be at B, and any change must involve an *earlier* state and a *later* state. But is time impossible without motion? Can we not conceive of a static, or indeed empty, universe enduring over a longer or shorter period of time?

Aristotle believed not: where there was no motion there was no time (4. 11. 219^{a}1). Not that time is identical with motion: motions are motions of particular things, and different kinds of changes are motions of different kinds, but time is universal and uniform. Motions, again, may be faster or slower; not so time. Indeed it is by the time they take that the speed of motions is determined (4. 10. 218^{b}9; 14. 223^{b}4). Nonetheless, Aristotle says, 'we perceive motion and time together' (4. 11. 219^{a}4).

We tell how much time has passed by observing the process of some change. We, nowadays, find out what the time is by finding out what point the fingers of the clock have reached in their journey round the clock face. Analogous points can be made about whatever processes are being used as clocks in hourglasses or clepsydras. More importantly, for Aristotle, we measure days and months and years by observing the sun and moon and stars upon their celestial travels.

The part of a journey that is nearer its starting point comes before the part that is nearer its end. This spatial relation of nearer and further underpins the relation of before and after in motion; and this is the 'before' and 'after' that appears in Aristotle's definition of time. It is the *before* and *after* in motion that provides the *earlier* and *later* in time. Thus temporal order is, on Aristotle's view, derived from the ultimately spatial ordering of stretches of motion.

When Aristotle says that time is the number of motion, this ordering is no doubt one of the things he has in mind: we can list parts of the motion as first, second, third, and so on. But he may well have in mind cardinal as well as ordinal numbering, since time has a metric as well as a topological element. We can often say not only that A came before B, but also *how long* before. This seems implicit when Aristotle explains that when he speaks of 'number' he means what is counted, not the unit of counting (*Ph.* 4. 11. 219^{a}9). To make it explicit he might have added to his definition that time is numbering not only in respect of before and after, but also in respect of faster and slower. For as a proof of the universality of time he offers the fact that any change whatever can be measured in terms of velocity (*Ph.* 4. 13. 222^{b}30).

What is the relationship between time as it appears in Aristotle's definition (the earlier–later series) and time as expressed by tense (past, present, and future)? Aristotle links the two by his concept of 'the now' (*to nun*).

We say 'earlier' and 'later' with reference to distance from the now; and the now is the boundary between the past and the future...But 'earlier' is used in opposite ways in respect to past time and future time: in the past we call earlier that which is further from the now, and later that which is nearer to the now; in the future we call earlier that which is nearer to the now, and later that which is further away. (*Ph.* 4. 14. 223^{a}5–14)

Aristotle frequently talks of the 'now'. He seems to use it for two different purposes: one, the most natural usage, to indicate present time; another, more technical one, in which it seems to mean 'instant' or 'moment'. In this second use one can speak of earlier and later nows (*Ph.* 4. 10. 218^{b}24; 11. 220^{a}21). In the passage just quoted he appears to be amalgamating the two uses, to mean 'the present instant'. This is unfortunate, because *the present instant* is an incoherent notion. 'Present' is an adjective applicable only to periods, such as the present year or the present century. Instants are the boundaries of periods, and future periods are bounded by future instants, and past intervals by past instants. But present periods are bounded not by present instants, but by two instants, one of which is past and the other future. There is no instantaneous present.[3]

The thesis that the present is an instant sorts ill with another thesis to which Aristotle attaches considerable importance, namely his claim that there can be no motion at an instant. If now is an instant, and there is no motion at an instant, then nothing is in motion now. This argument can be repeated at any time whatever; so it seems that motion must be forever unreal. But what, in any case, are we to make of this second thesis in its own right?

We can readily agree that no object can move at an instant. There cannot be movement between *t* and *t*, any more than there can be

---

[3] G. E. L. Owen ('Aristotle on Time', in J. Barnes, M. Schofield, and R. Sorabji (eds.), *Articles on Aristotle*, iii: *Metaphysics* (London: Duckworth, 1975), 151) suggests that the confusion here originates in Plato's *Parmenides* 152a–e and is not dispelled until Chrysippus.

movement from A to A. But it does not follow from that that no object can *be moving* at an instant, any more than that no object can be moving at a point. Aristotle, however, is not just making a fallacious inference from one acceptation of the Greek present tense to another; as we have seen, he is well capable of steering his way through any possible semantic confusion of this kind. He offers an argument for the stronger conclusion, based on the premiss we have already seen: that whatever is moving has already been moving. But the correct conclusion to draw from this argument is not that nothing can be moving at a moment, but that nothing can be moving for a single moment only.

The truth that lies behind Aristotle's claim is that we can only talk of X moving at time t if t is a moment within a period of time, t' to t'', during which X is in movement; just as we can only talk of X moving at point p if p is a point on a track between p' and p'' along which X is in movement. The notion of velocity at a point is then a derivative (which may be simple or complex, depending on the movement's uniformity or lack of it) from the length of time, t' to t'', that X takes to get from p' to p''.

Aristotle on Causation and Change

In his philosophical lexicon in *Metaphysics Δ*, and also in *Physics* 2. 3 (194^{b}16–195^{b}30), Aristotle distinguishes four types of cause, or explanation. First, he says, there is that of which and out of which a thing is made, such as the bronze of a statue and the letters of a syllable. This is called the material cause. Secondly, he says, there is the form and pattern of a thing, which may be expressed in its definition: his example is that the proportion of the length of two strings in a lyre is the cause of one note being an octave away from the other. The third type of cause is the origin of a change or state of rest in something; Aristotle's followers often called it the 'efficient cause'. Aristotle gives as examples a person reaching a decision, a father who begets a child, a sculptor carving a statue, a doctor healing a patient, and in general anyone who makes a thing or changes a thing. The fourth and last type of cause is the end or goal, that for the sake of which something is done; it is the type of explanation we give if someone asks us why we are taking a walk, and we reply 'In order to keep healthy'. This last kind of cause became known as the 'final cause'.

In modern philosophy causation is standardly thought of as a relation between two events, one being cause and the other effect. Clearly, Aristotle structures causation rather differently. He does occasionally speak of events causing events (the Athenian expedition to Sardis caused the war with Persia; *APo.* 2. 11. 94^{a}36), but none of the causes he mentions in his canonical list are episodic events. Most are substantial entities, human beings, for instance, or chunks of bronze; some are enduring states, such as the proportion between the strings of the lyre, or the skill of the sculptor (which is the more immediate cause of the statue; *Ph.* 2. 3. 195^{a}6). Effects, too, as he describes them, may be in many categories: states, actions, and products. The effects of the third type of cause, efficient causes, as stated include substances (a child), artefacts (a statue), and events (the healing of a patient). But it would not do violence to Aristotle's concept to say that, in the case of efficient causation, what is brought about is always an event, either a change in something (the recovery of the patient) or the coming into being of something (the procreation of the child, the fabrication of the statue).

The difference between Aristotelian and modern notions of cause is so notable that some scholars reject the traditional translation of *aitia* as cause; they prefer other terms such as 'explanation', or speak of the four becauses rather than the four causes. Aristotle himself tells us that they are four types of answer to the question 'why?'

The ultimate answer to a 'why' may take us, in the case of unchanging things like mathematics, to the 'what' (to the definition of straight, or commensurable, or the like); or it may take us to the originating change (why did they go to war? because there had been a raid), or to the purpose (so as to come into power) or, in the case of things that come into being, to the matter. (*Ph.* 2. 7. 198^{a}14–21)

Here we meet the same four items, but in the order: formal, efficient, final, material.

When listing his four causes, Aristotle gives mathematical examples of formal causes. But the forms whose causation interests him most are the forms or natures of living beings: it is these that provide the internal explanation for the life-cycles and characteristic activities of plants and animals. In these cases, formal and final causes coincide: the mature realization of natural form being the end to which the activities of the organism tend. But he was also interested in the explanation of interchanges between non-living substances, of which he would give as an example the turning of water into steam. In such cases he uses the formal and material causes as explanatory principles.

Change, for Aristotle, could take place in many different categories: growth, for instance, was change in the category of quantity, and a change in a quality (e.g. of colour) was called an alteration (*GC* 1. 5. 320ª13). Local motion, as we have seen, is change in the category of place. But change in the category of substance, where there is a change from one kind of thing into another, was a very special kind of change. When a substance undergoes a change of quantity or quality, the same substance remains throughout, with its substantial form. But if one kind of thing turns into another, does anything remain throughout? Aristotle answers: matter.

We have a case of alteration when the subject of change is perceptible and persists, and merely changes its properties...A body, for instance, while remaining the same body, is now healthy and now ill; some bronze may be now circular and now angular, and yet the same bronze. But when nothing perceptible persists in its identity as a subject of change, and the thing changes as a whole (when e.g. semen becomes blood, or water changes into air, or air totally into water), such an occurrence is a case of one substance coming to be and another substance ceasing to be...Matter, in the most proper sense of the term, is to be identified with the underlying subject which is receptive of coming-to-be and passing away. (*GC* 1. 4. 319ᵇ8–320ª2)

What is the nature of this matter that underlies substantial change? Aristotle constantly explains the relationship of matter to form in living things (e.g. in the formation of a foetus, as he archaically described it above) by analogy with artefacts. 'As the bronze is to the statue, the wood is to the bed, or the formless before receiving form is to the formed object, so is the underlying nature to the substance' (*Ph.* 1. 7. 191ª9–12). The analogy is not easy to grasp. What is the underlying nature that remains through substantial change in the way in which wood remains wood before and after being made into a bed? Surely the reshaping of wood or bronze is an example of an accidental, not a substantial change.

Things do not yet get any clearer when Aristotle tells us,

By matter I mean what in itself is neither of any kind nor of any size nor describable by any of the categories of being. For it is something of which all these things are predicated, and therefore its essence is different from that of all the predicates. All the other categories are predicated of substance, but substance of matter. Therefore the ultimate subject is of itself neither of any kind or any size nor anything else. (*Metaph. Z* 3. 1029ª21–5)

An entity that is not of any kind or any size or any shape, and of which nothing at all can be said, appears to be highly mysterious. But that is not what Aristotle is inviting us to accept. His ultimate matter (he sometimes calls it prime matter) is not *in and of itself* of any kind. It is not in and of itself any particular size, because it can grow or shrink; it is not in and of itself water, and it is not in and of itself steam, because it is each of these in turn. This does not mean that there is any time at which it is not of any size, or any time in which it is neither water nor steam nor anything else.

How then is a chunk of matter to be identified? Well, in everyday life we are familiar with the idea that one and the same parcel of stuff may be first one kind of thing, and then another kind of thing. A bottle containing a pint of cream may be found, after shaking, to contain not cream but butter. The stuff that comes out of the bottle is the same stuff as the stuff that went into the bottle: nothing has been added to it and nothing has been taken from it. But what comes out is different in kind from what goes in. It is from cases such as this that the Aristotelian notion of matter is derived.

The Stoics on Causality

The Stoic account of causes is both simpler and more complex than the Aristotelian one. It is simpler in that the Stoics do not count the material, formal, and final causes as causes properly so called, and they mock Aristotle's followers' 'crowd of causes' (Seneca, Ep. 65. 4). Their treatment of efficient causes, however, is more complex, in that they adopt a canonical form for the description of causation, and they offer a rich classification of different kinds of cause. Most importantly, unlike Aristotle, they offer a law of universal causation, which needs to be spelt out and defended.

The Stoics' standard analysis of causation was of the following form: A brings it about that B is F. A, the cause, must be a body, and so must B; but the effect, B's being F, is not a body but an abstract entity, a *lekton*. This is explained by Sextus:

The Stoics say that every cause is a body that becomes for another body a cause of something non-bodily. For instance a scalpel, which is a body, becomes for the flesh, another body, a cause of the non-bodily predicate *being cut*. Again a fire, which is a body, becomes for the wood, another body, a cause of the non-bodily predicate *being burnt*. (M. 9. 211)

While A and B are both material entities, the Stoics used the term 'matter' specially to refer to B, the passive element in causation (Seneca, Ep. 65. 2 LS 55E). So in Stoic causation we have a triad of cause, matter, and effect.

The Stoics introduced the notions of joint causes (*sunaitia*) and auxiliary causes (*sunerga*). Two oxen are joint causes of the movement of the plough if neither of them can pull it alone; I am an auxiliary cause if I help you lift a load which you can, at a pinch, manage by yourself (LS 55I). The recognition of joint and auxiliary causes was important, because it shows that it can often be misleading to speak of *the* cause of a particular state or event. Causes form not a chain, but a network.

For the Stoics it is not only changes and beginnings of existence that need causes: there are also sustaining causes (*aitiai synektikai*) that bring it about that things continue in existence. Bodies of all kinds, for instance, are held together by an active and tenuous fluid called *pneuma*, literally 'breath', which is responsible for the cohesion of the universe. Living bodies are kept alive by the soul, which is their sustaining cause. It is characteristic of such causes that if they cease to operate, their effects cease to obtain.

Zeno, indeed, stated this characteristic as a feature of all causes (LS 55A); but other Stoics seem to have allowed another category of antecedent (*prokatarktikai*) causes, whose effect remained after they had been removed (LS 55I). It seems obvious enough that a house may remain in existence long after the builder has ceased working. What Zeno seems to have had in mind were sustaining causes that sustained something other than existence or life: it is prudence, for instance, that brings it about that a man is prudent, and he is prudent only for so long as his prudence lasts. Prudence, it must be remembered, was for Stoic materialists a physical ingredient of a person (LS 55A).

The way in which the existence of antecedent causes is to be reconciled with Zeno's theory of sustaining causes seems to have been this: an antecedent cause brings it about that an object possesses an internal feature that is itself a sustaining cause simultaneous with the effect to be explained. This, certainly, was the form the theory took when it was employed to underpin medical practice: when a patient catches a chill, the coldness of the air is an antecedent cause, and the patient's fever is the internal and enduring state that is the sustaining cause of his symptoms.[4]

Chrysippus was famous for using the illustration of a garden roller or a child's spinning top. The top will not move unless the child strikes it: but once struck it will continue to spin 'of its own force and nature' (Cicero, *Fat.* 43). The crack of the whip is an antecedent cause, but the top's internal force is the principal cause. Likewise the roller, once pushed, will continue to roll of its own accord. This illustration was used in an attempt to reconcile the Stoic theory of causality with the possibility of human responsibility.

Causation and Determinism

The Stoics believed not just in universal causation, that is to say, the thesis that everything has a cause; they believed also in universal causal determinism, that is to say, that everything has a cause by which it was determined. Alexander reports them thus:

Nothing in the world is or comes about without a cause, because nothing of what it contains is independent from, or isolated from, all that has gone before. For the world would be torn apart and shattered, and no longer remain a unity under the governance of a single order and policy, if any uncaused motion were introduced. That would be the case unless all the things that are and come about have preceding causes from which they follow of necessity. (Alexander of Aphrodisias, *Fat.* 191. 30 LS 55N)

Note the extreme position of the Stoics. They claim not just that every beginning of existence has a cause, but that everything that happens has a cause. Further they claim that every cause is a necessitating cause: given the cause, the effect cannot but happen. They maintain not just universal causation, but universal determinism. This doctrine, which was to be hugely influential henceforth, is a Stoic invention. It lurks no doubt in ancient atomism (Cicero, *Fat.* 23), but Democritus does not spell it out with anything like Stoic clarity. Neither of the Stoics' causal claims was accepted by Aristotle, and the Epicureans, while accepting the universality of causation, did not accept the universality of necessity.

[4] See texts in Hankinson, *CHHP* 487–91.

This unified, successive, inescapable series of necessitating causes was called, by the Stoics and their critics, Fate (LS 55F). The doctrine of fate was immediately subjected to philosophical criticism from several quarters, and Cicero's *On Fate* gives a lively account of arguments levelled against it and Stoic responses to those arguments. One famous argument was called the Lazy Argument (*argos logos*); its purpose was to show that if determinism was true, there was no point in doing anything whatever.

The argument imagines someone addressing a Stoic patient on his sickbed. 'If it is fated that you will recover from this illness, then whether or not you call a doctor you will recover; likewise, if it is fated that you will not recover from this illness, then whether or not you call a doctor you will not recover. One or the other is your fate: so there is no point in calling a doctor' (*Fat.* 29 LS 55s0). Obviously, an argument of the same kind can be applied to any of the normal actions of life: another source imagines it being used to persuade a boxer that there is no point in putting up his guard.

In response, Chrysippus made a distinction between simple and complex facts. 'Socrates will die on such and such a day' may be true whatever Socrates does; but 'Laius will beget Oedipus' cannot be true unless Laius copulates with his wife. If the patient's recovery is a complex fact linked to calling a doctor, then calling the doctor will be no less fated than the eventual recovery.

If the history of the world is a single tissue of interconnected events, it is not clear how far Chrysippus is entitled to make his distinction between simple and complex facts: perhaps Socrates' death is co-fated (to use Chrysippus' term) with several of his actions, such as his behaviour when on trial. Indeed, perhaps everything is co-fated with everything else.

Nonetheless, Chrysippus is entitled to reject the Lazy Argument. Consider the propositions

(1) If I call the doctor, I will recover.
(2) If I do not call the doctor, I will recover.

If I am fated to recover, then the consequent of each of these propositions is true; and if we interpret each of the propositions truth-functionally, in the manner of Philo, each of them will on that supposition be true. In that sense it will be true that whether or not I call the doctor I will recover. But as these propositions are normally used in guiding behaviour, they must be understood not simply truth-functionally, but also as supporting the corresponding counterfactuals

(3) If I called the doctor, I would recover.
(4) If I did not call the doctor, I would recover.

But a Stoic has no reason to accept (4).[5]

Determinism and Freedom

More serious was the argument that if determinism is true, human responsibility for action evaporates, and praise and blame become pointless. This argument was mounted both by Epicureans and by Academics. Necessity is accountable to no one, Epicurus said, and what depends on us, what attracts blame and its converse, must be free of the overlordship of fate (LS 20A). To reconcile this freedom with their own atomistic system, Epicureans hypothesized that atoms engaged in unpredictable swerves. Thus Lucretius:

> Lest mind should suffer from compulsive force
> And helpless trace a predetermined course
> A travelling atom deviates a space
> And swerves at no fixed time and no fixed place.   (2. 290)

Neither in antiquity nor in modern times has it been clear how such a random quantum jerk would be a sufficient condition for human freedom; and not only Stoics, but Academics too, considered the swerve not only insufficient but unnecessary.

Carneades, Cicero tells us,

showed that the Epicureans could defend their case without this fictitious swerve. They taught that some voluntary motion of the mind was possible, and a defence of this doctrine was better than the introduction of the swerve, especially as they could assign no cause to it. By defending it they had an answer to Chrysippus: they could agree that no motion lacks a cause without conceding that everything that happens is a result of antecedent causes. For there are no external antecedent causes of the operation of our will. (*Fat.* 33)

---

[5] The Lazy Argument appears across the centuries in many different contexts, e.g. in John Milton's *de Doctrina Christiana* in an argument against Calvinist predestination.

Voluntary motion, by its intrinsic nature, is in our power and obedient to us; and it is this intrinsic nature that is its cause.

Carneades is here offering the Epicureans an answer to Chrysippus; yet Chrysippus is reported as stating his own position in a way very similar to that of Carneades. Chrysippus, as I remarked earlier, was fond of using the examples of the spinning top and the garden roller to explain causation; and he uses them to make room for responsible action. Our assent to any proposition or proposal is triggered by external stimuli, as the top begins to spin only when the child whips it. But the actual assent is in our power, and this preserves responsibility without violating fate. 'If something could be brought about without an antecedent cause, it would be false that everything happens through fate; but if it is probable that there is an antecedent cause for whatever happens, what possible reason is there for denying that all things happen through fate?' (Cicero, *Fat.* 43).

The difference appears to be this. Carneades denies that voluntary actions have an external antecedent cause; Chrysippus affirms that they have, but appears here to deny that they are necessitated by it. How is this to be reconciled with the universal determinism the Stoics maintained elsewhere? To answer this question we must look more closely at the analogy with the top. The top is set in motion by the whip, but it moves in the way it does (a way different from the motion, say, of a garden roller) because of its own nature. Similarly, the mind's assent, when a stimulus is presented to it, is given because of its own nature. The assent falls under the overarching rule of fate if it is the only possible outcome of the joint causes, the external stimulus and the agent's own nature. But it is not necessitated by the external, antecedent cause, and in this sense Chrysippus can deny that it is necessary.

Many philosophers in later ages have claimed that if a human agent is responsible for an action X, it must have been possible for her, at the moment of action, both to do and not to do X. Such freedom of alternative choice was later given the technical name of 'liberty of indifference'. Chrysippus is not claiming that liberty of indifference is compatible with fate: he is interested rather in what later philosophers called 'liberty of spontaneity'. An agent enjoys liberty of spontaneity if he does X because he wants to do X. Chrysippus' humans do enjoy liberty of spontaneity, because they do X because they assent to X, and they assent to X because of their own nature and character. The responsibility that he defends is the autonomy of the agent to act unforced by external causes and stimuli.

From the time of Chrysippus up to the present day philosophers have debated how far it is possible to reconcile determinism and freedom. One of the most interesting contributions in the ancient world was made by St Augustine, in his work on the freedom of the will, written in the year of his conversion to Christianity. However, since he locates his discussion in an ethical and theological context, we shall wait to consider it until Chapter 8.

6

What There Is: Metaphysics

The central topic of metaphysics is ontology: the study of Being. The word 'ontology' derives from the Greek word 'on' (in the plural 'onta'), which is the present participle of 'einai', the verb 'to be'. In Greek, as in English, a definite article can be placed in front of a participle to mark out a class of people or things: as when we talk of the living or of the dying, meaning all the people who are now living or all the people who are now dying. The founder of ontology was Parmenides, and he defined his topic by placing the definite article 'to' in front of the participle 'on'. 'To on', literally 'the being', on the model of 'the living', means: all that is. It is customary to translate the expression into English as 'Being' with an initial capital. Without a capital, the English word 'being' has, in philosophy, two uses, one corresponding to the Greek participle and one to the Greek infinitive. A being, we can say, using the participle, is an individual that is; whereas being (using the verbal noun) is, as it were, what any individual being is engaged in. The totality of individual beings make up Being.

These rather tedious grammatical distinctions need making, because neglect of them can lead, and has led, even great philosophers into confusion. In order to understand Parmenides, one further important distinction has to be made: between being and existence.

'To be' in English, and its equivalent in Greek, can certainly mean 'to exist'. Thus, Wordsworth tells us, 'She lived unknown, and few could know | When Lucy ceased to be.' In English the use is largely poetic, and it is not natural to say such things as 'The pyramids are, but the Colossus of Rhodes is not', when we mean that the pyramids are still in existence, while the Colossus is not. But analogous statements would be quite natural in ancient Greek, and this sense of 'be' is certainly involved in Parmenides' talk of Being. All that there is, all that exists, is included in Being.

However, the Greek verb 'to be' occurs not only in sentences such as 'Troy is no more' but also in sentences of many different kinds, such as 'Helen is beautiful', 'Aphrodite is a goddess', 'Achilles is brave', and so on through all the different modes that Aristotle was to dignify as categories. For Parmenides, Being is not just that which exists, but that of which any sentence containing 'is' is true. Equally, being is not just existing (being, period) but being anything whatever: being hot or being cold, being earth or being water, and so on. Thus interpreted, Being is a realm both richer and more puzzling than the totality of existents.

Parmenides' Ontology

Let us now look in detail at some of Parmenides' mysterious claims, expressed in his rugged verse, which I have tried to render in an equally clumsy translation.

> What you can call and think must Being be
> For Being can, and nothing cannot, be.   (DK 28 B6)

The first line (literally: 'What is for saying and for thinking must be') expresses the universality of Being: whatever you can call by any name, whatever you can think of, must be. Why so? Presumably because if I utter a name or think a thought, I must be able to answer the question 'What *is* it that you are talking about or thinking of?' The message of the second line (literally 'It is for being be but nothing is not') is that anything that can be at all must be something or other; it cannot be just nothing.

The matter becomes clearer when Parmenides, in a later fragment, introduces a negative notion to correspond to Being.

> Never shall this prevail, that Unbeing is;
> Rein in your mind from any thought like this.   (DK 28 B7, 1–2)

My 'Unbeing' represents the negation of Parmenides' participle (*me eonta*). I use the word instead of some formula such as 'not-being' because the context makes clear that Parmenides' Greek expression, though a perfectly

Parmenides and Heraclitus, neighbours in Raphael's School of Athens

natural one, is meant to designate a polar opposite of Being. If Being is that of which something or other, no matter what, is true, then Unbeing is that of which nothing at all is true. And that, surely, is nonsense: not only can it not exist, it cannot even be thought of.

> Unbeing you won't grasp—it can't be done—
> Nor utter; being thought and being are one.

If we understand 'Unbeing' as meaning that to which no predicate can be attached, then it is surely correct to say that it is something unthinkable. If, in answer to your question 'What kind of thing are you thinking of?', I say that it isn't any kind of thing, you will be puzzled. If, further, I cannot tell you what it is like, or indeed tell you anything at all about it, you may justly conclude that I'm not thinking of anything, indeed not really thinking at all. If we understand Parmenides in this sense, we can agree that to be thought of and to be go together.

But granting this much, we may still want to protest against the sweeping claim that being thought and being are one. It may be the case that if I am to think of X I must be able to attach, in thought, some predicate to X. But it is not the case that any thought I have about X must be true: I can think that X *is* P when X *is not* P. If we take the dictum in that way, then it is false: being thought and being true are two very different things.

Again, we can agree that Unbeing cannot be thought of without agreeing that what does not exist cannot be thought of. We can think of fictional heroes and chimerical beasts who never existed. If it were true that what does not exist cannot be thought of, we could prove that things exist simply by thinking of them. Did Parmenides believe we could? Given the contortions of his language, it is hard to be sure. Some scholars claim that he confused the 'is' of predication (involved in the true claim that Unbeing cannot be thought of) with the 'is' of existence (involved in the false claim that the non-existent cannot be thought of). It is, I think, more helpful to say rather that Parmenides always treats 'to be'—in any of its uses—as a fully fledged verb. That is to say, he thinks of 'being water' or 'being air' as related to 'being' in the same way as 'running fast' and 'running slowly' is related to 'running'. In a sentence of the form 'S is P', instead of thinking of the 'is' as a copula and the 'P' as a predicate, he thinks of the 'is' as a verb and the 'P' as analogous to an adverb. A person who first runs fast and then runs slowly is running all the time. Similarly, for Parmenides, stuff which is first water and then air goes on be-ing all the time. Change is never from not-being to being, or vice versa; the most there can ever be is variation of being.

Interpreting Parmenides in this way helps us to understand how he draws some very remarkable conclusions from the theses of the universality of Being and the inconceivability of Unbeing.

> One road there is, signposted in this wise:
> Being was never born and never dies.
> Four-square, unmoved, no end it will allow.
> It never was, nor will be; all is now,
> One and continuous. How could it be born
> Or whence could it be grown? Unbeing?—No—
> That mayn't be said or thought; we cannot go
> So far ev'n to deny it is. What need,
> Early or late, could Being from Unbeing seed?
> Thus it must altogether be or not.
>
> (DK 28 B8. 1–11)

From the principle 'Nothing can come from nothing' many philosophers of different persuasions have drawn the conclusion that the world must always have existed. Other philosophers, too, have offered as a supporting argument that there could be no sufficient reason for a world to come into existence at one moment rather than another, earlier or later. But Parmenides' claim that Being has no beginning and no end takes a much more sweeping form. Being is not only everlasting, it is not subject to change ('four-square, unmoved') or even to the passage of time (it is all now, and has no past or future). What could differentiate past from present and future? If it is no kind of being, then time is unreal; if it is some kind of being, then it is all part of Being. Past, present, and future are all one Being.

By similar arguments Parmenides seeks to show that Being is undivided. What could separate Being from Being? Being? In that case there is no division, but continuous Being. Unbeing? In that case any division is unreal (DK 28 B8. 22–5). We might expect him to argue in a parallel fashion that Being is unlimited. What could set limits to Being? Unbeing cannot do anything to anything; and if we imagine that Being is limited by Being, then Being has not yet reached its limits. Some of Parmenides' followers argued thus (Aristotle, *GC* 1.8. 325^{a}15), but this is not how Parmenides himself seems to have seen matters. When he comes to sum up his teaching, starting from premises that are by now familiar he reaches a rather startling conclusion.

> To think a thing's to think it is, no less.
> Apart from Being, whate'er we may express
> Thought does not reach. Naught is or will be
> Beyond Being's bounds, since Destiny's decree
> Fetters it whole and still. All things are names
> Which the credulity of mortals frames—
> Birth and destruction, being all or none,
> Changes of place, and colours come and gone.
> But since a bound is set embracing all
> Its shape's well rounded like a perfect ball.

(DK 28 B8, 34–43)

It is not at all clear how the concept of the universe as a perfect sphere is either coherent in itself or reconcilable with the rest of Parmenides' teaching. However that may be, there is a more pressing question. If this is the nature of Being, uniform, unchanging, immobile, and timeless, what are we to make of the multiplicity of changing properties that we normally attribute to items in the world on the basis of sense-experience? These, for Parmenides, belong to the Way of Seeming. If we want to follow the Way of Truth, we must keep our minds fixed on Being.

While Parmenides and his disciples, in Greek Italy, were stressing that only what is utterly stable is real, Heraclitus, across the seas in Greek Asia, was stressing that what is real is in total flux. Heraclitus was given to speaking in riddles: to express his philosophy of universal change he used both fire and water as images. The world is an ever-living fire, now flaring up, now dying down; fire is the currency into which everything can be converted just as gold and goods are exchanged for each other (DK 22 B30, B90). But the world is also an ever-flowing river. If you step into a river, you cannot put your feet twice into the same water. Getting rather carried away by his metaphor, Heraclitus went on to say—if Plato reports him honestly—that you cannot step twice into the same river (*Cra.* 402a). However that may be, he seems undoubtedly to have claimed that all things are in motion all of the time (Aristotle, *Ph.* 8. 3. 253^{b}9). If we do not notice this, it is because of the defects of our senses. For Heraclitus, then, it is change that is the Way of Truth, and stability that is the Way of Seeming.

Plato's Ideas and their Troubles

Parmenides and Heraclitus laid out a battlefield for centuries of philosophical warfare. Much of Plato's most energetic philosophizing was devoted to the task of reconciling, or disarming, these two champions. One of his characters tells us that the true philosopher must refuse to accept either the doctrine that all reality is changeless, or the doctrine that reality is everywhere changing. 'Like a child who wants to have his cake and eat it he must say that Being, the sum of all, is both at once—all that is unchangeable, and all that is in change' (*Sph.* 249c–d).

Aristotle tells us that Plato began to philosophize under the influence of Heraclitean ideas, and retained them well on in life (*Metaph. A* 6. 987^{a}31–3). In the *Theaetetus* Plato offers a theory of perception that endeavours to preserve the truth in Heraclitus' insights without accepting the universal flux. We will consider this in Chapter 7, concentrating for the present on his treatment of Parmenidean problems.

During his life Plato made three systematic attempts to cope with the metaphysical issues raised by the two giants. The first is the Theory of Ideas, as presented in the *Symposium*, *Phaedo*, and *Republic*. Very crudely, one can say that in this phase Plato's Socrates divided the realm of philosophy in two, and handed over the intelligible universe of the Ideas to Parmenides, and the perceptible universe of the senses to Heraclitus. In the second phase Parmenides himself, in the dialogue named after him, is represented as exposing for Socrates some unacceptable consequences of the Ideal theory. In the final phase, in the *Sophist*, a third protagonist, an unnamed stranger from Elea, leads us to disown not only Parmenides and Heraclitus, but also Plato's own Theory of Ideas, in favour of an elaborate solution that will supersede all three and enable us to have our metaphysical cake and eat it.

As we have seen, the Ideas, as represented in the early middle dialogues, belong in an eternal world that is as unchanging as the Being revealed by Parmenides' way of Truth. The entities that inhabit the empirical world, on the other hand, are in a Heraclitean flux, constantly flitting between being and non-being. Plato is not, however, even-handed between the two protagonists: the Parmenidean world is far superior to the Heraclitean one; the unchanging world of Ideas is more real, and contains more truth, than the flickering world of experience. Only intellectual insight

Plato, here idealized in a head from the Vatican, had a gift almost unique among philosophers for criticizing and revizing his own most cherished ideas

into Ideas gives knowledge; the senses can provide nothing better than true belief.

But while the realm of the Ideas is unchanging, it is not uniform or homogeneous like Parmenides' Being. Being is undifferentiated and single, whereas there are many different Ideas in some kind of relation to each other. They appear to be hierarchically ordered, under the Idea of Good, which appears to trump any notion of Being (*Rep.* 6. 509b). No doubt the other Ideas owe it to the Idea of Good that they are Ideas at all: a bed is a Perfect or Ideal Bed because it participates in Perfection and is the best possible bed. But the relations between the different subordinate ideas are not at all spelt out; there is certainly no suggestion that they are all one with each other in some sublime Parmenidean sphere.

It is not surprising, then, that when Plato comes to place a critical evaluation of the Theory of Ideas in the mouth of Parmenides, it is the One, the Idea of Unity, that is the focus of discussion.

The *Parmenides* is the most difficult of Plato's dialogues to interpret, and many scholars have confessed themselves baffled by it. It falls into two parts. The first part resembles one of the earlier Socratic dialogues in which a self-styled expert is shown to be unqualified to hold forth on the topic of his alleged expertise. The startling thing is that the usual roles are reversed. Instead of the inquiring Socrates puncturing the pretensions of some famous sophist, it is the young Socrates himself who is put to the question, and the topic of the quiz from which he emerges humiliated is none other than the Theory of Ideas. Parmenides, who is the successful inquisitor, tells Socrates that he is insufficiently trained in dialectic, and needs further exercise. The second part of the dialogue purports to illustrate the kind of exercise that Socrates needs. Starting from a pair of hypotheses about One and Being, which appear between them to exhaust the possibilities, Parmenides shows by a series of tight but often implausible arguments that whichever arm of the contradiction we accept we are led to wholly unpalatable conclusions.

Scholars disagree about both the nature of each of the two parts and their relation to each other. Are the criticisms of the Ideas in the first part regarded by Plato as seriously damaging to his theory? If so, does he have a remedy to propose, or is he just candidly confessing his perplexity? Are the proofs in the second part meant as jokes or as serious arguments? If the latter, did Plato mean us to detect fallacies in them, or did he himself regard them as valid? Either way, what is the relevance of the second part to the assault on the Ideas in the first part?[1]

Before outlining the main problems for the Theory of Ideas that are put forward in the first part, it is worth repeating at this point the six principles that we identified in Chapter 1 as constituting the core of the classical Theory.

(1) *The Principle of Commonality.* Wherever several things are F, this is because they participate in or imitate a single Idea of F (*Rep.* 5. 476a).
(2) *The Principle of Separation.* The Idea of F is distinct from all the things that are F (*Phd.* 74c).
(3) *The Principle of Self-Predication.* The Idea of F is itself F.
(4) *The Principle of Purity.* The Idea of F is nothing but F (*Phd.* 74c).
(5) *The Principle of Uniqueness.* Nothing but the Idea of F is really, truly, altogether F (*Phd.* 74d; *Rep.* 5. 479a–d).
(6) *The Principle of Sublimity.* Ideas are everlasting, they have no parts and undergo no change, and they are not perceptible to the senses (*Phd.* 78d).

The problems set out in the first part of the dialogue are as follows.

1. According to the theory, particular Fs are F because they participate in the Idea of F. But what does 'participation' mean? Does a particular F share only a part of the Idea, or does it contain the whole of the Idea? There are difficulties either way. If a particular large thing L has the whole Idea of Large, then the Idea seems to be scattered and lack the unity of an Idea; but if L shares only a part of the Large, then it is large by something which is itself small, because being only a part it must be smaller than the Large (131a ff.).

2. It is essential to the theory that wherever several things are F they derive this from some other entity which is the Idea of F. Thus, the several large things derive their largeness from the Idea of Large. But if we put together the original set of large things plus the Idea, we have a new set of large things, which must derive their largeness from some other entity. 'So another form of largeness will appear, alongside the Idea of Large and the things that participated in it, and then another again over all of these'—so that we are set off on an infinite regress (132b). This line of thought much

---

[1] In what follows I am indebted to Constance C. Meinwald's *Plato's Parmenides* (New York: Oxford University Press, 1991), though I differ from her on important points of interpretation.

impressed Aristotle, who, substituting 'man' instead of 'large' for F in the original premiss, named it the Third Man argument, after the Man who would appear as a Super-idea, after (*a*) the men in the world and (*b*) the Ideal Man.

3. There is a special difficulty with relational predicates. Suppose I am a slave. According to the theory, that must be because I resemble the Ideal Slave. But who is the Ideal Slave's owner? Surely, the Ideal Owner. But I am not a slave of the Ideal Owner but of whoever is my terrestrial slave-owner. So the relationships between entities in the world cannot be explained by relationships between the Ideas (133e).

These difficulties are genuine problems for the Theory of Ideas, and surely Plato means us to realize this. At the very least they demand substantial modification of the theory, and in other dialogues Plato undertakes such modification. In the *Parmenides*, however, he does not explicitly present the necessary modifications. We might expect, though, that the second part of the dialogue offers some guidance over the lines the modification needs to take.

A major problem with the second part is that it is not clear exactly what is the pair of hypotheses from which Parmenides starts his argument (137b). He describes the hypotheses as hypotheses about the One itself, but the Greek in which they are stated can be rendered in several ways. The two following pairs are the most promising translations:

(1) If the One is   v.   If the One is not.
(2) If it is one   v.   If it is not one.

(2) is the reading that best fits the Greek of the received text of this passage of the dialogue, where no definite article occurs before the word 'one' (*hen*). Indeed, even the most enthusiastic partisans of the first reading agree that it can only be sustained if one amends the text at this point. On the other hand, (1) seems to be a better fit not only to the immediately preceding wording, but to the whole series of subsequent arguments, which quite frequently unambiguously refer to the One, with a definite article. Moreover, anyone who accepts reading (2) has to answer the question what the 'it' stands for.

On my view, there is no need to amend the text. The second reading, which is the most natural translation, can easily be reconciled with the subsequent argument. There are two ways to do this.

The first is to take the 'it' in question to be the same as the 'it' which is the subject of the Way of Truth in the poem of the historical Parmenides: namely, Being. The references to the One in the course of the subsequent arguments are easy to account for. They occur in the course of following out the hypothesis that 'It (sc. Being) is One'. If that hypothesis is true, then there is one pre-eminent subject to which the predicate 'One' applies, namely Being itself. This subject can quite naturally be referred to as 'the One', and it is proleptically so referred to by Parmenides at 137b3. However, this interpretation becomes harder to sustain when Parmenides proceeds to examine the negative hypothesis, which on this account would be 'that Being is not one'.

A second interpretation, therefore, is preferable. The 'it' should be read as 'the One'. In that case, the two hypotheses are 'The One is one' and 'The One is not one'. Initially, this may seem a very implausible reading: surely the second hypothesis rules itself out instantly as being self-contradictory. But if we reflect, we see that this is not so. Some of the major problems with the Theory of Ideas that were laid out in the first part of the dialogue derived from the principle of self-predication, namely that the Idea of F is itself F (see p. 208 above). It is appropriate that the second part of the dialogue should not take self-predication for granted, but explore the consequences, in the case of one pre-eminent Idea, of its denial as well as of its affirmation.

The dialectic begins with the protagonist Parmenides inquiring what predicates attach to the One, and what predicates attach to other things, on the basis of the first hypothesis. If the One is one, then the One is not a whole with parts (137d). It is without limit and without place (138b). It is unchanging, but it is also not at rest (139b). It is neither different from, nor the same as, itself or another (139e), and it is neither like nor unlike itself or anything else (140b). It is neither greater nor less than itself or anything else (140d). It is not situated in time, and since it does not belong in the past, present, or future, it cannot have any share in being at all. The conclusion is this:

Therefore the One in no way is. Therefore it is not in such a way as to be one, because in that case it would be a being and a partaker of being. But, as it seems, the One is not one and is not at all, if we have to trust this argument. But if something is not, then nothing can belong to it or be about it. So it has no name, no sentence or thought can be about it, and there can be no sensation or knowledge of it. (142a)

We are pretty clearly not intended to accept this conclusion as a true statement about the One. Parmenides' interlocutor in the dialogue, Aristotle (no relation), who is commonly a complete yes-man, interposes a rare note of dissent when asked if this conclusion is possible. If it were true, it would cut the ground from under the arguments that lead to it, since they all purport to speak about the One, which according to this conclusion cannot be done. The dialectic up to this point must be intended as a *reductio ad absurdum*: but a *reductio* of what? Surely of the hypothesis that the One is one *and nothing but one*. But of course an important part of the Theory of Ideas was the Principle of Purity: that the Idea of F was F and nothing but F. So the dialectic, to this point, is a recantation of an important element in the theory.

At this point Parmenides makes a fresh start from the hypothesis that the One is one and proves that the One is a whole with ever so many parts (142b, 143a), bounded and shaped (145b), located both in itself and elsewhere, both in motion and at rest, both the same as and different from itself and from other things (146b), both like and unlike itself and other things (148c), simultaneously equal to, greater than, and less than itself and other things (151b). It is and becomes older and younger than itself and other things, but equally it neither is nor becomes older or younger than itself nor other things (155c). It belongs to past, present, and future, and it partakes in being, though being and oneness are not the same (if they were, Plato argues, 'is one' would mean the same as 'one one') (142c). So there is no problem in naming it, speaking of it, and arguing about it (155e).

There is clearly a close parallel between these two first sections of the dialectic. At each stage of each argument we are presented with a pair of opposite predicates (e.g. in motion, at rest). In the first section Parmenides argues that neither of these predicates apply to the One. In the second section he argues that both of these predicates apply to the One. Between them, the two sections throw a damaging light on the Theory of Ideas. The first section shows the folly of holding that the Idea of F is nothing but F (the Principle of Purity). The second section shows the falsehood of holding that nothing but the Idea of F is F (the Principle of Uniqueness).

But the two sections are not meant to be on all fours with each other. The conclusion of the first section is, as we have seen, self-stultifying and the whole argument can only be taken seriously as a *reductio ad absurdum*. The second section, however, leads to a conclusion that, though it may be surprising, can be understood in a way which is in no way self-refuting.

Summing up the results of this section, Parmenides says that the One sometimes partakes of being and sometimes does not. His words echo the complaint made in the *Republic* about the ordinary objects of sense-perception, namely that they roll about between being and non-being. But now it is a form that displays this pattern, whereas in the heyday of the theory what marked off Ideas from common or garden objects was that they did not roll about. The Idea of F was not sometimes F and sometimes not F, nor was it F in one respect and not F in another respect. What is now said about the One marks a very significant departure from the original Theory of Ideas.

In the case of the sensible particulars, we could specify the times, respects, relations, and so forth that made them—without any violation of the principle of non-contradiction—both F and not F. What we now have to do is to draw appropriate distinctions to see how both a predicate and its opposite can be true in different respects, of the One, and by implication, of other Forms. It is to be noted that the subjects of all Parmenides' predications are Ideas, or at least they are all items referred to by universal terms, not individual names: the expressions for them are things like 'the same', 'the other', not 'Callias', or 'Dio'.

In order to resolve some of the problems about Ideas, Plato introduces a distinction between two types of predication. Using a terminology which belongs to a later period, we can say that he makes a distinction between predication per se and predication *per accidens*. The difference between the two can be brought out thus: S is P per se if being P is part of what it is to be S. Thus, an oak is a tree per se. (If we allow improper as well as proper parts of what it is to be S, then an oak is oak per se.) S is P *per accidens*, on the other hand, if S is as a matter of fact P, but it is no part of being S to be P. Thus, if oaks are as a matter of fact plentiful in a certain area, 'plentiful' is predicated only *per accidens*.[2]

We have seen that Plato, in the *Parmenides*, abandoned the Principles of Purity and Uniqueness. With respect to the Principle of Self-predication he makes use of his distinction between types of predicate. The Large is indeed

---

[2] The Latin terms are meant to correspond to, though they are not translations of, Plato's Greek terms *pros heauto* (with respect to itself) and *pros alla* (with respect to others).

large: being large is an improper part of what it is to be large. But other things are not large per se. If my house is large, that is not because being large is part of what it is to be a house. Hence 'large' is not predicated in the same way of large things and of the Large; and hence the Large and the other large things cannot be grouped together to form a set as they have to be in order to generate the regress nicknamed the Third Man.

Similarly, the Slave belongs per se to the Owner: for belonging to an owner is part of what it is to be a slave. But the relations between human slaves and human owners, and the relations between both and the Ideal Slave and the Ideal Owner are not per se but *per accidens*. Both sets of relationship, relationships between individuals and between forms, can function side by side without conflict.

Finally, we can revisit the notion of participation. A major difficulty in understanding how many things can share in a single Idea was that this seemed to divide an Idea into parts. We can now say that a Form is one per se if it is part of what it is to be a Form that it should be single and unique: otherwise it will not achieve the purpose for which it was invented, to mark what is common to things bearing the same name. But if there are many individuals instantiating the Form, then it will be many *per accidens*.

The common thread that runs through the dialectical arguments and the suggested solutions to the Parmenidean difficulties about the Theory of Forms is this: nothing can be predicated in the same way of individuals and of the Forms in which the individuals partake. One modern analogue of the Platonic notion of participation is that of class membership: if x participates in the Form of F, x is a member of the class of Fs. Equally, a modern analogue of the message of the *Parmenides* is that one cannot simply predicate of classes what one predicates of individuals. The paradox that results if we talk of the class of all classes that are not members of themselves is the lineal descendant of the paradoxes of the *Parmenides*.

The adaptation of the Theory of Ideas into a Theory of Forms is carried out further in the dialogue the *Sophist*. The official purpose of the dialogue is to find a definition of a sophist. The definition eventually offered is clearly intended as a joke. What the search for the definition is meant to illustrate is a method of definition that is still popular in parlour games. In such games the respondent thinks of an object that it is the questioner's task to identify by putting a series of questions offering a dichotomy. Is it living or non-living? If living, is it an animal or a plant? If an animal, is it human or non-human? And so on. In the course of the dialogue Plato examines the metaphysical presuppositions of such a style of definition.

What the pursuit of a definition by division will reveal, if it is carried out in a serious manner, is a tree structure in which species will appear under genera, and narrower genera under broader genera: human under animal, animal under living being, and so on. This tree structure is related to the predication per se which we found an important feature of the *Parmenides*. For anything that appears above F in a genus–species tree structure will be something that is predicated per se. Thus, being an animal is part of what it is to be human; being a living thing is part of what it is to be an animal.

On the way to the definition of the sophist we have to address the problem of false thought and false discourse. One cannot distinguish the fraudulent sophist from the true philosopher without discussing the nature of falsehood. But how can we talk about falsehood without falling into the traps set out by the historical Parmenides in his poem (237a)? To say what is false is to say what is not. But what is not is surely Unbeing, and Unbeing is nonsense for reasons that Parmenides gave (238e). It seems to be impossible, therefore, to say what is false without talking nonsense. Shall we revise our account, then, and maintain that to say what is false is to say that what is, is not, or that what is not, is? Will this avoid Parmenides' censure?

To deal with this problem we have to disarm Parmenides by forcing him to agree that what is not, in some respect is, and what is, in a manner is not (241d). Motion, for instance, is not rest, but that does not mean that motion is not anything at all (250b). There are many things that even Being is not: for instance, Being is not motion and Being is not rest (250c–e).

In the *Sophist* as in the *Parmenides* Plato is interested in the relationships between different Forms. Here, he describes this topic as 'the interweaving of Forms', which he says is what underpins language (259e). We dig a pit for ourselves if we assume either that no Forms can combine with each other or that all can (251e–252e). Clearly, some can and some cannot, and we need to inquire which Forms can combine with which other Forms. Being (*to on*) here occupies the central role in this inquiry that the One (*to hen*) occupied in the *Parmenides*. But in addition to Being four other forms— motion, rest, sameness, and difference—are considered and their interrelations explored.

Difference turns out to have a crucial relationship to Being (256d–e). When we speak of what is not, we are not talking of Unbeing, the contrary of Being: we are speaking simply of something that is different from one of the things there are (257b). The non-beautiful differs from the beautiful and the unjust differs from the just; but the non-beautiful and the unjust are no less real than the beautiful and the just (257e–258a). If we lump together all the things that are non-something, or unsomething, then we get the category of non-being, which is just as real as the category of Being. So we have blown open the prison into which Parmenides had confined us (258c).

We are now in a position to give an account of falsehood in thought and speech. The problem was that it was not possible to think or say what was not, because Unbeing was nonsense. But now that we have found that non-being is perfectly real, we can use this to explain false thoughts and false sentences.

A typical sentence consists of a noun and a verb, and it says something about something (262a–e). 'Theaetetus is sitting' and 'Theaetetus is flying' are both sentences about Theaetetus, but one of them is true and one false (263b). They say different things about Theaetetus, and the true one says a thing about him that is among the things that he is, while the false one says a thing about him that is among the things that he is not. Flying is not Unbeing, it is a thing that is—there is quite a lot of it about—but it is a thing that is different from the things that Theaetetus is, the things that can truly be said of Theaetetus (263b).

From time to time in the *Sophist* Plato describes the controversy over the nature of Being in terms of a battle between groups of philosophical adversaries. In one place it is a battle between giants and gods, giants being materialists who think there is nothing but bodies, and gods being idealists who accept non-bodily Forms as described in the Theory of Ideas (246a ff.). Elsewhere the materialists appear, under the leadership of Heraclitus, as the proponents of universal flux (since all bodies are constantly changing) while the chief of the friends of Forms appears to be Parmenides, with his doctrine that all reality is changeless. Finally we are told that the true philosopher must turn a deaf ear to Heraclitus, and also reject the doctrine that all true reality is changeless, whether put forward by the champion of a single Form (Parmenides) or the champion of many Forms (the Plato of the theory).

The *Sophist* shows us the way to have our cake and eat it and say that Being encompasses all that is unchangeable and all that is in change (271d).

Aristotelian Forms

Aristotle was a severe critic of the Theory of Ideas. Sometimes he criticizes it respectfully (e.g. *NE* 1. 6. 1096ª11 ff.: Plato is my friend, but truth is a greater one), and sometimes contemptuously (e.g. *APo.* 1. 22. 83ª28: farewell to such tarradiddle). His critique, whether rude or civil, always seem directed to the theory as presented in the middle dialogues, and not to

Whether or not Aristotle refuted Platonism, Filippino Lippi was in no doubt that Aquinas had done so (Caraffa Chapel, S. Maria sopra Minerva, Rome)

216

the developments of the Theory of Forms in the *Parmenides* and the *Sophist*. He does, however, often tacitly make use of Plato's later thoughts in his own writings, in particular when developing his own theory of forms in *Metaphysics Z*. There, he treats on equal terms problems with Plato's theory and difficulties in his own. The book is dense and difficult, and the account of it I now give can only claim to be one possible thread to guide us through its labyrinth.

The difference between Aristotelian forms and Platonic Forms is that for Aristotle forms are not separate (*chorista*): any form is the form of some actual individual. As we have seen in our account of Aristotelian physics, form is paired with matter, and the paradigm examples of forms are the substantial or accidental forms of material substances. Aristotle cannot avoid, however, the questions for which Plato sought a solution in his theory. He must, for instance, provide his own answer to someone who asks what is common to the many things that are called by the same name or fall under the same predicate. He must, that is, offer an account of universal terms.

In *Metaphysics Z* Aristotle discusses the relationships between being, substance, matter, and form. He there works to relate the teaching of the *Categories* on substance and predication with the teaching of the *Physics* on matter and form, and he combines the two together, with modification and amplification, into a treatise on Being. 'The question that was asked of old, and is asked now, and always will be asked and always will be a problem is "what is Being?" And this is the question; "what is substance?" ' (*Z* 1. 1028^{b}2–4).

The reason he gives for eliding the two questions recalls the *Categories*. Whatever there is must be either a substance or something that belongs to a substance, such as a quantity or a quality of it. When we are listing the things that there are, we may count, if you like, health and goodness; but any actual health is someone's health, and any actual goodness is the goodness of something or other. If we ask, in such cases, what really and truly is, the answer will be: this healthy person, this good dog (*Z* 1. 1028^{a}24–30).

So Aristotle can regard it as obvious that material entities like animals and plants and earth and water and the sun and the stars are substances (*Δ* 8. 1017^{b}8; *Z* 3. 1028^{b}8). He puts on one side, for later treatment that we have no space to follow, a number of further questions. Are surfaces, lines, and points substances? Are numbers substances? But he addresses right away, though in a roundabout manner, the great Platonic question: Are there separate substances of any kind, distinct from those we can perceive with our senses? (*Z* 3. 1028^{b}8–32).

Essence and Quiddity

We saw that in the *Parmenides* Plato introduced a form of predication per se: S is P per se if being P is part of what it is to be S. Aristotle is keenly interested in this form of predication. In the *Categories* it is predication in the category of (second) substance. In the *Metaphysics* it is predication that answers the question what kind of thing something is (*ti esti*). Sometimes Aristotle speaks of the 'what-is-it?' of a thing; and in the context of the present discussion he often uses an almost untranslatable expression, *to ti en einai*, composed of the definite article, the question 'what-is-it?' and the infinitive of the verb 'to be'. This translates literally as 'the what-is-it to be' of a thing, i.e. the type of being that answers the question 'What is it?'

Latin commentators on Aristotle sometimes used the word 'quidditas' to correspond to this Greek expression; the Latin question 'Quid est?' corresponds to the Greek question 'Ti esti'. Many English scholars use 'essence' as a translation. That is quite possible; but I shall take my cue from the Latin and use the word 'quiddity'. 'Essence' is, of course, itself a Latinism, deriving from the Latin verb for being, 'esse', just as the Greek 'ousia' derives from the Greek word for being. There is good reason, however, to stick with the traditional translation 'substance' for 'ousia'. We can then use the word 'essence' to cope with another crabbed Aristotelian construction. We can speak, for example, of the essence of gold where Aristotle would speak of 'the for-gold being', using the infinitive after the Greek dative case, meaning 'what it is for gold to be gold'. This last construction, again, is descended from Plato's concern with questions about what is and what is not part of what being gold involves. For most purposes, 'quiddity' and 'essence' can be treated as synonyms.

With these preliminaries, we can state the agenda that Aristotle sets for himself at the beginning of the central section of *Metaphysics Z*. 'Substance', he says, has four principal meanings: the quiddity, the universal, the genus, and the subject. He treats of each of these four items in later chapters: the subject in chapter 3, the quiddity in chapters 4 and 5, the genus not until chapter 12, and finally the universal in chapter 14.

The subject (*to hypokeimenon*) turns out to be the same as the first substance of the *Categories*: it is that of which everything is predicated and which is itself predicated of nothing. Such first substances, we are told, are composites of matter and form; in the way that a statue is related to its bronze and its shape (1029^{a}3–5): so much is familiar to us from the *Physics*. But matter is not substance (because pure matter cannot exist alone; 1029^{a}27), and if we are to discover whether form is substance, we have to investigate its relation to quiddity.

In treating of quiddity Aristotle makes use of a distinction he drew in his lexicon in *Metaphysics Δ* (1017^{a}7) between being per se (*kath'auto*) and being *per accidens* (*kata sumbebekos*). I have already used these expressions in giving an account of the *Parmenides*, though Plato's Greek expressions are not quite the same. The Latin phrases are simply transverbalizations of Aristotle's Greek expressions. It is futile to seek to render them into English, since the meaning of any English equivalents, as of the Latin and Greek phrases, would have to be gleaned from the contexts in which they occur. The phrases are used in various contexts, for instance in that of causation. A builder is a per se cause of a house: he builds it *qua* builder. But if the builder happens also to be blind, then the headline 'Blind man builds house' gives not the per se but the *per accidens* cause of the house.

The distinction is applied to the case of being in the following way. Entities in all ten of the categories, he tells us, are examples of per se beings: a thing's colour or shape is as much a per se being as the thing itself (*Δ* 7. 1017^{a}22). Clearly, the distinction between per se and *per accidens* is not the same as that between substance and accident. Accidents, confusingly, are per se beings. It is a substance-qualified-by-an-accident that is a *per accidens* being. So while the wisdom of Socrates is a per se being, wise Socrates is not; he is a being *per accidens*.

Aristotle uses his definition in defining quiddity: a quiddity is what a thing is said to be per se. You may be a scholar, but you are not a scholar per se as you are a person per se (*Z* 4. 1029^{b}15). 'The scholar Theophrastus' names a *per accidens* being. However, 'the man Theophrastus' names a per se being, and 'Theophrastus is a man' is a per se predication. Being a man is the quiddity or essence of Theophrastus.

A quiddity, we are further told, is what is given by a definition. This is puzzling, for surely not only per se beings have definitions. No doubt, for Aristotle, a postman would be a *per accidens* being: but can we not define 'postman' as 'man who brings the post' (cf. 1029^{b}27)? Aristotle responds that we do not always have a definition of X when we have a series of words equivalent to 'X': otherwise the whole epic would be a definition of the word 'Iliad' (*Z* 4. 1030^{a}9). A definition must be in terms of species and genus, and only such a definition will generate a quiddity (*Z* 4. 1030^{a}12).

Accidents as well as substances can be defined in this way: we can ask what 'triangular' means as well as asking what a horse is. To allow for this Aristotle is willing to soften his original strict account of definition. 'Definition', he says, like 'being', 'quiddity', and 'essence', are all analogous terms: all four of them belong primarily only to substances, just as 'health' is predicated primarily of patients and only secondarily of medicines and instruments. Secondarily, they can be applied to accidents, and thirdly even to *per accidens* beings (*Z* 4. 1030^{b}1; 5. 1031^{a}9).

Aristotle next asks: what is the relation between a thing and its quiddity? His answer is that they are identical: and this takes us by surprise, since a thing is surely concrete and a quiddity is surely abstract. His initial justification of his surprising claim is that a thing is surely the same substance as itself, and a thing's quiddity is called its substance. The *Categories* seems to offer a fairly straightforward way of sorting out the mystery here: Socrates, for example, is identical with a first substance, and his quiddity is his second substance. But here in *Metaphysics Z* Aristotle is looking for the answer to the question, what is really meant by 'second substance'? In 'Socrates is human' what does 'human' signify?

The first answer Aristotle considers is that of Plato: it stands for a Humanity that is something distinct from Socrates. Aristotle uses a variant of the Third Man argument to show that this will not do. If a horse was distinct from its quiddity, the horse's quiddity would have its own distinct quiddity, and so on for ever. The chapter ends with the remark, 'It is clear then that for things that are primary and spoken of per se the thing and its essence are one and the same' (*Z* 6. 1032^{a}8).

What this seems to mean is this. In a sentence such as 'Socrates is wise' the word 'wise' signifies an accident, the wisdom of Socrates, which is distinct from Socrates. But in 'Socrates is human' the word 'human' does not signify anything distinct from Socrates himself. We need to distinguish between Socrates and his wisdom because they have two different histories: as Socrates gets older, Socrates' wisdom may increase or perhaps evaporate. But Socrates and his humanity do not have two different histories: to be Socrates is to be human, and if Socrates ceases to be a human being he ceases to exist.

But is there not still the difference between concrete and abstract to be taken account of? Aristotle helps us with this in his discussion of coming-into-being in chapters 7 and 8, where he makes the point that when a thing comes into being, neither its form nor its quiddity begins to exist. Using his long-overworked analogy, he says that if I manufacture a bronze sphere, I do not thereby make either the bronze or the spherical shape. He goes on to generalize:

What comes into existence must always be divisible, and there must be two identifiable components, one matter and the other form. . . . it is clear from what has been said that the part which is called form or substance does not come into existence; what comes into existence is the composite entity which bears its name. (Z 8. 1033^{b}16–19)

He goes on to draw an anti-Platonic conclusion: if everyday enmattered forms do not come into existence at all, there is no need to invoke separate, Ideal, Forms to explain how forms come into existence (Z 8. 1033^{b}26).

We do not even need to invoke Forms to explain how an individual substance gets its form. Human beings derive their form not from an Ideal Human, but from their parents (Z 8. 1033^{b}32). The father (plus the mother, though Aristotle was ignorant of this) is responsible for introducing form into the appropriate matter. 'The final product, a form of such-and-such a kind in this flesh and these bones, is Callias or Socrates. What makes them distinct is their matter, which is distinct; but they are the same in form (for that is not subdivided)' (Z 8. 1034^{a}8). In this passage Aristotle enunciates a thesis that was to have a long history, namely the thesis that matter is the principle of individuation. According to this thesis, however different two things may be from each other, it is not the differences between their properties or characteristics that make them distinct from each other. For it is possible for things to resemble each other totally without being identical with each other. Two peas, for instance, however alike they are, are two peas and not one pea because they are two different parcels of matter.

In some places Aristotle identifies form and quiddity (e.g. Z 7. 1032ª33) and he goes on to say that in the case of humans and other animals, the form and the quiddity are to be identified with the soul (Z 10. 1035ᵇ14). This presents a problem: if the soul is the quiddity, and the quiddity is the same as what has the quiddity, does this mean that Socrates is identical with Socrates' soul? Aristotle seems briefly ready to contemplate this possibility (Z 11. 1037ª8), but that is not his considered opinion, and he goes on to qualify his identification of soul, form, and quiddity. 'Man and horse and whatever is predicated universally of individuals are not substance. Substance is the composite of this definition and this matter taken universally' (Z 10. 1035ᵇ27). That means that having flesh and blood is indeed part of being human; but having *this* particular flesh and blood is not part of being human. It is part, however, of being Socrates.

We may wonder what is the relationship between the pair matter–form and the pair body–soul. Aristotle at Z 11. 1037ª5 says that an animal is composed of body and soul, and he clearly identifies body with matter, but at that point he says not that the soul is form, but that it is first substance. He goes on shortly afterwards to say that the primary substance is the form inherent in the thing, and that substance (of another kind) is the composite of this and the matter (Z 11. 1037ª29). To make this cohere with his earlier teaching, we have to assume that he is here calling 'first substance' what in the *Categories* he called 'second substance'!

We are left, however, with a serious problem. In studying an earlier passage of the *Metaphysics* we had good reason to conclude that Aristotle was teaching that in 'Socrates is human' the predicate 'human' signified nothing other than Socrates. Now it seems to be suggested that it signifies Socrates' form or soul: it is that which provides the definition of Socrates, and it is here being distinguished from Socrates' matter. Socrates' body is clearly part of Socrates: but is it part of Socrates' definition or quiddity?

Some light is thrown on this by Aristotle's treatment of definition. Definitions have parts, and the substances they define also have parts: Aristotle takes a chapter to explain that if A is a part of X this does not always mean that the definition of A has to be part of the definition of X. (You don't have to mention an acute angle in defining a right angle; just the reverse, in fact; Z 11. 1035ᵇ6.) The definition has to mention parts of the form, but not parts of the matter. Parts of the form are to be identified by the method of definition by division, into genus and species, that we met in Plato's later dialogues.

We can now see why it is misguided to ask whether Socrates' body is part of his quiddity. Body and soul are parts of Socrates (parts of a rather special kind, as will be explained in the next chapter). Being rational and being animal are parts of the quiddity of Socrates, and being animal includes having a body (an organic body of a particular kind). But *having a body* is not at all the same as a body. To ask whether Socrates' body is part of his quiddity is to fall into the confusion of concrete and abstract of which we were earlier tempted to accuse Aristotle himself. On the other hand, we must say something similar about soul. The soul cannot simply be identified with the quiddity, as Aristotle sometimes incautiously suggests: to be human is to have a soul of an appropriate kind incarnate in an organic body.

We have done our best to make sense of the doctrine of substance in the *Metaphysics*. The topic was introduced by Aristotle as a method of answering the fundamental question, What is being? It is now time to address that question frontally.

Being and Existence

It is clear that Aristotle uses the expression *to on* in the same manner as Parmenides: Being is whatever is anything whatever. Whenever Aristotle explains its meaning he does so by explaining the sense of the Greek verb 'to be' (e.g. $\varDelta$ 7. 1017^{a}6 ff.; Z 2. 1028^{a}19 ff.).

Being contains whatever items can be the subjects of true sentences containing the word 'is', whether or not the 'is' is followed by a predicate. Both 'Socrates is' and 'Socrates is wise' tell us something about Being. Predicates in all the categories, Aristotle tells us, signify being, because any verb can be replaced by a predicate that will contain the copula 'is': 'Socrates runs', for instance, can be replaced by 'Socrates is a runner'. Every being in any category other than substance is a property or modification of substance. That is why the study of substance is the way to understand the nature of Being.

With Aristotle, as with Parmenides, it is a mistake to equate being with existence. In the dictionary entry for 'being' in the philosophical lexicon

Metaphysics Δ existence is not even mentioned as one of the senses of the word. This is surprising, for from time to time in his logical works he seems to have identified it as a special sense. Thus in *Sophistical Refutations* he makes the point that 'to be something is not the same as to be, period', i.e. to be and to be F are not the same (5. 167ª2). He uses this principle to dissolve fallacious inferences such as 'What is not is, because what is not is thought of' or 'X is not, because X is not a man'. He makes a similar move in connection with the being F of that which has ceased to be: e.g. from 'Homer is a poet' it does not follow that he is (*Int.* 11. 21ª25).

In a famous passage of *Posterior Analytics* (11. 7. 92ᵇ14) Aristotle says 'to be is not part of the substance (*ousia*) of anything, because what is (*to on*) is not a genus'. This can be taken as saying that existence is not part of the essence of anything: i.e. *that there is* such a thing is not *what* anything is. If that is what it means, then it deserves the compliment paid by Schopenhauer when he said that with prophetic insight Aristotle forestalled the Ontological Argument.[3] But it is not clear that this is the only sense that can be given to the passage.

The premiss that *to on* is not a genus need not mean that there is no such kind of thing as *the things that there are*, true though that may be. Aristotle elsewhere argues that being is not a genus because a genus is differentiated into species by differences that are distinct from it, whereas any differentia is a being of some kind (*Metaph. B* 3. 998ᵇ21). The clearest case where 'be' must mean 'exist' is when it is attached to 'entia per accidens': when he says 'wise Socrates is' and distinguishes it from 'Socrates is wise' he can hardly mean anything else than that wise Socrates exists, and is among the things that there are. It is much more difficult to decide, when Aristotle writes simply 'Socrates is', whether this means that Socrates exists or that Socrates is a subject of predication: we cannot pin him down to the distinction that seems so clear to us between the copula 'is' and the 'is' of existence.

When 'is' does occur as a copula, joining subject and predicate, we may ask what it signifies. Two possible accounts are suggested by the Aristotelian texts. One is that it has no signification: it is an incomplete symbol, not to be construed by itself, but to be taken with the predicate-term that follows it, so that ' . . . is white' is to be taken as standing for the accidental form being

---

[3] See G. E. M. Anscombe, in Anscombe and P. T. Geach, *Three Philosophers* (Oxford: Blackwell, 1961), 20–1.

'white'. There will then be no general answer to the question what 'is' denotes, but there will in general be an answer to the question what ' . . . is P' denotes, namely an entity in one of the ten categories.

The other, which is easier to fit to the texts, is that it stands for *being*, where 'being' is to be taken as a verbal noun like 'running'. If we say this, it seems that we must add that there are various types of being: the being that is denoted by 'is' in the substantial predicate ' . . . is a horse' is substantial being, whereas the being that is denoted by 'is' in the accidental predicate ' . . . is white' is accidental being of a kind corresponding to the category of quality. Further, more detailed, difference can be drawn between different kinds of being and therefore different senses of 'is'.

A passage that strongly supports this reading is the second chapter of *Metaph*. H. Here Aristotle says that there are many ways in which things differ from each other. Sometimes it is because there are different ways in which their components are combined: sometimes these are mingled, as in a punch, sometimes they are tied together, as in a sheaf, sometimes they are glued together, as in a book. Sometimes the difference is one of position: a stone block may be a threshold or a lintel according as it is above or below a door. Time makes the difference between breakfast and supper, and direction makes the difference between one wind and another. He goes on to say that 'is' is said in as many different senses. A threshold *is* because it is placed in such and such a position, and so its being is to be so placed. For ice to be is for it to be solidified in such and such a way (H 3. $1043^{b}15$ ff.).

While it is a mistake to look to Aristotle's treatment of being for an account of existence, it would be wrong to think that he is unaware of the issues that have exercised philosophers in this area. When philosophers ask themselves which things really exist and which do not, they may be worrying about the contrast between the concrete and the abstract (e.g. Socrates v. wisdom, Socrates v. humanity), or the contrast between the fictional and the factual (e.g. Pegasus v. Bucephalus), or the contrast between the extant and the defunct (the Great Pyramid v. the Pharos of Alexandria). In different places Aristotle treats of all three problems.

We have seen at length how Aristotle deals with abstractions by introducing the categories. Accidents are modifications of substance, so that statements about abstractions, such as colours, actions, and changes, are analysable into ones about first substances. Predicates in the category of substance, on the other hand, do not involve the existence of any entity—such as a Form of Humanity—distinct from the individual substance of the appropriate kind.

Aristotle provides himself with the means to deal with the problems about fictions by introducing a sense of 'is' in which it means 'is true' (*Δ* 7. 1017ᵃ31). A fiction *is* a genuine thought, but it *is not*, i.e. is not true. With regard to the extant and the defunct, Aristotle solves problems about things that come into existence and go out of existence by means of the doctrine of matter and form. To exist is to be matter under a certain form, to be a thing of a certain kind. Socrates ceases to exist if he ceases to possess his form, that is, if he ceases to be a human being.

We have still not explicitly considered the most important of Aristotle's contributions to metaphysics, namely the doctrine of actuality and potentiality. If we consider any item, from a pint of milk to a policeman, we shall find a number of things true of that item and a number of other things which, though not at that time true of it, can become true of it at some other time. Thus, the pint of liquid *is* milk, but it *can be* turned into butter; the policeman *is* fat, prone, and speaks only English, but if he wants to he *can* become slim, start mowing the lawn, and learn French. The things that something currently is, or is doing, are called by Aristotle its actualities (*energeiai*); the things that it can be, or can do, are its potentialities (*dynameis*). Thus the liquid is actually milk but potentially butter; the policeman is actually fat but potentially slim; and so on. Potentiality, in contrast to actuality, is the ability to undergo a change of some kind, whether through one's own action or through the action of other agents upon oneself. A change from fat to slim is an accidental change: in such a case a substance has the potentiality to be now F and now not F. A change, however, from milk to butter would be, for Aristotle, a substantial change. It is not the substance, but the matter, that has the potentiality to take on different substantial forms.

Of course in studying the pairs matter–form and substance–accident, we have in fact become acquainted with particular types of potentiality and actuality. The importance of the analysis in the history of metaphysics is that Aristotle saw it as a way of disarming the challenges of Parmenides, Heraclitus, and Plato. The early metaphysicians had spelt out the paradoxes that could be generated either by saying that being came from being, or that being came from non-being. Aristotle wants to cut between the two by saying that actual being comes from potential being. This, of course, is not a magic formula that will dissolve all philosophical puzzlement: but it is an appropriate template in which to insert detailed analyses of different types of possible change.

Aristotle did not call his own investigations 'Metaphysics'; that name initially just meant 'After Physics' and was given it by his editors to mark the text's place in the corpus. He does, however, say that there is a discipline 'which theorizes about Being *qua* being, and the things which belong to Being taken in itself' (*Γ* 1. 1003ᵃ21). This discipline is called 'first philosophy', and it interests itself in first principles and supreme causes. Aristotle seems to give two conflicting accounts of its subject matter: one that, unlike the special sciences, it deals with Being as a whole; the other that it deals with a particular kind of being, namely divine, independent, and immutable substance (for this reason he sometimes calls it 'theology'). Are we to say that these are two different accounts of Being *qua* being?

No: there is no such thing as Being *qua* being: there are only different ways of studying Being. You can study Being *qua* being, but that is not to study a mysterious object but rather to undertake a particular sort of study. This study, like all Aristotelian sciences, is an inquiry into causes: and when we study Being *qua* being we are looking for the most universal and primary causes. Contrast this with the other disciplines: when we study human physiology, we study humans *qua* animals, that is to say we study the structures and functions that humans have in common with animals. But of course there is no such entity as a human *qua* animal.

To study something as a being is to study it in virtue of what it has in common with all other things. (Precious little, you might think: and Aristotle himself says, as we have seen, that nothing can have being as its essence or nature.) But a study of the universe *as being* is to study it as a single overarching system embracing all the causes of things coming into being and remaining in existence. At the supreme point of the hierarchy of Aristotelian causes—as we shall see more fully in Chapter 9—are the heavenly moved and unmoved movers that are the final causes of all generation and corruption. When Aristotle says that first philosophy studies the whole of Being, he is assigning to it the field it is to explain; when he says that it is the science of the divine, he is assigning to it its ultimate principles of explanation. Thus Aristotle's first philosophy is both the science of Being *qua* being, and also theology.

Epicureans and Stoics devoted little attention to the ontological questions that preoccupied Plato and Aristotle. One development, however, deserves a brief remark.

In one of his letters Seneca writes to explain to a friend how things are classified by species and genus: man is a species of animal, but above the genus *animal* there is the genus *body*, since some bodies are animate and others (e.g. rocks) are not. Is there a genus above *body*? Yes: there is the genus of what there is (*quod est*): for of the things there are, some are bodily and some are not. This, according to Seneca, is the supreme genus.

The Stoics want to place above this yet another, more primary genus. To these Stoics the primary genus seems to be 'something'—let me explain why. In nature, they say, some things are and some things are not, and nature includes even those things that are not—things that enter the mind, like Centaurs, giants and whatever other delusory fictions take on an image although they lack substance. (Ep. 58. 11–15)

Here, we can see clearly identified a use of the verb 'to be' in the sense of 'exist' without any of the complications dating from Parmenides.[4] This is a great advance. On the other hand, in treating the existent and the non-existent as two species of a single supreme ontological genus, namely 'something' (*ti, quid*), the Stoics sowed the seed of centuries of philosophical confusion. We shall meet the fruits of this confusion in later volumes. Its most elaborate product is the ontological argument for the existence of God; its most fashionable offspring is the distinction between worlds that are actual and worlds that are possible.

Despite the significance of this Stoic development, it is not until we come to the Neoplatonists that metaphysics resumes its importance in the ancient world as the prime element of philosophy. But in an author such as Plotinus, metaphysics has taken such a theological turn that his teaching is best considered in Chapter 9 devoted to the philosophy of religion.

---

[4] See LS i. 163.

7

Soul and Mind

The soul is much older than philosophy. In many places and in many cultures human beings have imagined themselves surviving death, and the ancient equivalents of the world 'soul' first appear as an expression for whatever in us is immortal. Once philosophy began, the possibility of an afterlife and the nature of the soul came to be one of its central concerns, straddling the boundary between religion and science.

Pythagoras' Metempsychosis

Pythagoras, often venerated as the first of philosophers, was also renowned as a champion of survival after death. He did not, however, believe as many others have done that at death the soul entered a different and shadowy world; he believed that it returned to the world we all live in, but it did so as the soul of a different body. He himself claimed to have inherited his soul from a distinguished line of spiritual ancestors, and reported that he could remember fighting, some centuries earlier, as a hero at the siege of Troy. Such transmigration (which need not continue for ever) was quite different from the blessed immortality of the gods, altogether exempt from death (D.L. 8. 45).

Souls could transmigrate in this way, according to Pythagoras, not only between one human and another, but also across species. He once stopped a man whipping a puppy because he claimed to have recognized in its whimper the voice of a dead friend (D.L. 8. 36). Shakespeare was struck by this doctrine, and refers to it several times. Malvolio, catechized about Pythagoras in *Twelfth Night*, tells us that his belief was

Pythagoras calculating for his disciples the height of long-dead Hercules (from a fifteenth-century manuscript of Aulus Gellius)

That the soul of our grandam might haply inhabit a bird.

(IV. ii. 50–1)

And when Shylock is abused in *The Merchant of Venice*, the possibility is raised of migration in the reverse direction.

> Thou almost mak'st me waver in my faith
> To hold opinion with Pythagoras
> That souls of animals infuse themselves
> Into the trunks of men.   (IV. i. 130–3)

Pythagoras did not offer philosophical arguments for survival and transmigration; instead he claimed to prove it in his own case by identifying his belongings in a previous incarnation. He was thus the first of a long line of philosophers to take memory as a criterion of personal identity (Diodorus 10. 6. 2). His contemporary Alcmaeon seems to have been the first to offer a philosophical argument in this area, claiming, by a dubious inference from an obscure premiss, that the soul must be immortal because it is in perpetual motion like the divine bodies of the heavens (Aristotle, *de An.* 1. 2. 405^{a}29–^{b}1).

Empedocles adopted an elaborate version of Pythagorean transmigration as part of his cyclical conception of history. As a result of a primeval fall, sinners such as murderers and perjurers survive as wandering spirits for thrice ten thousand years, incarnate in many different forms, exchanging one hard life for another (DK 31 B115). Since the bodies of animals are thus the dwelling places of punished souls, Empedocles told his followers to abstain from eating living things. In slaughtering an animal you might even be attacking your own son or mother (DK 31 B137). Moreover, transmigration is possible not only into animals but also into plants, so even vegetarians should be careful what they eat, avoiding in particular beans and laurels (DK 31 B141). After death, if you had to be an animal, it was best to become a lion; if a plant, best to become a laurel. Empedocles himself claimed to have experienced transmigration not only as a human but also in the vegetable and animal realm.

> I was once in the past a boy, once a girl, once a tree,
> Once too a bird, and a silent fish in the sea.

(DK 31 B117)

In this early period, inquiry into the nature of the soul in the present life seems to have been subsequent to speculation on its location in an afterlife. All the earliest thinkers seem to have taken a materialist view: the soul consisted either in air (Anaximenes and Anaximander) or fire (Parmenides and Heraclitus). It took some time, however, for the problem to be addressed: how does a material element, however fine and fluid, perform the soul's characteristic functions of feeling and thought?

Heraclitus offers only a splendid simile:

As a spider in the middle of its web notices as soon as a fly damages any of its threads, and rushes thither as though grieving for the breaking of the thread, so a person's soul, if any part of the body is hurt, hurries quickly thither as if unable to bear the hurt of the body to which it is tightly and harmoniously joined. (DK 22 B67a)

This paragraph is the ancestor of many philosophical attempts to explain the capacities and behaviour of humans as the activities of a tiny animal within—though later philosophers were more inclined to view the soul as an internal homunculus than as an internal arthropod.

Perception and Thought

Empedocles was the first philosopher to offer a detailed account of how perception takes place. Like his predecessors he was a materialist. The soul, like everything else in the universe, was a compound of earth, air, fire, and water. Sensation takes place by a matching of each of these elements, as they occur in the objects of perception, with their counterparts in our sense-organs. Strife and Love, the forces that in Empedocles' system operate upon the elements, also have their part in this matching procedure, which is governed by the principle that like is perceived by like.

> We see the earth by earth, by water water see,
> The air of the sky by air, by fire the fire in flame,
> Love we perceive by love, strife by sad strife, the same.

(DK 31 B109)

The process seems to take place like this. Objects in the world give off an effluence that reaches the pores of our eyes; sound is an effluence that penetrates our ears. If perception is to take place, the pores and the effluences have to match each other (DK 31 A86). This matching must, of course, take place at the level of the elements, the fundamental principles of explanation in Empedocles' system. In some cases this is simple: sound is carried by air, which is echoed by the air in the inner ear. In the case of sight it is more complicated, and must be a matter of the proportions of each of the elements, as suggested in the fragment above. The most complex mixture of all the elements is blood, and as the blood churns round the heart this produces thought. The refined nature of the blood's constitution is what explains the wide-ranging nature of thought (DK 31 B105, 107).

The crude nature of Empedocles' materialism made him easy game for later philosophers of mind. Aristotle complained that he had not distinguished between perception and thought. Others pointed out that other things besides eyes and ears had pores: why then were sponges and pumices not capable of perception? The atomist Democritus offered an answer to this question. The visual image was the product of an interaction between effluences from the seen object and effluences from the person seeing: this image or impression was formed in the intervening air, and then entered the pupil of the eye (KRS 589). But Democritus, like Empedocles, was unable to offer any remotely convincing account of thought, and so, like him, fell foul of Aristotle's criticism.

The Presocratic whom later Greeks revered as a philosopher of mind was Anaxagoras. Anaxagoras believed that the universe began as a tiny complex unit which expanded and evolved into the world we know, but that at every stage of evolution every single thing contains a portion of everything else. This development is presided over by Mind (*nous*), which is itself outside the evolutionary process.

Other things have a portion of everything, but Mind is unlimited and independent and is unmixed with any kind of stuff, but stands all alone by itself. For if it was not by itself, but was mixed with anything else, it would have a share in every kind of stuff, since as I said earlier in everything there is a portion of everything. The things mixed with it would prevent it from controlling everything in the way it does now when it is alone by itself. For it is the finest and purest of all things, and it has all knowledge of and all power over everything. All things that have souls, the greater and the lesser, are governed by Mind. (KRS 476)

Anaxagoras distinguishes between souls, which are part of the material world, and a godlike Mind, which is immaterial, or at least is made of a unique, ethereal, kind of matter. Whereas for Empedocles like was known by like, Anaxagoras' Mind can know everything only because it is unlike anything. There is not only the one grand cosmic Mind: some other things (presumably humans) have a share in mind, so that there are lesser minds as well as greater (KRS 476, 482).

Immortality in Plato's Phaedo

Among those influenced by Anaxagoras was Socrates; but it is difficult to be sure what the historic Socrates truly thought about the soul and the mind. Socrates in Plato's *Apology* appears to be agnostic about the possibility of an afterlife. Is death, he wonders, a dreamless sleep or is it a journey to another world to meet the glorious dead? 'We go our ways, I to die and you to live: which is better, only God knows' (40c–42a). The Platonic Socrates in the *Phaedo*, however, is a most articulate protagonist of the thesis that the soul not only survives death, but is better off after death (63e).

The starting point of his discussion is the conception of a human being as a soul imprisoned in a body. True philosophers care little for bodily pleasures such as food and drink and sex, and they find the body a hindrance rather than a help in philosophic pursuits (64c–65c). 'Thought is best when the mind is gathered into itself, and none of these things trouble it—neither sounds nor sights nor pain, nor again any pleasure— when it takes leave of the body and has as little as possible to do with it' (65c). So philosophers in pursuit of truth keep their souls detached from their bodies. But death is the separation of soul from body: hence a true philosopher has throughout his life in effect been craving for death (67e).

Socrates' interlocutors, Simmias and Cebes, find his words edifying: but Cebes feels obliged to point out that most people will reject the idea that the soul can survive the body. They believe that at death the soul ceases to exist, vanishing into nothingness like a puff of smoke (70a). Socrates agrees that he needs to offer proofs that after a man's death his soul still exists.

First he offers an argument from opposites. If two things are opposites, each of them comes from the other. If you go to sleep, you must have been awake; if you wake up, you must have been asleep. If A becomes larger than

234

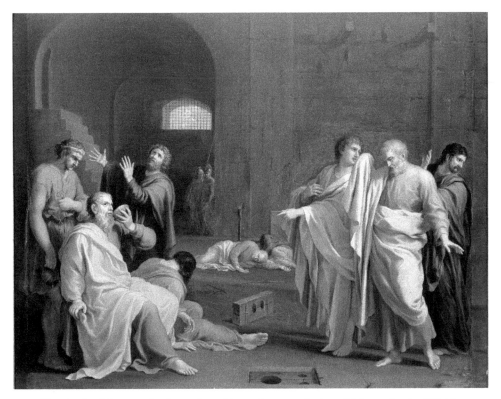

The death of Socrates has been the subject of many paintings. This one in the Uffizi is by Claude Dufresnoy (1611–68).

B, A must have been smaller than B; if A becomes better than B, A must have been worse than B. So opposites like *larger* and *smaller*, *better* and *worse*, come into being from each other. But death and life are opposites, and the same holds here. If death comes from life, must not life in turn come from death? Since life after death is not visible, it must be in another world (70c–72e).

Socrates' next argument sets out to prove the existence of a non-embodied soul not after, but before, its life in the body. He argues first that knowledge is recollection, and then that recollection involves pre-existence. We often see things, he says, that are more or less equal in size; but we never see any two things in the world absolutely equal to each other. Our idea of equality, therefore, cannot be derived from experience. The approximately equal things we see are simply reminders of an absolute

235

equality we have encountered earlier. But this encounter did not take place in our present life, nor by means of the senses: it must have taken place in a previous life and by the operation of pure intellect. What goes for the Idea of absolute equality must work also for other similar Ideas, like absolute goodness and absolute beauty (73a–77d).

Thirdly, Socrates argues from the concepts of dissolubility and indissolubility. Whatever can disintegrate, as the body does at death, must be composite and changeable. But the Ideas with which the soul is concerned are unchangeable, unlike the visible and fading beauties we see with our eyes. Within the visible world of flux, the soul staggers like a drunkard; it is only when it returns within itself that it passes into the world of purity, eternity, and immortality in which it is at home. If even bodies, when mummified in Egypt, can survive for many years, it is hardly credible that the soul dissolves at the moment of death. Instead, provided it is a soul purified by philosophy, it will depart to an invisible world of bliss (78b–81a).

In response to these arguments, Simmias offers a different conception of the soul. Consider, he says, a lyre made out of wood and strings, which is tuned by the tension of the strings. A living human body may be compared to a lyre in tune, and a dead body to a lyre out of tune. It would be absurd to argue that because attunement is not a material thing like wood and strings, it could survive the smashing of the lyre. When the strings of the body lose their tone through injury or disease, the soul must perish like the tunefulness of a broken lyre (84c–86e).

Cebes, too, has an objection to make. He agrees that the soul is tougher than the body and need not come to an end when the body does; in the normal course of life, the body suffers frequent wear and tear and needs constant repair by the soul. But a soul might be immortal, in the sense that it can survive death, without being imperishable, in the sense that it will live for ever. Even if it transmigrates from body to body, perhaps one day it will pass away, just as a weaver, who has made and worn out many coats in his lifetime, one day meets his death and leaves a coat behind (86e–88b).

Socrates produces several reasons for rejecting Simmias' analogy. Being in tune admits of degrees; but no soul can be more or less a soul than another. It is the tension of the strings that causes the lyre to be in tune, but in the human case the relationship goes in the other direction: it is the soul that keeps the body in order (92a–95e).

In response to Cebes, Socrates introduces a distinction between what later philosophers would call the necessary and contingent properties of things. Human beings may or may not be tall: tallness is a contingent property of humans. The number three, however, cannot but be odd, and snow cannot but be cold: these properties are necessary to them and not just contingent. Coldness cannot turn into heat, and consequently snow, which is necessarily cold, must either retire or perish at the approach of heat (103a–105c).

We can generalize: not only will opposites not receive opposites, but nothing that necessarily brings with it an opposite will admit the opposite of what it brings. Now the soul brings life, just as snow brings cold. But death is the opposite of life, so that the soul can no more admit death than snow can admit heat. But what cannot admit death is immortal, and so the soul is immortal. Unlike the snow, it does not perish, but retires to another world (105c–107a).

Socrates' arguments convince Simmias and Cebes in the dialogue, but surely they should not have done so. Is it true that opposites always come from opposites? And even when opposites do come from opposites, must the cycle continue for ever? Even if sleeping has to follow waking, may not one last waking be followed (as the Socrates of the *Apology* surmised) by everlasting sleep? And however true it may be that the soul cannot abide death, why must it retire elsewhere when the body dies, rather than perish like the melted snow?

The Anatomy of the Soul

In the *Phaedo* the soul is treated as a single, unified entity. Elsewhere, Plato offers us accounts of the soul in which it has different parts with different functions. In the *Phaedrus*, having offered a brief proof, reminiscent of Alcmaeon, that soul must be immortal because it is self-moving, Plato turns to describing its structure. Think of it, he says, as a triad: a charioteer with a pair of horses, one good and one bad, driving towards a heavenly banquet (246b). The good horse strives upwards, while the bad horse constantly pulls the chariot downwards. The horses are clearly meant to represent two different parts of the soul, but their exact functions are never made clear. Plato applies his analogy mainly in the course of setting out the

Plato's vision of the soul as charioteer, as illustrated by Donatello in a medallion on a portrait bust

lineaments of his ideal philosophical type of homoerotic love. When we reach the point where we have a man and a boy and four horses all in bed together, the metaphor has obviously got quite out of hand (256a).

The anatomy of the soul is more soberly described in the *Republic*. In book 4 Socrates suggests that the soul contains three elements, just as his imaginary state contains three classes. 'Do we learn things with one part,' he asks, 'feel anger with another, and with yet a third desire the pleasures of food and sex and the like? Or when we have such impulses are we operating with our whole soul?' (436a–b). He finds his answer by attending to the phenomena of mental conflict. A man maybe thirsty and yet unwilling to drink (perhaps because of doctor's orders): this shows that there is one part of the soul that reflects and a different one that feels bodily desires. The first can be called reason (*to logistikon*) and the second appetite (*to epithymetikon*; 439d). Now anger cannot be attributed to either of these elements: not to appetite, for we may feel disgust at our own perverted desires; not to reason, because children have tantrums before they reach

238

the age of discretion. Since anger can conflict with reason and appetite, we have to attribute it to a third element in the soul, which we can call temper (*to thymoeides*; 441b). Justice in the soul is the harmony of these three elements.

We meet the tripartite soul again in book 9 of the *Republic*. The lowest element in it can be called the avaricious element, since money is the principal means of satisfying the desires of appetite. Temper seeks power, victory, and repute, and so may be called the honour-loving or ambitious part of the soul. Reason pursues knowledge of truth: its love is learning. In each man's soul one or other of these elements may be dominant: he can be classed accordingly as avaricious, ambitious, or academic. Each type of person will claim their own life is the best life: the avaricious man will praise the life of business, the ambitious man will praise a political career, and the academic man will praise knowledge and understanding and the life of learning. Naturally, Plato awards the palm to the philosopher: he has the broadest experience and the soundest judgement, and the objects to which he devotes his life are much more real than the illusory pleasures pursued by his competitors (587a).

There are differences, it will be seen, between the accounts of the soul in book 4 and in book 9. In the meantime Plato has introduced the Theory of Ideas and has set out his plan of education for philosopher kings. Reason's task is no longer just to take care of the body: it is exercised in the ascending scale of mental states and activities described in the Line: imagination, belief, and knowledge. At the end of book 9 we bid farewell to the tripartite soul with a vivid picture. Appetite is a many-headed beast, constantly sprouting heads of tame and wild animals; temper is like a lion, and reason like a man. The beast is larger than the other two, and all three are stowed away within a human being. We have come a long way from the humble spider of Heraclitus.

The tripartite soul is not Plato's last word in the *Republic*. In book 10 he makes a contrast between different elements in the reasoning part: one that is confused by optical illusions, and another that measures, counts, and weighs. Whereas in the earlier books the parts of the soul were distinguished by their desires, we now have a difference of cognitive power presented as a basis for distinguishing parts.

In the same book Socrates offers a new proof of immortality. Each thing is destroyed by its characteristic disease: eyes by ophthalmia, and iron by rust. Vice is the characteristic disease of the soul: but it does not destroy the soul. If the soul's own disease cannot kill it, then it cannot be killed by bodily disease and must be immortal (609d). But what is immortal cannot be an uneasily composite entity like the threefold soul. Such a soul is like a statue in the sea covered with barnacles. The element of the soul that loves wisdom and has a passion for the divine must be stripped of extraneous elements if we are to see it in all its loveliness. Whether the soul seen in its true nature would prove manifold or simple is left an open question (611b ff., 612a3).

In the *Timaeus*, however, the tripartite soul reappears, and its parts are given corporeal locations. Reason sits in the head, the other two parts are placed in the body, with the neck as an isthmus to keep the divine and the mortal elements of the soul apart from each other. Temper is located around the heart, and appetite in the belly, with the midriff separating the two like the partition between the men's and women's quarters in a house. The heart is the guardroom from which commands can be transmitted around the body, via the circulating blood, when reason for some purpose or other orders combat stations. The lowest part of the soul is kept under control by the liver, which is particularly susceptible to the influence of mind. The coiling of the bowels has the function of preventing appetites from becoming insatiable (69c–73b).

Plato on Sense-Perception

While the *Timaeus*, like the earlier books of the *Republic*, anatomizes the soul on the basis of desire rather than cognition, the dialogue does deal at some length with the mechanisms of perception. The status of sense-perception also attracted Plato's attention in the *Theaetetus* in the course of the discussion of Protagoras' thesis that whatever seems to a particular person is true for that person. Behind Protagoras Plato detects Heraclitus' doctrine of universal flux.

If everything in the world is in constant change, then the colours we see and the qualities we detect with our other senses cannot be stable, objective realities. Rather, each of them is a meeting between one of our senses and some appropriate transitory item in the universal maelstrom. When the eye, for instance, comes into contact with a suitable visible counterpart, the eye begins to see whiteness, and the object begins to look white. The whiteness itself is generated by the intercourse between these two parents, the eye and the object. The eye and its object are themselves subject to perpetual change, but their motion is slow by comparison with the speed with which the sense-impressions come and go. The eye's seeing of the white object, and the whiteness of the object itself, are two twins which are born and can die together (156a–157b).

A similar tale can be told of other senses: but it is not clear how seriously Plato means us to take this account of sensation. It occurs, after all, in the course of a *reductio ad absurdum* argument against the Heraclitean thesis that everything is always changing both in quality and in place. If something stayed put, Socrates argues, we could describe how it looked, and if we had a patch of constant colour, we could describe how it moved from place to place. But if both kinds of change are taking place simultaneously, we are reduced to speechlessness: we cannot say *what* is moving, or *what* is changing colour. Each episode of seeing will turn instantly into an episode of non-seeing, and perception becomes impossible (182b–e).

Nonetheless, the principle that seeing is an encounter between eye and object is stated by Plato on his own account in the *Timaeus* and an explanation is there offered of the mechanism of vision. Within our heads there is a gentle fire, akin to daylight: this fire flows through our eyes and makes a uniform column with the surrounding light: when this strikes an object, shivers are sent back along the column, through the eyes, and into the body to produce the sensation we call sight (45d). Colours are a kind of flame that streams off bodies and is composed of particles so proportioned to our sight as to yield sensation. These flames travel towards the eye using the original light column as a kind of carrier wave. Individual colours are the product of different mixtures of particles of four basic kinds: black, white, red, and bright (67b–68d).

Aristotle's Philosophical Psychology

Plato's philosophy of mind has to be pieced together from fragments of various dialogues, largely concerned with ethical and metaphysical issues. The case is very different when we come to Aristotle's philosophical psychology. Here, in addition to material from ethical writings, we have a systematic treatise on the nature of the soul (*de Anima*) and a number of minor monographs on topics such as sense-perception, memory, sleep, and dreams. Aristotle took over and developed some of Plato's ideas, such as the division of the soul into parts and faculties and the philosophical analysis of sensation as encounter, but his fundamental approach differs by being rooted in the study of biology. The way in which he structured the soul and its faculties influenced not only philosophy but science for nearly two millennia.

For Aristotle the biologist the soul is not, as in the *Phaedo*, an exile from a better world ill-housed in a base body. The soul's very essence is defined by its relationship to an organic structure. Not only humans, but beasts and plants have souls—not second-hand souls, transmigrants paying the penalty of earlier misdeeds, but intrinsic principles of animal and vegetable life. A soul, Aristotle says, is 'the actuality of a body that has life', where life means the capacity for self-sustenance, growth, and decay. If we regard a living substance as a composite of matter and form, then the soul is the form of a natural, or as Aristotle sometimes says, organic, body (*de An.* 2.1. 412^{a}20,^{b}5–6).

Aristotle gives several definitions of 'soul' which have seemed to some scholars inconsistent with each other.[1] But the differences between the definitions arise not from an incoherent notion of soul, but from an ambiguity in Aristotle's use of the Greek word for 'body'. Sometimes the word means the living compound substance: in that sense, the soul is the form of a body that is alive, a self-moving body (2.1. 412^{b}17). Sometimes the word means the appropriate kind of matter to be informed by a soul: in that sense, the soul is the form of a body that *potentially* has life (2. 1. 412^{a}22; 2. 2. 414^{a}15–29). The soul is the form of an organic body, a body that has organs, that is to say parts which have specific functions, such as the mouths of mammals and the roots of trees.

The Greek word 'organon' means a tool, and Aristotle illustrates his notion of soul by comparison both with inanimate tools and with bodily organs. If an axe were a living body, its power to cut would be its soul; if an eye were a whole animal, its power to see would be its soul. A soul is an actuality, Aristotle tells us, but he makes a distinction between first and

---

[1] On this see J. Barnes, 'Aristotle's Concept of Mind' (*Proceedings of the Aristotelian Society* (1972), 101–14); J. L. Ackrill, 'Aristotle's Definitions of *Psyche*' (*Proceedings of the Aristotelian Society* (1973), 119.

second actuality. When the axe is actually cutting, and the eye is actually seeing, that is second actuality. But an axe in a sheath, and the eye of a sleeper, retain a power that they are not actually exercising: that active power is a first actuality. It is that kind of actuality that the soul is: the first actuality of a living body. The exercise of this actuality is the totality of the vital operations of the organism (2. 1. 412^{b}11–413^{a}3).

The soul is not only the form, or formal cause, of the living body: it is also the origin of change and motion in the body, and above all it is also the final cause that gives the body its teleological orientation. Reproduction is one of the most fundamental vital operations. Each living thing strives 'to reproduce its kind, an animal producing an animal, and a plant a plant, in order that they may have a share in the everlasting and the divine so far as they can' (2. 4. 415^{a}26–9, ^{b}16–20).

The souls of living beings can be ordered in a hierarchy. Plants have a vegetative or nutritive soul, which consists of the powers of growth, nutrition, and reproduction (2. 4. 415^{a}23–6). Animals have in addition the powers of perception, and locomotion: they possess a sensitive soul, and every animal has at least one sense-faculty, touch being the most universal. Whatever can feel at all can feel pleasure: and hence animals, who have senses, also have desires. Humans in addition have the power of reason and thought (*logismos kai dianoia*), which we may call a rational soul.

Aristotle's theoretical concept of soul differs from that of Plato before him and Descartes after him. A soul, for him, is not an interior, immaterial agent acting on a body. 'We should not ask whether body and soul are one thing, any more than we should ask that question about the wax and the seal imprinted on it, or about the matter of anything and that of which it is the matter' (2. 1. 412^{b}6–7). A soul need not have parts in the way that a body does: perhaps they are no more distinct than concave and convex in the circumference of a circle (*NE* 1. 13. 1102^{a}30–2). When we talk of parts of the soul we are talking of faculties: and these are distinguished from each other by their operations and their objects. The power of growth is distinct from the power of sensation because growing and feeling are two different activities; and the sense of sight differs from the sense of hearing not because eyes are different from ears, but because colours are different from sounds (*de An.* 2. 4. 415^{a}14–24).

The objects of sense come in two kinds: those that are proper to particular senses, such as colour, sound, taste, and smell, and those that are perceptible by more than one sense, such as motion, number, shape, and size. You can tell, for instance, if something is moving either by watching it or by feeling it, and so motion is a 'common sensible' (2. 6. 418^{a}7–20). We do not have a special organ for detecting common sensibles, but Aristotle says that we do have a faculty which he calls *koine aisthesis*, literally 'common sense', but better translated, because of English idiom, 'general sense' (3.1. 425^{a}27). When we encounter a horse, we may see, hear, feel, and smell it: it is the general sense that unifies these as perceptions of a single object (though the knowledge that this object is a horse is, for Aristotle, a function of intellect rather than sense). The general sense is given by Aristotle several other functions: for instance, it is by the general sense that we perceive that we are using the particular senses (3. 1. 425^{b}13 ff.), and it is by the general sense that we tell the difference between sense objects proper to different senses (e.g. between white and sweet) (3. 4. 429^{b}16–19). This last move seems ill-judged: telling the difference between white and sweet is surely not an act of sensory discrimination like telling the difference between red and pink. What would it be like to mistake white for sweet?

Aristotle's most interesting thesis about the operation of the individual senses is that a sense-faculty in operation is identical with a sense-object in action: the actuality of the sense-object is one and the same as the actuality of the sense-faculty (3. 2. 425^{b}26–7, 426^{a}16). Aristotle explains his thesis by using sound and hearing as an example; because of differences between Greek and English idiom I will try to explain what he means in the case of the sense of taste.[2] The sweetness of a cup of tea is a sense-object, something that can be tasted. My ability to taste is a sense-faculty. The operation of the sense of taste upon the object of taste is the same thing as the action of the object upon my sense. That is to say, the tea's tasting sweet to me is one and the same event as my tasting the sweetness of the tea.

Aristotle is applying to the case of sensation his scheme of layers of potentiality and actuality (2. 5. 417^{a}22–30, ^{b}28–418^{a}6). The tea is actually sweet, whereas before the sugar was put in, it was only potentially sweet. The sweetness of the tea in the cup is a first actuality: the tea's actually tasting sweet to me is a second actuality. Sweetness is nothing other than

---

[2] Aristotle complains that Greek lacks a word for what an object does to us when we taste it (3. 2. 426^{a}17). English does not, but it does lack a single word corresponding to the Greek word for what a sound does to us when it makes us hear it.

the power to taste sweet to suitable tasters; and the faculty of taste is nothing other than the power to taste such things as the sweetness of sweet objects. Thus we can agree that the sensible property in operation is the same thing as the faculty in operation, though of course the power to taste and the power to be tasted are two different things, one in an animal and the other in a substance.

This seems a sound and important philosophical analysis of the concept of sensation: it enables one to dispense with the notion, which has misled many philosophers, that sensation involves a transaction between the mind and some *representation* of what is sensed. Aristotle's detailed explanations of the chemical vehicles of sensory properties and the mechanism of the organs of sensation are very different matters, speculative theories long since super-annuated. Though Aristotle is very critical of his predecessors in this area, such as Democritus and the Plato of the *Timaeus*, his own accounts are no less distant than theirs from the truth as discovered by the progress of science.

Besides the five senses and the general sense, Aristotle recognizes other faculties which later came to be grouped together as the 'inner senses': notably imagination (*phantasia*) (*de An*. 3. 3. 427^{b}28–429^{a}9), and memory, to which he devoted an entire opuscule (*de Memoria*). Corresponding to the senses at the cognitive level, there is an affective part of the soul, the locus of spontaneous felt emotion. This is introduced in the *Nicomachean Ethics* as part of the soul that is basically irrational but which is, unlike the vegetative soul, capable of being controlled by the reason. It is the part of the soul for desire and passion, corresponding to appetite and temper in the Platonic tripartite soul. When brought under the sway of reason it is the home of the moral virtues such as courage and temperance (1. 13. 1102^{a}26–1103^{a}3).

For Aristotle as for Plato the highest part of the soul is occupied by mind or reason, the locus of thought and understanding. Thought differs from sense-perception, and is restricted—on earth at least—to human beings (*de An*. 3. 3. 427^{a}18–^{b}8). Thought, like sensation, is a matter of making judgements; but sensation concerns particulars, while intellectual knowledge is of universals (2. 5. 417^{b}23). Aristotle makes a distinction between practical reasoning and theoretical reasoning, and makes a corresponding division of faculties within the mind. There is a deliberative part of the rational soul (*logistikon*) which is concerned with human affairs, and there is a scientific part (*epistemonikon*) that is concerned with eternal truths (*NE* 6. 1. 1139^{a}16; 12. 1144^{a}2–3). This distinction is easy enough to understand; but in a famous passage of the *de Anima* Aristotle introduces a different distinction between two kinds of mind (*nous*) which is very difficult to grasp. Everywhere in nature, he says, we find a material element, which is potentially anything and everything, and there is also a creative element that works upon the matter. So it is too with mind.

There is a mind of such a kind as to become everything, and another for making all things, a positive state like light—for in a certain manner light makes potential colours into actual colours. This mind is separable, impassible, and unmixed, being in essence actuality; for the agent is always superior to the patient, and the principle to the matter. Knowledge in actuality is the very same thing as the object of knowledge. (*de An.* 3. 5. 430ᵃ14–21)

In antiquity and the Middle Ages this passage was the subject of sharply different interpretations. Some—particularly among Arabic commenta-

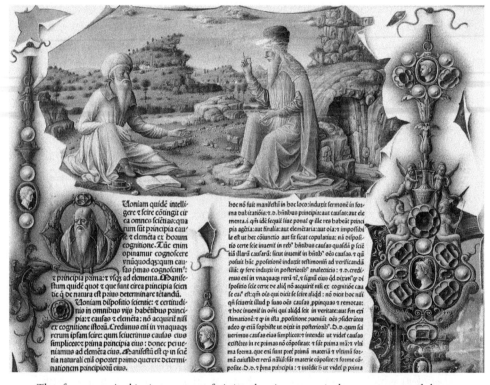

The foremost Arabic interpeter of Aristotle, Averroes, is here represented by a sixteenth-century illuminator of his commentary as receiving instruction from the Philosopher

tors—identified the separable, active agent, the light of the mind, with God or with some other superhuman intelligence. Others—particularly among Latin commentators—took Aristotle to be identifying two different faculties within the human mind: an active intellect, which formed concepts, and a passive intellect, which was a storehouse of ideas and beliefs.

The theorem of the identity in actuality of knowledge and its object—parallel to the corresponding thesis about sense-perception—was understood, on the second interpretation, in the following manner. The objects we encounter in experience are only potentially, not actually, thinkable, just as colours in the dark are only potentially, not actually, visible. The active intellect creates concepts—actually thinkable objects—by abstracting universal forms from particular experience. These matterless forms exist only in the mind: their actuality is simply to be thought. Thinking itself consists of nothing else but being busy about such universals. Thus the actualization of the object of thought, and the operation of the thinker of the thought, are one and the same.

If the second interpretation is correct, then Aristotle is here recognizing a part of the human soul that is separable from the body and immortal. In a similar vein, in the *Generation of Animals* (2. 3. 736^{b}27) Aristotle says that reason enters the body 'from out of doors', being the sole divine element in the soul and being unconnected with any bodily activity. These passages remind us that in addition to the official, biological notion of the soul that we have been studying, there is detectable from time to time in Aristotle a Platonic residue of thought according to which the intellect is a distinct entity separable from the body.

This line of thought is nowhere more prominent than in the final book of the *Nicomachean Ethics*. Whereas in the *Eudemian Ethics* and in the books that are common to the two treatises, the theoretical intellect is clearly a faculty of the soul, and there is no suggestion that it is transcendent or immortal, in book 10 of the *Nicomachean Ethics* the life of intellect is described as superhuman and is contrasted with that of the *syntheton*, or body–soul compound. The moral virtues and practical wisdom are virtues of the compound, but the excellence of intellect is capable of separate existence (10. 7. 1177^{a}14, ^{b}26–9; 1178^{a}14–20). It is in this activity of the separable intellect that, for the *Nicomachean Ethics*, human happiness supremely consists.

It is difficult to reconcile the biological and the transcendent strains in Aristotle's thought. No theory of chronological development has succeeded in doing so. The *de Anima* itself, as we have seen, contains a passage that strongly suggests an immortal element in the human soul; and in the very section of the work that sets out most clearly the theory of the soul as the form of an organic body, Aristotle tells us that it is an open question whether the soul is in the body as a sailor in a ship (2. 1. 413^{a}9). But that is a classic formulation of the dualist conception of the relation of soul to body.

Hellenistic Philosophy of Mind

No ancient author between Aristotle and Augustine formulated a comparably rich philosophy of mind. The philosophical psychology of Epicurus shows little advance on that of Democritus. For him the soul, like everything else, consists of atoms, which differ from other atoms only in being smaller and subtler, more finely structured even than those that constitute the winds. It is nonsense to say that the soul is incorporeal: whatever is not body is merely empty void. The soul has the major responsibility for sensation, but only through its position in the body—soul compound. At death its atoms are dispersed and cease to be capable of sensation because they no longer occupy their appropriate place in a body (LS 14B).

The third book of Lucretius' great poem *On the Nature of Things* is devoted to psychology. He distinguishes initially between a*nimus* and *anima* (34–5). The *animus*, or mind, is a part of the body just like a hand or foot; this is shown by the fact that a body becomes inert once it has breathed its last breath. The mind is a part of the *anima*, or soul; it is the dominant part, located in the heart. The rest of soul is spread throughout the body and moves at the behest of mind. Mind, soul, and body are closely interwoven, as we see when fear causes the body to tremble and bodily wounds cause the mind to grieve. Mind and soul must be corporeal or they could not move the body—to move it they must touch it, and how could they touch it unless they were themselves bodily (160–7)? Mind is very light and fine textured, like the bouquet of wine—a dead body, after all, weighs little less than a live one. It is composed of fire, air, wind, and a fourth nameless element. Mind is more important than soul; once mind goes, soul follows soon after, but mind can survive great damage to soul (402–5).

Some say that the body does not perceive or sense anything, but only the soul, conceived as an inner homunculus. Lucretius argues ingeniously against this primitive view. If the eyes are not doing any seeing, but are merely doors through which the mind sees, then we ought to be able to see more clearly if our eyes have been torn out, because a man in a house can see out much better if doors and doorposts are removed (367–9).

The goal of Lucretius' discussion of mind and soul is to prove that they are both mortal, and thus to take away the grounds on which people fear death. Water flows out of a smashed vessel: how much faster must soul's tenuous fluid leak away once the body is broken! The mind develops with the body and will decay with the body. The mind suffers when the body is sick, and is cured by physical medicine. These are all clear marks of mortality.

> What has this bugbear, death, to frighten man,
> If souls can die, as well as bodies can?
> For, as before our birth we felt no pain,
> When Punic arms infested land and main,
> When heaven and earth were in confusion hurled,
> For the debated empire of the world,
> Which awed with dreadful expectation lay,
> Sure to be slaves, uncertain who should sway:
> So, when our mortal frame shall be disjoined,
> The lifeless lump uncoupled from the mind,
> From sense of grief and pain we shall be free;
> We shall not feel, because we shall not be.
>
> (830–40, trans. Dryden)

We are only we, Lucretius says in conclusion, while souls and bodies in one frame agree.

The Epicureans gave an atomistic account of sense-perception, in particular of vision. Bodies in the world throw off thin films of the atoms of which they are made, which retain their original shape and thus serve as images (*eidola*). These fly around the world with astonishing speed, and perception occurs when they make contact with atoms in the soul. When we see mental images, this is the result of even more tenuous filaments joining together in the air, like spider's web or gold leaf. Thus, the image of a centaur is the result of the interweaving of a human image and a horse image; it can enter the mind during sleep as well as when awake. We are always surrounded by countless such fine images, but we are only aware of those on which the mind turns the beam of its attention (Lucretius 4. 722–85).

The Stoics, like the Epicureans, had a materialist concept of soul. We live to the extent that we breathe, Chrysippus argued; soul is what makes us live, and breath is what makes us breathe, so soul and breath are identical (LS 53G). The heart is the seat of the soul: there resides the soul *par excellence*, the master-faculty (*hegemonikon*) which sends out the senses to bring back reports on the environment for it to evaluate. Sense-perception itself takes place exclusively within the master-faculty (LS 53M). The master-faculty is material like the rest of the soul, but it is capable of surviving, at least temporarily, separation from the body at death (LS 53w). There is not, however, any real personal immortality for the Stoics: at best, the souls of the wise after death can be absorbed into the divine World Soul that permeates and governs the universe.

Some Stoics compared the human soul to an octopus: eight tentacles sprouted out from the master-faculty into the body, five of them being the senses, one being a motor agent to effect the movement of the limbs, one controlling the organs of speech, and the final one a tube to carry semen to the generative organs. Each of these tentacles was made out of breath (LS 53H, L).

It will be noted that of the eight tentacles five are afferent, and three efferent. This reflects an important clarification the Stoics introduced into philosophical psychology. Plato and Aristotle had been principally interested in dividing faculties of the soul hierarchically, on the basis of the cognitive or ethical value of the objects of the faculty: thus intellect came above sensation, and rational choice above animal desire. The Stoics were well aware of the difference between the capacities of rational language users and dumb animals (LS 53T) but they regarded as equally important a division of faculties that is vertical rather than horizontal. The distinction is thus stated by Cicero, quoting Panaetius:

Minds' movements are of two kinds: some belong to thought, and some to appetition. Thought is principally concerned with the investigation of truth and appetition is a drive to action. (Off 1. 132).

The distinction between cognitive and appetitive faculties cuts across the distinction between sensory and intellectual faculties. In later antiquity and in the Middle Ages philosophers came to accept the following scheme:

Intellect	Will
Sensation	Desire

This combines the Aristotelian distinction between the rational and the animal level, with the Stoic distinction between the cognitive and appetitive dimension.

Will, Mind, and Soul in Late Antiquity

It is often said that in classical philosophy there is no concept of the will. Some have gone so far as to say that in Aristotle's psychology the will does not occur at all, and the concept was invented only after eleven further centuries of philosophical reflection. Certainly, it is undeniable that there is no Aristotelian expression that exactly corresponds to the English expression 'freedom of the will', and scholars have concluded that he had no real grasp of the issue.

This criticism of Aristotle depends on a certain view of the nature of the will. In modern times philosophers have often thought of the will as a phenomenon of introspective consciousness. Acts of the will, or volitions, are mental events that precede and cause certain human actions; their presence or absence make the difference between voluntary and involuntary actions. The freedom of the will is to be located in the indeterminacy of these introspectible volitions.

It is not clear how far the Epicureans and Stoics shared this conception of the causation of human action, but it is certain that this concept of the will is not to be found in Aristotle. But this is to his credit, for the concept is radically flawed and has been discredited in recent times. A satisfactory philosophical account of the will must relate human action to ability, desire, and belief. It must contain a treatment of voluntariness, a treatment of intentionality, and a treatment of rationality. Aristotle's treatises contain ample material relevant to the study of the will thus understood, even though his concepts do not exactly coincide with those that it would nowadays be natural to employ.

Aristotle defined voluntariness as follows: something was voluntary if it was originated by an agent free from compulsion or error (NE 3. 1. 1110^{a}1 ff.). In his moral system an important role was also played by the concept of *prohairesis*, or purposive choice: the choice of an action as part of an overall plan of life (*NE* 3. 2. 1111^{b}4 ff.). His concept of the voluntary was too clumsily defined, and his concept of *prohairesis* too narrowly defined, to demarcate the everyday moral choices that make up our lives. The fact that there is no English word corresponding to 'prohairesis' is itself a mark of the awkwardness of the concept: most of Aristotle's moral terminology has been naturalized into all European languages.

Though he has a rich and perceptive account of practical reasoning, Aristotle has no technical concept corresponding to our concept of intention: that is to say, of doing A *in order to* bring about B, of choosing means to ends as well as pursuing ends for their own sake. Voluntariness is a broader concept than intention: it includes whatever we bring about knowingly but unintentionally, as an undesired consequence of action. *Prohairesis* is a narrower concept: it restricts the goal of the intention to the enactment of a grand pattern of life.

These defects in Aristotle's treatment of the appetitive side of human life are the truth behind the exaggerated claim that he had no concept of the will. It was, indeed, the reflection of Latin philosophers which led to the full development of the concept, and this reflection can be seen in copious form in the writings of Augustine.

In the second and third centuries further developments called for modification of Aristotelian philosophy of mind. The physician Galen (129–99) discovered that for the operation of the muscles nerves arising from the brain and spinal cord have to be active. Thus the brain, rather than the heart, should be regarded as the principal seat of the soul. But like the Stoics, Galen distinguished between a sensory soul and a motor soul, the former associated with afferent nerves travelling to the brain, the latter with motor nerves originating in the spinal cord.[3]

The peripatetic commentator Alexander of Aphrodisias, who flourished in the first decades of the third century, identified the Active Intellect of the *de Anima* with the unmoved mover of *Metaphysics Λ*. Alexander thus began a long tradition of interpretation which flourished, in different forms, among later commentators, especially in the Arab world. A human being at birth, he maintained, had only a material or physical intellect; true intelligence is acquired only under the influence of the

---

[3] M. R. Bennett, and P. M. S. Hacker, *Philosophical Foundations of Neuroscience* (Oxford: Blackwell, 2003), 20.

supreme divine mind. In consequence, the human soul is not immortal: the best it can do is to think immortal thoughts by meditating on the Motionless Mover (*de An.* 90. 11–91. 6).

In reaction to the mortalism of the Epicureans, Stoics, and later Peripatetics, Plotinus set out, in Plato's footsteps, to prove that the individual soul is immortal. He sets out his case in one of his earliest writings, Ennead 4. 7 (2), *On the Immortality of the Soul*. If the soul is the principle of life in living beings, it cannot itself be bodily in nature. If it is a body, it must be either one of the four elements, earth, air, fire, and water, or a compound of one or more of them. But the elements are themselves lifeless. If a compound has life, this must be due to a particular proportion of the elements in the compound: but this must have been conferred by something else, the cause that provides the recipe for and combines the ingredients of the mixture. This something else is soul (4. 7. 2. 2).

Plotinus argues that none of the functions of life, from the lowliest form of nutrition and growth to the highest forms of imagination and thought, could be carried out by something that was merely bodily. Bodies undergo change at every instant: how could something in such perpetual flux remember anything from moment to moment? Bodies are divided into parts and spread out in space: how could such a scattered entity provide the unified focus of which we are aware in perception? We can think of abstract entities, like beauty and justice: how can what is bodily grasp what is non-bodily? (4. 7. 5–8). The soul must belong, not to the world of becoming, but to the world of Being (4. 8. 5).

Plotinus is aware that there are those who say that the soul, though not a body itself, nonetheless is dependent on body for its existence. He recalls Simmias' contention in the *Phaedo* that the soul is nothing more than an attunement of the body's sinews. He neatly turns the tables on that argument. When a musician plucks the strings of a lyre, he says, it is the strings, not the melody that he acts upon; but the strings would not be plucked unless the melody called for it (3. 6. 4. 49–80; 4. 7. 8).

Plotinus clearly maintains the personal immortality of individuals. It would be absurd to suggest that Socrates will cease to be Socrates when he goes from hence to a better world hereafter. Minds will survive in that better world, because nothing that has real being ever perishes (4. 3. 5). However, the exact significance of this claim is unclear, since Plotinus also maintains that all souls form a unity, bound together in a superior World-

Soul, from which they have originated and to which they return (3. 5. 4). We shall learn more about this World-Soul in Chapter 9, when we come to discuss Plotinus' theology.

One of those who learnt most from Plotinus' speculations was the young Augustine. His own original contribution to philosophy of mind, however, is to be found in his writing on freedom. In his *de Libero Arbitrio*, written in the year of his conversion to Christianity, he defends a form of libertarianism that differs both from the compatibilism we saw in an earlier chapter when considering Chrysippus, and from the predestinarianism for which the later, Christian, Augustine is notorious.

In the third book the question is raised whether the soul sins by necessity. We have to distinguish, we are told, three senses of 'necessity': nature, certainty, and compulsion. Nature and compulsion are incompatible with voluntariness, and only voluntary acts are blameable. If a sinner sins by nature or by compulsion, the sin is not voluntary. But certainty is compatible with voluntariness: it may be certain that X will sin, and yet X will sin voluntarily and will rightly be blamed.

St Augustine in his study (Vittorio Carpaccio, S. Giorgio, Venice)

Consider first the necessity of nature. The soul does not sin by necessity in the way that a stone falls by necessity of nature: the soul's action in sinning is voluntary. Both the soul and the stone are agents, but the soul is a voluntary and not a natural agent. The difference is this: 'it is not in the stone's power to arrest its downward motion, but unless the soul is willing it does not so act as to abandon what is higher for what is lower' (III. 2).

As we saw in considering Chrysippus, voluntariness can be defined by reference to the power to do otherwise (liberty of indifference) or by reference to the power to do what one wants (liberty of spontaneity). In the *de Libero Arbitrio* Augustine combines the two approaches. The soul's motions are voluntary, because the soul is doing what it wants. 'I do not know what I can call my own', Augustine says, 'if the will by which I want or reject is not my own.' But the power to want is itself a two-way power. 'The motion by which the will turns in this or that direction would not be praiseworthy unless it was voluntary and placed within our power.' Nor could the sinner be blamed when he turns the hinge (*cardo*) of the will towards the nether regions (III. 3).

Augustine offers to prove that wanting is in our power. The exact lines of his proof are not clear. On one interpretation it goes like this. Doing X is in our power if we do X whenever we want. But whenever we want, we want. Therefore wanting is in our power. This seems too easy: surely the first premiss is incomplete. It should read: Doing X is in our power if we do X whenever we want to do X. The second premiss would then have to read: Whenever we want to want to do X we want to do X. This would give us Augustine's conclusion: whatever X is, wanting X is in our power. But one may question the second premiss. May we not have a second-order want to want something, without having the first-order want itself? When Augustine wanted to be chaste, but not yet, was he really wanting to be chaste, or only wanting to want to be chaste?

If it is in my power to do X, in the sense earlier outlined by Augustine, then it must be in my power not to do X. This weakens his argument to show that wanting is in our power. For whatever plausibility there is in the claim that if I want to want something I want it, there is none in the claim that if I want not to want something then I do not want it. I may very sincerely want to give up smoking: that does not prevent my passionate want for a cigarette at this moment.

No doubt Augustine can respond by making distinctions between different kinds of wanting: but in the present context it would not be profitable to follow further his analysis of volition. The part of the *de Libero Arbitrio* most relevant to the issue of determinism and freedom is his consideration of the foreknowledge of God. Augustine believed that at any moment God foreknew all future events. He can then construct the following argument against the possibility of voluntary sin.

(1) God foreknew that Adam was going to sin.
(2) If God foreknew that Adam was going to sin, necessarily Adam was going to sin.
(3) If Adam was necessarily going to sin, then Adam sinned necessarily.
(4) If Adam sinned necessarily, Adam did not sin of his own free will.
(5) Adam did not sin of his own free will.

The line of argument here is clearly the Christian heir to the discussion of the sea-battle in Aristotle and the Master Argument of Diodorus: in each case, in different ways, the necessity of a past state or event is used as a starting point from which to derive the necessity of a future event. In the Greeks the starting premiss is logical, here it is theological.

Augustine proposes to disarm the argument by the distinction between certainty, on the one hand, and natural causation or compulsion, on the other. I can know something without causing it (as when I know it because I remember it). I can be certain that someone is about to do something without in any way compelling him to do it. Accordingly, we can distinguish the senses of 'necessity' in the argument above. In the second premiss, and the antecedent of the third premiss 'necessarily' must be taken as 'certainly'. In the fourth premiss and the consequent of the third premiss 'necessarily' must be taken as 'under compulsion'. Because of the resulting equivocation in the third premiss, the argument fails.

Augustine's response does not wholly convince: there is surely no exact analogy between conjectural human knowledge of the future and omni-temporal divine omniscience. The difficulties that his treatment leaves unsolved were taken up by many future generations of Christian theologians; but his discussion can fittingly be taken as representative of the final stage of reflection on determinism in antiquity.

8

How to Live: Ethics

Among the sayings attributed to the earliest Greek philosophers, many have a moral content. Thales, for instance, is credited with an early version of 'Do as you would be done by': asked how we could best live, he replied, 'if we do not ourselves do what we blame others for doing'. In more ambiguous vein, when asked by an adulterer if he should swear he was innocent, he replied, 'Well, perjury is no worse than adultery' (D.L. 1. 37). Oracular utterances of a similar kind are to be found in Heraclitus: 'It is not good for men to get all they want' (DK 22 B110); 'a man's character is his destiny' (DK 22 B117). Other philosophers took stances on particular moral issues: thus Empedocles attacked meat-eating and animal sacrifice (DK 31 B128, 139). But it is not until Democritus that we find any sign of a philosopher with a moral system.

Democritus the Moralist

Democritus was eloquent on ethical topics: sixty pages of his fragments, as recorded in Diels–Kranz, are devoted to moral counsel. Much of it is of a homespun, agony-aunt type: don't take on tasks above your power, don't be envious of the rich and famous: think of all the people who are worse off than you are, and be contented with your lot (DK 68 B91). Do not try to know everything, or you will end up knowing nothing (DK 68 B69). Don't blame bad luck when things go wrong through your own fault: you can avoid drowning by learning to swim (DK 68 B119, 172). Accept favours only if you plan to do greater favours in return (DK 68 B92). A remark that has been garbled at many a wedding breakfast is fragment 272: 'One who is lucky in his son-in-law gains a son, one who is unlucky loses a daughter.'

Sometimes Democritus' advice is more controversial. It is better not to have any children: to bring them up well takes great trouble and care, and seeing them grow up badly is the cruellest of all pains (DK 68 B275). If you must have children, adopt them from your friends rather than beget them yourselves. That way, you can choose the kind of child you want, whereas in the normal way you have to put up with what you get (DK 68 B277).

From Plato onwards there have been moral philosophers who have despised the body as a corrupter of the soul. Democritus took just the opposite view. If a body, at the end of life, were to sue the soul for the pains and ills it had suffered, a fair judge would find for the body. If some parts of the body have been damaged by neglect or ruined by debauchery, that is the soul's fault. Maybe you think that the body is no more than a tool used by the soul: well and good, but if a tool is in a bad shape you blame not the tool but its owner (DK 68 B159).

Democritus' moral views have come down to us as a series of aphorisms, but there is some evidence that he developed a systematic ethics, though it is obscure what relation, if any, it had to his atomism. He wrote a treatise on the purpose of life and inquired into the nature of happiness (*eudaimonia*): it was to be found not in riches but in the goods of the soul, and one should not take pleasure in mortal things (DK 68 B37, 171, 189). The hopes of the educated, he put it, were better than the riches of the ignorant (DK 68 B285). But the goods of the soul in which happiness was to be found do not seem to have been of any exalted mystical kind: rather, his ideal was a life of cheerfulness and quiet contentment (DK 68 B188). For this reason he was known to later ages as the laughing philosopher. He praised temperance, but was not an ascetic. Thrift and fasting were good, he said, but so was banqueting; the difficulty was judging the right time for each. A life without feasting was like a highway without inns (DK 68 B229, 230).

In some ways Democritus set an agenda for succeeding Greek thinkers. In placing the quest for happiness in the centre of moral philosophy he was followed by almost every moralist of antiquity. When he said, 'the cause of sin is ignorance of what is better' (DK 68 B83), he formulated an idea that was to be central in Socratic moral thought. Again, when he said that you are better off being wronged than doing wrong (DK 68 B45), he uttered a

Bramante here represents Democritus as the laughing philosopher and Heraclitus as the weeping philosopher

thought that was developed by Socrates into the principle that it is better to suffer wrong than to inflict wrong—a principle incompatible with the influential moral systems that encourage one to judge actions only by their consequences and not by the identity of their agents. Others of his offhand remarks, if taken seriously, are sufficient to overturn whole ethical systems. For instance, when he says that a good person not only refrains from wrongdoing but does not even want to do wrong (DK 68 B62), he sets himself against the often held view that virtue is at its highest when it triumphs over conflicting passion.

Democritus did not explore, however, the most important concept of all for ancient ethics: that is, *arete*, or virtue. The Greek word does not match precisely any single English word, and in recent scholarly writing the traditional translation 'virtue' is often replaced by 'excellence'. 'Arete' is the abstract noun corresponding to the adjective 'agathos', the most general word for 'good'. Whatever is good of its kind has the corresponding *arete*. It is archaic in English to speak of the virtue of a horse or a knife, which is no doubt one reason for preferring the translation 'excellence'; and some of the *aretai* of human beings, such as scientific expertise, fit uncomfortably into the description 'intellectual virtue'. But it is perhaps equally odd to call a character trait like gentleness an 'excellence'; so I shall make use of the traditional translation of *arete*, having given fair warning that it is far from a perfect fit. The matter is not merely one of idiom: it reveals a conceptual difference between ancient Greeks and modern Westerners about the appropriate way to group together different desirable properties of human beings. The difference between the two conceptual structures both accounts for the difficulty, and provides a great deal of the value, of the study of ancient moral philosophy.

Socrates on Virtue

It was Socrates who initiated systematic inquiry into the nature of virtue; he placed it in the centre of moral philosophy, and indeed of philosophy as a whole. In the *Crito* his own acceptance of death is presented as a martyrdom to justice and piety (54b). In the Socratic dialogues particular virtues are subjected to detailed examination: piety (*hosiotes*) in the *Euthyphro*, temperance (*sophrosyne*) in the *Charmides*, fortitude (*andreia*) in the *Laches*, and justice in the first book of the *Republic* (which most probably began existence as a separate dialogue, *Thrasymachus*). Each of these dialogues follows a similar pattern. Socrates seeks a definition of the respective virtue, and the other characters in the dialogue offer definitions in response. Cross-examination (*elenchus*) forces each of the protagonists to admit that their definitions are inadequate. Socrates, however, is no better able than his opponents to offer a satisfactory definition, and each dialogue ends inconclusively.

The pattern can be illustrated from the first book of the *Republic*, where the virtue to be defined is justice. The aged Cephalus proposes that justice is telling the truth and returning what one has borrowed. Socrates refutes this by asking whether it is just to return a borrowed weapon to a friend who has gone mad. It is agreed that it is not just, because it cannot be just to harm a friend (331d). The next proposal, from Cephalus' son Polem-archus, is that justice is doing good to one's friends and harm to one's enemies. This is rejected on the grounds that it is not just to harm anyone: justice is a virtue and it cannot be an exercise of virtue to make anyone, friend or foe, worse rather than better (335d).

Another character in the dialogue, Thrasymachus, now questions whether justice is a virtue at all. It cannot be a virtue, he argues, for it is not in anyone's interest to possess it. On the contrary, justice is simply what is to the advantage of the powerful; law and morality are systems to protect their interests. By complicated, and often dubious, arguments Thrasymachus is eventually brought to concede that the just man will have a better life than the unjust man, so that justice is in the interest of the person who possesses it (353e). Yet the dialogue closes on an agnostic note. 'The upshot of the discussion in my case', says Socrates, 'is that I have learned nothing. Since I don't know what justice is, I will hardly know whether it is a virtue or not, and whether its possessor is happy or unhappy' (354c).

The profession of ignorance which Plato places in Socrates' mouth in these dialogues does not mean that Socrates has no convictions about moral virtue: it means rather that a very high threshold is being set for something to count as knowledge. In these dialogues Socrates and his interlocutors can often agree whether particular actions would or would not count as instances of the virtue in question: what is lacking is a formula that would cover all and only acts of the relevant virtue. Moreover, Socrates, in the course of discussion, defends a number of substantive theses both about virtues in particular (e.g. that it is never just to harm anyone) and about virtue in general (e.g. that it must always be a benefit to its possessor).

In inquiring into the nature of a virtue, Socrates' regular practice is to compare it with a technical skill or craft, such as carpentry, navigation, or medicine, or with a science such as arithmetic or geometry. Many readers, ancient and modern, find the comparison bizarre. Surely knowledge and virtue are two totally different things, one is a matter of the intellect and another a matter of the will. In response to this two things can be said. First, if we make a sharp distinction between the intellect and the will, that is because we are the heirs to many generations of philosophical reflection to which the initial impetus was given by Socrates and Plato. Secondly, there are indeed important similarities between virtues and forms of expertise. Both, unlike other properties and characteristics of mankind, are acquired rather than innate. Both are valued features of human beings: we admire people both for their skills and for their virtues. Both, Socrates claims, are beneficial to their possessors: we are better off the more skills we possess and the more virtuous we are.

But in important respects skills and virtues are unlike each other, at least prima facie. Socrates is well aware of this, and one reason for his constant recourse to the analogy between the two is to contrast them as well as to compare them. He is anxious to test how significant are the differences. One difference is that arts and sciences are transmitted through teaching by experts: but there do not seem to be any experts who can teach virtue. There are not, at any rate, genuine experts, though some sophists falsely hold themselves out to be such (*Prt.* 319a–320b; *Men.* 89e–91b). Another difference is this. Suppose someone goes wrong: we may ask whether he did it on purpose or not, and whether, if he did, that makes things better or worse. If the going wrong was making a mistake in the exercise of a skill—e.g. playing a false note on the flute, or missing the mark in archery—then it is better if it was done on purpose: that is to say, a deliberate mistake is not a reflection on one's skill. But things seem different when the going wrong is a failure in virtue: it is odd to say that someone who violates my rights on purpose is less unjust than someone who violates them unwittingly (*Hp. Mi.* 373d–376b).

Socrates believes he can deal with both of these objections to assimilating virtue to expertise. In response to the second point, he flatly denies that there are people who sin against virtue on purpose (*Prt.* 358b–c). If a man goes wrong in this way he does so through ignorance, through lack of knowledge of what is best for him. We all wish to do well and be happy: it is for this reason that people want things like health, wealth, power, and honour. But these things are only good if we know how to use them well; in the absence of this knowledge they can do us more harm than good. This knowledge of how best to use what one possesses is wisdom (*phronesis*) and it is the only thing that is truly good (*Euthd.* 278e–282e). Wisdom is the science of what is good and what is bad, and it is identical with virtue— with all the virtues.

The reason why there are no teachers of virtue is not that virtue is not a science, but that it is a science impossibly difficult to master. This is because of the way in which the virtues intertwine and form a unity. Actions that exhibit courage are of course different actions from those that exhibit temperance; but what they express is a single, indivisible state of soul. If we say that courage is the science of what is good and bad in respect of future dangers, we have to agree that such a science is only possible as part of an overall science of good and evil (*La.* 199c). The individual virtues are parts of this science, but it can only be possessed as a whole. No one, not even Socrates, is in possession of this science.[1]

We are, however, given an account of what it would look like, and it is rather a surprising account. Socrates asks Protagoras, in the dialogue named after him, to accept the premiss that goodness is identical with pleasure and evil is identical with pain. From this premiss he offers to prove his contention that no one does evil willingly. People are often said to have done evil in the knowledge that it was evil because they yielded to temptation and were overcome by pleasure. But if 'pleasure' and 'good' mean the same, then they must have done evil because they were overcome by goodness. Is not that absurd (354c–5d)?

Knowledge is a powerful thing, and the knowledge that something is evil cannot be pushed about like a slave. Given the premiss that Protagoras has accepted, knowledge that an action is evil must be knowledge that, taken with its consequences, the action will lead to an excess of pain over pleasure. No one with such knowledge is going to undertake such an action; hence the person acting wrongly must lack the knowledge. Nearby objects seem larger to vision than distant ones, and something similar happens in mental vision. The wrongdoer is suffering from the illusion that the present pleasure outweighs the consequent pain. What is needed is a science that measures the relative sizes of pleasures and pains, present and future, 'since our salvation in life has turned out to lie in the correct choice of pleasure and pain' (356d–357b). This is the science of good and evil that is identical with each of the virtues, justice, temperance, and courage (361b).

---

[1] Here I am indebted to a number of articles by Terry Penner, summed up in his essay 'Socrates and the Early Dialogues', in R. Kraut (ed.), *The Cambridge Companion to Plato* (Cambridge: Cambridge University Press, 1992).

Plato on Justice and Pleasure

Scholars are not agreed whether Socrates seriously thought that the hedonic calculus was the answer to 'What is virtue?' Whether Socrates did so or not, Plato certainly did not, and in the *Republic* we are given a different account of justice—indeed, more than one different account. The main body of the dialogue begins in book 2 with two challenges set by Plato's brothers Glaucon and Adeimantus. Glaucon wants to be shown that justice is not just a method of avoiding evils, but something worthwhile for its own sake (358b–362c). Adeimantus wants to be shown that quite apart from any rewards or sanctions attached to it, justice is as preferable to injustice as sight is to blindness and health is to sickness (362d–367d).

The Socrates of the dialogue introduces his answer by setting out the analogy between the soul and the city. In his imagined city the virtues are allotted to the different classes of the state: the city's wisdom is the wisdom of its rulers, its courage is the courage of its soldiers, and its temperance is the obedience of the artisans to the ruling class. Justice is the harmony of the three classes: it consists in each citizen, and each class, doing that for which they are most suited. The three parts of the soul correspond to the three classes in the state, and the virtues in the soul are distributed like the virtues in the state (441c–442d). Courage belongs to temper, temperance is the subservience of the lower elements, wisdom is located in reason, which rules and looks after the whole soul. Justice is the harmony of the psychic elements. 'Each of us will be a just person, fulfilling his proper function, only if the several parts of our soul fulfil theirs' (441e).

If injustice is the hierarchical harmony of the soul's elements, injustice and all manner of vice occur when the inferior elements rebel against this hierarchy (443b). Justice and injustice in the soul are like health and disease in the body. Accordingly, it is absurd to ask whether it is more profitable to live justly or to do wrong. All the wealth and power in the world cannot make life worth living when the body is ravaged by disease. Can it be any more worth living when the soul, the principle of life, is deranged and corrupted (445b)?

That is the first account of justice and virtue given in answer to Glaucon and Adeimantus. It differs from the account in the *Protagoras* in several ways. The thesis of the unity of virtue has been abandoned, or at least modified, as a result of the tripartition of the soul. Pleasure appears not as the object of virtue, but as the crony of the lowest part of the soul. The conclusion that justice benefits its possessor, however, is common ground both to the *Republic* and to the earlier Socratic dialogues. Moreover, if justice is psychic health, then everyone must really want to be just, since everyone wants to be healthy. This rides well with the Socratic thesis that no one does wrong on purpose, and that vice is fundamentally ignorance.

However, the conclusion drawn at the end of *Republic* 4 is only a provisional one, for it makes no reference to the great Platonic innovation: the Theory of Ideas. After the role of the Ideas has been expounded in the middle books of the dialogue, we are given a revised account of the relation between justice and happiness. The just man is happier than the unjust, not only because his soul is in concord, but because it is more delightful to fill the soul with understanding than to feed fat the desires of appetite. Reason is no longer the faculty that takes care of the person, it is akin to the unchanging and immortal world of truth (585c).

Humans can be classified as avaricious, ambitious, or academic, according to whether the dominant element in their soul is appetite, temper, or reason. Men of each type will claim that their own life is best: the avaricious man will praise the life of business, the ambitious man will praise a political career, and the academic man will praise knowledge and understanding. It is the academic, the philosopher, whose judgement is to be preferred: he has the advantage over the others in experience, insight, and reasoning (580d–583b). Moreover, the objects to which the philosopher devotes his life are so much more real than the objects pursued by the others that their pleasures seem illusory by comparison (583c–587a). Plato has not altogether said goodbye to the hedonic calculus: he works out for us that the philosopher king lives 729 times more pleasantly than his evil opposite number (587e).

Plato returns to the topic of happiness and pleasure in the mature dialogue *Philebus*. One character, Protarchus, argues that pleasure is the greatest good; Socrates counters that wisdom is superior to pleasure and more conducive to happiness (11a–12b). The dialogue gives an opportunity for a wide-ranging discussion of different kinds of pleasure, very different from the *Protagoras* treatment of pleasure as a single class of commensurable items. At the end of the discussion Socrates wins his point against Protarchus: on a well-considered grading of goods even the best of pleasures come out below wisdom (66b–c).

The most interesting part of the dialogue, however, is an argument to the effect that neither pleasure nor wisdom can be the essence of a happy life, but that only a mixed life that has both pleasure and wisdom in it would really be worth choosing. Someone who had every pleasure from moment to moment, but was devoid of reason, would not be happy because he would be able neither to remember nor to anticipate any pleasure other than the present: he would be living not a human life but the life of a mollusc (21a–d). But a purely intellectual life without any pleasure would equally be intolerable (21e). Neither life would be 'sufficient, perfect, or worthy of choice'. The final good consists in a harmonious proportion between pleasure and wisdom (63c–65a).

Aristotle on Eudaimonia

The criteria for a good life set out in the *Philebus* reappear in Aristotle's account of the good life. The good we are looking for, he says, at the beginning of the *Nicomachean Ethics*, must be perfect by comparison with other ends—that is, it must be something sought always for its own sake and never for the sake of something else; and it must be self-sufficient, that is, it must be something which taken on its own makes life worthwhile and lacking in nothing. These, he goes on, are the properties of happiness (*eudaimonia*) (*NE* 1. 7. 1097^{a}15–^{b}21).

In all Aristotle's ethical treatises the notion of happiness plays a central role. This is brought out more clearly, however, in the *Eudemian Ethics*, and in my exposition I will begin by following this rather than the more familiar text of the *Nicomachean Ethics*. The treatise begins with the inquiry: what is a good life and how is it to be acquired? (*EE* 1. 1. 1214^{a}15). We are offered five candidate answers to the second question (by nature, by learning, by discipline, by divine favour, and by luck) and seven candidate answers to the first (wisdom, virtue, pleasure, honour, reputation, riches, and culture) (1. 1. 1214^{a}32, ^{b}9). Aristotle immediately eliminates some answers to the second question: if happiness comes purely by nature or by luck or by grace, then it will be beyond most people's reach and they can do nothing about it (1. 3. 1215^{a}15). But a full answer to the second question obviously depends on the answer to the first: and Aristotle works on that by asking the question: what makes life worth living?

There are some occurrences in life, e.g. sickness and pain, that make people want to give up life: clearly these do not make life worth living. There are the events of childhood: these cannot be the most choiceworthy things in life since no one in his right mind would choose to go back to childhood. In adult life there are things that we do only as means to an end; clearly these cannot, in themselves, be what makes life worth living (1. 5. 1215^{b}15–31).

If life is to be worth living, it must surely be for something that is an end in itself. One such end is pleasure. The pleasures of food and drink and sex are, on their own, too brutish to be a fitting end for human life: but if we combine them with aesthetic and intellectual pleasures we find a goal that has been seriously pursued by people of significance. Others prefer a life of virtuous action—the life of a real politician, not like the false politicians, who are only after money or power. Thirdly, there is the life of scientific contemplation, as exemplified by Anaxagoras, who when asked why one should choose to be born rather than not replied, 'In order to admire the heavens and the order of the universe.'

Aristotle has thus reduced the possible answers to the question 'What is a good life?' to a shortlist of three: wisdom, virtue, and pleasure. All, he says, connect happiness with one or other of three forms of life, the philosophical, the political, and the voluptuary (1. 4. 1215^{a}27). This triad provides the key to Aristotle's ethical inquiry. Both the *Eudemian* and the *Nicomachean* treatises contain detailed analyses of the concepts of virtue, wisdom (*phronesis*), and pleasure. And when Aristotle comes to present his own account of happiness, he can claim that it incorporates the attractions of all three of the traditional forms of life.

A crucial step towards achieving this is to apply, in this ethical area, the metaphysical analysis of potentiality and actuality. Aristotle distinguishes between a state (*hexis*) and its use (*chresis*) or exercise (*energeia*).[2] Virtue and wisdom are both states, whereas happiness is an activity, and therefore cannot be simply identified with either of them (*EE* 2. 1. 1219^{a}39; *NE* 1. 1. 1098^{a}16). The activity that constitutes happiness is, however, a use or exercise of virtue. Wisdom and moral virtue, though different *hexeis*, are exercised inseparably in a single *energeia*, so that they are not competing but collaborating contributors to happiness (*NE* 10. 8. 1178^{a}16–18). Moreover,

---

[2] The *EE* prefers the distinction in the form: virtue–use of virtue; the *NE* prefers it in the form: virtue–activity in accord with virtue (*energeia kat'areten*).

This may not have been Aristotle's idea of a happy life, but this was how it seemed to a fifteenth-century illuminator of his text

pleasure, Aristotle claims, is identical with the unimpeded exercise of an appropriate state: so that happiness, considered as the unimpeded exercise of these two states, is simultaneously the life of virtue, wisdom, and pleasure (*EE* 7. 15. 1249^{a}21; *NE* 10. 7. 1177^{a}23).

To reach this conclusion takes many pages of analysis and argument. First, Aristotle must show that happiness is activity in accordance with virtue. This derives from a consideration of the function or characteristic activity (*ergon*) of human beings. Man must have a function, the *Nicomachean Ethics* argues, because particular types of men (e.g. sculptors) do, and parts and organs of human beings do. What is this function? Not growth and nourishment, for this is shared by plants, nor the life of the senses, for this is shared by animals. It must be a life of reason concerned with action: the activity of soul in accordance with reason. So human good will be good human functioning, namely, activity of soul in accordance with virtue (*NE* 1. 7. 1098^{a}16). Virtue unexercised is not happiness, because that would be compatible with a life passed in sleep, which no one would call happy (1. 8. 1099^{a}1).

Secondly, Aristotle must analyse the concept of virtue. Human virtues are classified in accordance with the division of the parts of the soul outlined in the previous chapter. Any virtue of the vegetative part of the soul, such as soundness of digestion, is irrelevant to ethics, which is concerned with specifically human virtue. The part of the soul concerned with desire and passion is specifically human in that it is under the control of reason: it has its own virtues, the moral virtues such as courage and temperance. The rational part of the soul is the seat of the intellectual virtues.

Aristotle on Moral and Intellectual Virtue

The moral virtues are dealt with in books 2 to 5 of the *Nicomachean Ethics* and in the second and third books of the *Eudemian*. These virtues are not innate, but acquired by practice and lost by disuse: thus they differ from faculties like intelligence or memory. They are abiding states, and thus differ from momentary passions like anger and pity. What makes a person good or bad, praiseworthy or blameworthy, is neither the simple possession of faculties or the simple occurrence of passions. It is rather a state of character which is expressed both in purpose (*prohairesis*) and in action (*praxis*) (*NE* 2. 1. 1103^{a}11–^{b}25; 4. 1105^{a}19–1106^{a}13; *EE* 2. 2. 1220^{b}1–20).

Virtue is expressed in good purpose, that is to say, a prescription for action in accordance with a good plan of life. The actions which express moral virtue will, Aristotle tells us, avoid excess and defect. A temperate person, for instance, will avoid eating or drinking too much; but he will also avoid eating or drinking too little. Virtue chooses the mean, or middle ground, between excess and defect, eating and drinking the right amount. Aristotle goes through a long list of virtues, beginning with the traditional ones of fortitude and temperance, but including others such as liberality, sincerity, dignity, and conviviality, and sketches out how each of them is concerned with a mean.

The doctrine of the mean is not intended as a recipe for mediocrity or an injunction to stay in the middle of the herd. Aristotle warns us that what constitutes the right amount to drink, the right amount to give away, the right amount of talking to do, may differ from person to person, in the way that the amount of food fit for an Olympic champion may not suit a novice athlete (2. 6. 1106^{b}3–4). Each of us learns what is the right amount by experience: by observing, and correcting, excess and defect in our conduct.

Virtue is concerned not only with action but with passion. We may have too many fears or too few fears, and courage will enable us to fear when fear is appropriate and be fearless when it is not. We may be excessively concerned with sex and we may be insufficiently interested in it: the temperate person will take the appropriate degree of interest and be neither lustful nor frigid (*NE* 2. 7. 1107^{b}1–9).

The virtues, besides being concerned with means of action and passion, are themselves means in the sense that they occupy a middle ground between two contrary vices. Thus courage is in the middle, flanked on one side by foolhardiness and on the other by cowardice; generosity treads the narrow path between miserliness and prodigality (*NE* 2. 7. 1107^{b}1–16; *EE* 2. 3. 1220^{b}36–1221^{a}12). But while there is a mean of action and passion, there is no mean of virtue itself: there cannot be too much of a virtue in the way that there can be too much of a particular kind of action or passion. If we feel inclined to say that someone is too courageous, what we really mean is that his actions cross the boundary between the virtue of courage and the vice of foolhardiness. And if there cannot be too much of a virtue, there cannot be too little of a vice: so that there is no mean of vice any more than there is a mean of virtue (*NE* 2. 6. 1107^{a}18–26).

While all moral virtues are means of action and passion, it is not the case that every kind of action and passion is capable of a virtuous mean. There are some actions of which there is no right amount, because any amount of them is too much: Aristotle gives murder and adultery as examples. There is no such thing as committing adultery with the right person at the right time in the right way. Similarly, there are passions that are excluded from the application of the mean: there is no right amount of envy or spite (*NE* 2. 6. 1107^{a}8–17).

Aristotle's account of virtue as a mean seems to many readers truistic. In fact, it is a distinctive ethical theory that contrasts with other influential systems of various kinds. Moral systems such as traditional Jewish or Christian doctrine give the concept of a moral law (natural or revealed) a central role. This leads to an emphasis on the prohibitive aspect of morality, the listing of actions to be altogether avoided: most of the commands of the Decalogue, for instance, begin with 'Thou shalt not'. Aristotle does believe that there are some actions that are altogether ruled out, as we have just seen; but he stresses not the minimum necessary for moral decency but rather the conditions of achieving moral excellence (that is, after all, what *ethike arete* means). He is, we might say, writing a text for an honours degree, rather than a pass degree, in morality.

But it is not only religious systems that contrast with Aristotle's treatment of the mean. For a utilitarian, or any kind of consequentialist, there is no class of actions to be ruled out in advance. On a utilitarian view, since the morality of an action is to be judged by its consequences there can, in a particular case, be the right amount of adultery or murder. On the other hand, some secular ascetic systems have ruled out whole classes of actions: for a vegetarian, for instance, there can be no right amount of the eating of meat. We might say that from Aristotle's point of view utilitarians go to excess in their application of the mean, whereas vegetarians are guilty of defect in its application. Aristotelianism, naturally, hits the happy mean in application of the doctrine.

Aristotle sums up his account of moral virtue by saying that it is a state of character expressed in choice, lying in the appropriate mean, determined by the prescription that a wise person would lay down. In order to complete this account, he has to explain what wisdom is, and how the wise person's prescriptions are reached. This he does in a book that is common to both ethics (*NE* 6; *EE* 5) in which he treats of the intellectual virtue.

Wisdom is not the only intellectual virtue, as he explains at the beginning of the book. The virtue of anything depends on its *ergon*, its function or job. The job of the reason is the production of true and false judgements, and when it is doing its job well it produces true judgements (6. 2. 1139^{a}29). The intellectual virtues are then excellences that make reason come out with truth. There are five states, Aristotle says, that have this effect: skill (*techne*), science (*episteme*), wisdom (*phronesis*), understanding (*sophia*), and intuition (*nous*). (6. 3. 1139^{b}17). These states contrast with other mental states such as belief or opinion (*doxa*) which may be true or false. There are, then, five candidates for being intellectual virtues.

Techne, however, the skill exhibited by craftsmen and experts such as architects and doctors, is not treated by Aristotle as an intellectual virtue. As we have seen, Socrates and Plato delighted in assimilating virtues to skills; but Aristotle emphasizes the important differences between the two. Skills have products that are distinct from their exercises—whether the product is concrete, like the house built by an architect, or abstract, like the health produced by the doctor (6. 4. 1140^{a}1–23). The exercise of a skill is evaluated by the excellence of its product, not by the motive of the practitioner: if the doctor's cures are successful and the architect's houses are splendid, we do not need to inquire into their motives for practising their arts. Virtues are not like this: virtues are exercised in actions that need not have any further outcome, and an action, however objectively irreproachable, is not virtuous unless it is done for the right motive, that is say, chosen as part of a worthwhile way of life (*NE* 2. 4. 1105^{a}26–^{b}8). It need not count against a person's skill that he exercises it reluctantly; but a really virtuous person, Aristotle maintains, must enjoy doing what is good, not just grudgingly perform a duty (*NE* 2. 3. 1104^{b}4). Finally, though the possessor of a skill must know how it should be exercised, a particular exercise of a skill may be a deliberate mistake—a teacher, perhaps, showing a pupil how a particular task should *not* be performed. No one, by contrast, could exercise the virtue of temperance by, say, drinking himself comatose.

It turns out that the other four intellectual virtues can be reduced to two. *Sophia*, the overall understanding of eternal truths that is the goal of the philosopher's quest, turns out to be an amalgam of intuition (*nous*) and science (*episteme*) (6. 7. 1141^{a}19–20). Wisdom (*phronesis*) is concerned not with unchanging and eternal matters, but with human affairs and matters that can be objects of deliberation (6. 7. 1141^{b}9–13). Because of the different objects with which they are concerned, understanding and wisdom are virtues of two different parts of the rational soul. Understanding is the virtue of the theoretical part (the *epistemonikon*), which is concerned with the eternal truths; wisdom is the virtue of the practical part (the *logistikon*), which deliberates about human affairs. All other intellectual virtues are either parts of, or can be reduced to, these two virtues of the theoretical and the practical reason.

The intellectual virtue of practical reason is inseparably linked with the moral virtues of the affective part of the soul. It is impossible, Aristotle tells us, to be really good without wisdom, or to be really wise without moral virtue (6. 13. 1144^{b}30–2). This follows from the nature of the kind of truth that is the concern of practical reason.

What affirmation and negation are in thinking, pursuit and avoidance are in desire: so that since moral virtue is a state which finds expression in purpose, and purpose is deliberative desire, therefore, both the reasoning must be true and the desire right, if the purpose is to be good, and the desire must pursue what the thought prescribes. This is the kind of reasoning and the kind of truth that is practical. (6. 2. 1139^{a}21–7)

Virtuous action must be based on virtuous purpose. Purpose is reasoned desire, so that if purpose is to be good both the reasoning and the desire must be good. It is wisdom that makes the reasoning good, and moral virtue that makes the desire good. Aristotle admits the possibility of correct reasoning in the absence of moral virtue: this he calls 'intelligence' (*deinotes*). (6. 12. 1144^{a}23). He also admits the possibility of right desire in the absence of correct reasoning: such are the naturally virtuous impulses of children

(6. 13. 1144^{b}1–6). But it is only when correct reasoning and right desire come together that we get truly virtuous action (*NE* 10. 8. 1178^{a}16–18). The wedding of the two makes intelligence into wisdom and natural virtue into moral virtue.

Practical reasoning is conceived by Aristotle as a process starting from a general conception of human well-being, going on to consider the circumstances of a particular case, and concluding with a prescription for action.[3] In the deliberations of the wise person, all three of these stages will be correct and exhibit practical truth (6. 9. 1142^{b}34; 13. 1144^{b}28). The first, general, premiss is one for which moral virtue is essential; without it we shall have a perverted and deluded grasp of the ultimate grounds of action (6. 12. 1144^{a}9, 35).

Aristotle does not give a systematic account of practical reasoning comparable to the syllogistic he constructed for theoretical reasoning. Indeed, it is difficult to find in his writings a single virtuous practical syllogism fully worked out. The clearest examples he gives all concern reasonings that are in some way morally defective. Practical reasoning may be followed by bad conduct (*a*) because of a faulty general premiss, (*b*) because of a defect concerning the particular premiss or premisses, (*c*) because of a failure to draw, or act upon, the conclusion. Aristotle illustrates this by considering a case of gluttony.

We are to imagine someone presented with a delicious sweet from which temperance (for some reason which is not made clear) commands abstention. Failure to abstain will be due to a faulty general premiss if the glutton is someone who, instead of the life-plan of temperance, adopts a regular policy of pursuing every pleasure that offers itself. Such a person Aristotle calls 'intemperate'. But someone may subscribe to a general principle of temperance, thus possessing the appropriate general premiss, and yet fail to abstain on this occasion through the overwhelming force of gluttonous desire. Aristotle calls such a person not 'intemperate' but 'incontinent', and he explains how such incontinence (*akrasia*) takes different forms in accordance with the various ways in which the later stages of the practical reasoning break down (7. 3. 1147^{a}24–^{b}12).

From time to time in his discussion of the relation of wisdom and virtue Aristotle pauses to compare and contrast his teaching with that of Socrates.

---

[3] See A. Kenny, *Aristotle's Theory of the Will* (London: Duckworth, 1979), 111–54.

Socrates was correct, he said, to regard wisdom as essential for moral virtue, but he was wrong simply to identify virtue with wisdom (*NE* 6. 13. 1144^{b}17–21). Again, Socrates had denied the possibility of doing what one knows to be wrong, on the grounds that knowledge could not be dragged about like a slave. He was correct about the power of knowledge, Aristotle says, but wrong to conclude that incontinence is impossible. Incontinence arises from deficiencies concerning the minor premisses or the conclusion of practical reasoning, and does not prejudice the status of the universal major premise which alone deserves the name 'knowledge'. (*NE* 7. 3. 1147^{b}13–19).

Pleasure and Happiness

The pleasures that are the domain of temperance, intemperance, and incontinence are pleasures of a particular kind: the familiar bodily pleasures of food, drink, and sex. If Aristotle is to carry out his plan of explicating the relationship between pleasure and happiness, he has to give a more general account of the nature of pleasure. This he does in two passages, in *NE* 7 = *EE* 6 (1152^{b}1–54^{b}31) and in *NE* 10. 1–5 (1172^{a}16–1176^{a}29). The two passages differ in style and method, but their fundamental content is the same.[4]

In each treatise Aristotle offers a fivefold classification of pleasure. First of all, there are the pleasures of those who are sick (either in body or soul); these are really only pseudo-pleasures (1153^{b}33, 1173^{b}22). Next, there are the pleasures of food and drink and sex as enjoyed by the gourmand and the lecher (1152^{b}35 ff., 1173^{b}8–15). Next up the hierarchy are two classes of aesthetic sense-pleasures: the pleasures of the inferior senses of touch and taste, on the one hand, and on the other the pleasures of the superior senses of sight, hearing, and smell (1153^{b}26, 1174^{b}14–1175^{a}10). Finally, at the top of the scale, are the pleasures of the mind (1153^{a}1–20, 1173^{b}17).

Different though these pleasures are, a common account can be given of the nature of each genuine pleasure.

Each sense has a corresponding pleasure, and so does thought and contemplation. Each activity is pleasantest when it is most perfect, and it is most perfect when the

---

[4] See A. Kenny, *The Aristotelian Ethics* (Oxford: Clarendon Press, 1978), 233–7.

organ is in good condition and when it is directed to the most excellent of its objects; and the pleasure perfects the activity. The pleasure does not however perfect the activity in the same way as the object and the sense, if good, perfect it; just as health and the physician are not in the same way the cause of someone's being in good health. (*NE* 10. 4. 1174^{b}23–32)

The doctrine that pleasure perfects activity is presented in different terms in another passage in which pleasure is defined as the unimpeded activity of a disposition in accordance with nature (*NE* 7. 12. 1153^{a}14).

To see what Aristotle had in mind, consider the aesthetic pleasures of taste. You are at a tasting of mature wines; you are free from colds, and undistracted by background music; then if you do not enjoy the wine either you have a bad palate ('the organ is not in good condition') or it is a bad wine ('it is not directed to the most excellent of its objects'). There is no third alternative. Pleasure 'perfects' activity in the sense that it causes the activity—in this case a tasting—to be a good one of its kind. The organ and the object—in this case the palate and the wine—are the efficient cause of the activity. If they are both good, they will be the efficient cause of a good activity, and therefore they too will 'perfect' activity, i.e. make it be a good specimen of such activity. But pleasure causes activity not as efficient cause, but as final cause: like health, not like the doctor.

After this analysis, Aristotle is in a position to consider the relation between pleasure and goodness. The question 'Is pleasure good or bad?' is too simple: it can only be answered after pleasures have been distinguished and classified. Pleasure is not to be thought of as a good or bad thing in itself: the pleasure proper to good activities is good and the pleasure proper to bad activities is bad (*NE* 10. 5. 1175^{b}27).

If certain pleasures are bad, that does not prevent the best thing from being some pleasure—just as knowledge might be, thought certain kinds of knowledge are bad. Perhaps it is even necessary, if each state has unimpeded activities, that the activity (if unimpeded) of all or one of them should be happiness. This then would be the most worthwhile thing of all; and it would be a pleasure. (*NE* 7. 13. 1153^{b}7–11)

In this way, it could turn out that pleasure (of a certain kind) was the best of all human goods. If happiness consists in the exercise of the highest form of virtue, and if the unimpeded exercise of a virtue constitutes a pleasure, then happiness and that pleasure are one and the same thing.

Plato, in the *Philebus*, proposed the question whether pleasure or *phronesis* constituted the best life. Aristotle's answer is that properly understood the two are not in competition with each other as candidates for happiness. The exercise of the highest form of *phronesis* is the very same thing as the truest form of pleasure; each is identical with the other and with happiness. In Plato's usage, however, 'phronesis' covers the whole range of intellectual virtue that Aristotle distinguishes into wisdom (*phronesis*) and understanding (*sophia*). If we ask whether happiness is to be identified with the pleasure of wisdom, or with the pleasure of understanding, we get different answers in Aristotle's two ethical treatises.

The *Nicomachean Ethics* identifies happiness with the pleasurable exercise of understanding. Happiness, we were told earlier, is the activity of soul in accordance with virtue, and if there are several virtues, in accordance with the best and most perfect virtue. We have, in the course of the treatise, learnt that there are both moral and intellectual virtues, and that the latter are superior; and among the intellectual virtues, understanding, the scientific grasp of eternal truths, is superior to wisdom, which concerns human affairs. Supreme happiness, therefore, is activity in accordance with understanding, an activity which Aristotle calls 'contemplation'. We are told that contemplation is related to philosophy as knowing is to seeking: in some way, which remains obscure, it consists in the enjoyment of the fruits of philosophical inquiry (*NE* 10. 7. 1177^{a}12–^{b}26).

In the *Eudemian Ethics* happiness is identified not with the exercise of a single dominant virtue but with the exercise of all the virtues, including not only understanding but also the moral virtues linked with wisdom (*EE* 2. 1. 1219^{a}35–9). Activity in accordance with these virtues is pleasant, and so the truly happy man will also have the most pleasant life (*EE* 7. 25. 1249^{a}18–21). For the virtuous person, the concepts 'good' and 'pleasant' coincide in their application; if the two do not yet coincide then a person is not virtuous but incontinent (7. 2. 1237^{a}8–9). The bringing about of this coincidence is the task of ethics (7. 2. 1237^{a}3).

Though the *Eudemian Ethics* does not identify happiness with philosophical contemplation it does, like the *Nicomachean Ethics*, give it a dominant position in the life of the happy person. The exercise of the moral virtues, as well as intellectual ones, is, in the *Eudemian Ethics*, included as part of happiness; but the standard for their exercise is set by their relationship to contemplation—which is here defined in theological rather than philosophical terms.

Whatever choice or possession of natural goods—health and strength, wealth, friends, and the like—will most conduce to the contemplation of God is best: this is the finest criterion. But any standard of living which either through excess or defect hinders the service and contemplation of God is bad. (*EE* 7. 15. 1249^{b}15–20)

The *Eudemian* ideal of happiness, therefore, given the role it assigns to contemplation, to the moral virtues, and to pleasure, can claim, as Aristotle promised, to combine the features of the traditional three lives, the life of the philosopher, the life of the politician, and the life of the pleasure-seeker. The happy man will value contemplation above all, but part of his happy life will be the exercise of political virtues and the enjoyment in moderation of natural human pleasures of body as well as of soul.

The Hedonism of Epicurus

In making an identification between the supreme good and the supreme pleasure, Aristotle entitles himself to be called a hedonist: but he is a hedonist of a very unusual kind, and stands at a great distance from the most famous hedonist in ancient Greece, namely Epicurus. Epicurus' treatment of pleasure is less sophisticated, but also more easily intelligible, than Aristotle's. He is willing to place a value on pleasure that is independent of the value of the activity enjoyed: all pleasure is, as such, good. His ethical hedonism resembles that of Democritus or of Plato's *Protagoras* rather than that of either Aristotelian ethical treatise.

For Epicurus, pleasure is the final end of life and the criterion of goodness in choice. This is something that needs no argument: we all feel it in our bones (LS 21A).

We maintain that pleasure is the beginning and end of a blessed life. We recognize it as our primary and natural good. Pleasure is our starting point whenever we choose or avoid anything and it is this we make our aim, using feeling as the criterion by which we judge of every good thing. (D.L. 10. 128–9)

This does not mean that Epicurus, like Aristotle's intemperate man, makes it his policy to pursue every pleasure that offers. If pleasure is the greatest good, pain is the greatest evil, and it is best to pass a pleasure by if it would lead to long-term suffering. Equally, it is worth putting up with pain if it will bring great pleasure in the long run (D.L. 10. 129).

These qualifications mean that Epicurus' hedonism is far from being an invitation to lead the life of a voluptuary. It is not drinking and carousing, nor tables laden with delicacies, nor promiscuous intercourse with boys and women, that produce the pleasant life, but sobriety, honour, justice, and wisdom. (D.L. 10. 132) A simple vegetarian diet and the company of a few friends in a modest garden suffice for Epicurean happiness.

What enables Epicurus to combine theoretical hedonism with practical asceticism is his understanding of pleasure as being essentially the satisfaction of desire. The strongest and most fundamental of our desires is the desire for the removal of pain (D.L. 10. 127). Hence, the mere absence of pain is itself a fundamental pleasure (LS 21A). Among our desires some are natural and some are futile, and it is the natural desires to which the most important pleasures correspond. We have natural desires for the removal of the painful states of hunger, thirst, and cold, and the satisfaction of these desires is naturally pleasant. But there are two kinds of pleasure involved, for which Epicurus framed technical terms: there is the kinetic pleasure of quenching one's thirst, and the static pleasure that supervenes when one's thirst has been quenched (LS 21Q). Both kinds of pleasure are natural: but among the kinetic pleasures some are necessary (the pleasure in eating and drinking enough to satisfy hunger and thirst) and others are unnecessary (the pleasures of the gourmet) (LS 21I, J).

Unnecessary natural pleasures are not greater than, but merely variations on, necessary natural pleasures: hunger is the best sauce, and eating simple food when hungry is pleasanter than stuffing oneself with luxuries when satiated. But of all natural pleasures, it is the static pleasures that really count. 'The cry of the flesh is not to be hungry, not to be thirsty, not to be cold. Someone who is not any of these states, and has good hope of remaining so, could rival even Zeus in happiness' (LS 21G).

Sexual desires are classed by Epicurus as unnecessary, on the grounds that their non-fulfilment is not accompanied by pain. This may be surprising, since unrequited love can cause anguish. But the intensity of such desire, Epicurus claimed, was due not to the nature of sex but to the romantic imagination of the lover (LS 21E). Epicurus was not opposed to the fulfilment of unnecessary natural desires, provided they did no harm—which of course was to be measured by their capacity for producing pain (LS 21F). Sexual pleasure, he said, could be taken in any way one wished, provided one respected law and convention, distressed no one, and did no damage to one's body or one's essential resources. However, these qualifications added up to substantial constraint, and even when sex did no harm, it did no good either (LS 21G).

Epicurus is more critical of the fulfilment of desires that are futile: these are desires that are not natural and, like unnecessary natural desires, do not cause pain if not fulfilled. Examples are the desire for wealth and the desire for civic honours and acclaim (LS 21G, 1). But so too are desires for the pleasures of science and philosophy: 'Hoist sail', he told a favourite pupil 'and steer clear of all culture' (D.L. 10. 5). Aristotle had made it a point in favour of philosophy that its pleasures, unlike the pleasures of the senses, were unmixed with pain (cf. *NE* 10. 7. 1177ª25); now it is made a reason for downgrading the pleasures of philosophy that there is no pain in being a non-philosopher. For Epicurus the mind does play an important part in the happy life: but its function is to anticipate and recollect the pleasures of the senses (LS 21L, T).

On the basis of the surviving texts we can judge that Epicurus' hedonism, if philistine, is far from being licentious. But from time to time he expressed himself in terms that were, perhaps deliberately, shocking to many. 'For my part I have no conception of the good if I take away the pleasures of taste and sex and music and beauty' (D.L. 10. 6). 'The pleasure of the stomach is the beginning and root of all good' (LS 21M). Expressions such as these laid the ground for his posthumous reputation as a gourmand and a libertine. The legend, indeed, was started in his lifetime by a dissident pupil, Timocrates, who loved to tell stories of his midnight orgies and twice-daily vomitings (D.L. 10. 6–7).

More serious criticism focused on his teaching that the virtues were merely means of securing pleasure. The Stoic Cleanthes used to ask his pupils to imagine pleasure as a queen on a throne surrounded by the virtues. On the Epicurean view of ethics, he said, these were handmaids totally dedicated to her service, merely whispering warnings, from time to time, against incautiously giving offence or causing pain. Epicureans did not demur: Diogenes of Oenoanda agreed with the Stoics that the virtues were productive of happiness, but he denied that they were part of happiness itself. Virtues were a means, not an end. 'I affirm now and always, at the top of my voice, that for all, whether Greek or barbarian, pleasure is the goal of the best way of life' (LS 21P).

Stoic Ethics

In support of the central role they assigned to pleasure, Epicureans argued that as soon as every animal was born it sought after pleasure and enjoyed it as the greatest good while rejecting pain as the greatest evil. The Stoic Chrysippus, on the contrary, argued that the first impulse of an animal was not towards pleasure, but towards self-preservation. Consciousness begins with awareness of what the Stoics called, coining a new word, one's own *constitution* (LS 57A). An animal accepted what assisted, and rejected what hampered, the development of this constitution: thus a baby would strive

Zeno and Epicurus (plus swine) represented on a silver cup from Boscoreale, first century AD

to stand unsupported, even at the cost of falls and tears (Seneca, Ep. 121, 15 LS 57B). This drive towards the preservation and progress of the constitution is something more primitive than the desire for pleasure, since it occurs in plants as well as animals, and even in humans is often exercised without consciousness (D.L. 8. 86 LS 57A). To care for one's own constitution is nature's first lesson.

Stoic ethics attaches great importance to Nature. Whereas Aristotle spoke often of the nature of individual things and species, it is the Stoics who were responsible for introducing the notion of 'Nature', with a capital 'N', as a single cosmic order exhibited in the structure and activities of things of many different kinds. According to Diogenes Laertius (D.L. 7. 87), Zeno stated that the end of life was 'to live in agreement with Nature.' Nature teaches us to take care of ourselves through life, as our constitution changes from babyhood through youth to age; but self-love is not Nature's only teaching. Just as there is a natural impulse to procreate, there is a natural impulse to take care of one's offspring; just as we have a natural inclination to learn, so we have a natural inclination to share with others the knowledge we acquire (Cicero, *Fin.* 3. 65 LS 57E). These impulses to benefit those nearest to us should, according to the Stoics, be extended outward to the wider world.

Each of us, according to Hierocles, a Stoic of the time of Hadrian, stands at the centre of a series of concentric circles. The first circle surrounding my individual mind contains my body and its needs. The second contains my immediate family, and the third and fourth contain extensions of my family. Then come circles of neighbours, at varying distances, plus the circle that contains all my co-nationals. The outermost and largest circle encompasses the whole human race. If I am virtuous I will try to draw these circles closer together, treating cousins as if they were brothers, and constantly transferring people from outer circles to inner ones (LS 57G).

The Stoics coined a special word for the process thus picturesquely described: 'oikeiosis', literally 'homification'. A Stoic, adapting himself to cosmic nature, is making himself at home in the world he lives in. *Oikeiosis* is the converse of this: it is making other people at home with oneself, taking them into one's domestic circle. The universalism is impressive, but its limitations were soon noted. It is unrealistic to think that, however virtuous, a person can bestow the same affection on the most distant foreigner as one can on one's own family. *Oikeiosis* begins at home, and even within the very first circle we are more troubled by the loss of an eye than by the loss of a nail. But if the benevolence of *oikeiosis* is not universally uniform, it cannot provide a foundation for the obligation of justice to treat all human beings equally (LS 57H). Moreover, the Stoics believed that it was praiseworthy to die for one's country: but is not that preferring an outer circle to an inner one?

Again, the universe of nature contains more than the human beings who inhabit the concentric circles: what is the right attitude to those who share the cosmos with us? Stoics, in some moods, described the universe as a city or state shared by men with gods, and it was to this that they appealed in order to justify the self-sacrifice of the individual for the sake of the community. In their practical ethical teaching there is little concern with non-human agents. Animals, certainly, have no rights against mankind: Chrysippus was sure that humans can make beasts serve their needs without violating justice (Cicero, *Fin.* 3. 67 LS 57G).

The cosmic order does, however, provide not only the context but the model for human ethical behaviour. 'Living in agreement with nature' does not mean only 'living in accordance with human nature'. Chrysippus said that we should live as taught by experience of natural events, because our individual natures were part of the nature of the universe. Consequently, Stoic teaching about the end of life can be summed up thus:

We are to follow nature, living our lives in accordance with our own nature and that of the cosmos, doing no act that is forbidden by the universal law, that is to say the right reason that pervades all things, which is none other than Zeus, who presides over the administration of all that exists. (D.L. 7. 87)

The life of a virtuous person will run tranquilly beneath the uniform motion of the heavens, and the moral law within will mirror the starry skies above.

Living in agreement with nature was, for the Stoics, equivalent to living according to virtue. Their best-known, and most frequently criticized, moral tenet was that virtue alone was necessary and sufficient for happiness. Virtue was not only the final end and the supreme good: it was also the only real good.

Among the things there are, some are good, some are evil, and some are neither the one nor the other. The things that are good are the virtues: wisdom, justice, fortitude, temperance, and so on. The things that are evil are the opposites of these: folly, injustice, and so on. The things that are neither one nor the other are all those things that neither help nor harm: for instance, life, health, pleasure, beauty, strength, wealth, fame, good birth, and their opposites, death, disease, pain, ugliness, weakness, poverty, disrepute, and low birth. (D.L. 7.101 LS 58A)

The items in the long list of 'things that neither help nor harm' were called by the Stoics 'indifferent matters' (*adiaphora*). The Stoics accepted that these were not matters of indifference like whether the number of hairs on one's head was odd or even: they were matters that aroused in people strong desire and revulsion. But they were indifferent in the sense that they were irrelevant to a well-structured life: it was possible to be perfectly happy with or without them (D.L. 7. 104–5 LS 58B–C).

Like the Stoics, Aristotle placed happiness in virtue and its exercise, and counted fame and riches no part of the happiness of a happy person. But he thought that it was a necessary condition for happiness to have a sufficient endowment of external goods (*NE* 1. 10. 1101^{a}14–17; *EE* 1. 1. 1214^{b}16). Moreover, he believed that even a virtuous man could cease to be happy if disaster overtook himself and his family, as happened to Priam (*NE* 1. 10. 1101^{a}8). By contrast, the Stoics, with the sole exception of Chrysippus, thought that happiness, once possessed, could never be lost, and even Chrysippus thought it could be terminated only by something like madness (D.L. 7. 127).

Indifferent matters, the Stoics conceded, were not all on the same level as each other. Some were popular (*proegmena*) and others unpopular (*apoproegmena*). More importantly, some went with nature and some went against nature: those that went with nature had value (*axia*) and those that went against nature had disvalue (*apaxia*). Among the things that have value are talents and skills, health, beauty, and wealth; the opposites of these have disvalue (D.L. 7. 105–6). It seems clear that, according to the Stoics, all things that have value are also popular; it is not so clear whether everything that is popular also has value. Virtue itself did not come within the class of the popular, just as a king is not a nobleman like his courtiers, but something superior to a nobleman (LS 58E). Chrysippus was willing to allow that it was permissible, in ordinary usage, to call 'good' what strictly was only popular (LS 58H); and in matters of practical choice between indifferent matters, the Stoics in effect encouraged people to opt for the popular (LS 58c).

An action may fall short of being a virtuous action (*katorthoma*) and yet be a decent action (*kathekon*). An action is decent or fitting if it is appropriate to one's nature and state of life (LS 59B). It is decent to honour one's parents and one's country, and the neglect of parents and failure to be patriotic is something indecent. (Some things, like picking up a twig, or going into the country, are neither decent nor indecent.) Virtuous actions are, a fortiori, decent actions: what virtue adds to mere decency is first of all purity of motive and secondly stability in practice (LS 59G, H, I). Here Stoic doctrine is close to Aristotle's teaching that in order to act virtuously a person must not only judge correctly what is to be done, but choose it for its own sake and exhibit constancy of character (*NE* 2. 6. 1105ª30–ᵇ1). Some actions, according to the Stoics, are not only indecent but sinful (*hamartemata*) (LS 59M). The difference between these two kinds of badness is not made clear: perhaps a Stoic sinner is like Aristotle's intemperate man, while mere indecency may be parallel to incontinence. For while the Stoics, implausibly, said that all sinful actions were equally bad, they did regard those that arose from a hardened and incurable character as having badness of a special kind (LS 59o).

The Stoic account of incontinence, however, differs from Aristotle in an important respect. They regard it not as arising from a struggle between different parts of the soul but rather as the result of intellectual error. Incontinence is the result of passion, which is irrational and unnatural motion of the soul. Passions come in four kinds: fears, desires, pain, and pleasure. According to Chrysippus passions were simply mistaken judgements about good and evil; according to earlier Stoics they were perturbations arising from such mistaken judgements (LS 65G, K). But all agreed that the path of moral progress lay in the correction of the mistaken beliefs (LS 65A, K). Because the beliefs are false, the passions must be eliminated, not just moderated as on the Aristotelian model of the mean.

Desire is rooted in a mistaken belief that something is approaching that will do us good; fear is rooted in a mistaken belief that something is approaching that will do us harm. These beliefs are accompanied by a further belief in the appropriateness of an emotional response, of yearning or shrinking as the case may be. Since according to Stoic theory, nothing can do us good except virtue, and nothing can do us harm except vice, beliefs of the kind exhibited in desire and fear are always unjustified, and that is why the passions are to be eradicated. It is not that emotional responses are always inappropriate: there can be legitimate joy and justified apprehension. But if the responses are appropriate, then they do not count as passions (LS 65F). Again, even the wise man is not exempt from irregular bodily arousals of various kinds: but as long as he does not consent to them, they are not passions (Seneca, *de Ira* 2. 3. 1).

When Chrysippus says that passions are beliefs, there is no need to regard him as presenting the passions, implausibly, as calm intellectual assessments: on the contrary he is pointing out that the assents to propositions that set a high value on things are themselves tumultuous events. When I lose a loved one, it appears to me that an irreplaceable value has left my life. Full assent to this proposition involves violent internal upheaval. But if we are ever to be happy, we must never allow ourselves to attach such supreme value to anything that is outside our control.[5]

The weakness in the Stoic position is, in fact, its refusal to come to terms with the fragility of happiness. We have met a parallel temptation in classical epistemology: the refusal to come to terms with the fallibility of judgement. The epistemological temptation is embodied in the fallacious argument from 'Necessarily, if I know that p, then p' to 'If I know that p, then necessarily p'. The parallel temptation in ethics is to argue from 'Necessarily, if I am happy, I have X' to 'If I am happy, I have X necessarily'. This argument, if successful, leads to the denial that happiness can be constituted by any contingent good that is capable of being lost (Cicero, *Tusc.* 5. 41). Given the frail, contingent natures of human beings as we know ourselves to be, the denial that contingent goods can constitute happiness is tantamount to the claim that only superhuman beings can be happy.

The Stoics in effect accepted this conclusion, in their idealization of the man of wisdom. Happiness lies in virtue, and there are no degrees of virtue, so that a person is either perfectly virtuous or not virtuous at all. The most perfect virtue is wisdom, and the wise man has all the virtues, since the virtues are inseparable (LS 61F). Like Socrates, the Stoics thought of the virtues as being sciences, and all of them as making up a single science (LS 61H). One Stoic went so far as to say that to distinguish between courage and justice was like regarding the faculty for seeing white as different from the faculty of seeing black (LS 61B). The wise man is totally

---

[5] Here I am indebted to an unpublished paper by Martha Nussbaum.

free from passion, and is in possession of all worthwhile knowledge: his virtue is the same as that of a god (LS 61J, 63F).

The wise man whom we seek is the happy man who can think no human experience painful enough to cast him down nor joyful enough to raise his spirits. For what can seem important in human affairs to one who is familiar with all eternity and the vastness of the entire universe? (Cicero, *Tusc.* 4. 37).

The wise man is rich, and owns all things, since he alone knows how to use things well; he alone is truly handsome, since the mind's face is more beautiful than the body's; he alone is free, even if he is in prison, since he is a slave to no appetite (Cicero, *Fin* 3. 75). It was unsurprising, after all this, that the Stoics admitted that a wise man was harder to find than a phoenix (LS 61N). They thus purchase the invulnerability of happiness only at the cost of making it unattainable.

Since a wise man is not to be found, and there are no degrees of virtue, the whole human race consists of fools. Shall we say, then, that the wise man is a mythical ideal held up for our admiration and imitation (LS 66A)? Hardly, because however much we progress towards this unattainable goal, we have still come no nearer to salvation. Someone who is only two feet from the surface is drowning as much as anyone who is 500 fathoms deep in the ocean (LS 61T).

The Stoics' doctrine of wisdom and happiness, then, offers us little encouragement to strive for virtue. However, later Stoics made a distinction between doctrine (*decreta*) and precepts (*praecepta*), the one being general and the other particular (Seneca, Ep. 94, 1–4). While the doctrine is austere and Olympian, the precepts, by an amiable inconsistency, are often quite liberal and practical. Stoics were willing to give advice on the conduct of marriage, the right time for singing, the best type of joke, and many other details of daily life (Epictetus, discourses 4. 12. 16). The distinction between doctrine and precepts is matched by a distinction between choice and selection: virtue alone was good and choiceworthy (D.L. 7. 89), but among indifferent matters some could be selected in preference to others. Smart clothes, for instance, were in themselves worthless; but there could be good in the selection of smart clothes (Seneca, Ep. 92, 12). Critics said that a selection could be good only if what was selected was good (LS 64C). Sometimes, again, Stoics spoke as if the end of life was not so much the actual attainment of virtue as doing one's best to attain virtue. At this point critics complained that the Stoics could not make up their minds whether the end of life was the unattainable target itself, or simply ineffective assiduousness in target practice (LS 64F, C).

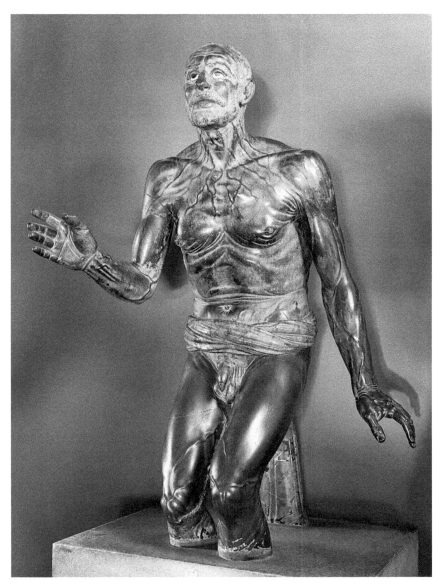

A Roman statue in the Louvre, traditionally entitled 'The Death of Seneca'

One of the best-known and most controversial of Stoic precepts was that suicide could sometimes be permissible. The Stoics 'say that the wise man may reasonably make his own exit from life, for the sake of his country or dear ones, or if he suffer intolerable pain, handicap, or disease' (D.L. 7. 130). It is difficult to see how this can be reconciled with the Stoic picture of the wise man. No amount of pain or suffering can impair the wise man's happiness, we have been told; and indeed when recommending reasonable suicide the Stoics agree that it will be the suicide of a happy man (Cicero, *Fin*, 3. 60). But then what can be the motive that provides the reason for leaving life, since virtue and happiness are supposed to be that for the sake of which everything is to be chosen?

Given that the Stoic wise man is an idealization, it is an academic issue whether his suicide would be a virtuous act. What is of practical importance is whether, for the rest of us, suicide can be a decent act. Many in antiquity believed that the Stoics taught this principle and some famous Stoics seem to have acted on it. However, it is oddly difficult to find the principle stated in our sources in a clear and unambiguous way. The most famous Stoic suicide, that of Seneca, was not a matter of his choice, but the execution of the death sentence of a tyrant.

9

God

In Homer's poems gods and goddesses figure prominently among the cast of characters. Zeus, the king of the gods, with his consort, Hera, and ten members of their extended family, including his daughter Athena, Aphrodite the goddess of love, and Poseidon the sea-god, all live together in a blissful abode on Mount Olympus. They take a keen partisan interest in the doings of the human heroes of the *Iliad* and the *Odyssey*. These gods and goddesses are simply human beings writ large, with all the emotions and vices of human beings. They interact both mentally and physically with ordinary humans, often with disastrous results. The only fundamental difference between gods and men is that men die while gods are immortal.

Xenophanes' Natural Theology

This conception of the divine was attacked by the first philosopher of religion, Xenophanes. Xenophanes savaged Homeric theology in satirical verses of which only fragments remain. Homer's stories, he complained, attributed to the gods theft, adultery, deception, and everything that, among humans, would be considered a shame and a reproach (KRS 166). But even if Homer's gods had behaved honourably, they would still resemble humans too much to be credible. Men fashion gods in their own image: Ethiopians believe in gods that are dark and snub-nosed, while the gods worshipped by the Thracians have red hair and blue eyes (KRS 168). 'If cows and horses or lions had hands and could draw, then horses would draw the forms of gods like horses, cows like cows, making their bodies similar in shape to their own' (KRS 169).

Instead of this childish anthropomorphism, Xenophanes offered a sophisticated monotheism.

He believed in

> One god, lord over gods and human kind,
> Like mortals neither in body nor in mind.   (DK 24 B23)

There could be only one God, because God is the most powerful of all things; if there were more than one god, none of them could be more powerful than the others, and none of them would be able to do whatever he wished. God must always have existed: he could not come into being from something like himself (for there cannot be anything equal to him), nor could he come into being from something unlike himself (for the greater cannot be brought into being by the lesser) (Aristotle, *MXG* 976^{b}14–36). God is a living being, but not an organic being like humans and animals: there are no parts in God, and 'he sees as a whole, he thinks as a whole, and he hears as a whole' (DK 21 B24). He has no physical contact with anything in the world, but 'remote and effortless, with his mind alone he governs all there is' (DK 21 B25).

Though he is willing to state and argue for such substantive theses about God, Xenophanes' theology is largely negative. He finds it difficult to accept either that God is finite, or that he is infinite. Similarly, when he asks whether God is changing or changeless, he finds equally balanced arguments on each side. Some of our sources leave it obscure whether his God is really transcendent or is to be identified in some mysterious way with the entire Eleatic universe. 'The clear truth about the gods no man has ever seen nor any man will ever know' (DK 21 B34).

Xenophanes was not, of course, the first monotheist. He had been anticipated much earlier in Egypt by Akhenaten and more recently in Israel by the Hebrew prophets. But he presents his monotheism not as an oracular revelation, but as the result of rational argument. In terms of a distinction not drawn until centuries later, the prophets proclaimed a revealed religion, while Xenophanes was a natural theologian.

Socrates and Plato on Piety

Plato, in the *Republic*, follows up Xenophanes' attack on the disgusting stories of the gods told by Homer and Hesiod. The stories must be eliminated from the educational curriculum, because they are false in themselves and encourage evil behaviour in their readers. Children must be told no tales of battles between the gods, or of gods changing shapes and taking human and animal form (377e–381d). God is good, and does no harm to anyone. Only the goods things in life come from God, and if the gods punish people that is for their own benefit (379c–380b). Again, God is unchanging, and does not deceive others by falsehood or disguise (382e).

Plato's assault on Homer and the poets often seems exaggerated to a modern reader. It can only be understood if we recall the centrality of the *Iliad* and the *Odyssey* in Greek education, and the importance of religion in Greek everyday life. It is true that the Greeks were never a 'people of the book', and the Homeric poems never commanded in Greek life and religion an authority similar to that which has been exercised by the Hebrew Bible, the Gospels, and the Koran. None the less, the stories of Homer and Hesiod exercised an influence in education much more powerful than that of fairy stories and children's books in our society. In that context, Plato's polemic is understandable. It must also have taken courage: after all, Socrates had been put to death on a charge of teaching the young not to believe in the gods in whom the city believes (*Apol.* 26b).

Socrates was also charged with introducing new divinities. This must be a reference to his *daimon*, an inner divine voice which, he claimed, used to warn him off wrongdoing (*Apol.* 40b). Otherwise he seems to have been respectful of conventional Greek religion. Of course he claimed not to know what piety was, just as he claimed not to know what any other virtue was. But the Socratic dialogue *Euthyphro* contains an interesting discussion of a proposed definition of piety or holiness as 'that which the gods love'.

Socrates puts the question: do the gods love what is holy because it is holy, or is it holy because the gods love it? Euthyphro responds that the holy is not so called because the gods love it; rather, the gods love what is holy because it is holy. Socrates then offers 'godly' as an abbreviation for 'what is loved by the gods'. Accordingly, Euthyphro's thesis can be stated in the following terms, substituting 'godly' for 'holy':

(A) The godly is loved by the gods because it is godly.

On the other hand, it seems clear that

(B) The godly is godly because it is loved by the gods

since 'godly' was introduced as a synonym for 'loved by the gods'. So Socrates claims to have reduced Euthyphro to inconsistency, and urges him to give up the claim that holiness is what the gods love (10a–11b).

However, there is no real inconsistency between A and B: 'because' is used in two different senses in the two theses. In (A) it introduces the gods' motive; in (B) it recalls our stipulation about meaning. A parallel point can be made in English by pointing out that it is true both that

(C) A judge judges because he is a judge

(i.e. he does it because it is his job); and also that

(D) A judge is a judge because he judges

(that is why he is called a judge).

Euthyphro, however, gives up his proposed definition and offers another: holiness is justice in the service of the gods. This too is shot down: what service can we render the gods? Socrates mocks at the idea of sacrifice as a form of trading with the gods when we have nothing worthwhile to offer them in exchange for the favours we ask them (14e–15a). If Plato's *Euthyphro* gives a realistic picture of Socrates' methods of cross-examination, we can understand why religious folk in Athens might regard him as a purveyor of impiety and a danger to the young.

Another Socratic dialogue (this time probably not by Plato), *Second Alcibiades*, contains a deflationary discussion of the practice of prayer. When we pray for something that we want, we may be asking for something that will harm us: an answer to prayer may be a disaster. Since we lack the knowledge of what is best for us, it is better not to ask for anything; or, like the Spartans, simply to pray for what is good and noble, without specifying further (148c). In terms of sacrifice and worship the Athenians are far more religious than the Spartans, and yet the Spartans always come off better in battle. Is this surprising? 'It would be a strange and sorry thing if the gods took more account of our gifts and sacrifices than of our souls and whether there is holiness and justice to be found in them' (150a).

Plato's Evolving Theology

Plato's own attitude to religion evolved along with his other metaphysical beliefs. In the central part of the *Republic* the summit of the universe is occupied not by a personal God but by the Idea of the Good, which plays the part in the ideal world of Being that is played by the sun in our everyday world of becoming (508c–e). Everything ultimately owes its being to this absolute goodness, which is itself beyond and superior to being (509b). In the *Symposium* it is the Idea of Beauty that is supreme, and the priestess Diotima describes to Socrates, in terms appropriate to the religious initiation of mystery cults, the soul's ascent to the lofty raptures of its vision. Humans crave immortality: this craving drives them to procreate and cherish their offspring, to strive for exploits that will go down in history, and to create works of art of everlasting value. But these are only the lesser mysteries of love. To reach the greatest mysteries, the candidate should rise above beautiful bodies, above beautiful souls, above the beauty of sciences and institutions, to reach an eternal and unchanging absolute beauty. The most noble life consists in the intellectual contemplation of beauty divine, absolute, and unalloyed. These rites of love will make the initiate as immortal as any human being can be (206b–212a).

Despite the religious context and phraseology, the Idea of Beauty in the *Symposium* is no more personal than the Idea of the Good in the *Republic*. But in the *Sophist* this very fact is given as a reason for a substantial overhaul of the Theory of Ideas. 'Shall we be easily persuaded', asks the Eleatic Visitor, 'that change and life and soul and wisdom do not belong to the most perfect being, and that it neither lives nor thinks, but remains motionless and stately and sacred but mindless?' (248e).

By the time he wrote the *Timaeus* Plato had reached a conception of God close to that of the major monotheistic religions. The topic of the dialogue is the origin of the world we live in: did it always exist, or did it come into being? Because it is visible and tangible it must have come into being; but it is no easy task 'to find the maker and father of this universe' (28c). Why should such a one have brought it into being? 'He was good, and what is good has no particle of jealousy in it; and so, being free of jealousy, he wanted all things to be as much like himself as possible' (29e).[1] God

---

[1] Cf. Kretzmann, *The Metaphysics of Creation* (Oxford: Oxford University Press, 1999). 101–4.

is not conceived by Plato as the creator of the universe out of nothing; rather, he established the cosmos by bringing order out of chaos. 'God, therefore, wishing that all things should be good, and nothing any less perfect than was necessary, finding the visible universe not at rest but in discordant and disorderly motion, brought it from a state of disorder into one of order, an order that he judged altogether better' (30a). The dialogue then takes us through the stages of this ordering: first soul was created and then matter, with soul incarnate in the visible body of the heavens (34e, 36e). Within the universe there are four kinds of living beings: gods, birds, fish, and animals (40a). Gods, we are told, come in two kinds: visible and invisible. The visible gods are the fixed stars, living beings divine and eternal; invisible gods appear to humans from time to time at their own discretion (40b, 41a). The father of the universe delegates to these created but immortal beings the task of making the inferior living things. In the case of human beings, he himself made the immortal soul, leaving it to the lesser gods to encase this in a skull and add the rest of the body below it (69c–d). The dialogue ends by describing the visible universe as being itself a perceptible god, the image of the God who is known only by the mind (92c).

In the last of Plato's dialogues, *The Laws*, religion is prominent, and the whole of the tenth book is devoted to it. In the ideal city of Magnesia atheism is prohibited under severe penalties. The fifty-eighth of the city's laws instructs officials to bring before a court any act of impiety that is brought to their notice. Those convicted of impiety should be sent to a penitentiary for five years' solitary confinement; anyone who relapses after release is to be punished by death. Aggravated impiety, which is atheism accompanied by fraudulent claims to supernatural powers, is to be punished by life imprisonment (907e–909c).

The legislators for Magnesia believe that it is preferable to use argument and persuasion rather than sanctions to ensure compliance with the laws, and accordingly they preface these severe prohibitions with the following preamble:

No one who believes in gods as directed by law ever voluntarily commits an act of impiety or utters any lawless word. If he does so it is due to one of three possible errors. Either he does not believe that gods exist; or he believes that they exist but have no interest in the human race; or he believes that they can be won round by sacrifice and prayer. (885b)

The lawgivers accept an obligation to cure people of these errors by offering proofs of the three truths that contradict them.

To prove the existence of gods it is not enough to point to the wonders of the universe or the order of the seasons. Atheists will say that the sun and moon and stars are only unfeeling earth and stones, and that elements and their compounds owe their existence to nature and chance (886d, 889a). Nor can one appeal to the unanimous agreement of Greeks and barbarians that gods exist: such beliefs, the atheists maintain, are simply the result of indoctrination from childhood, and in any case there is no unanimity about the nature of the gods (887c, 889e).

A refutation of atheism must take a longer way round. The fundamental error of those who think that random evolution produced the furniture of the world is that they have not grasped the priority of soul over body. Soul was created long before any bodies, and it is soul that causes the development and transformation of physical things (892a). The priority of soul is proved by an analysis of the different possible kinds of motion. There are ten such kinds, but the most important of them are just two: (*a*) one that imparts motion to other things, itself being moved by something else; and (*b*) one that imparts motion to itself as well as to other things. Obviously, a motion of the former type could not be the origin of motion in the world: motion in the universe must begin with self-generating motion. But self-generating motion is equivalent to soul: for 'that which moves itself' is a definition of 'living thing' (894c–896a).

Soul, then, is prior to body, and it is soul, or rather souls, that control the heavens. If we ask how soul controls the sun, there seem to be three possible answers: either the sun itself has a soul, which resides in its globe in the way that our souls reside in our bodies; or there is a soul with a different body of its own, which is in contact with the sun and impels it on its course; or the soul is entirely immaterial, and guides the sun on its path by some spiritual force. However it does it, the soul is clearly a god of some kind, and Thales was right that the world is full of gods (898e–899b).

It remains to be proved both that the gods care for mankind and that they are not to be swayed by prayers or gifts. The main reason for doubting their care is that they seem to allow scoundrels to prosper in spite of their wickedness. But we cannot doubt that the gods that watch over the universe possess the virtues of wisdom, temperance, and courage; they cannot be conceived as being lazy or self-indulgent. Moreover, they know and see and hear everything, and they can do whatever is in the power of mortals or immortals. If they neglect our needs it must be either because they do not know about them, or because they have allowed temptation to distract them from the knowledge. But this is absurd: after all, taking care of our tiny affairs is child's play compared with the creation of the universe (899d–903a).

The prosperity of the wicked is only temporary and apparent. It has its place in the grand divine design: but no one will forever escape punishment for misdeeds, whether he flies to heaven or hides in hell (905a). Those who say that punishment can be bought off by gifts and prayers are treating the gods as if they were sheepdogs who would yield to bribery by the wolf (906b).

Aristotle's Unmoved Movers

Plato's argument for the priority of soul over body was the progenitor of a long series of arguments for the existence of God based on an analysis of motion and change. One of the earliest and most elaborate is the argument for the existence of a cosmic unmoved mover in the last two books of Aristotle's *Physics*, which is given a highly theological interpretation in his *Metaphysics* Λ.

The basic principle of Aristotle's argument is that everything that is in motion is moved by something else. At the beginning of book 7 of the *Physics* he presents a *reductio ad absurdum* of the idea of self-movement. A self-moving object must (*a*) have parts, in order to be in motion at all; (*b*) be in motion as a whole, and not just in one of its parts; and (*c*) originate its own motion. But this is impossible. From (*b*) it follows that if any part of the body is at rest, the whole of it is at rest. But if the whole body's being at rest depends upon a part's being at rest, then the motion of the whole body depends upon the motion of the part; and thus it does not originate its own motion. So that which was supposed to be moved by itself is not moved by itself (*Ph.* 8. 241^{b}34–242^{a}49).[2]

---

[2] There is a problem with translating Aristotle's writings on motion. 'Move' in English may be transitive or intransitive: I may move someone out of my way, or move out of her way. The corresponding Greek verb has only a transitive sense, and to express the intransitive sense Greek uses the passive form of the verb. It is often therefore difficult to tell whether a particular sentence means 'X is moving' or 'X is being moved'—an ambiguity which is obviously crucial in a discussion of unmoved movement. To avoid the ambiguity in my discussion I use 'X is in motion' for the intransitive sense, and reserve 'X moves' for the transitive case in which an

This argument contains two fallacies. The first is represented in my paraphrase by an equivocation in the expression 'depends on'. The motion of the whole is logically dependent on the motion of the part, but it is not necessarily causally dependent on it.[3] Moreover, there is a confusion between necessary and sufficient conditions. The part's being at rest is a sufficient condition for the whole's being at rest; but from this it follows only that the motion of the part is a necessary condition for the motion of the whole. The argument fails to prove that the motion of the alleged self-mover must have something else, namely the motion of the part, as a causally sufficient condition.

Aristotle goes on to derive from the premiss that everything in motion must be moved by something else the conclusion that there must be a first mover. Rather than consider immediately his argument against an infinite regress, it is more profitable to examine the fuller argument against self-movement which is presented in the subsequent, and final, book of the *Physics*. Here Aristotle observes at the outset that it appears that some things in the world are self-moving, namely living beings (*empsycha*).

It sometimes happens that when there is no motion in us, from a state of rest we go into motion, that is to say motion originates in us from ourselves without any external agent moving us. This never happens with inanimate beings: it is always some other external thing that moves them; but an animal, we say, moves itself. Therefore, if an animal is ever completely at rest, we have a case of something motionless in which motion comes into being from the thing itself and not from without. Now if this can occur in an animal, why should not the same thing happen with the universe as a whole? ($252^b18–25$)

Aristotle goes on to offer a detailed and complicated argument to show that it cannot.

He offers a proof by cases that everything that is in motion is moved by something else. Motion may be divided into motion *per accidens* and motion per se. (If something is in motion because it is located in something else, like a sleeping man in a travelling ship, then its motion is *per accidens*. Another case of motion *per accidens* is where only a part of a thing is in motion, as when a man waves his hands.)

object could be supplied. Similarly with 'motion' and 'movement'. See my *The Five Ways* (London: Routledge, 1969), 8–9.

[3] See Sir David Ross, *Aristotle's Physics* (Oxford: Clarendon Press, 1936), 669.

Motion *per accidens*, he seems to take for granted, is not self-movement (254^b7–11). Things that are in per se motion may be in motion of themselves, or because of other things; in the former case their motion is natural while in the latter it may be either natural (e.g. the upward motion of fire) or violent (the upward movement of a stone). It is clear, Aristotle believes, that violent motion must be derived from elsewhere than the thing itself. We may agree right away that a stone will not rise unless somebody throws it; but it is not obvious that once thrown it does not continue in motion of itself. Not so, Aristotle says; a thrower imparts motion not only to a projectile, but to the surrounding air, and in addition he imparts to the air a quasi-magnetic power of carrying the projectile further (266^b28–267^a3). It is clear, he thinks, that not only the violent but also the natural motions of inanimate bodies cannot be caused by those bodies themselves: if a falling stone was the cause of its own motion, it could stop itself falling (255^a5–8). There are two ways in which heavy and light bodies owe their natural motions to a moving agent. First, they rise and fall because that is their nature, and so they owe their motion to whatever gave them their nature; they are moved, he says, by their 'generator'. Thus, when fire heats water, a heavy substance, it turns it into steam, which is light, and being light, naturally rises; and thus the fire is the cause of the natural motion of the steam and can be said to move it. The steam, however, might be prevented from rising by an obstacle, e.g. the lid of a kettle. Someone who lifted the lid would be a different kind of mover, a *removens prohibens*, which we might call a 'liberator' (255^b31–256^a2).

But what about the natural motions of an animal: are they not a case of self-movement? All such cases seem to be explained by Aristotle as the action of one part of the animal on another. If a whole animal moved its whole self, this, he implies, would be as absurd as someone being both the teacher and the learner of the same lesson, or the healer being identical with the person healed (257^b5). (But is this so absurd: may not the physician sometimes heal himself?) 'When a thing moves itself it is one part of it that is the mover and another part that is moved' (257^b13–14). But in the case of an animal, which part is the mover and which the moved? Presumably, the soul and the body.[4]

---

[4] See S. Waterlow, *Nature, Change, and Agency in Aristotle's Physics* (Oxford: Clarendon Press, 1982), 66.

Having established to his satisfaction that nothing is in motion without being moved by something else, Aristotle has a number of arguments to show that there cannot be an infinite series of moved movers: we have to come to a halt with a first unmoved mover which is itself motionless. If it is true that when A is in motion there must be some B that moves A, then if B is itself in motion there must be some C moving B and so on. This series cannot go on for ever and so we must come to some X which moves without being in motion (7. 242^{a}54–^{b}54, 256^{a}4–29).

The details of Aristotle's long arguments are obscure and difficult to follow, but the most serious problem with his course of reasoning is to discover what kind of series he has in mind. The example he most often gives—a man using his hands to push a spade to turn a stone—suggests a series of simultaneous movers and moved. We may agree that there must be a first term of any such series if motion is ever to take place: but it is hard to see why this should lead us to a single cosmic unmoved mover, rather than to a multitude of human shakers and movers.[5] But Aristotle might, I suppose, respond that a human digger is himself in motion, and therefore must be moved by something else. But his earlier arguments did not show that whatever is in motion is *simultaneously* being moved by something else: the generators and liberators that were allowed in as causes of motion may have long since ceased to operate, and perhaps ceased to exist, while the motion they cause is still continuing.

Is the argument from the impossibility of infinite regress, then, meant to apply to a series of causes of motion stretching back through time? It is hard to see how Aristotle, who believed that the world had no beginning, can contest the impossibility of an infinite series of causes of motion in an everlasting universe perpetually changing. So whichever series we start from, we fail to reach any unchanging, wholly simple, cosmic mover such as Aristotle holds out as resembling the great Mind of Anaxagoras (256^{b}28).

It is such a being that Aristotle, in *Metaphysics Λ*, describes in theological terms. There must, he says, be an eternal motionless substance, to cause everlasting motion. This must lack matter—it cannot come into existence or go out of existence by turning into anything else—and it must lack potentiality—for the mere *power* to cause change would not ensure the sempiternity of motion. It must be simply actuality (*energeia*) (1071^{b}3–22).

---

[5] Aristotle himself at one point seems to agree with this objection, and to treat a human digger as a self-mover (256^{a}8).

The concentric planetary spheres of the Aristotelian cosmos (under the influence of
the unmoved mover) as represented by Giovanni di Paolo in his illustration to Dante's
Paradiso

The revolving heavens, for Aristotle, lack the possibility of substantial
change, but they possess potentiality, because each point of the heavens
has the power to move elsewhere in its diurnal round. Since they are in
motion, they need a mover; and this is a motionless mover. Such a mover
could not act as an efficient cause, because that would involve a change in
itself; but it can act as a final cause, an object of love, because being loved does
not involve any change in the beloved, and so the mover can remain without
motion. For this to be the case, of course, the heavenly bodies must have
souls capable of feeling love for the ultimate mover. 'On such a principle',
Aristotle says, 'depend the heavens and the world of nature' (1072^b).

What is the nature of the motionless mover? Its life must be like the very
best in our life: and the best thing in our life is intellectual thought. The
delight which we reach in moments of sublime contemplation is a perpetual state in the unmoved mover—which Aristotle is now prepared to call
'God' (1072^b15–25). 'Life, too, belongs to God; for the actuality of mind is
life, and God is that actuality, and his essential actuality is the best and
eternal life. We profess then that God is a living being, eternal and most
good, so that life and continuous and eternal duration belong to God. That
is what God is' (1072^b13–30). Aristotle is surprisingly insouciant about how
many divine beings there are: sometimes (as above) he talks as if there was a
single God; elsewhere he talks of gods in the plural, and often of 'the

300

divine' in the neuter singular. Because of the intimate link between the celestial motions and the motionless mover(s) postulated to explain them, he seems to have regarded the question of the number of movers as a matter of astronomy rather than theology, and he was prepared to entertain the possibility of as many as forty-seven (1074ª13). This is far distant from the reasoned monotheism of Xenophanes.

Like Xenophanes, however, Aristotle was interested in the nature of the divine mind. A famous chapter (Λ 9) addresses the question: what does God think of? He must think of something, otherwise he is no better than a sleeping human; and whatever he is thinking of, he must think of throughout, otherwise he will be undergoing change, and contain potentiality, whereas we know he is pure actuality. Either he thinks of himself, or he thinks of something else. But the value of a thought is dictated by the value of what is thought of ; so if God were thinking of anything else than himself, he would be degraded to the level of what he is thinking of. So he must be thinking of himself, the supreme being, and his thinking is a thinking of thinking (*noesis noeseos*) (1074ᵇ).

This conclusion has been much debated. Some have regarded it as a sublime truth about the divine nature; others have thought it a piece of exquisite nonsense. Among those who have taken the latter view, some have thought it the supreme absurdity of Aristotle's theology, others have thought that Aristotle himself intended it as a *reductio ad absurdum* of a fallacious line of argument, preparatory to showing that the object of divine thought was something quite different.[6]

Is it nonsense? If every thought must be a thought of something, and God can think only of thinking, then a thinking of a thinking would have to be a thinking of a thinking of, and that would have to be a thinking of a thinking of a thinking of . . . ad infinitum. That surely leads to a regress more vicious than any that led Aristotle to posit a motionless mover in the first place. But perhaps it is unfair to translate the Greek 'noesis' as 'thinking of'; it can equally well mean 'thinking that'. Surely there is nothing nonsensical about the thought 'I am thinking'; indeed Descartes built his whole philosophy upon it. So why should God not be thinking that he is thinking? Only, if that is his only thought, then he seems to be nothing very grand, to use Aristotle's words about the hypothetical God who thinks of nothing at all.

[6] See G. E. M. Anscombe, in Anscombe and P. T. Geach, *Three Philosophers* (Oxford: Blackwell, 1961), 59.

Whatever the truth about the object of thought of the motionless mover, it seems clear that it does not include the contingent affairs of the likes of us. On the basis of this chapter, then, it seems that if Aristotle had lived in Plato's Magnesia, he would have been condemned as one of the second class of atheists, those who believe that the gods exist but deny that they have any care for human beings.

The Gods of Epicurus and the Stoics

Someone who certainly fell into this class was Epicurus. In the letter to Menoecus he wrote:

Think of God as a living being, imperishable and blessed, along the main lines of the common idea of him, but attach to him nothing that is alien to imperishability or incompatible with blessedness. Believe about him everything that can preserve this imperishable bliss. There are indeed gods—the knowledge of them is obvious—but they are not such as most people believe them to be, because popular beliefs do not preserve them in bliss. The impious man is not he who denies the gods of the many, but he who fastens on the gods the beliefs of the many. (D.L. 123 LS 23B)

The belief that endangers the gods' imperishable bliss is precisely the belief that they take an interest in human affairs. To favour some human beings, to be angry with others, would interrupt the gods' life of happy tranquillity (Letter to Herodotus, D.L. 10. 76; Cicero, *ND* 1. 45). It is folly to think that the gods created the world for the sake of human beings. What profit could they take from our gratitude? What urge for novelty could tempt them to venture on creation after aeons of happy tranquillity (Cicero, *ND* 1. 21–3; Lucretius, *RN* 5. 165–9)? Does the world look, the Epicurean Lucretius asks, as if it had been created for the benefit of humans? Most parts of the world have such inhospitable climates that they are uninhabitable, and the habitable parts yield crops only because of human toil. Disease and death carry off many before their time: no wonder that a newborn babe wails on entering this woeful world, in which wild beasts are more at home than human beings.

> Thus, like a sailor by the tempest hurled
> Ashore, the babe is shipwrecked on the world.

Naked he lies, and ready to expire,
Helpless of all that human wants require;
Exposed upon unhospitable earth,
From the first moment of his hapless birth.
Straight with foreboding cries he fills the room
(Too true presages of his future doom).
But flocks and herds, and every savage beast,
By more indulgent nature are increased:
They want no rattles for their froward mood,
Nor nurse to reconcile them to their food,
With broken words; nor winter blasts they fear,
Nor change their habits with the changing year;
Nor, for their safety, citadels prepare,
Nor forge the wicked instruments of war;
Unlaboured earth her bounteous treasure grants,
And nature's lavish hands supply their common wants.

(*RN* 5. 195–228, trans. Dryden)

The sorry lot of humans is made worse, not better, by popular beliefs about the gods. Impressed by the vastness of the cosmos and the splendour of the heavenly bodies, terrified by thunderbolts and earthquakes, we imagine that nature is controlled by a race of vengeful celestial beings bent on punishing us for our misdeeds. We cower with terror, live in fear of death, and debase ourselves by prayer, prostration, and sacrifice (*RN* 1194–1225).

Epicurus accepted the existence of gods because of the consensus of the human race: a belief so widespread and so basic must be implanted by nature and therefore be true. The substance of the consensus, he maintained, is that the gods are blessed and immortal, and therefore free from toil, anger, or favour. This knowledge is enough to enable human beings to worship with piety and without superstition. However, human curiosity wishes to go further and to find out what the gods look like, what they think, and how they live (Cicero, *ND* 1. 43–5).

The way in which nature imparts a conception of the gods, according to Epicurus, is this. Human beings had dreams, and sometimes saw visions, in which grand, handsome, and powerful beings appeared in human shape. These were then idealized, endowed with sensation, and conceived as immortal, blessed, and effortless (Lucretius, *RN* 1161–82). But even as idealized the gods retain human form, because that is the most beautiful of all animate shapes, and the only one in which reason is possible. The gods are not, however, beings of flesh and blood like us; they are made of tenuous quasi-flesh and quasi-blood. They are not tangible or visible, but perceptible only by the mind; and they do not live in any region of our world. Nonetheless, there are exactly as many immortals as there are mortals (Cicero, *ND* 1. 46–9; Lucretius, *RN* 5. 146–55).

It is not easy to harmonize all the elements of Epicurus' theology. One recent study attempts to do so by treating Epicurean gods as thought-constructs, the product of streams of images that by converging on our minds become our gods. The idealized concepts that result provide ethical paradigms for imitation; but there are no biologically immortal beings anywhere in the universe. On this interpretation, Epicurus would be an ancient anticipation of nineteenth-century thinkers such as George Eliot and Matthew Arnold, whose professed theism proves on inspection to be an essentially moral theory.[7] Ingenious and attractive though this interpretation is, it is clearly not how the matter was seen by either Lucretius or the Epicurean spokesman in Cicero's *On the Nature of the Gods*, who between them provide most of our information about his theology. These admirers both took Epicurus' repudiation of atheism at face value.

Undeniably, however, there were those in classical times who took the Epicurean system as tantamount to atheism, notably the Stoics (Cicero, *ND* 2. 25). Stoic piety itself, however, like Epicurean piety, was at some distance from popular polytheistic religion. From the point of view of the great monotheistic religions Epicureans and Stoics both err in theology: Epicureans by making God too distant from the real world and Stoics by making God too close to it. For the controlling thought of Stoic theology is the identification of God with providence, that is to say, the rationality of natural processes. This is an anticipation of Spinoza's *Deus sive Natura*.

Like the Epicureans, the Stoics began by appealing to the consensus of the human race that gods exist. The two schools also agree that one origin of popular belief in gods is terror of the violence of nature. From that point, however, the two theologies diverge. The Stoics, unlike the Epicureans, offered proofs of the existence of God, and sometimes the starting points of those proofs are the same as the starting point of Epicurean arguments against the operation of divine providence. Thus Cleanthes said

[7] See LS, i. 145–9.

that what brought the concept of God into men's minds was the benefit we gain from temperate climate and the earth's fertility (Cicero, *ND* 2. 12–13). Chrysippus, again, takes as a premiss that the fruits of the earth exist for the sake of animals, and animals exist for the sake of humans (*ND* 2. 37).

The most popular argument the Stoics offered was the one that later became known as the Argument from Design. The heavens move with regularity, and the sun and moon are beautiful as well as useful. Anyone entering a house, a gymnasium, or a forum, said Cleanthes, and seeing it functioning in good order, would know that there was someone in charge. A fortiori, the ordered progression of bodies so many and so great must be under the governance of some mind (*ND* 2. 15). The Stoics anticipated Paley's comparison of the world to a watch that calls for a watchmaker. The Stoic Posidonius had recently constructed a wondrous armillary sphere, modelling the movement of the sun and moon and the planets. If this was brought even to primitive Britain, no one there would doubt it was the product of reason. Surely the original thus modelled proclaims even more loudly that it is the product of a divine mind. Anyone who believes that the world is the result of chance might as well believe that if you threw enough letters of the alphabet into an urn and shook them out onto the ground you would produce a copy of the Annals of Ennius. So spoke Cicero's Stoic spokesman Balbus, centuries before anyone had though of the possibility of the works of Shakespeare being produced by battalions of typing monkeys (*ND* 2. 88).

Zeno, the founder of the Stoic school, was fertile in the production of arguments for the existence of God, or at least for the rationality of the world. 'The rational is superior to the non-rational. But nothing is superior to the world. Therefore the world is rational.' 'Nothing inanimate can generate something that is animate. But the world generates things that are animate; therefore the world is animate.' If an olive tree sprouted flutes playing in tune, he said, you would have to attribute a knowledge of music to the tree: why not then attribute wisdom to the universe which produces creatures that possess wisdom? (*ND* 2. 22).

One of Zeno's most original, if least convincing, arguments went like this. 'You may reasonably honour the gods. But you may not reasonably honour what does not exist. Therefore gods exist.' This recalls an argument I once came across in a discussion of the logic of imperatives: 'Go to church. If God does not exist, do not go to church. Therefore, God exists.'

We are used to hearing prohibitions on deriving an 'ought' from an 'is'. It is less usual to find philosophers seeking to derive an 'is' from an 'ought'. However, throughout the ages philosophers have been eager to derive an 'is not' from an 'ought not': those who have propounded the problem of evil have been in effect arguing that the world ought not to be as it is, and therefore there is no God.

This problem was of particular interest to the Stoics. On the one hand, the doctrine of divine providence played an important part in their system, and providence may seem incompatible with the existence of evil. On the other hand, since for the Stoics vice is the only real evil, the problem seems more restricted in scope for them than it does for theists of other schools. But even so limited, it calls for a solution, and this Chrysippus found by appealing to a principle that contraries can exist only in coexistence with each other: justice with injustice, courage with cowardice, temperance with intemperance, and wisdom with folly (LS 54Q). The principle (adapted from one of Plato's arguments for immortality in the *Phaedo*) seems faulty: no doubt the concept of an individual virtue may be inseparable from the concept of the corresponding vice, but that does not show that both of the concepts must be instantiated.

The Stoics offered other less metaphysical responses to the problem of evil. Because they were determinists, the Stoics could not offer the freewill defence which has been a mainstay of Christian treatments of the topic. Instead, they offered two principal lines of defence: either the alleged evils were not really evil (even from a non-Stoic point of view) or they were unintended but unavoidable consequences of beneficent providential action. Along the first line, Chrysippus pointed out that bedbugs were useful for making us rise promptly, and mice are helpful in encouraging us to be tidy. Along the second he argued (borrowing once again from Plato) that in order to be a fit receptacle for reason, the human skull had to be very thin, which had the inevitable consequence that it would also be fragile (LS 54O, Q). Sometimes Chrysippus falls back on the argument that even in the best-regulated households a certain amount of dirt accumulates (LS 54S).

Whatever pains and inconveniences we suffer, Chrysippus maintained, the world exists for the sake of human beings. The gods made us for our own and each other's sakes, and animals for our sakes. Horses help us in war, and dogs in hunting, while bears and lions give us opportunities for courage.

Other animals are there to feed us: the purpose of the pig is to produce pork. Some creatures exist simply so that we can admire their beauty: the peacock, for instance, was created for the sake of his tail (LS 54o, P).

Divine providence was extolled by Cleanthes in his majestic hymn to Zeus.

> O King of Kings
> Through ceaseless ages, God, whose purpose brings
> To birth, whate'er on land or in the sea
> Is wrought, or in high heaven's immensity;
> Save what the sinner works infatuate.
> Nay, but thou knowest to make the crooked straight:
> Chaos to thee is order: in thine eyes
> The unloved is lovely, who didst harmonise
> Things evil with things good, that there should be
> One Word through all things everlastingly.
>
> (LS 54I, trans. James Adam)

Cleanthes addresses Zeus in terms that would be appropriate enough for a devout Jew or Christian praying to the Lord God. But the underlying Stoic conception of God is very different from that of the monotheistic religions. God, according to the Stoics, is material, himself a constituent of the cosmos, fuelling it and ordering it from within as a 'designing fire'. God's life is identical with the history of the universe, as it evolves and develops.

The doctrine of Chrysippus is thus described by Cicero:

He says that divine power resides in reason, and in the soul and mind of the whole of nature. He calls the world itself god, and the all-pervasive World-Soul, or the dominant part of that soul that is located in mind and reason. He also calls god the universal, all-embracing, common nature of things, and also the power of fate and the necessity of future events. (ND 1. 39)

God can be identified with the elements of earth, water, air, and fire, and in these forms he can be called by the names of the traditional gods of Olympus. As earth, he is Demeter; as water and air, Poseidon; as fire or ether, he is Zeus, who is also identified with the everlasting law that is the guide of our life and the governess of our duties (ND 1. 40). As described by Cicero, Chrysippus' religion is neither monotheism nor polytheism: it is polymorphous pantheism.

On Divination and Astrology

One doctrine of the Stoics that Cicero vigorously contested was their belief in divination. His dialogue *On Divination* takes the form of a conversation between his brother and himself, with Quintus Cicero defending divination and claiming that religion stands or falls with the belief in it, while Marcus Cicero denies the equivalence and denounces divination as puerile superstition. Quintus draws some of his material from Chrysippus, who wrote two books on divination, and collected lists of veridical oracles and dreams (*D* 1. 6), while Marcus is indebted for many of his arguments to the Academic sceptic Carneades.

Divination—the attempt to predict future events which on the face of them are fortuitous—was practised in Rome in many ways: by the study of the stars, the observation of the flight of birds, by the inspection of the

Marcus Tullius Cicero as a diligent schoolboy, in a fresco by V. Foppa

entrails of sacrificed animals, by the interpretation of dreams, and by the consultation of oracles. Not all of these modes of divination are fashionable in the modern world, but Cicero's consideration of astrology is still, sadly, relevant.

Quintus heaps up anecdotes of remarkable predictions by augurs, sooth-sayers, and the like, and argues that in principle they are acting no differently from the rest of us when we predict the weather from the behaviour of birds and frogs or the copiousness of berries on bushes. In both cases we do not know the reason that links sign and signified, but we do know that there is one, just as when someone throws double sixes a hundred times in succession we know it is not pure chance. Not all soothsayers' predictions come true: but then doctors too make mistakes from time to time. We may not understand how they make their predictions, but then we don't understand the operation of the magnet either (*D* 1. 86).

Quintus confirms his empirical evidence with an a priori argument drawn from the Stoics. If the gods know the future, and do not tell it to us, then they do not love us, or they think such knowledge will be useless, or they are powerless to communicate with us. But each of these alternatives is absurd. They must know the future, since the future is what they themselves decree. So they must communicate the future to us, and they must give us the power to understand the communication: and that power is the art of divination (*D* 1. 82–3). Belief in divination is not superstitious but scientific, because it goes hand in hand with the acceptance of a single united series of interconnected causes. It is that series that the Stoics call Fate (*D* 1. 125–6).

Marcus Cicero begins his reply in a down-to-earth manner. If you want to know what colour a thing is, you had better ask somebody sighted rather than a blind seer like Tiresias. If you a sick, call a doctor, not a soothsayer. If you want cosmology, you should go to a physicist, and if you want moral advice, seek a philosopher, not a diviner. If you want a weather forecast trust a pilot rather than a prophet.

If an event is a genuine matter of chance, then it cannot be foretold, for in chance cases there is no equivalent of the causal series that enables astronomers to predict eclipses (*D* 2. 15). On the other hand, if future events are fated, then foreknowledge of a future disaster will not enable one to avoid it, and the gods are kinder to keep such knowledge from us. Julius Caesar would not have enjoyed a preview of his own body stabbed and untended at the foot of Pompey's statue. The predictions that divines offer us contradict each other: as Cato said, it is a wonder that when one soothsayer meets another they can keep a straight face (D 2. 52).

To match Quintus' list of prophecies, Marcus compiles a dossier of cases where the advice of divines was falsified or disastrous: both Pompey and Caesar, for instance, had happy deaths foretold to them. Cicero treats portents rather as Humeans were later to treat miracles. 'It can be argued against all portents that whatever was impossible to happen never in fact happened; and if what happened was something possible, it is no cause for wonder' (D 2. 49). Mere rarity does not make a portent: a wise man is harder to find than a mule in foal.

The best astronomers, Cicero says, avoid astrological prediction. The belief that men's careers are predictable from the position of stars at their birth is worse than folly: it is unbelievable madness. Twins often differ in career and fortune. The observations on which predictions are based are quite erratic: astrologers have no real idea of the distances between heavenly bodies. The rising and setting of stars is something that is relative to an observer: so how can it affect alike all those born at the same time? A person's ancestry is a better predictor of character than anything in the stars. If astrology was sound, why did not all the people born at the same moment as Homer write an *Iliad*? Did all the Romans who fell in battle at Cannae have the same horoscope (D 2. 94, 97)?

Finally, Cicero ridicules the idea that dreams may foretell the future. We sleep every night and almost every night we dream: is it any wonder that dreams sometimes come true? It would be foolish of the gods to send messages by dreams, even if they had time to flit about our beds. Most dreams turn out false, and so sensible people pay no attention to them. Since we possess no key to interpret dreams, for the gods to speak to us through them would be like an ambassador addressing the Senate in an African dialect.

With surprisingly little embarrassment, Cicero admits that he himself has acted as an augur—but only, he says, 'out of respect for the opinion of the masses and in the course of service to the state'. He would have sympathized with the atheist bishops of Enlightenment France. But he concludes by insisting that he is not himself an atheist: it is not only respect for tradition, but the order of the heavens and the beauty of the universe that makes him confess that there is a sublime eternal being that humans must look up to and admire. But true religion is best served by rooting out superstition (*D* 2. 149).

The Trinity of Plotinus

Philosophical theology in the ancient world culminates in the system of Plotinus. It is thus summed up by Bertrand Russell: 'The metaphysics of Plotinus begins with a Holy Trinity: The One, Spirit and Soul. These three are not equal, like the Persons of the Christian Trinity; the One is supreme, Spirit comes next, and Soul last.'[8] The comparison with the Christian Trinity is inescapable; and indeed Plotinus, who died before the church councils of Nicaea and Constantinople gave a definitive statement of the relationships between the three divine persons, undoubtedly had an influence on the thought of some of the Church fathers. But for the understanding of his own thought it is more rewarding to look backwards. With some qualification it can be said that the One is a Platonic God, Intellect (a more appropriate translation for *nous* than 'spirit') is an Aristotelian God, and Soul is a Stoic God.

The One is a descendant of the One of the *Parmenides* and the Idea of Good in the *Republic*. The paradoxes of the *Parmenides* are taken as adumbrations of an ultimately ineffable reality, which is, like the Idea of the Good, 'beyond being in power and dignity'. 'The One', it should be stressed, is not, for Plato and Plotinus, a name for the first of the natural number series: rather, it means that which is utterly simple and undivided, all of a piece, and utterly unique (Ennead 6, 9. 1 and 6). In saying that the One and the Good (Plotinus uses both names, e.g. 6. 9. 3) is beyond being he does not mean that it does not exist: on the contrary it is the most real thing there is. He means that no predicates can be applied to it: we cannot say that it *is* this, or it *is* that. The reason for this is that if any predicate was true of it, then there would have to be a distinction within it corresponding to the distinction between the subject and the predicate of the true sentence. But that would derogate from the One's sublime simplicity (5. 3. 13).

[8] A History of Western Philosophy (London: Allen & Unwin, 1961), 292.

Being has a kind of shape of being, but the One has no shape, not even intelligible shape. For since its nature is generative of all things, the One is none of them. It is not of any kind, has no size or quality, is not intellect or soul. It is neither moving nor stationary, and it is in neither place nor time; in Plato's words it is 'by itself alone and uniform'—or rather formless and prior to form as it is prior to motion and rest. For all these are properties of being, making it manifold. (6. 9. 3. 38–45)

If no predicates can be asserted of the One, it is not surprising if we enmesh ourselves in contradiction when we try to do so. Being, for a Platonist, is the realm of what we can truly know—as against Becoming, which is the object of mere belief. But if the One is beyond being, it is also beyond knowledge. 'Our awareness of it is not through science or understanding, as with other intelligible objects, but by way of a presence superior to knowledge.' Such awareness is a mystical vision like the rapture of a lover in the presence of his beloved (6. 9. 4. 3 ff.).

Because the One is unknowable, it is also ineffable. How then can we talk about it, and what is Plotinus doing writing about it? Plotinus puts the question to himself in Ennead 5, 3. 14, and gives a rather puzzling answer.

We have no knowledge or concept of it, and we do not say it, but we say something about it. How then do we speak about it, if we do not grasp it. Does our having no knowledge of it mean that we do not grasp it at all? We do grasp it, but not in such a way as to say it, only to speak about it.

The distinction between saying and speaking about is puzzling. Could what Plotinus says here about the One be said about some perfectly ordinary thing like a cabbage? I cannot say or utter a cabbage; I can only talk about it. What is meant here by 'say', I think, is something like 'call by a name' or 'attribute predicates to'. This I can do with a cabbage, but not with the One. And the Greek word whose standard translation is 'about' can also mean 'around'. Plotinus elsewhere says that we cannot even call the One 'it' or say that it 'is'; we have to circle around it from outside (6. 3. 9. 55).

Any statement about the One is really a statement about its creatures. We are well aware of our own frailty: our lack of self-sufficiency and our shortfall from perfection (6. 9. 6. 15–35). In knowing this we can grasp the One in the way that one can tell the shape of a missing piece in a jigsaw puzzle by knowing the shape of the surrounding pieces. Or, to use a metaphor closer to Plotinus' own, when we in thought circle around the

One we grasp it as an invisible centre of gravity. Most picturesquely, Plotinus says:

It is like a choral dance. The choir circles round the conductor, sometimes facing him and sometimes looking the other way; it is when they are facing him that they sing most beautifully. So too, we are always around him—if we were not we would completely vanish and no longer exist—but we are not always facing him. When we do look to him in our divine dance around him, then we reach our goal and take our rest and sing in perfect tune. (6. 9. 38–45)

We turn from the One to the second element of the Plotinian trinity, Intellect (*nous*). Like Aristotle's God, Intellect is pure activity, and cannot think of anything outside itself, since this would involve potentiality. But its activity is not a mere thinking of thinking—whether or not that was Aristotle's doctrine—it is a thinking of all the Platonic Ideas (5. 9. 6). These are not external entities: as Aristotle himself had laid down as a universal rule, the actuality of intellect and the actuality of intellect's object is one and the same. So the life of the Ideas is none other than the activity of Intellect. Intellect is the intelligible universe, containing forms not only of universals but also of individuals (5. 9. 9; 5. 7).

Despite the identity of the thinker and the thought, the multiplicity of the Ideas means that Intellect does not possess the total simplicity which belongs to the One. Indeed, it is this complexity of Intellect that convinced Plotinus that there must be something else prior to it and superior to it. For, he believed, every form of complexity must ultimately depend on something totally simple.[9]

The intellectual cosmos is, indeed, boundlessly rich.

In that world there is no stinting nor poverty, but everything is full of life, boiling over with life. Everything flows from a single fount, not some special kind of breath or warmth, but rather a single quality containing unspoilt all qualities, sweetness of taste and smell, wine on the palate and the essence of every aroma, visions of colours and every tangible feeling, and every melody and every rhythm that hearing can absorb. (6. 7. 12. 22–30)

This is the world of Being, Thought, and Life; and though it is the world of Intellect, it also contains desire as an essential element. Thinking is indeed itself desire, as looking is a desire of seeing (5. 6. 5. 8–10). Knowledge too is

---

[9] Dominic O'Meara, to whose *Plotinus: An Introduction to the Enneads* (Oxford: Clarendon Press, 1993) I am much indebted, calls this the Principle of Prior Simplicity (p. 45).

desire, but satisfied desire, the consummation of a quest (5. 3. 10. 49–50). In the Intellect desire is 'always desiring and always attaining its desire' (3. 8. 11. 23–4).

How does Intellect originate? Undoubtedly Intellect derives its being from the One: the One neither is too jealous to procreate, nor loses anything by what it gives away. But beyond that Plotinus' text suggests two rather different accounts. In some places he says that Intellect emanates from the One in the way that sweet odours are given off by perfume, or that light emanates from the sun. This will remind Christian readers of the Nicene Creed's proclamation that the Son of God is light from light (4. 8. 6. 10). But elsewhere Plotinus speaks of Intellect as 'daring to apostatize from the One' (6. 9. 5. 30). This makes Intellect seem less like the Word of the Christian Trinity, and more like Milton's Lucifer.

From Intellect proceeds the third element, Soul. Here too Plotinus talks of a revolt or falling away, an arrogant desire for independence, which took the form of a craving for metabolism (5. 1. 1. 3–5). Soul's original sin is well described thus by A. H. Armstrong:

It is a desire for a life different from that of Intellect. The life of Intellect is a life at rest in eternity, a life of thought in eternal, immediate, and simultaneous possession of all possible objects. So the only way of being different which is left for Soul is to pass from eternal life to a life in which, instead of all things being present at once, one thing comes after another, and there is a succession, a continuous series, of thoughts and actions.[10]

This continuous, restless, succession is time: time is the life of the soul in its transitory passage from one episode of living to the next (3. 7. 11. 43–5).

Soul is the immanent, controlling element in the universe of nature, just as God was in the Stoic system, but unlike the Stoic God Soul is incorporeal. Intellect was the maker of the universe, like the Demiurge of the *Timaeus*, but Soul is intellect's agent in managing its development. Soul links the intelligible world with the world of the senses, having an inner element that looks upwards to Intellect and an external element that looks downwards to Nature (3. 8. 3). Nature is the immanent principle of development in the material world: Soul, looking at it, sees there its own

---

[10] A. H. Armstrong (ed.), *The Cambridge History of Later Greek and Early Medieval Philosophy* (Cambridge: Cambridge University Press, 1970), 251.

reflection. The physical world that Nature weaves is a thing of wonder and beauty even though its substance is such as dreams are made of (3. 8. 4).

Plotinus' theological system is undoubtedly impressive: but we may wonder whatever kind of argument he can offer to persuade us to accept it. To understand this, we have to explore the system from the bottom up, instead of looking from the top down: we must start not with the One, but with matter, the outermost limit of reality. Plotinus takes his start from widely accepted Platonic and Aristotelian principles. He understands Aristotle as having argued that the ultimate substratum of change must be something which possesses none of the properties of the changeable bodies we see and handle. But a matter which possesses no material properties, Plotinus argued, is inconceivable.

If we dispense with Aristotelian matter, we are left with Aristotelian forms. The most important such forms were souls, and it is natural to think that there are as many souls as there are individual people. But here Plotinus appeals to another Aristotelian thesis: the principle that forms are individuated by matter. If we have given up matter, we have to conclude that there is only a single soul.

To prove that this soul is prior to and independent of body, Plotinus uses very much the same arguments as Plato used in the *Phaedo*. He neatly reverses the argument of those who claim that soul is dependent on body because it is nothing more than an attunement of the body's sinews. When a musician plucks the strings of a lyre, he says, it is the strings, not the melody, that he acts on: but the strings would not be plucked unless the melody called for it.

How can an incorruptible World-Soul be in any way present to individual corruptible bodies? Plotinus, who liked marine metaphors, explained this in two different ways. The World-Soul he once compared to a man standing up in the sea, with half his body in the water and half in the air. But he thought that we should really ask not how soul is in body, but how body is in soul. Body floats in soul, as a net floats in the sea (4. 3. 9. 36–42). Without metaphor, we can say that body is in soul by depending upon it for its organization and continued existence.

Soul governs the world wisely and well, but the wisdom that it exercises in the governance of the world is not native to it, but must come from outside. It cannot come from the material world, since that is what it shapes; it must come from something that is by nature linked to the Ideas that are the models or patterns for intelligent activity. This can only be a world-mind or Intellect.

We have already encountered the arguments whereby Plotinus shows that Intellect cannot be the ultimate reality because of the duality of subject and object and because of the multiplicity of the Ideas. Thus, at the end of our journey, we reach the one and only One.

Plotinus' theology continued to be taught, with modifications, until Western pagan philosophy came to an end with the closure of the school of Athens. But his influence lived on, and lives on, unacknowledged, through the ideas that were absorbed and transmitted by his first Christian readers. Most important of these was Augustine, who read him as a young man in the translation of Marius Victorinus. The reading set him on the course which led to his conversion to Christianity, and his *Confessions* and *On the Trinity* contain echoes of Plotinus on many a page. In the last days of his life, we are told, when the Vandals were besieging Hippo, he consoled himself with a quotation from the Enneads: 'How can a man be taken seriously if he attaches importance to the collapse of wood and stones, or to the death—God help us—of mortal creatures?' (1. 4. 7. 24–5).

CHRONOLOGY

585 BC	Thales predicts an eclipse
547	Anaximander dies
530	Pythagoras migrates to Italy
525	Anaximenes dies
500	Heraclitus in mid-life
470	Xenophanes dies
	Democritus born
469	Socrates born
450	Parmenides and Zeno visit Athens
	Empedocles in mid-life
444	Protagoras writes a constitution
427	Plato born
399	Socrates executed
387	Plato's Academy founded
384	Aristotle born
347	Plato dies
336	Alexander king of Macedon
322	Aristotle dies
313	Zeno of Citium comes to Athens
306	Epicurus founds the Garden
273	Arcesilaus becomes head of the Academy
263	Cleanthes becomes head of the Stoa
232	Chrysippus succeeds as head of the Stoa
155	Carneades heads the Academy and visits Rome
106	Cicero born
55	Lucretius' *De Rerum Natura*
44	Julius Caesar assassinated
30	Augustus becomes Emperor
52AD	St Paul preaches in Athens
65	Suicide of Seneca

161	Marcus Aurelius becomes Emperor
205	Plotinus born
387	St Augustine baptized

Many of these dates, particularly in earlier centuries, are conjectural and approximate.

ABBREVIATIONS AND CONVENTIONS

CHHP   K. Algra, J. Barnes, J. Mansfeld, and M. Schofield (eds.), *The Cambridge History of Hellenistic Philosophy* (Cambridge: Cambridge University Press, 1999)

CHLGP   A. H. Armstrong (ed.), *The Cambridge History of Later Greek and Early Medieval Philosophy* (Cambridge: Cambridge University Press, 1967)

DK   H. Diels and W. Kranz (eds.), *Die Fragmente der Vorsokratiker*, 6th edn., 3 vols. (Berlin: Wiedmann, 1951); cited as DK, followed by the chapter, letter, and the number of the fragment (e.g. DK 8 B115). Each chapter of this work is divided into two sections, A (which contains references in ancient authors) and B (which contains fragments that have been handed down verbatim)

D.L.   Diogenes Laertius, *Lives of the Philosophers*, trans. R. D. Hicks, Loeb Classical Library, 2 vols. (Cambridge, Mass.: Harvard University Press, 1972); cited by book and paragraph (e.g. 8. 8)

Ep.   Epistle

fr.   fragment

KRS   G. S. Kirk, J. E. Raven, and M. Schofield (eds.), *The Presocratic Philosophers*, 2nd edn. (Cambridge: Cambridge University Press, 1983); cited as KRS, followed by the number of the fragment in the single series that runs through the edition (e.g. KRS 433)

LS   A. A. Long and D. N. Sedley (eds.), *The Hellenistic Philosophers*, 2 vols. (Cambridge: Cambridge University Press, 1987); cited as LS, followed by the number of the chapter and the letter corresponding to the individual text (e.g. LS 30F)

S.E.   Sextus Empiricus

Alexander of Aphrodisias

de An.	*de Anima*
Fat.	*On Fate*

Aristotle

The standard form of reference is to the book and chapter of the individual work, followed by page, column, and line of the classic 1831 edition of Bekker (e.g. *Physics* 3. 1. 200^{b}32)

APo.	*Posterior Analytics*
APr.	*Prior Analytics*
Barnes	*The Complete Works of Aristotle*, ed. J. Barnes, Oxford Translation (Princeton: Princeton University Press, 1984)
Cael.	*On the Heavens*
Cat.	*Categories*
de An.	*On the Soul*
EE	*Eudemian Ethics*
GA	*On the Generation of Animals*
GC	*On Generation and Corruption*
HA	*History of Animals*
Int.	*de Interpretatione*
Metaph.	*Metaphysics*
Mete.	*Meteorologica*
MM	*Magna Moralia*
MXG	*de Melisso, Xenophane, et Gorgia*
NE	*Nicomachean Ethics*
PA	*On the Parts of Animals*
Ph.	*Physics*
Po.	*Poetics*
Pol.	*Politics*
Rh.	*Rhetorica*
SE	*Sophistical Refutations*
Top.	*Topics*

Cicero

Acad.	*Academica*
D.	*On Divination*

Fat.	*On Fate*
Fin.	*de Finibus*
ND	*On the Nature of the Gods*
Off.	*On Duties (de Officiis)*
Tusc.	*Tusculan Disputations*

Epictetus

| *Disc.* | *Discourses* |

Lucretius

| RN | *On the Nature of Things* |

Plato

It is the universal custom to refer to the works of Plato by the name of the work followed by the page, section, and line of the Stephanus edition of 1578 (e.g. *Phaedo* 64a5). This numeration is preserved in all editions and most translations of Plato.

Apol.	*Apologia Socratis*
Cra.	*Cratylus*
Euthd.	*Euthydemus*
Euthphr.	*Euthyphro*
Grg.	*Gorgias*
Hp. Ma.	*Hippias Major*
Hp. Mi.	*Hippias Minor*
La.	*Laches*
Men.	*Meno*
Phd.	*Phaedo*
Phdr.	*Phaedrus*
Phlb.	*Philebus*
Prm.	*Parmenides*
Prt.	*Protagoras*
Rep.	*Republic*
Smp.	*Symposium*
Sph.	*Sophist*
Tht.	*Theaetetus*
Ti.	*Timaeus*

Plotinus

Plotinus is standardly cited according to the schema of his pupil Porphyry, who divided his works into Enneads, or groups of nine. The number of the Ennead is given, followed by the number of the work, chapter, and line (e.g. Ennead 6, 1. 5. 27; or simply 6. 1. 5. 27)

Sextus Empiricus (S.E.)

Sextus Empiricus is cited as S.E., followed by an abbreviation for the work (e.g. S.E., *M.*)

M.	*Against the Professors*
P.	*Outlines of Pyrrhonism*

Xenophon

Mem.	*Memorabilia*

BIBLIOGRAPHY

This bibliography does not contain all the works cited in footnotes, nor all the works referred to in the course of writing the text. It is a selection of works that I believe readers will find particularly helpful in pursuing their interests in ancient philosophers and in the philosophical topics they discussed. The selection is limited mainly to works in English of an accessible kind; many such works themselves contain much fuller bibliographies.

General Works

BRUNSCHWIG, J., and LLOYD, G. E. R., *Greek Thought: A Guide to Classical Knowledge* (Cambridge, Mass.: Harvard University Press, 2000).

FREDE, M., *Essays in Ancient Philosophy* (Oxford: Clarendon Press, 1987).

GOTTLIEB, A., *The Dream of Reason: A History of Western Philosophy from the Greeks to the Renaissance* (London: Allen Lane, 2000).

IRWIN, T., *Classical Philosophy*, Oxford Readers (Oxford: Oxford University Press, 1999).

OWEN, G. E. L., *Logic, Science, and Dialectic: Collected Papers in Greek Philosophy*, ed. M. Nussbaum (London: Duckworth, 1986).

Routledge History of Philosophy, i: *From the Beginning to Plato*, ed. C. C. W. Taylor; ii: *From Aristotle to Augustine*, ed. D. Furley (London: Routledge, 1997, 1999).

Presocratic Philosophers (Chapter 1)

The standard collection of the original texts of the surviving fragments of the philosophers prior to Socrates is that of H. Diels and W. Kranz, *Die Fragmente der Vorsokratiker*, 6th edn., 3 vols. (Berlin: Wiedmann, 1951). Our main source for the biographies of the Presocratics, and many other ancient philosophers, is the *Lives of the Philosophers* by Diogenes Laertius, trans. R. D. Hicks, Loeb Classical Library, 2 vols. (Cambridge, Mass.: Harvard University Press, 1972).

There is a helpful, though less complete, collection which contains English translations in addition to the original texts: G. S. Kirk, J. E. Raven, and M. Schofield (eds.), *The Presocratic Philosophers*, 2nd edn. (Cambridge: Cambridge University Press, 1983).

An excellent collection of texts in translation alone is J. Barnes, *Early Greek Philosophy* (Harmondsworth: Penguin, 1987). A more recent translation is R. Waterfield, *The First Philosophers: The Presocratics and the Sophists*, World's Classics (Oxford: Oxford University Press, 2000).

BIBLIOGRAPHY

Barnes, J., *The Presocratic Philosophers*, rev. edn. (London: Routledge, 1982).

Cornford, F. M., *Plato and Parmenides* (London: Kegan Paul, 1939).

de Romilly, Jacqueline, *The Great Sophists in Periclean Athens* (Oxford: Clarendon Press, 1992).

Dodds, E. R. (ed.), *Plato: Gorgias*, text with introd. and comm. (Oxford: Clarendon Press, 1959).

Guthrie, W. K. C., *A History of Greek Philosophy*, vols. i–iii (Cambridge: Cambridge University Press, 1962–9).

Inwood, B., *The Poem of Empedocles* (Toronto: University of Toronto Press, 1992).

Kahn, C. H., *The Verb 'Be' in Ancient Greek* (Dordrecht: Reidel, 1973).

—— *The Art and Thought of Heraclitus* (Cambridge: Cambridge University Press, 1979).

—— *Anaximander and the Origins of Greek Cosmology*, repr. of 1960 edn. (Indianapolis: Hackett, 1994).

Kerferd, G. B., *The Sophistic Movement* (Cambridge: Cambridge University Press, 1981).

Mourelatos, A. P. D., *The Route of Parmenides* (New Haven: Yale University Press, 1970).

O'Brien, D., *Empedocles' Cosmic Cycle* (Cambridge: Cambridge University Press, 1969).

Osborne, C., *Rethinking Early Greek Philosophy: Hippolytus and the Pre-Socratics* (London: Duckworth, 1987).

Schofield, M., *An Essay on Anaxagoras* (Cambridge: Cambridge University Press, 1980).

Taylor, C. C. W. (ed.), *Plato: Protagoras*, trans. with notes, rev. edn. (Oxford: Clarendon Press, 1991).

Socrates and Plato (Chapter 1)

All the works of Plato in the original Greek are contained in five volumes of the series of Oxford Classical Texts (Oxford University Press) and, with an English translation on facing pages, in twelve volumes of the Loeb Classical Library (Harvard University Press). There is a convenient English single-volume edition of Plato's complete works edited by J. M. Cooper and D. S. Hutchinson (Indianapolis: Hackett, 1997).

The Clarendon Plato series (Oxford: Clarendon Press, 1973–) contains translations with notes of the major Platonic dialogues, notably *Theaetetus* (ed. J. McDowell, 1973), *Philebus* (ed. J. C. B. Gosling, 1975), and *Phaedo* (ed. D. Gallop, 1975). Many dialogues are translated in volumes of the Penguin Classics and of the Oxford World's Classics series.

The Socratic works of Xenophon appear in two volumes of the Loeb Classical Library: *Memorabilia* (trans. E. C. Marchant, London, 1923) and *Symposium and Apology* (trans. O. J. Todd, London, 1961). A good English translation is Xenophon,

BIBLIOGRAPHY

Conversations of Socrates, ed. H. Tredennick and R. Waterfield (Harmondsworth: Penguin, 1990).

ADAM, J. (ed.), *The Republic of Plato*, 2 vols. (Cambridge: Cambridge University Press, 1902).

ALLEN, R. E., *Plato's Euthyphro and the Earlier Theory of Forms* (London: Routledge & Kegan Paul, 1970).

—— (ed.), *Studies in Plato's Metaphysics* (London: Routledge & Kegan Paul, 1965).

ANNAS, J., *An Introduction to Plato's Republic* (Oxford: Oxford University Press, 1981).

BLONDELL, R., *The Play of Character in Plato's Dialogues* (Cambridge: Cambridge University Press, 2002).

BRANDWOOD, L., *The Chronology of Plato's Dialogues* (Cambridge: Cambridge University Press, 1990).

BRICKHOUSE, T. C., and SMITH, N. D., *Socrates on Trial* (Oxford: Oxford University Press, 1989).

—————— *Plato's Socrates* (New York: Oxford University Press, 1994).

DOVER, K. (ed.), *Plato: Symposium* (Cambridge: Cambridge University Press, 1980).

GOSLING, J. C. B., *Plato* (London: Routledge & Kegan Paul, 1973).

HACKFORTH, *Plato's Examination of Pleasure* (Cambridge: Cambridge University Press, 1945).

IRWIN, T., *Plato's Moral Theory: The Early and Middle Dialogues* (Oxford: Clarendon Press, 1977).

KAHN, C. H., *Plato and the Socratic Dialogue* (Cambridge: Cambridge University Press, 1996).

KRAUT, R. (ed.), *The Cambridge Companion to Plato* (Cambridge: Cambridge University Press, 1992).

LEDGER, G., *Re-counting Plato: A Computer Analysis of Plato's Style* (Oxford: Clarendon Press, 1989).

MEINWALD, C. C., *Plato's Parmenides* (New York: Oxford University Press, 1991).

MORROW, GLENN R., *Plato's Epistles*, a trans. with critical essays and notes, 2nd edn. (Indianapolis: Bobbs-Merill, 1962).

ROBINSON, R., *Plato's Earlier Dialectic* (Oxford: Clarendon Press, 1953).

ROWE, C. J. (ed.), *Plato: Phaedrus* (Warminster: Aris & Phillips, 1986).

RYLE, G., *Plato's Progress* (Cambridge: Cambridge University Press, 1966).

SAUNDERS, T. J., *Plato's Penal Code* (Oxford: Clarendon Press, 1991).

SAYRE, KENNETH M., *Plato's Late Ontology: A Riddle Resolved* (Princeton: Princeton University Press, 1983).

STONE, I. F., *The Trial of Socrates* (Boston: Little, Brown, 1988).

TAYLOR, C. C. W., *Socrates: A Very Short Introduction* (Oxford: Oxford University Press, 1998).

VLASTOS, G., *Platonic Studies*, 2nd edn. (Princeton: Princeton University Press, 1981).

VLASTOS, G., *Socrates, Ironist and Moral Philosopher* (Cambridge: Cambridge University Press, 1991).

WHITE, N. I., *A Companion to Plato's Republic* (Indianapolis: Hackett, 1979).

Aristotle (Chapter 2)

Most of Aristotle's works appear in the original in volumes of the Oxford Classical Texts series, and many of them appear with a translation in volumes of the Loeb Classical Library. All of the surviving works are to be found in English in the two-volume Oxford Translation, edited by J. Barnes (Princeton: Princeton University Press, 1984).

The Clarendon Aristotle series (Oxford: Clarendon Press, 1963–) contains translations of selected Aristotelian texts, with detailed philosophical notes. The series includes *Categories and de Interpretatione* (ed. J. L. Ackrill, 1963), *de Anima II and III* (ed. D. W. Hamlyn, 1968), *de Generatione et Corruptione* (ed. C. J. F. Williams, 1971), *de Partibus Animalium* (ed. D. M. Balme, 1972), *Eudemian Ethics I, II, VIII* (ed. M. Woods), *Metaphysics Γ, Δ and E* (ed. C. Kirwan, 1971, 1993), *Metaphysics Z and H* (ed. D. Bostock, 1994), *Metaphysics M and N* (ed. J. Annas, 1976), *Physics I and II* (ed. W. Charlton, 1970), *Physics III and IV* (ed. E. Hussey, 1983), *Posterior Analytics* (ed. J. Barnes, 1975, 1993), *Topics 1 and 8* (ed. R. Smith, 1994).

Many of Aristotle's works are available in translation in Penguin Classics or in Oxford World's Classics.

ACKRILL, J. L., *Aristotle the Philosopher* (Oxford: Oxford University Press, 1981).

ANSCOMBE, G. E. M., and GEACH, P. T., *Three Philosophers* (Oxford: Blackwell, 1961).

BAMBROUGH, R. (ed.), *New Essays on Plato and Aristotle* (London: Routledge & Kegan Paul, 1965).

BARNES, J. (ed.), *The Cambridge Companion to Aristotle* (Cambridge: Cambridge University Press, 1995).

—— *Aristotle: A Very Short Introduction* (Oxford: Oxford University Press, 2000).

—— SCHOFIELD, M., and SORABJI, R. (eds.), *Articles on Aristotle*, i: *Science*; ii: *Ethics and Politics*; iii: *Metaphysics*; iv: *Psychology and Aesthetics* (London: Duckworth, 1975).

BROADIE, S., and ROWE, C., *Aristotle: Nicomachean Ethics*, trans., introd., and comm. (Oxford: Oxford University Press, 2002).

IRWIN, T. H., *Aristotle's First Principles* (Oxford: Oxford University Press, 1988).

JAEGER, W., *Aristotle: Fundamentals of the History of his Development*, trans. R. Robinson, 2nd edn. (Oxford: Clarendon Press, 1948).

KENNY, A., *The Aristotelian Ethics* (Oxford: Clarendon Press, 1978).

—— *Aristotle on the Perfect Life* (Oxford: Clarendon Press, 1992).

KRAUT, R., *Aristotle:Political Philosophy* (Oxford: Oxford University Press, 2002).

LEAR, J., *Aristotle and Logical Theory* (Cambridge: Cambridge University Press, 1980).

LLOYD, G. E. R., *Aristotle: The Growth and Structure of his Thought* (Cambridge: Cambridge University Press, 1968).

MEIKLE, S., *Aristotle's Economic Thought* (Oxford: Clarendon Press, 1995).

Ross, W. D., *Aristotle's Metaphysics* (Oxford: Clarendon Press, 1924).

—— *Aristotle's Physics* (Oxford: Clarendon Press, 1936).

SORABJI, R., *Time, Creation and the Continuum* (London: Duckworth, 1983).

—— *Matter, Place and Motion: Theories in Antiquity and their Sequel* (London: Duckworth, 1988).

WATERLOW, S., *Passage and Possibility: A Study of Aristotle's Modal Concepts* (Oxford: Clarendon Press, 1982).

Hellenistic Philosophy (Chapter 2)

Much of our information about these philosophers derives from later writers such as Cicero, Lucretius, and Sextus Empiricus, whose works have been published as Oxford Classical Texts or in the Loeb Classical Library.

The most helpful collection of the extant fragments and of references in ancient authors is *The Hellenistic Philosophers* by A. A. Long and D. N. Sedley, 2 vols. (Cambridge: Cambridge University Press, 1987). One volume of this work gives translations of the principal sources, and another gives an annotated edition of the Greek and Latin texts.

The classic edition of surviving Stoic texts was for long J. von Arnim, *Stoicorum Veterum Fragmenta*, 3 vols. (Leipzig, 1903–5) (*SVF*). It has been superseded by K. Hulser, *Die Fragmente zur Dialektik der Stoiker* (Stuttgart: Frommann-Holzboog, 1987). For Epicureanism the fundamental collection is H. Usener, *Epicurea* (Leipzig, 1887).

ALGRA, K., BARNES, J., MANSFELD, J., and SCHOFIELD, M., *The Cambridge History of Hellenistic Philosophy* (Cambridge: Cambridge University Press, 1999).

ANNAS, J. E., and BARNES, J., *The Modes of Scepticism: Ancient Texts and Modern Interpretations* (Cambridge: Cambridge University Press, 1985).

ASMIS, E., *Epicurus' Scientific Method* (Ithaca, NY: Cornell University Press, 1984).

BARNES, J., BRUNSCHWIG, J., BURNYEAT, M., and SCHOFIELD, M., *Science and Speculation: Studies in Hellenistic Theory and Practice* (Cambridge: Cambridge University Press, 1982).

BURNYEAT, M., *The Sceptical Tradition* (Berkeley: University of California Press, 1983).

FURLEY, D. J., *Two Studies in the Greek Atomists* (Princeton: Princeton University Press, 1967).

LONG, A. A., *Hellenistic Philosophy*, 2nd edn. (Berkeley: University of California Press, 1986).

RIST, J. M., *Stoic Philosophy* (Cambridge: Cambridge University Press, 1969).

—— *Epicurus: An Introduction* (Cambridge: Cambridge University Press, 1972).

SHARPLES, R. W., *Stoics, Epicureans and Sceptics* (London: Routledge, 1994).

Roman and Imperial Philosophy

The works of Epictetus, Marcus Aurelius, and Plotinus have appeared in the Loeb Classical Library, and those of Plotinus as an Oxford Classical Text edited by P. Henry and H.-R. Schyzer, which has become the standard edition (Oxford: Oxford University Press, 1964–82).

O'DONNELL, J. J., *Augustine: Confessions*, 3 vols. (Oxford: Clarendon Press, 1992). There are many translations of *Confessions*, notably H. Chadwick in the World's Classics series (Oxford: Oxford University Press, 1991).

ARMSTRONG, A. H. (ed.), *The Cambridge History of Later Greek and Early Medieval Philosophy* (Cambridge: Cambridge University Press, 1970).

BAILEY, C., *Titi Lucreti Cari de Rerum Natura Libri Sex*, 3 vols. (Oxford: Oxford University Press, 1947).

BARNES, J., and GRIFFIN, M., *Philosophia Togata*, vols. i and ii (Oxford: Clarendon Press, 1989, 1997).

CLARK, G., and RAJAK, T., *Philosophy and Power in the Graeco-Roman World* (Oxford: Oxford University Press, 2002).

DILLON, J., *The Middle Platonists* (Ithaca: Cornell University Press, 1977).

DODDS, E. R., *Proclus: The Elements of Theology*, ed., trans., and comm., 2nd edn. (Oxford: Clarendon Press, 1992).

GRIFFIN, M. T., *Seneca, a Philosopher in Politics* (Oxford: Oxford University Press, 1976).

LLOYD, A. C., *The Antomy of NeoPlatonism* (Oxford: Clarendon Press, 1990).

O'BRIEN, D., *Plotinus on the Origin of Matter* (Naples: Bibliopolis, 1991).

O'MEARA, D. J., *Plotinus: An Introduction to the Enneads* (Oxford: Clarendon Press, 1993).

RIST, J., *Plotinus: The Road to Reality* (Cambridge, Cambridge University Press, 1967).

SEDLEY, D., *Lucretius and the Transformation of Greek Wisdom* (Cambridge: Cambridge University Press, 1998).

STUMP, E., and KRETZMANN, N., *The Cambridge Companion to Augustine* (Cambridge: Cambridge University Press, 2001).

Logic (Chapter 3)

KNEALE, W. C., and KNEALE, M., *The Development of Logic* (Oxford: Clarendon Press, 1962).

ŁUKASIEWICZ, J., *Aristotle's Syllogistic from the Standpoint of Modern Formal Logic*, 2nd edn. (Oxford: Clarendon Press, 1957).

MATES, B., *Stoic Logic*, 2nd edn. (Berkeley: University of California Press, 1961).

NUCHELMANS, G., *Theories of the Proposition* (Amsterdam: North-Holland, 1973).

PATZIG, *Aristotle's Theory of the Syllogism* (Dordrecht: Reidel, 1968).

PRIOR, A. N., *Time and Modality* (Oxford: Clarendon Press, 1957).

BIBLIOGRAPHY

Epistemology (Chapter 4)

BOSTOCK, D., *Plato's Theaetetus* (Oxford: Clarendon Press, 1988).

HANKINSON, R. J., *The Sceptics* (London: Routledge, 1994).

McKIRAHAN, R. D., *Principles and Proofs: Aristotle's Theory of Demonstrative Science* (Princeton: Princeton University Press, 1992).

SCHOFIELD, M., BURNYEAT, M., and BARNES, J., *Doubt and Dogmatism: Studies in Hellenistic Epistemology* (Oxford: Clarendon Press, 1980).

WHITE, N. P., *Plato on Knowledge and Reality* (Indianapolis: Hackett, 1976).

Philosophy of Physics (Chapter 5)

BOBZIEN, S., *Determinism and Freedom in Stoic Philosophy* (Oxford: Clarendon Press, 1998).

HANKINSON, R. J., *Cause and Explanation in Ancient Greek Thought* (Oxford: Clarendon Press, 1998).

HOENEN, P., *Cosmologia* (Rome: Pontifical Gregorian University, 1949).

SORABJI, R., *Necessity, Cause, and Blame* (London: Duckworth, 1980).

—— *Time, Creation and the Continuum* (London: Duckworth, 1983).

WATERLOW, S., *Nature, Change, and Agency in Aristotle's Physics* (Oxford: Clarendon Press, 1982).

Metaphysics (Chapter 6)

BARNES, J., and MIGNUCCI, M. (eds.), *Matter and Metaphysics* (Naples: Bibliopolis, 1988).

FINE, GAIL, *On Ideas: Aristotle's Cricitism of Plato's Theory of Forms* (Oxford: Clarendon Press, 1993).

GRAHAM, D. W., *Aristotle's Two Systems* (Oxford: Oxford University Press, 1987).

MALCOLM, J., *Plato on the Self-Predication of Forms* (Oxford: Clarendon Press, 1991).

SCALTSAS, T., *Substances and Universals in Aristotle's Metaphysics* (Ithaca: Cornell University Press, 1994).

Philosophy of Mind (Chapter 7)

ANNAS, J. E., *Hellenistic Philosophy of Mind* (Berkeley: University of California Press, 1992).

BRUNSCHWIG, J., and NUSSBAUM, M. (eds.), *Passions and Perceptions: Studies in Hellenistic Philosophy of Mind* (Cambridge: Cambridge University Press, 1993).

HICKS, R. D. (ed.), *Aristotle: De Anima*, with trans., introd., and comm. (Cambridge: Cambridge University Press, 1907).

NUSSBAUM, M. C. (ed.), *Aristotle: De Motu Animalium*, with trans., introd., and essays (Princeton: Princeton University Press, 1978).

—— and RORTY, A. O. (eds.), *Essays on Aristotle's Philosophy of Mind* (Oxford: Oxford University Press, 1992).

Ethics (Chapter 8)

ANNAS, J., *Platonic Ethics Old and New* (Ithaca: Cornell University Press, 1999).

BROADIE, S., *Ethics with Aristotle* (New York: Oxford University Press, 1991).

GOSLING, J. C. B., and TAYLOR, C. C. W., *The Greeks on Pleasure* (Oxford: Clarendon Press, 1982).

INWOOD, B., *Ethics and Human Action in Early Stoicism* (Oxford: Clarendon Press, 1985).

NUSSBAUM, M. C., *The Fragility of Goodness* (Cambridge: Cambridge University Press, 1986).

PRICE, A., *Love and Friendship in Plato and Aristotle* (Oxford: Clarendon Press, 1989).

SCHOFIELD, M., and STRIKER, G., *The Norms of Nature: Studies in Hellenistic Ethics* (Cambridge: Cambridge University Press, 1986).

Philosophy of Religion (Chapter 9)

FESTUGIERE, A. J., *Epicurus and his Gods* (Oxford: Blackwell, 1955).

KENNY, A., *The Five Ways* (London: Routledge, 1969).

KRETZMANN, NORMAN, *The Metaphysics of Theism* (Oxford: Oxford University Press, 1999).

ILLUSTRATIONS

Page

6   Anaximander with his sundial, in a Roman mosaic
Rheinisches Landesmuseum Trier

10   Pythagoras commending vegetarianism, as imagined by Rubens
The Royal Collection © 2003, Her Majesty Queen Elizabeth II

38   Socrates and Plato as portrayed by Matthew Paris in the thirteenth century
The Bodleian Library, University of Oxford/Ms Ashmole 304 fol 31v

47   A herm of Socrates, bearing a quotation from Plato's *Crito*
© Soprintendenza Archeologica, Naples

59   Crates and Hipparchia, in a fourth-century-BC fresco
Archivi Alinari

66   The location of the philosophical schools of Athens
Candace H Smith

70   The frontispiece of a fifteenth-century manuscript translation of Aristotle's *History of Animals*
© Biblioteca Apostolica Vaticana (Vat.Lat.2094)

83   Aristotle ridden by his wife, Phyllis
Bibliothèque nationale de France

92   A Venetian representation of King Ptolemy and his library at Alexandria
© Biblioteca Nazionale Marciana, Venice (cod.Gr.Z.388 c. VI)

97   Alexander standing in Diogenes' light (Rome, Villa Albani)
Archivi Alinari

110   The campaigns of Marcus Aurelius, depicted on his column in Rome
Fototeca Unione, American Academy in Rome

ILLUSTRATIONS

122   Aristotle, attributed to Lysippus (fourth century BC)
      Kunsthistorisches Museum, Vienna

137   Chrysippus, in a statue in the Louvre (third century AD)
      Giraudon/Bridgeman Art Library

149   Socrates in a wall-painting from Ephesus
      Sonia Halliday Photographs

158   Plato's cave (Flemish school, sixteenth century)
      Giraudon/Bridgeman Art Library

167   The opening of a book of Lucretius' *De Rerum Natura* in an illuminated
      manuscript
      British Library (Add ms 11912 f 2)

182   Alexander the Great and Aristotle
      British Library ((Royal ms 20Bxx f77v)

201   Parmenides and Heraclitus
      Archivi Alinari

206   Plato (Museo Vaticano)
      Archivi Alinari

216   Plato trodden by Aquinas (Caraffa Chapel, S. Maria sopra Minerva,
      Rome)
      Archivi Alinari

230   Pythagoras calculating the height of Hercules (from a fifteenth-
      century manuscript of Aulus Gellius)
      © Biblioteca Ambrosiana, Milan (cod.S/P 10/28, 90v)

235   The death of Socrates, as depicted by Claude Dufresnoy
      Archivi Alinari/Giraudon

238   Plato's vision of the soul as charioteer, as illustrated by Donatello
      Archivi Alinari/Giraudon

246   Aristotle teaching Averroes, represented by a sixteenth-century illu-
      minator
      The Pierpont Morgan Library, New York: PML 21194

ILLUSTRATIONS

254 St Augustine in his study (Vittorio Carpaccio, S. Giorgio, Venice)
    Archivi Alinari, Florence

259 Democritus and Heraclitus, as imagined by Bramante
    Archivi Alinari

268 Detail of illumination from Petrus de Abano, *Conciliator differentiarum philosophorum et medicorum* (Venice: Herbort, 1483), attributed to the Master of the Seven Virtues
    Koninklijke Bibliotheek, The Hague (169 D 3, f, a2r)

280 Zeno and Epicurus (plus swine) represented on a silver cup from Boscoreale, first century AD
    Lauros/Giraudon/Bridgeman Art Library

287 A Roman statue in the Louvre, traditionally entitled 'The Death of Seneca'
    Giraudon/Bridgeman Art Library

300 Aristotle's cosmology, as represented by Giovanni di Paolo in his illustration to Dante's *Paradiso*
    British Library (Yates-Thompson ms 36 f 169r canto XXII)

308 Marcus Tullius Cicero as a schoolboy, in a fresco by V. Foppa
    Trustees of the Wallace Collection, London

INDEX

Academy 66–9, 100–101, 173–5
accidents 220
Achilles 19
active intellect 246
actuality 88, 186, 226–7, 244
Adeimantus 48, 57
adiaphora 283
adultery 257, 270
Aenesidemus 176
affirmative propositions 117
akrasia 273
Alcibiades 35
Alexander of Aphrodisias xi, 112, 194, 252
Alexander the Great 73, 86, 89, 96, 182
alteration 191
Ambrose, St 114
anachronism xxiii
analysis 155
anatomy 71
Anaxagoras 24–6, 34, 233
Anaximander 5–7
Anaximenes 8
Andronicus of Rhodes 93
anger 76, 106
anthropomorphism 290
Anytus 34
apeiron 7
appearance vs reality 145, 170
appetite 238
Aquinas, St Thomas xviii, 216
Arcesilaus 94, 100, 172–3
arete 164, 259–77
argument from design 305
Aristophanes 34–5
Aristotle xi, xv, 1–4, 23, 65–91, 112,
    116–36, 161–6, 178–92, 216–28,
    296–302
    Categories 116, 124–7

Constitution of Athens 82
De Anima 241–7
De Interpretatione 116, 123–4
Eudemian Ethics 79–81, 266–77
Eudemus 66
Generation and Corruption 179–80
History of Animals 69, 70
Magna Moralia 79, 81
Metaphyiscs 69, 161, 217–23, 299–301
Nicomachean Ethics 69, 79–81, 164–6,
    247–8, 266–77
Organon 68
Parts of Animals 69
Physics 88, 178–92, 296–299
Poetics 75–8
Politics 82–7
Posterior Analytics 116
Prior Analytics 67, 116–121
Problems 88–9
Protrepticus 67
Rhetoric 73, 75
Sophistical Refutations 67, 116
Topics 67, 116
Arnold, Matthew 24, 304
art xvi–xix
asceticism 278
Aspasius 80, 112
aspect 186
assent 197
Assos 69
astrology 30811
atheism 294–6
Athens 33, 66, 89, 94
atomism 27, 63, 95, 168, 179–80
attunement 236, 253
augury 310
Augustine, St xxiii, 103, 113–5, 198, 254–6,
    316

Augustus 104
auxiliaries 57–8
axioma 140

beauty 156
Being 75, 199–228
Being *qua* being 227–8
biology 69–73
Bolt, Robert 16
Bruno, Giordano 25

Caesar, Julius 103–4
Callicles 32
Callisthenes 87
canon xviii
canonic 166
Cantor, Georg 20
Carneades 100, 104, 173–5, 196–7, 308
Case, Thomas 80
categories 124–7, 191
Cato the Censor 100
causes 1, 87, 189–96
cave 158
Celsus 111
Chalcidius 64
change 226
character 78
charioteer 237–8
choir 313
Christianity, 109
Chrysippus 98–100, 137, 194–6, 254–5, 282, 306–8
Cicero xii, 100–104, 286, 303, 308–1
circle 50
classes 54, 213
Cleanthes 98, 105, 279, 307
Clement of Alexandria 110
Cleopatra 93
clocks 187
cognition 170
cognitive appearance 171
Coleridge, S.T. 90
commerce 86
common sensibles 244
commonality, principle of 51–2, 208

communism 58, 98
compass, points of 56
compatibilism 254
compulsion 254
concepts 168, 170
concrete universals 55
concrete vs abstract 221, 225
conjectures 169
consequentialism 270
constitution 280
contemplation 81, 276
contingency 130–4
continuum 178–81
contradictories 123
contraries 123
conversion 121
cosmology 62, 87–9
crafts 44, 261–3
Crates 59, 96
creation 294
Critias 48

Dante 91, 300
Darwin, Charles 23
death 94, 107, 249
definite description 156
definition 50, 222
deliberation 133
Delphic oracle 42
Demetrius of Phaleron 93
demiurge 37, 63
democracy 34, 59, 82, 84
Democritus 26–8, 95, 257–9
Demosthenes 68
Descartes, R. 301
determinism 196–8, 306
diagrams 26
dialectic 159–60, 210–11
Diodorus Cronos 97, 136–8
Diogenes Laertius 48, 82, 91, 94, 140
Diogenes of Oenoanda 279
Diogenes of Synope 96–7
Dion 48
Dionysius II 48
disciplines 74, 91

divination 308–11
doctrine vs precepts 286
doxa 154–7
drama 77, 79
dreams 153, 310
Dryden, John 101

Eco, Umberto 76
education 58, 61
effects 190
efficient cause 1–2
eidola 249
elements 21, 63, 87
elenchus 37, 43
emotions 76
Empedocles, 20–4, 231–3
energeiai 185
envy 62
Epictetus xii, 107–8
Epicurus 94–6, 101–3, 166–9, 196, 277–9,
    302–4
episteme 164–6
epistemological fallacy 177
ergon 164, 268
essence 218–25
Etruscan torture 67
Euclid 166
eudaimonia 81, 258, 266–77
Eudemus 80
events 190
evidence 169
evil, problem of 306
evolution 22
existence 199, 223–6
expansion of universe 25
experience 163

falsehood 214–5
family 83
Fate 309
fate 31 195
fiction 79, 226
figures of syllogism 119
final cause 1–3
fire, 14–16, 22

first philosophy 75
fish 72
flux 14, 205
formal cause 1–2
forms (Aristotelian) 222–3
Forms (Platonic) 50, 213–6, 243–4
fortune 31
fossils 11
Frede, Michael xxi
free will xx
Frege, Gottlob xxi, 128, 166

Galen 109
garden roller 194, 197
garlic 89
Geminus 173
general sense 244
Genesis 3, 63
genus 224
Giovanni di Paolo 300
Glaucon 48, 57
gnome 157
God 36, 99, 289–316
gods, Homeric 64, 289–90
Good, Idea of 53
Gorgias 30
grammar 29
guardians 57–8

happiness 81, 258
harmony 14
hedonic calculus 263–5
hedonism 277–9
Hegel xv, 13
Helen of Troy 30
Heraclitus 11–17, 201, 204–5, 215, 232
heresy 62
Hermias 69
Hippias 29
history 79
holidays 26
Homer 13, 58, 76, 289–90
homonymy 127
homosexuality 62
horme 175

hunting 61
hypotheses 158–60

Ideas (Platonic) 2, 46–56, 68–9, 156–60, 205–16, 313–4
identity of indiscernibles 173
illusion 161–3, 176–8
imitation 51
immortality 234–7, 253–4
impulse 175
inclusive "or" 142
incontinence 273, 284
individuation 221
induction 44
infallibility of senses 162–3, 166–8
inference 143
infinite 179–81
infinite series 299
innate ideas xvii
instants 188
intellect 246–7, 313–4
intellectual virtue 271–4
intelligence, 272
intemperance 273

Jaeger, Werner 80
jealousy 293
Jerome, St 102
Jesus 104–5
jigsaw 312
Justin Martyr 109

Kant, Immanuel 121
katalepsis 170
katharsis 77
katorthoma 284
kinetic pleasures 278
Kneale, Martha 135
knowledge 145–177

law, divine 16
lazy argument 195
lekton 139, 192
Leucippus 26
lexicography 30

lexis 139
liberty of indifference xx, 197
liberty of spontaneity xx, 197
libraries 90–2
Lippi, Filippino 216
logic 67, 116–44
logos 14, 139, 154–5
love 22, 31
Lucifer 314
Lucretius xii, 94, 101–2, 166–8, 196, 248–9, 302–3
Lyceum 66, 73

Macedonia 65, 68
madness 171
Magnesia 60
magnitudes 178–81
major term 118
Manicheism 114
Marcus Aurelius 107–110
marriage 5, 61, 98
Master Argument 136, 256
material cause 1–2
material implication 138
mathematics xviii, 2, 157–8
matter 191–2, 221
means 269–71
Melissus 19
memory 163, 231
metaphysics 75, 119–228
metempsychosis 10, 23, 229–31
Michelangelo 181
microscope 73
middle term 118
Mind 25–6, 229–256
minor term 118
modal syllogistic 135
modality 130–3
monarchy 59, 82–6
monotheism 290
moods of inference 144
moods of syllogism 120
moral virtue 269–71
More, Thomas 16
Morning Star 19

motion 19, 182–6
music 2, 9
myth 8, 58
Mytilene 69

names 123, 128
natural motion 87
natural place 183
nature 88, 99, 281
necessity 130–4
negative propositions 117
Neleus of Skepsis 93
Newton, I. 183
Nicomachus 65
Nocturnal Council 61
noesis noeseos 301
nothing 203
nouns 215
now 188

objects of senses 161–2
Oedipus 78
oikeiosis 281–2
oligarchy 59, 82
One, the 209–10, 311–3
ontological argument 224
ontology 199
opinion 154
opposites 7, 15, 235
Orestes 168
organism 242
Origen 111

pain 19
Pantheia 23
pantheism 307
paradigms 55
Parmenides xix, 17–19, 199–204, 214
participation 51, 213
particular propositions 118
passions 284–5
passive intellect 247
Paul St, 13, 98, 105
Peloponnesian War 33

per se vs per accidens 212, 219
Pericles 24, 33
Peripatetics 73
peripeteia 78
Philip II 68
Philo of Alexandria 105, 111
Philo of Megara 97, 138–9, 142
philosopher kings 60
phronesis 164, 262
piety 289–90
place 182–4
plasma physics 22
Plato xii, xix, 2, 35–66, 205–216, 234–41, 260–1, 276
  Apology 42
  Crito 47
  Euthyphro 49, 290–2
  Gorgias 45
  Hippias Minor 45
  Ion 43
  Laches 43
  Laws 60–2, 294–6
  Meno 45
  Parmenides 53, 66, 207–212
  Phaedo 26, 45–9, 66, 234–7
  Phaedrus 237–8
  Philebus 265, 276
  Protagoras 45
  Republic 43–4, 56–60, 76–7, 83, 156–60, 207, 237–9, 260–1, 290–6
  Second Alcibiades 292
  Seventh Letter 49
  Sophist 32, 205, 213–6, 293
  Symposium 205
  Theaetetus 152–7
  Timaeus 62, 293
pleasure 95–6, 263–8, 274–9
plot 77–8
Plotinus xiii, 111–3, 311–6
plurality of worlds 25, 28
Plutarch 111
pneuma 99
political philosophy 16
Posidonius 103, 172, 305
potentiality 88, 226–7, 244

powers 157
practical reasoning 273–4
praxis 164
precepts vs doctrines 107
predicate calculus 144
predication 51, 54, 118, 125 133
premisses 117
prime matter 7, 63, 192
prime mover 88
private property 61, 84
Prodicus 30
progress in philosophy xvi–xx
prohairesis 252
projectiles 298
prolepsis 168, 170
proper sensibles 243
proposition 117
propositional calculus 141
Protagoras 28–30, 152–3
providence 99, 306
Ptolemy II 92–3
purity, principle of 52, 211
pyramids 4
Pyrrho of Elis 100, 175
Pythagoras 2–3, 9–11, 229–231

quality 126
quantity 126, 178
quiddity 218–25
quintessence 88

rainbow 12
Raphael 17
reason 238
recollection 160, 235
reincarnation 23
relations 209
religion 101–2
representation 245
rhetoric 30
Rubens 10
rules of syllogism 120
Russell, Bertrand 20
Ryle, Gilbert 90

sawdust 180
scepticism 172–6
Schopenhauer 224
science xvi–xix, 73, 91
sciences: productive, practical,
    theoretical 75
scope 142
sea-battle 133–4
self-predication, 52, 55, 208, 210
self-preservation 280
Seneca 105–7, 192, 228, 287
sense-data 161–2
sense-impression 168
sense-perception 143–5, 152–3, 161–4,
    166–9, 232–4, 249–51
senses 95, 243–5
sensitive soul 243
separation of powers 85
separation, principle of 52, 208
sex 37, 58, 61–2, 89, 102, 278–9
Sextus Empiricus xiii, 139, 142
Shylock 86
Sicily 48
singular propositions 124
skills 261–3
slavery 85–6
sleep 89
Socrates 13, 26, 32–45, 260–3, 290–2
Socratic fallacy 151
solstices 4
sophia 165, 272
Sophists 28–32
soul 16
soundness 144
Speusippus 69
sphere 204
spider 232
square of opposition 124
standard metre 55
state 57–8, 82–6, 264
static pleasures 278
Stoa Poikile 66, 96
Stoics 96–100, 136–44, 169–73, 192–6, 228,
    280–8, 304–8

Strife 22
sublimity, principle of 52–3, 208
substance 125, 217–25
substance, first vs second 126
suicide 288
sun 12, 13, 26, 34
sundial 5
superstition 303
swerve of atoms 95
syllogism 117–21
synonymy 127

tarradiddle 216
taste 275
techne 44, 164, 271
teeth 72
teleology 23, 26
temper 238
tenses 130, 185
terms 118, 128
testicles 71
Thales, 2–5, 257
theology xviii, 289–316
Theophrastus 90–3, 135
Theory of Ideas 2
therapy xix
Third Man 69, 209, 213
Thompson, D'Arcy 72
thought 154, 202, 245, 301
Thrasymachus 32, 159
time 179, 186–9
Timon 100
tragedy 77
transmigration of souls 10, 229–31
trinity 311–16
tripartite soul 160, 237–40
truth-conditions 143
truth-functions 141
truth-values 129

twins 173
two-way possibilities 135
tyranny 84–5

Unbeing 200–3, 215
understanding 81, 157, 272
uniqueness, principle of 52–3, 208
unity of virtues 263, 285
universal propositions 117
unmoved movers 296–9
usury 86
utilitarianism 270

vacuum 19, 27, 183
validity 143
vegetarianism 10, 270–1, 282
vegetative soul 243
verbs 123, 128, 215
virtue 44, 58–9, 81, 164–6, 259–77,
    282–8
voluntariness 251–2

will 251–6
wisdom 81, 164, 271
Wittgenstein, Ludwig xvi, xxiii, 151
women 58–9, 61, 78, 83–4, 89, 98
Wordsworth, W. 199
world-soul 63, 314–5
worship 30

Xanthippe 35
Xenophanes 11–12, 17, 289–90
Xenophon xiii, 35–7

Zeno of Citium 96–8, 172, 193, 280,
    305
Zeno of Elea 19
Zeus 15
zoology 71

9 780198 752721